The Worldwide Aeronautical Communications Frequency Directory

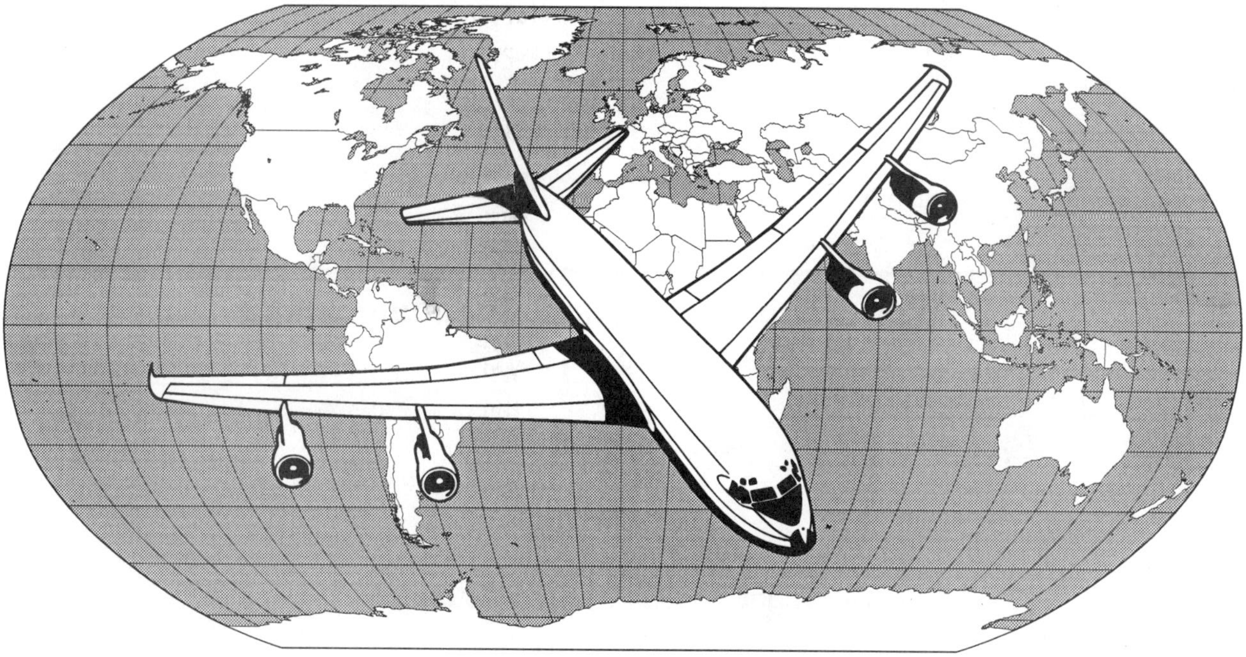

Robert E. Evans

Universal Radio Research

Second Edition

The Worldwide Aeronautical Communications Frequency Directory

SECOND EDITION

First Printing

Published By:
Universal Radio Research
6830 Americana Pkwy.
Reynoldsburg, Ohio, 43068

Printed in the United States of America

ISBN 1-882123-33-6

Preface

Five years have passed since the *Aeronautical Communications Handbook - HF Edition* was first published. During this time several global changes have ensued. The demise of the Soviet Block, the unification of the two Germany's and the fragmentation of the Czech and Yugoslav Republics have kept cartographers busy.

With the redrawing of terrestrial boundaries, the aeronautical Major World Air Route Areas have also been redefined. New ground stations have been added while others have been closed or their airspace assigned to another facility. World events, such as the Gulf War, have resulted in the creation of a new enroute sector in the North Atlantic.

Major airline carriers, both scheduled and charter, continue to experience tough economic times. Once familiar names no longer fly the "friendly" skies. Solar Cycle 22, with its increased sunspot activity, precipitated a need to allocate more frequencies in the 21 and 23 mHz bands in order to maintain effective communications. Now that this current cycle has "bottomed out", aeronautical radio communications have reverted to the lower bands once more.

Satellite technology has also taken its toll on the traffic that we used to monitor. Many of the Aeronautical Fixed Telecommunications Network stations no longer propagate their signals on the shortwave bands. In addition, much of the standard VHF aero band voice traffic has also been converted to digital mode, in the form of ACARS.

However, don't sell your radios just yet. There is still a plethora of aeronautical communications out there in the airwaves, if you know where to tune. That's the focus that this publication is intended to address. Of the 2,350 frequencies found in this book, 2,000 of them carry voice traffic in the shortwave bands.

Every attempt was made to include all extant frequencies and facilities currently active on the airwaves. To this end, not only were official sources consulted, but the individual loggings of aeronautical DX'ers have been closely monitored over the past year as they appeared in DX Club publications on five continents. To those listeners who have contributed logs to any of these sources, the author wishes to acknowledge your contribution to this directory. The author makes no claim that this is "the definitive work" with regards to aeronautical frequencies and ground facilities. If anything, it may simply be the most complete list published to-date. Approximately half of the frequencies (1,000) have been personally monitored from the author's listening post.

The dream to soar, unfettered, in a ocean of blue, has long captured mankind's imagination since the early dawn of our prehistoric beginnings. Within the course of a century we have progressed from the Wright Brothers to the "Right Stuff". To paraphrase J. G. Magee's immortal sonnet "High Flight", each time we sit behind the radio dial, as "armchair" pilots, we can

Slip the surly bonds of earth
And dance the skies on laughter-silvered wings;
Sunward climb and join the tumbling mirth
Of sun-split clouds - and do a hundred things
We had not dreamt of - wheel and soar and swing
High in the sunlit silence.

Robert E. Evans

Acknowledgements

The author is indebted to the following individuals and sources that were consulted in the preparation of this publication:

• Larry Van Horn	Grove Shortwave Directory, 8th Edition Utility World column, Monitoring Times
• Marcelo Toniolo Dos Anjos	Aero Monitor, Sao Paulo, Brazil
• Joerg Klingenfuss	Air and Meteo Code Manual, 13th Edition Guide to Utility Stations, 12th Edition
• Poly-Verlag	Internationales Kurzwellen-Frequenz-Handbuch
• Don Schimmel	Communications Confidential column, Popular Communications
• Fred Osterman	The RTTY Listener (Universal Radio)
• David Ross	Monitoring Services column, DX Ontario, ODXA
• John Evans & Ian Baxter	Utility Shack column, Danish Shortwave Club International
• Dick Moon	Utility Safari column, South African DX Club
• Spence Naylor	Utility column, Association of DX Reporters
• John Smith	HF Utilities column, DX Post of Australia
• Chuck Yarbrough	former editor, Utility World column, SPEEDX
• Ed Flynn	ACARS Monitor Emeritus

Foreword

Scope

This publication covers aeronautical radio communications, both voice and digital, within the range of the HF (Shortwave) and VHF/UHF frequency bands. Commercial, Military and Para-military operations are included.

Audience

Shortwave radio and VHF/UHF monitors.

Organization

This publication is organized into four major sections:

1. HF (Shortwave) Voice Communications
2. HF (Shortwave) Digital Communications
3. VHF/UHF Voice Communications
4. VHF Digital Communications

Comprehensive frequency listings are included that are applicable to each section.

The initial chapter of Section 1 presents general background information that may be helpful to the novice monitor.

Inasmuch as the digital VHF ACARS mode is relatively new, and may be unfamiliar, even to the most experienced of monitors, an "ACARS Primer" has been included with this section.

The Glossary contains the abbreviations used in this work as well as information on common aeronautical terms and tactical identifiers you may encounter on the airwaves.

The Appendices contain a cross-referenced listing of all the major identifiers, codes and designators introduced in the first chapter.

An up-to-date source of books, magazines, club publications, and other aeronautical materials completes this section.

Methodology

For the sake of clarity and brevity, certain conventions have been used in the various frequency listings. Please refer to the appropriate sections beginning on the next page for an explanation of their usage.

Foreword

Conventions

• *Master HF Voice Frequency List*

a) Frequency Order

This list is organized in numerical frequency order by Frequency, Type of Service and Station/Location. All Service abbreviations can be found in the Glossary. Within Frequency order, the Service abbreviation is sorted alphabetically. If more than one station/facility applies to the Service, they are likewise listed in alphabetical order. The frequency and service is listed for only the first item in the series. All frequencies are listed in kilohertz to one decimal place of precision.

FREQ.	SERVICE	STATION/LOCATION
5526.0	NAT-RDARA	Greenland - Nerlit linatt Constable Pynt, Godthab, Gronnedal, Julianehab, Maarmorlick & Sondre Stromfjord aeradios
	NCA-RDARA	CIS - Yeniseysk Aeradio
	SAM-C MWARA	Belem, Bogota, Brasilia, Leticia, Manaus, Maiquetia, Porto Velho, Rio de Janeiro
	SAM-NE MWARA	Belem, Cayenne, Georgetown, Maiquetia, Paramaribo, Piarco, Recife
	SAM-RDARA	Bolivia - Santa Cruz Aeradio
		Brazil - Belem, Brasilia, Campo Grande Curitiba , Manaus, Porto Velho FIR's
		Colombia - Arauca (Santiago Perez), Cucuta (Camilo Daza), Mitu, Puerto Carreno, San José del Guaviare, Tame, Trinidad & Villavicencio (Vanguardia) Aeradios
		Uruguay - Velasquez (Calderon)
	SAM-SE MWARA	Asuncion, Belem, Brasilia, Buenos Aires, Campo Grande, Curtiba, La Paz, Montevideo, Porto Alegre, Porto Velho, Recife, Salvador Dois De Julho, Santa Cruz
	SAUDI-AF	Saudi Air Force, Riyadh (Hotel 2), Tabuk (Hotel 8)
	SEA-LDOC	Singapore (Singapore Airlines)
	SEA-RDARA	Australia HF Network - South Eastern region - Dubbo, Melbourne, Midura & Sydney Aeradios
		Myanmar - Heho, Hommalin, Kengtung, Kawthoung, Kyauktu, Loikaw, Mong-Hsat, Mong-Tong, Magwey, Hpa-An, Hpapun, Sittwe, Thandwe, Tachilek, Tanai & Yangon Aeradios

b) MWARA

Stations belonging to a Major World Air Route Area are listed alphabetically. Note that some stations may belong to other MWARA's as well.

SAM-C MWARA	**Belem**, Bogota, Brasilia, Leticia, Manaus, **Maiquetia**, Porto Velho, Rio de Janeiro
SAM-NE MWARA	**Belem**, Cayenne, Georgetown, **Maiquetia**, Paramaribo, Piarco, Recife

A complete list by country/city/Area/Frequency for each of the MWARA locations can be found in the MWARA Country/City Listing in Section 1.

Brazil							
Belem	SAM-C	3479.0	5526.0	8855.0	10096.0	13297.0	17907.0
	SAM-NE	3479.0	5526.0	8855.0	10096.0	13297.0	17907.0
	SAM-SE	3479.0	5526.0	8855.0	10096.0	13297.0	17907.0

c) Airport Names

Many aeronautical facilities are named for their local airports. Some of the more common ones you will encounter are:

Boyeros (Havana)	Maiquetia (Caracas)
Piarco (Port of Spain)	Roberts (Monrovia)

For less known facilities, especially in RDARA sectors, the city name appears first, followed by the airport name in parenthesis.

SAM-RDARA	Colombia - Arauca **(Santiago Perez)**, Cucuta **(Camilo Daza)**, Mitu, Puerto Carreno, San José del Guaviare, Tame, Trinidad & Villavicencio **(Vanguardia)** Aeradios

d) RDARA

Where a Regional and Domestic Air Route area applies to one country only, the country name precedes the list of stations.

Greenland - Nerlit Iinatt Constable Pynt, Godthab, Gronnedal, Julianehab, Maarmorlick & Sondre Stromfjord aeradios

e) LDOC

Company Operations services (LDOC - Long Distance Operational Control) contain the location name followed by the name of the airline carrier in parenthesis.

8921.0	CWP-LDOC	Hong Kong **(Dragonair)**
	EU-LDOC	Dusseldorf **(LTU)**
		Frankfurt **(Lufthansa)**
		Speedbird London **(British Airways)**
	RAF	Hong Kong Air
	SEA-LDOC	Colombo **(Air Lanka)**
		Jakarta
		Sydney **(Qantas)**

A complete listing of all LDOC frequencies listed alphabetically by carrier can be found in the LDOC - Long Distance Operational Control section.

Lufthansa	Dusseldorf	13324.0			
	Frankfurt	3010.0	4687.0	5645.0	6637.0
		8921.0	8983.0	10018.0	10065.0
		10072.0	10078.0	11190.0	13213.0
		13248.0	13324.0	13327.0	17931.0
		21967.0	21979.0		

f) Special Airline Call-Signs

Some airline companies utilize their own special call-sign names rather than use the actual name of the airline. Some of the more notable ones include:

Speedbird (British Airways)	Springbok (South African Airways)
Clipper (Pan American)	Sabena (Belgian World Airlines)

In Appendix C, Airline Carriers, the special call-sign, if one exists, will be found after the carrier name in quotation marks.

AIRLINE CARRIER	COUNTRY	IATA	IACO
British Airways, "**Speedbird**"	United Kingdom	BA	BAW
British Midland Airways, "**Midland**"	United Kingdom	BD	BMA

g) Aviation Weather Broadcasts

VOLMET stations broadcast aviation weather at specific times during the course of an hour. Normally several stations in a sector may be involved. The fixed broadcast times are indicated in parenthesis after the station name as (Hour + minutes past the hour) when the broadcast is made. For example, (H+00,30) indicates the broadcast is made on the hour and half-hour.

6676.0	SEA-VOL	Sydney **(H+00,30)**, Calcutta **(H+05,35)**, Bangkok **(H+10,40)**, Karachi **(H+15,45)**, Singapore **(H+20,50)**, Bombay **(H+25,55)**
6679.0	PAC-VOL	Honolulu **(H+00,30)**, Tokyo **(H+10,40)**, Hong Kong **(H+15,45)**, Auckland **(H+20,50)**
6680.0	MID-VOL	Karachi Volmet **(H+15,45)**

h) FOXTROT Frequency Designators

Military and government services often assign "channel designators" to their frequencies. These channel identifiers are known as "Foxtrot Designators" since they normally use the characters of the phonetic "Foxtrot" alphabet. (See the Glossary for a complete listing of the International Phonetic Alphabet). These channel designators will be found after the station name(s) enclosed in quotation marks.

6693.0	CANFORCE	Air/Ground - Halifax, St. John's & Vancouver Military **"Delta One Golf"**
	RAF	UKADGE **"Delta Sierra"**

i) EAM Broadcasts

Emergency Action Broadcasts are still made by many USAF stations. The convention used to indicate the broadcast time is the same as that used for VOLMET stations.

9017.0	USAF-ACC	Former SAC "Giant Talk" Network **(EAM + 42)** "XRAY-904"

j) Country and City Names

All country and city names used in this publication conform to the 1994 ICAO standards. The reader should be aware that the growing spirit of nationalism has resulted in the renaming of many of the old familiar place names we had come to recognize. Perhaps the most striking example of this is the former country of Burma, now known as Myanmar. Approximately 97% of its city names were also changed. Rangoon, the capital, is now Yangon.

You may also notice that the spellings adopted for many place names are now more closely identified with the language of the region and are less "anglicized" than before. For example, Ulan Bator in Mongolia is spelled Ulaanbaatar.

The break-up of the Soviet Union, Czechoslovakia and Yugoslavia and the unification of the two Germanys and the two Yemens have also resulted in change. By way of example, Leningrad, USSR is now St. Petersburg, Russia, Belgrade, Yugoslavia is now Beograd, Serbia.

• *MWARA Maps*

The maps found in the Major World Air Route Area section have been logically grouped in order by geographical sector. All maps appear on the left page while the accompanying text is found on the right. Maps that appear in "landscape" format have been deliberately aligned so that the bottom of map faces the center binding. This arrangement should alleviate the need to constantly re-orient the publication when viewing the maps and reading the associated text.

Foreword

This publication was produced using an Apple Macintosh Quadra 650. Database information was entered and maintained through Microsoft Works and then ported to MicroSoft Word. Text entry and final page assembly was accomplished using Aldus PageMaker. Maps were rendered from Cartesia CD-ROM-based map templates using Adobe Illustrator. Photographs were taken from Corel's Professional Photos CD-ROM "Aviation Photography", imported into Adobe Photoshop, cropped and enhanced. The final assembled master page was printed on the Apple SelectWriter 360 600 dpi laser printer.

Table of Contents

Section 1 HF (Shortwave) Voice Communications

• Introduction to Aero Monitoring

Table of Contents

Section 3 VHF/UHF Voice Communications

• VHF/UHF

Section 4 VHF Digital Communications

• Aircraft Communications Addressing and Reporting System

Table of Contents

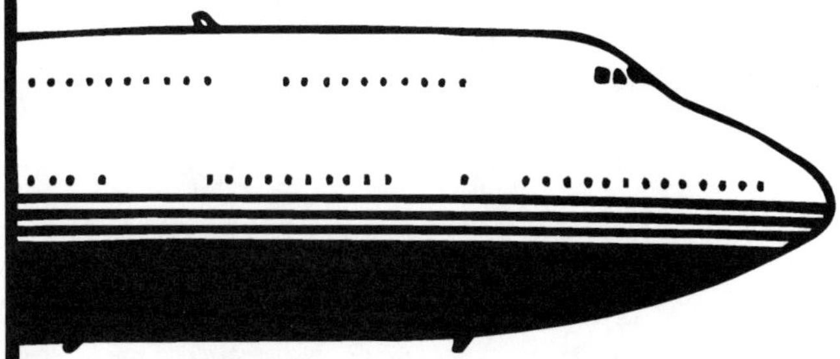

Section 1

HF (Shortwave) Voice Communications

Introduction to Aero Monitoring

What Can You Hear?

Welcome to the exciting past-time of monitoring aeronautical air/ground communications. Monitor conversations between high-flying passenger aircraft and ground stations on all five continents. Follow the progress of transatlantic flights or fly a search and rescue mission with the U.S. Coast Guard.

Join the astronauts on-board the Space Shuttle or fly copilot in the cockpits of the world's major air forces. Fly jump-seat on the flight deck of the NOAA "Hurricane Hunters" as they repeatedly traverse the walls of a hurricane, in and out of its eye, collecting important meteorological data. Join the U.S. Customs Service as they interdict drug smugglers in the Caribbean, both on the water and in the air.

All these adventures, and more await you as an aeronautical communications monitor.

With a few exceptions, English is the primary language of international aeronautical community. For regional flights, you can expect to hear Portuguese in Brazil, Spanish in South America and French in West Africa. Conversations between aircraft and their company operations (LDOC) will normally take place in the native language of the country. (It should come as no surprise that a KLM pilot would talk to his base in Amsterdam in Dutch, for example).

The following table summarizes the major worldwide voice traffic you can expect to monitor from the comfort of your listening post.

Aircraft/Ground Control (IFSS/ATCC)
Aircraft/Company Operations (LDOC)
Aviation Weather Broadcasts (VOLMET)
Point-to-Point Ground Station Traffic
Aeronautical Flight Tests
Military/Air Force Flights and Bases
Aero Search and Rescue Operations
Aero Law Enforcement Activities
Coast Guard Aircraft Operations
NASA Shuttle Flight Support
Offshore Drilling Rigs Helicopter Support

Where Do You Listen?

By international agreement, specific band segments have been reserved in the high frequency (HF) radio spectrum for commercial voice aeronautical communications. These bands are to be found in the 2.0 to 23.0 Megahertz (MHz) frequency range as described below.

BAND (MHz)	FREQUENCY RANGE (kHz)
2	2850 - 3155
3	3400 - 3500
4	4650 - 4750
5	5450 - 5730
6	6525 - 6765
8	8815 - 9040
10	10005 - 10100
11	11175 - 11400
13	13200 - 13360
15	15010 - 15100
17	17900 - 18030
21	21850 - 22000
23	23200 - 23350

Almost all voice transmissions take place in Upper Side Band (USB). The lone exception is the U.S. Air Force Mystic Star service used to transport VIP's onboard Special Air Mission (SAM) flights, and their use of Lower Side Band (LSB) has noticeably diminished over the past year.

Military/Air Force transmissions can generally be found at the bottom and top edge of the frequency ranges, but a slow migration to out-of-band frequencies also seems to be taking place.

Most ground facilities have from four to six frequencies allocated for their use in the various bands. Generally they will use the higher frequencies during their local day, moving to the lower ones during their period of darkness. During the high solar activity experienced in Solar Cycle 22, the traditional 5 MHz and lower band frequencies were abandoned in favour of higher ones. As of 1994, most aero traffic can now be found on the 5, 6, 8, 11, and 13 MHz bands.

What Equipment Do You Need?

To monitor HF communications, you require a shortwave radio capable of tuning the band segments and frequency ranges previously listed. It also must be capable of tuning SSB (Single Sideband) in USB (Upper Sideband) mode. It may be a portable or a more expensive tabletop receiver. Naturally, the better the radio, the better its selectivity, and improved reception of distant stations will result.

Not even the most expensive shortwave radio will perform properly if it does not have an adequate antenna system. While an out-of-doors long wire antenna (70 to 100 feet in length) is most often preferred by DXers, believe it or not, many air/ground stations are within the reach of the whips provided on the better portable shortwave radios. The Sony 2010 is a good example of this point. If you live in eastern North America, you can expect to hear aircraft working Gander, New York Oceanic, Santa Maria and Shanwick, as well as hearing the ground stations themselves.

You'll probably even get Sydney VOLMET in the mornings, but don't expect to get Ho-Chi-Minh, Bali or Jakarta without an external antenna.

For apartment dwellers and people with limited space, the new breed of electronic active antennas performs very well.

A good cassette tape recorder is another indispensable tool for aeronautical monitoring. Often transmissions are so fast and brief, you may miss part of the message. The tape recorder allows you to replay and relisten.

Serious aerocomm monitors often have two or more receivers, so they can sit on one frequency waiting for traffic while they "dial-twiddle" on the other. Two or more antennas, oriented in different receiving directions, selectable by a coax switch can dramatically improve signal strength and clarity. An antenna oriented towards Africa, does a lousy job at picking up South American traffic and vice-versa.

When Should You Listen?

The time of day and the season of the year will be a major factor in determining the locations of air/ground traffic that you can monitor. Two major factors that effect what you'll hear are airline flight schedules and shortwave propagation conditions.

Don't expect to hear what isn't there. For example, trying to monitor eastbound flights to Europe from North American in the mornings is a waste of time - most of these flights only take place in the afternoon and evenings. Don't expect to hear a lot of European ATC stations - aircraft flying in their airspace use VHF, not shortwave.

Predicting propagation conditions is akin to fortune telling, as an exact science. Since the shortwave signal you receive is constantly at the mercy of a churning mass of electrons forming the refractive ionosphere, and there seems to be more than enough solar and terrestrial influences capable of disturbing its mirroring qualities, the stations you hear today, may be totally inaudible tomorrow, or for that matter, 30 minutes from now.

As anyone who has ever monitored the aeronautical bands knows, transmissions tend to be very short and brief on many frequencies. How can you determine if it is worthwhile to chase a particular area of the world. The answer can be found in what shortwave listeners have referred to over the years as 'beacon" or "indicator" stations. For the aeronautical monitor, these are the VOLMET stations that broadcast as specified time periods past the hour.

For example, suppose you are interested in tuning in to the Far East air routes early in the morning. You switch on your radio at 6:00 am local time. Sydney VOLMET is coming through loud and clear on 11387 kHz. If you don't hear Bangkok at 6:10 or Singapore at 6:20, your chances of picking up more elusive stations in that part of the world on other frequencies are rather slim.

Transatlantic conditions can be checked by noting stations such as Shannon VOLMET, Santa Maria and Dakar IFSS or Brazzaville VOLMET.

West coast listeners will normally have little difficulty monitoring the Pacific and South East Asia. To them, transatlantic, African and Middle Eastern catches are notable. The opposite is true for east coast dwellers.

Transatlantic and African traffic is normally at its best between 2200 to 0200 UTC. Summer months are noticeably better than winter ones.

Best openings for the Pacific and South East Asia occur around local dawn on the east coast (0900 to 1200 UTC). Winter months present more favourable propagation conditions for this part of the world.

Where Should You Tune?

A quick glance at the HF frequencies in this directory will show that many ground stations have been allocated more than one frequency. The general rule of thumb is that the higher frequencies are used during their local day, and as the bands drop-off, they will move to lower ones, until by late evening, they are on the lowest useable frequency that propagation conditions will allow.

This general rule applies to their location, not necessarily to your listening post. It may be high noon at the transmitter sight and the middle of the night at your listening post. For example, very often Honolulu Radio can be heard on 21964 kHz late at night from eastern North America. On other nights, the high bands may be dead and you won't hear a thing.

Ground stations may also change their frequencies depending on the part of the world they wish to contact. Speedbird London (British Airways Company Operations) is a good example. Transatlantic flights enroute to the UK from North America can normally be found on 8921 or 10072 kHz during early evening hours EST. Flights calling in from Africa or the Middle East may use 5535 kHz since that area of the world has been in darkness for a much longer period of time.

Prior to the current Solar Cycle, there was very little aero traffic above the 13 megaHertz band. Cycle 22 changed all of that. Now that Cycle 22 activity is on the decline and Solar Flux numbers have fallen below 100, traffic on the lower bands has returned.

Except for VOLMET broadcasts, aeronautical communications may take place at any time. The trick, if there is one, is to be on the right frequency at the right time. This is no easy chore if you are trying to monitor several hundred frequencies.

Take Springbok Jo'burg (South African Airways Company Ops in Johannesburg, South Africa) for example. At ten minutes past the hour, you tune to 8933 kHz hoping to hear air/ground LDOC traffic. In all probability, you may have to wait to the top of the next hour for all the Springbok flights to check in. Traffic for the entire airborne fleet may be handled in a matter of 5 to 6 minutes.

On another occasion, things can be significantly different. In-flight emergencies may occupy all of the air time. A case in point was the death of a passenger on a flight from London to Cape Town a few years ago. The captain and passenger agent could be heard discussing plans to put the body in a body bag and move it to the cargo hold so it could be unloaded at the back door. The flight attendants were instructed to move passengers forward or aft and to search the man's pockets for id and a passport.

Once identified, the passenger agent was instructed to locate and notify the next of kin. At the top of the hour, other aircraft were requested to maintain radio silence until this matter had been dealt with.

How Should You Start?

Assemble your reference materials, maps, charts, logging sheets/notebook before you start. If you're a new aero monitor - sit back and just listen for a while. Listen not so much for what is said, but how it is said. Become familiar with the communications format flow. (You'll soon find that there are standard methods used reporting waypoint positions, maintenance status, etc.)

Keep logs of what you hear, even if they are only scribbled in a notebook. Record the frequency, UTC time, flight name and number, SELCAL and ground station worked. Try monitoring the progress of a flight over a period of a couple of hours as it calls in for waypoint checks. Make a note of the time the aircraft expects to cross the next co-ordinate or waypoint and tune back to the frequency a few minutes before the estimated time. You usually will be rewarded with another position report and details of the next set of co-ordinates.

ICAO HF Enroute Networks

For the purposes of aeronautical radio communications, the world has been divided into specific regions known as Major World Air Route Areas (MWARA). The table below lists the major divisions and their appropriate abbreviations.

Because of the vast areas covered, several of these MWARAs may be further subdivided into smaller units. For example, the African MWARA is divided into four separate units AFI-1 to AFI-4. Each group has its owned assigned air space, frequencies and ground stations associated with it. Sometimes a particular ground station may be found in more than one group, depending on its location.

In parts of Africa, the Pacific and the Indian Oceans, special regional areas have been set up. They are known as Regional and Domestic Air Route Areas (RADARA) and are represented in frequency lists with the letter R - example AFI-4(R). Since these frequencies are regional/domestic in nature, the local vernaculars of the individual countries often replace English as the language for traffic.

DESIG.	REGION
AFI	Africa
CAR	Caribbean
CEP	Central East Pacific
CWP	Central West Pacific
EA	Eastern Asia
EUR	Europe
INO	Indian Ocean
MID	Middle East
NAT	North Atlantic
NCA	North Central Asia
NP	North Pacific
SAM	South America
SAT	South Atlantic
SEA	South East Asia
SP	South Pacific

Aeronautical Traffic Types

• International Flight Service Stations (IFSS)/Air Traffic Control Centres (ATCC)

Air/ground communications between in-flight aircraft and Air Traffic Control Centres (ATCC) and International Flight Service Stations (IFSS) are used to keep commercial aircraft on conflict-free, fuel efficient routes during their flights. All commercial airliners fly established routes (airways) with waypoint reporting positions. Waypoints may be designated by a five-letter name or by geographic coordinates of latitude and longitude. As the aircraft passes each waypoint on its route, it reports to the ground station that currently has its "guard" Normally, estimates for the next two or three waypoints are also given as well as flight level, wind direction/speed, outside air temperature and possibly fuel consumption.

Each ground facility has specific geographical airspace boundaries known as a Flight Information Region (FIR).

• Point-to-Point ATC Messages

As a rule, most IFSS/ATC facilities maintain communications with aircraft directly in their zone. In parts of the Third World, Africa in particular, the radio equipment is often so old or poorly maintained that aircraft are unable to read ground-to-air transmissions. This results in a barrage of messages on aircraft positions being passed from one control center to the next. (Tune to 11300 kHz around 2300 UTC for a graphic example of this practice).

• Long Distance Operational Control (LDOC)

Special frequencies are allocated to international carriers for company operations. Transmissions typically cover arrival and departure times, passenger and fuel loads, flight progress reports, aircraft maintenance problems and crew scheduling. Frequencies are often shared by more than one carrier, and some carriers provide LDOC services for carriers that do not have their own LDOC facilities. The majority of traffic is in English as well as the national language of the airline. LDOC transmissions can be far more interesting in content than aircraft position reports.

• Common Carrier

Not all commercial airline companies have the facilities to maintain an LDOC set-up. Many rely on common carriers such as ARINC (Aeronautical Radio Inc., New York, San Francisco & Honolulu), Houston Radio (Universal Aviation, TX), Rainbow Radio (Canada), Portishead Radio (England), Berna Radio (Switzerland) and Stockholm Radio (Sweden). Airlines subscribe to these message handling services and are charged accordingly. Phone patches to company dispatch and engineering form the majority of this traffic. Corporate business and private aircraft often use these facilities as well.

• VOLMET Stations

These stations are transmit-only facilities that broadcast airport forecast weather conditions for specific parts of the world on special frequencies at designated times past the hour. Normally they broadcast twice per hour. Broadcast times may range from two to several minutes. Usually several stations in the region share the same frequencies. The times they broadcast are indicated in minutes past the hour (for example, H+00, 30 indicates broadcasts on the hour and half-hour).

Flight Service Stations

All commercial airline carriers navigate established flyways in the sky. Although invisible to the naked eye, these air routes (airways), defined by geographical coordinates, are much the same as automobile highways.

At predetermined positions along these flyways, commercial aircraft are required to report to an ATC (Air Traffic Control) ground station.

Those flight stations primarily involved with domestic or regional flights are designated as Flight Service Stations (FSS) and normally operate on VHF frequencies, although some regional stations may also be found in the HF bands as well. The long range route stations are called International Flight Service Stations (IFSS) and operate on frequencies between 2 and 23 mHz in the HF bands.

Each of these FSS/IFSS ATC facilities has geographical boundaries assigned to their airspace (FIR - Flight Information Region) and any aircraft, commercial or military, flying within or through their areas must establish their *guard* with that ground facility.

Flight Plans

All commercial airline flights must file a flight plan. This includes the flyways it will follow, planned cruising speed and altitude, departure and destination and a wealth of other data.

Once airborne, an aircraft must obtain prior clearance to deviate from this preplanned arrangement. Normally adverse weather conditions and inflight emergencies are the only instances when such deviations are allowed.

The best route may ride the jet stream, a fast moving river of air, which offers the most economical way of getting from point A to point B at high altitudes. It will be high above the weather, around the 250 millibar level at 34,000 feet. Wind speed of 250 knots are not uncommon. Jet streams are Nature's way of equalizing weather conditions across the globe.

Several airline crews may want to fly the same airway at the same time; routes are allocated on a first-come, first-served basis. Aircraft usually follow airways which are divided into three main altitude layers.

DESIGNATION	RANGE	USAGE
Supersonic	45,000 to 75,000	Concordes, Military Jets
Enroute High Altitude	20,000 to 41,000	Commercial Jets
Low Altitude	18,000 and below	Turboprop Aircraft, Propeller Aircraft

Commercial Aero Traffic Layers

Airways

Airways are corridors within which aircraft are protected by internationally agreed rules of separation. Other aircraft must be at least 1000 feet above or below, 10 minutes flying time in front or behind, and 10 miles on either side of any aircraft flying on the same flyway. The 10 minute/ 10 mile restriction may be relaxed to 3 miles under radar control.

Until recently, all airways (routes) were numbered and color-coded. B646 (Blue 646) for example, is an airway that passes from southern Florida through Bermuda. Because B646 is also used for low altitude flights, commercial aircraft flying above 18,000 feet refer to it as Upper Blue 646 (UB646). There is a move afoot to replace the color designation with the appropriate letter from the international phonetic alphabet. Thus Upper Blue 646 would be known as Upper Bravo 646 instead. Both systems of designation are currently in use.

Airways over the continental United States are referred to as a "Jet Route" followed by a number (J50 for example). In Canadian airspace, they are designated as "Victor" plus a number (V30), although there is increasing pressure to accept the "Jet Route" designation.

Airways are further subdivided into area sectors. Aircraft may change sectors only when their entry into a new one has been coordinated by ATC. Many sectors are restricted to military use (rocket launchings, naval gunnery exercises, etc.) and civil airways are often channelled into narrow gaps between them. At times, they may be completely closed off and flights will have to be rerouted to avoid them.

Waypoints - Enroute High Altitude Positions

In order to navigate the predefined air routes, commercial pilots make use of high altitude enroute maps and charts. These serve as roadmaps with numbered airways and pre-arranged reporting positions.

By international agreement, a series of checkpoint positions (Waypoints) have been established along the numbered airways. Each position name is five characters long which leads to some interesting spellings. FISSH and OYSTR are two examples.

Most of the named positions are close to land masses. Once over the world's oceans, aircraft report their positions in degrees of latitude and longitude. The Concordes use pre-arranged latitude positions of SM (Sierra Mike) for flights to Europe and SN (Sierra November) for flights from Europe.

Route numbers are revised and changed periodically.

Flight Levels

All aircraft flying at levels above 18,000 feet are under positive control of the Air Traffic Control System, even on days with the highest visibility.

Above 18,000 feet, all aircraft refer to Flight Level rather than height above sea level. Flight Level 195 (FL 195) refers to an altimeter reading of 19,500 feet, with the barometric adjustment always set to 29.92 inches of mercury. Thus Flight Levels always refer to altimeter readings and never to absolute height above sea level.

In this way, all aircraft are using the same instrument setting and calibration factor to maintain separation. This means that all altimeters will be affected uniformly by localized non-standard conditions. It makes no difference if an aircraft is really 200 feet below the 19,500 foot level as long as all other altimeters in the area also read 200 below as well.

As barometric pressure drops, those aircraft above 18,000 feet do not adjust their altimeters. They remain set a 29.92 Hg. An aircraft at FL 200 would not really be flying at 20,000 feet if the actual barometric pressure were 27.92 Hg. It would actually be flying at 18,000 feet, but so would all other aircraft in the area flying at FL 200. Under these conditions, a Lowest-Useable Flight Level (LUFL) is computed. This allows a flight level computation that will always keep the aircraft above 18,000 feet.

The LUFL computation is dependent solely on the barometric pressure. If B, the barometric pressure in inches of mercury (Hg), is greater than 29.92, the Lowest Usable Flight Level (LUFL) will be 18,000 feet. If B is less than 29.92 inches then the following formula applies:

$$\text{LUFL} = 18000 + 500 \times \text{INT}(60.82 - 2B)$$

Great Circle Routes

Pilots planning long distance transoceanic flights may take a great circle route, the shortest distance between departure and destination points, especially if no airway links the two. The latest navigation systems that do not depend on ground station locations make this possible.

The shortest distance between any two points on a sphere such as the Earth lies on a great circle, which if marked on the surface of the globe, would divide it into two equal halves.

The Equator, the zero degrees latitude line, is the only parallel of latitude that is a great circle; all other parallels are smaller circles. Latitude is measured north and south from the Equator through 90 degrees in each direction. All meridians of longitude are great circles. By international agreement, the zero degrees or Prime Meridian passes through Greenwich, near London in the United Kingdom. Longitude is measured east and west from the Prime Meridian through 180 degrees in each direction.

Pilots calculate great circle routes and distances using simple trigonometry. Shortwave signals also follow great circle routes.

North Atlantic Tracks

The North Atlantic Track system consists of about six approximately parallel tracks active from entry points on the coast of the UK and Ireland to exit points on the Canadian coast and vice-versa.

Westbound (Europe to America) flights are made mostly by day, while eastbound (America to Europe) are usually made afternoons and evenings. The tracks are selected twice daily by computer to avoid strong headwinds when flying from Europe to America and to follow the best tailwinds when travelling in the opposite direction.

Eastbound tracks are usually designated with the letters A, B, C, D, E, and F. Westbound tracks are U, V, W, X, Y and Z. The track an aircraft requests depends on the departure time and destination of the flight. Pilots usually look for the shortest and fastest route. It is usually the most economical in terms of fuel consumption.

Airlines tend to schedule departures to similar destinations at much the same time. Since all big jet aircraft prefer to operate at flight levels within the narrow 11,000 foot band from 28,000 to 39,000 feet, congestion over the North Atlantic can easily result.

The Captain programs the INS (Inertial Navigation System) for the first nine waypoints along the route. The North Atlantic Tracks do not follow Great Circle routings, but use best time paths for wind conditions. When progressing from one position to another along the Track, however, the INS routes the aircraft along a Great Circle (the shortest distance between two points) and the compass continually changes heading as the aircraft maintains the Great Circle path.

Track coordinates currently in use are broadcast over the ICAO AFTN RTTY network and can easily be received with appropriate RTTY decoding equipment. Similar track systems exist in the high Arctic for northern polar routes as well.

Selective Call Paging

A system known as SELCAL (Selective Call) Paging is used to alert a specific aircraft when a ground station wishes to contact them. Each aircraft (actually the aircraft's HF radios) has its own unique four-letter code which is transmitted by the ground station. This in turn, produces a "ding-dong" sound on the flight deck and an amber IFSS light flashes on the overhead panel. The pilot/communications officer can then replace his headset and answer the call. The crew who fly aircraft that are not SELCAL equipped must wear their headsets at all times.

SELCALs are always pronounced phonetically - BDFH is bravo delta foxtrot hotel (this SELCAL is assigned to one of the Speedbird Concordes - aircraft registration G-BOAC).

You should normally try to record an aircraft's SELCAL in your logs. It is usually always given at the beginning or end of traffic messages. In this way, you can observe when the same aircraft is used. Since flight crew information is generally not broadcast, the aircraft SELCAL is the most unique piece of information you can normally gather for a specific flight.

Squawk Codes/Secondary Surveillance Radar

Secondary Surveillance Radar (SSR) involves a ground-transmitted radar signal being received onboard an aircraft by a small receiver/transmitter device called a **transponder**. Once the initial signal is received, the transponder transmits a second signal which in turn is received by the ground-based radar. The resultant signal received by the ground station is much stronger than the weak echo detected using primary radar.

Transponders transmit on a different frequency than the ground-based radar transmitter. Thus ghost-images from clouds and the like never occur. The transponder can also transmit code signals that positively identify the aircraft on a controller's radar screen.

Almost all air traffic control in congested airspace today involves aircraft fitted with transponders. Unlike the SELCAL which is permanently assigned to the HF radio, transponder or Squawk Codes are assigned by the local ATC Controller. The pilot then dials the four digit number into the unit. When requested, the pilot can press an identification button on the transponder. This produces an enlarged blip on the controller's screen. If identification is required, the ground station will use the word *Ident* when assigning the Squawk Code.

You will normally hear Squawk Codes being assigned to transoceanic flights as they approach the coast of North America.

Certain codes are memorized by pilots and are used in cases of emergency, complete radio failure or hijack.

CODE	MEANING
7500	Hijack
7600	Communications Failure
7700	In-flight Emergency
7500 followed by 7700	Situation Desperate Captain Requesting Armed Intervention Upon Landing

Periodically a pilot will dial an emergency code by mistake. The ground controller will usually request a verification.

The transponder can also transmit aircraft altitude which appears as a number beside the aircraft blip on the ATC radar screen. Transponders are used extensively in North American and European airspace, but most of the remaining parts of the world do not have the necessary ground equipment.

• Velocity Measurements

Aircraft Speed

Aircraft speed is measured in knots, one knot being equal to one nautical mile per hour. One nautical mile (nm) is equivalent to the distance subtended by one minute of arc of a meridian on the Earth's surface (ie. one nautical mile is equal to minute of latitude).

The shape of the Earth is an oblate spheroid, being slightly flatter than a sphere at the top and bottom. One minute of arc at the North and South Poles is therefore different from one minute of arc at the Equator, so the average distance of one minute of arc (6080 feet) is taken as the measurement of the nautical mile. It is approximately 15% longer than the statute mile (5280 feet).

Ground Speed (G/S) is the speed of the aircraft relative to the ground and True Air Speed (TAS) is the speed of the aircraft relative to the air through which it is flying.

Indicated Airspeed

An aircraft inflight is subject to a pressure force from the air known as dynamic pressure and to the influence of static pressure. The dynamic pressure experienced is an indication of airspeed and is measured by a device known as a Pitot Tube named after its French inventor.

The tube is usually mounted near the nose of the aircraft. The Indicated Air Speed (IAS) obtained and displayed on the Air Speed Indicator (ASI) instruments (in knots) is subject to a number of errors.

At high altitudes the air is very thin and of low density which results in airspeed under-reading. At aircraft speeds over 300 knots, compressibility of air results in ASI over-read. Corrections have to be made to determine the True Airspeed (TAS) of the aircraft. The under/over-read errors can be significant. For example, an aircraft flying at 35,000 feet with an outside air temperature (OAT) of -60° Celsius, the IAS reading would be 280 knots while the TAS is actually 480 knots, a difference of 200 knots.

Mach Number

Because of the density error effect mentioned previously, the airspeed indicator is not suitable for speed indication above the 25,000 foot level. Instead, the speed of the aircraft is given as a ratio of the True Airspeed (TAS) of the aircraft to the local speed of sound. This value, known as the **Mach Number**, is named after the Austrian physicist, Ernst Mach.

The speed of sound is not constant, but decreases with drop in temperature, which normally occurs with increase in altitude. It is 661 knots at sea level in the standard atmosphere and 589 knots at 30,000 feet. The speed of sound is given the value 1.0 at any height and therefore an indicated Mach Number of 0.82 for example, at 35,000 feet, indicates that the aircraft is travelling at 82 per cent of the value of the speed of sound at that height. The Mach Number is recorded on an instrument in the cockpit known as a Mach meter.

Cruise Mach Numbers for large jets at levels from 28,000 to 39,000 feet range from about Mach 0.80 to Mach 0.85. The maximum for a Boeing 747 is Mach 0.90. The Concordes reach a speed of Mach 2.0 or roughly 1340 miles per hour.

Airspeed Envelope

All aircraft operate within a specific airspeed envelope. If the aircraft flies too fast, the airflow over the top surface of the wings reaches a point where its speed becomes supersonic, producing shock waves that result in a condition known as **High-Speed Buffet**, the effects of which can be felt and which may damage the aircraft as well. The speed at which this occurs varies with altitude and is indicated on the ASI instruments. Speed control is usually the responsibility of the flight engineer and an audible alarm is sounded if the aircraft exceeds maximum speed.

At the other extreme, if the aircraft flies too slow, the smooth air flow over the top surface of the wings starts to break away and turbulence results. This condition is known as **Low Speed Buffet**. This value is likewise calculated and marked on the ASI instruments and is frequently recalculated and reset as aircraft weight reduces with fuel consumption or the aircraft climbs or descends to a different flight level.

Thus all cruise speeds for a particular height and aircraft weight lie within the range of speeds encompassed by the Low and High Speed Buffet markers on the ASI dial. As height increases, the aircraft has to fly faster to maintain the same lift in the thinner air to stay above the Low Speed Buffet value. The higher speed brings the aircraft closer to the High Speed Buffet value for that particular height. If it continues to accelerate, a point is reached at which High Speed Buffet occurs if it flies faster and Low Speed Buffet occurs if it slows down. At this point the aircraft has reached its theoretical maximum operating height and in flying jargon is referred to as *Coffin-Corner.*

• Aircraft Weight Computations

Aircraft Weight and Loading

All aircraft have a maximum **Take-Off Weight** (TOW). To this basic weight is added the weight of special equipment, the crew and their baggage. This resultant figure is known as the **Dry Operating Weight** (DOW).

To this weight is added the **Payload Weight**, which consists of the weight of the cargo (including passenger baggage) and the weight of the passengers. The following average passenger weights are used for computation:

- Males - 182 lbs
- Females - 135 lbs
- Children - 75 lbs
- Infants - 10 lbs

These values also include carry-on hand luggage as well.

The Dry Operating Weight plus the Payload Weight account for all weights excluding fuel and are known as the **Zero Fuel Weight** (ZFW). The weight of the fuel is then added to the Zero Fuel Weight to obtain the final Take-Off Weight. The total aircraft weight at any point in the flight is known as the **All Up Weight** (AUW).

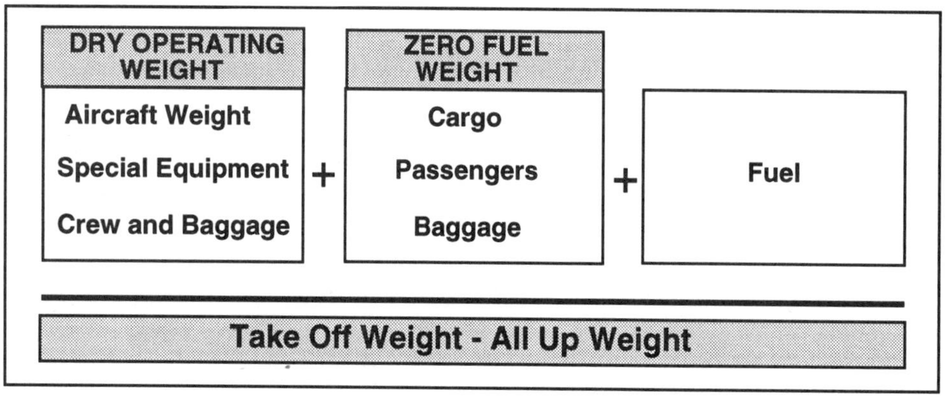

As an example, the approximate Boeing 747-100 series Dry Operating Weight is 165 tons. Since the maximum structural Take-Off Weight for the aircraft is 333 tons, it can carry 168 tons of fuel and payload combined. The maximum fuel load depends on the specific gravity of the fuel and the capacity of the fuel tanks which is about 140 tons. Average weights for a Boeing 747 at the start of an 8 hour flight are:

- 165 tons Dry Operating Weight
- 35-40 tons payload
- 105-110 tons fuel (90 tons are used, the rest is reserve)
- 305-315 tons Take-Off Weight

Aircraft also have a maximum structural landing weight. In cases of emergency, when an aircraft must return to its departure airport, the dumping of fuel is undertaken to reduce the AUW to within landing tolerance. The maximum structural landing weight of the Boeing 747-100 series is 265 tons.

Weight and Balance

Weight distribution on an aircraft is very important; incorrect loading can result in the aircraft being too nose or tail heavy and beyond the ability of controls for correction. All payload weights and their distribution are carefully preplanned and are normally accomplished with the help of a computer.

The computer calculates the centre of gravity and checks that it is within limits. Aircraft are designed to cope with a range of movement of the center of gravity to allow for take-off at different weights and with varying weight distribution. Similar calculations are made by the flight engineer throughout the progress of the flight as fuel is burned and redistributed from tank to tank.

Aircraft Fuel

Commercial jet airliners burn various grades of jet fuel of the kerosene (paraffin) type. They are colored to identify different types and you may well hear pilots refer to them as type Alpha or Bravo as well.

For an average transatlantic flight of 7 to 8 hours, a Boeing 747 requires about 80 to 90 tons. Diversion fuel together with an alternate reserve is always carried just in case and is in the range of an additional 10 to 15 tons. Contingency fuel is also carried which may be used in the event of significant flight plan changes and holding delays at the destination. Any remaining fuel carried is known as excess fuel.

In this day and age with escalating aviation fuel prices, commercial airlines carefully plan the locations where they fill up their aircraft. Too much excess fuel is not economical because you use more fuel carrying the extra weight. On the other hand, too little contingency fuel can result in serious fuel shortage problems. A common safety factor used by many airlines with respect to fuel is the amount you need plus 15% more.

The fuel requirements and associated flying times for a Boeing 747 enroute from London to New York are illustrated below.

Description	Fuel (Tons)	Time (Hours)
Fuel and time to New York	80.0	7.00
Diversion Fuel (Boston)	13.0	1.10
Contingency Fuel	4.0	0.25
Excess Fuel	0.0	0.00
TOTAL	**97.0**	**8.35**

The maximum time an aircraft can remain aloft is known as **Endurance**. The altitudes of many international airports do not permit a full load of fuel to be carried and midway stops have been prearranged for the aircraft to refuel. This is especially true for flights out of many parts of Africa to Europe.

• City/Airport Identifiers

IATA City/Airport Three Letter Identifiers

IATA (the International Air Transport Association) has defined a set of three letter codes that are used by the airline industry to designate cities and airports. These three-character codes are used in reservations, timetables, tickets, tariffs, air waybills, schedule publications and other airline industry applications.

Some of these codes bear a resemblance to the actual city name. For example, MIA stands for Miami. Others have been allocated according to a different method. YYZ is the code for Toronto. The code for most major Canadian airports starts with the letter Y.

Some cities have more than one airport. In this case a separate code is used for each. Consider the following examples:

SFO	San Francisco
YYZ	Toronto
JFK	New York - Kennedy
LGA	New York - La Guardia
LHR	London - Heathrow
LGW	London - Gatwick

Most ticketing agents will know several hundred of these codes off by heart. The general public is also exposed to them via the baggage tags that are affixed to their luggage indicating the destination of the flight.

ICAO Four-Letter Location Indicators

Four-letter Location Indicators are formulated and arranged to identify the geographical location of stations that are part of the Aeronautical Fixed Telecommunications Network (AFTN).

For AFTN purposes, the world is divided in 22 geographic regions, with each region assigned a letter of the alphabet. (Letters I, J, Q and X are not used.)

For many parts of the world, the four-letter Location Indicator is formed by adding the appropriate one-letter geographic prefix to the three-letter IATA city/airport identifier. For example, "K" is assigned to the United States, while "C" is applied to Canada.

IATA 3-Letter	IATA 4-Letter	City/Airport
SFO	KSFO	San Francisco
JFK	KJFK	New York - Kennedy
LGA	KLGA	New York - La Guardia
YYZ	CYYZ	Toronto

However, such is not he case for Europe and other parts of the world. Consider the following:

IATA 3-Letter	IATA 4-Letter	City/Airport
LHR	EGLL	London Heathrow
CDG	LFPG	Charles de Gaulle
BDU	TXKF	Bermuda
TKO	RJAA	New Tokyo International

The four-letter indicators are always used in AFTN radioteletype circuit traffic.

IATA Two-character Airline Designators

IATA also has assigned two-letter designators to all airlines and air carriers for commercial purposes.

These two-letter codes are used in reservations, timetables, tickets, tariffs, air waybills, schedule publications and in airline interline telecommunications, as well as other airline industry applications.

IATA assigns three types of two-character airline designators: unique, numeric/alpha and controlled duplicate. The definition of a controlled duplicate is when two carriers have the same designator, but operate different services (and are also generally located in a different geographic region).

Some examples follow:

AA	American Airlines
UA	United Airlines
AC	Air Canada
AF	Air France
BA	British Airways

ICAO Three-character Airline Designators

Prior to October 25, 1987, all commercial airline carriers (scheduled and non-scheduled) were assigned a two letter designator code by IATA (International Air Transport Association). As far back as 1981, the ICAO (International Civil Aviation Organization) had decided that it would be necessary to convert to a three letter code in order to prevent duplication or meaningless codes.

In conjunction with the Aeronautical Fixed Telecommunications Network (AFTN), every aircraft operating agency, aeronautical authority and aviation service using the AFTN network switched to the new approved ICAO three letter designators.

The general public, however, is not aware of this fact as airlines continue to use their previously assigned two letter IATA designators for tickets, boarding passes, baggage tags and terminal arrival/departure display systems.

Some examples of the old two and the new three letter designator codes appear below.

Old 2 Letter Designator	New 3 Letter Designator	Airline Carrier
AC	ACA	Air Canada
AF	AFR	Air France
BA	BAW	British Airways

Aircraft Registration Prefixes

An aircraft's country of registration is readily identifiable from its registration number prefix. The Prefix may be a one to four character code, with two characters being the most common for most countries. Consider the following examples:

Registration #	Country	Carrier/Aircraft Type
C-FBEF	Canada	Air Canada Boeing 767 250ER
G-BOAC	Great Britain	British Airways Concorde
LV-LOA	Argentina	Aerolineas Argentinas Fokker F.28 1000
N712DA	United States	Delta Airlines Lockheed 1011 Tristar 1
PP-VPJ	Brazil	VARIG McDonnell Douglas MD-11
ZS-SPF	South Africa	South African Airways Boeing 747SP 44
4X-ELB	Israel	El Al Boeing 747 458
5W-1LF	Western Samoa	Polynesian Airlines Boeing 737 3Q8
9V-STZ	Singapore	Singapore Airlines Airbus A.310 324

NOTE: *The Appendices contain complete cross listings of Location Identifiers, Airline Designators, Registration Prefixes and international High Altitude Enroute Waypoints.*

Master Frequency List

FREQ.	SERVICE	STATION/LOCATION
2020.0	AUS-RFDS	Royal Flying Doctor Service
2141.0	USCG-AIR	USCG-Air/Ground - Alaska
2182.0	SP-RDARA	Koror (Babelthuap), Majuro (Marshall Is), Ponape Int'l, Truk Int'l (Moen Is) & Yap Radios
	USCG-AIR	Air/Ground
2260.0	AUS-RFDS	Royal Flying Doctor Service
2261.0	USCG-AIR	Air/Ground
2280.0	AUS-RFDS	Royal Flying Doctor Service
2326.0	USN	Air/Ground/Ship
2371.0	US-CAP	Civil Air Patrol
2374.0	US-CAP	Civil Air Patrol
2405.0	NASA	Cape Radio
2426.0	USN	Air/Ground/Ship
2476.0	USN	Air/Ground/Ship
2505.0	NASA	Cape Radio
2576.0	USN	Air/Ground/Ship
2622.0	NASA	Cape Radio
2641.0	RAF	UKADGE "Kilo Papa"
2656.0	AUS-RFDS	Royal Flying Doctor Service
2664.0	NASA	Cape Radio
2678.0	NASA	Cape Radio
	USCG-AIR	Air/Ground
2716.0	NASA	Cape Radio
2728.0	CAR-RDARA	Cuba - Boyeros, Camaguey & Santiago de Cuba Aeradios
2744.0	NASA	Cape Radio
2760.0	AUS-RFDS	Royal Flying Doctor Service
2764.0	NASA	Cape Radio
2789.0	USN	Air/Ground/Ship
2800.0	NASA	Cape Radio
2805.0	AUS-RFDS	Royal Flying Doctor Service
2808.5	US-DOD	Counterdrug Network "Xray Alpha"
2811.0	CAR-RDARA	Cuba - Baracoa, Bayamo, Guantanamo, Holguin, Manzanillo, Moa & Nicaro Aeradios
2836.0	NASA	Cape Radio
2851.0	AFI-RDARA	AFI-4 RDARA, Cabinda, Luanda (4 de Fevereiro), Kinshasa
	NCA-2 MWARA	Barnaul, Irkutsk, Khanty Mansiysk, Kirensk, Kolpashevo, Krasnoyarsk, Novosibirsk, Podkamennaya, Surgut, Yeniseysk
	U.S. Flight Test	Boeing Company
		Falcon Jet Corp
		McDonnel Douglas
		Rockwell International
2854.0	SAT-2 MWARA	Canarias, Cayenne, Dakar, Manaus, Paramaribo, Recife, Rio de Janeiro, Sal Island, Salvador
2860.0	OD-RDARA	North Sea Oil Rig Helicopters (Beccles Aeradio)
2861.0	CAR-RDARA	Cuba - Manzanillo Aeradio
	NA-RDARA	Alaska - Intra-Alaska Air to Ground, Anchorage Radio
2862.0	NAT-C MWARA	Gander, Iceland (Reykjavik), Shannon (Shanwick)
2863.0	PAC-VOL	Honolulu (H+00,30), Tokyo (H+10,40), Hong Kong (H+15,45), Auckland (H+20,50)
2865.0	NA-RDARA	Alaska - Yakutat Aeradio
2866.0	NA-RDARA	Alaska - Barrow (Wiley Post/Will Rogers), Cold Bay, Cordova, Ketchikan, Kotzebue (Ralph Wien Memorial), McGrath & Point Barrow Dew Station Radios
2868.0	AFI-RDARA	Angola - Luanda ACC
	NCA-RDARA	CIS - Khabarovsk ACC
2869.0	CEP-1/2 MWARA	Honolulu, San Francisco
	NCA-VOL	Russian Network C, Syktyvkar, Russia (H+00,30), Sverdlovsk, Russia (H+05,35), Novosibirsk, Russia (H+10,40), Kuybyshev, Russia (H+15,45), Tyuman, Russia (H+20,50)
	SEA-RDARA	Australia HF Network - South Eastern region
	U.S. Flight Test	Rockwell International
2872.0	MID-RDARA	India - several aeradios
2875.0	NA-RDARA	Alaska - Central and Southeast

Master Frequency List

FREQ.	SERVICE	STATION/LOCATION
2878.0	AFI-4 MWARA	Accra, Bangui, Brazzaville, Bulawayo, Contonou, Douala, Entebbe, Franceville, Francistown, Garoua, Goma, Johannesburg, Kano, Kinshasa, Kisangani, Lagos, Libreville, Lomé, Luanda, Lumbumbashi, Lusaka, Maroua, Maseru, Nairobi, N'djamena, N'djili, Niamey, Niamtougou, Port Gentil, Roberts (Monrovia), Salisbury, Salazar, Seychelles, Windhoek, Yaounde
	OD-RDARA	Offshore Drilling Rigs & Helicopters
	SAM-RDARA	Brazil - Navegantes FIS & several others
2881.0	SAM-VOL	Buenos Aires (Ezeiza) Volmet (H+15)
2887.0	CAR-A MWARA	Barranquilla, Boyeros, Guatemala City, Merida, New York, Panama, Piarco, San Andres Is (Sesquicentenario), San Jose, Tegucigalpa (Toncontin Int'l)
2893.0	NCA-RDARA	Ukraine - Kiev Aeradio
2896.0	CAR-LDOC	Boyeros (Aeroflot)
	CWP-RDARA	Japan - Naha ACC
	NCA-LDOC	Moscow (Aeroflot)
2899.0	NAT-B MWARA	Gander, Iceland (Reykjavik), New York, Santa Maria, Shannon (Shanwick)
2902.0	NCA-RDARA	Byelorussia - Minsk & Vitebsk ACC's
2905.0	SP-RDARA	Maldive Islands - Gan FIS (Addu Atoll)
2910.0	EA-RDARA	Nepal - Kathmandu Aeradio
2911.0	NA-RDARA	Alaska - Central and Southeast , Aleutians
2914.0	SAM-RDARA	Brazil - Santa Cruz Aeradio
2920.0	AFI-RDARA	Swaziland - Manzini/Manzapa Aeradio
	NCA-RDARA	CIS - Moscow Aeradio
2923.0	MID-RDARA	Pakistan - Gilgit, Jiwani, Karachi, Pasni, Peshawar, Rawalpindi/Islamabad (Chaklala), Skardu, & Turbat Aeradios
2926.0	NCA-RDARA	CIS - Mineralyne-Vody, Rostov-na-Donu, Sochl, Sukhumi & Tbilisi ACC's
2931.0	MID-RDARA	India - Agartala, Ahmadabab, Amritsar, Baghdogra, Bangalore, Bhubaneswar, Bombay, Calcutta, Delhi, Dibrugarh, Gauhati, Hyderabad (Begumpet), Lucknow, Madras, Nagpur, Patna, Port Blair, Varanasi, Vijayawada & Vishakhapatnam Radios
	PAK-AF	Sargodha Radio (Pakistani Air Force)
	SAM-RDARA	Uruguay - Montevideo (Carrasco) & Vichadero Aeradios
		Venezuela - Upata Radio
2932.0	NCA-RDARA	CIS - Khabarovsk ACC
	NP-3/4 MWARA	Honolulu , Tokyo
2933.0	MID-RDARA	India - several aeradios
2941.0	NCA-VOL	Russian Network A, Riga, Latvia (H+00,30), St. Petersburg, Russia (H+05,35), Moscow, Russia H+10,15,40,45), Kiev, Ukraine (H+20,50), Rostov, Ukraine (H+25,55)
2943.5	MID-RDARA	India - Hyderabad (Begumpet) Radio
2944.0	MID-3 MWARA	Aktyubinsk, Alma Ata, Dushanbe, Frunze, Kuybyshev, Kzyl-Orda, Moscow, Samarkand, Tashkent, Uralsk, Yevevan
	SAM-NW MWARA	Barranquilla, Bogota, Caracas (Maiquetia), Lima, Quito
	SAM-SW MWARA	Antofagasta, Asuncion, Bariloche, Buenos Aires (Ezeiza), Comodoro Rivadavia, Cordoba, Easter Is (Pascua), La Paz, Lima, Mendoza, Puerto Montt, Punta Arenas, Resistencia, Salta, Santa Cruz (El Trompillo), Santiago, Talara, Ushuaia
	SP-RDARA	Australia - Dubbo, Melbourne & Midura ACC's
2945.0	SEA-RDARA	Myanmar - Heho, Kawthoung, Kengtung, Kyaukpyu, Loikaw, Magwey, Mong-Hsat, Mawlamyine, Hpapun, Hpa-an, Yangon, Thandwe & Sittwe Aeradios
	SP-RDARA	Australia - Sydney Aeradio
2950.0	USAF	Greenland - Sondre Stromford Aeradio
2952.0	CAM-RDARA	Guatemala - Carmelita Aeradio
	NCA-RDARA	CIS - Frunze, Samarkand, Tashkent & Termez ACC's
2956.0	NA-RDARA	Alaska - Aleutians
	SEA-RDARA	Indonesia - Biak, Ujung Pandang & several other ACC's
2962.0	NAT-E MWARA	New York, Santa Maria
2965.0	SAM-RDARA	Argentina - Buenos Aires (Ezeiza) & Comodoro Rivadavia ACC's
	SEA-VOL	Sydney (H+00,30), Calcutta (H+05,35), Bangkok (H+10,40), Karachi (H+15,45), Singapore (H+20,50), Bombay (H+25,55),
2966.0	NA-RDARA	Mexico - Mazatlan Aeradio
	NCA-RDARA	Afghanistan - Kabul ACC
	SAM-RDARA	Argentina - Bahia Blanca Naval (Commandante Espora), Comodoro Rivadavia, Rio Gallegos, San Carlos de Bariloche, Santa Rosa & Trelew Aeradios
2971.0	NAT-D MWARA	Bodo, Cambridge Bay, Churchill, Iqaluit (Frobisher Bay), Gander, Iceland (Reykjavik), Sondrestrom

FREQ.	SERVICE	STATION/LOCATION
2972.0	AUS-RFDS	Royal Flying Doctor Service
2973.0	SEA-RDARA	Myanmar - Banmaw, Htilin, Kyauktu, Lashio, Mandalay, Momeok, Myitkyina & Putao
2980.0	NCA-RDARA	CIS - Dushanbe Radio
	SAM-RDARA	Venezuela - Bruzal & Upata Aeradios
2983.0	EU-RDARA	Norway - Bodo ACC
2986.0	NCA-RDARA	CIS, Eastern region - Chulman, Vitim & other ACC's
2989.0	EU-RDARA	Greece - several aeradios
2992.0	MID-1 MWARA	Aden, Amman, Ankara, Baghdad, Basrah, Beirut, Cairo, Damascus, Jeddah, Kuwait, Manama, Odessa, Sana'a, Simferopol, Tehran, Tbilisi, Yerevan
	MID-RDARA	Bahrain ACC
	MID-VOL	Damascus Volmet (H+30)
2994.0	U.S. Flight Test	Boeing Company
		Rockwell International
2998.0	CWP-1/2 MWARA	Guam, Honolulu, Manila, Naha, Port Moresby, Seoul, Taipei, Tokyo
3001.0	MID-VOL	Beirut Volmet (H+15,45)
3004.0	NCA-3 MWARA	Chita, Chulman, Ekimchan, Irkutsk, Kirensk, Khabarovsk, Pyongyang, Ulaanbaatar, Ulan Ude
	U.S. Flight Test	Boeing Company
		McDonnel Douglas
		Rockwell International
3007.0	CAR-LDOC	Boyeros (Cubana Airlines)
		Merida, Mexico City, Tijuana (AeroMexico)
		Willemstad (ALM Antillean)
	CWP-LDOC	Hong Kong (Dragonair)
		Manila (Philippines Air)
		Seoul (KAL-Korean Airlines)
	EA-LDOC	Beijing
	MID-LDOC	Bombay (Air India)
	RAF	Hong Kong Air
	SEA-CC-LDOC	Sydney SkyComms
	SEA-LDOC	Bangkok (Thai Airways)
		Jakarta
		Sydney (Qantas)
		Yangon (Myanma Airways)
	SP-LDOC	Auckland (Air New Zealand)
3008.0	SAM-RDARA	Argentina - Cordoba, Monte Caseros, Resistencia & Salta ACC's
	SP-RDARA	Nauru - Nauru Island Aeradio
3010.0	EU-LDOC	Amsterdam (KLM-Royal Dutch Airlines)
		Athens (Olympic Airlines)
		Belgrade (Serbia Aerotransport)
		Berne ("Berna") Radio
		Brussels (Sabena)
		Dublin (Aer Lingus)
		Frankfurt (Lufthansa)
		Lisbon (TAP-Air Portugal)
		Paris Radio (Air France)
	MID-LDOC	Tel Aviv (El Al)
	MID-RDARA	India - several aeradios
	SAM-LDOC	Buenos Aires (Aerolineas Argentinas)
		Caracas (AVENSA)
		Lima (American Airlines)
		Montevideo (PLUNA)
		Piarco (West Indian)
		Rio de Janeiro & several others (VARIG)
		San Salvador
		Santiago
	SP-LDOC	Easter Island
3013.0	AFI-LDOC	Addis Ababa, Asmara (Ethiopian Airlines - Holloway)
		Algiers (Air Algerie)
		Blantyre (Air Malawi)
		Cairo (Egypt Air)
		Dar es Salaam (Air Tanzania)
		Djibouti (Air Djibouti)

Master Frequency List

FREQ.	SERVICE	STATION/LOCATION
3013.0	AFI-LDOC	Entebbe (Uganda Airlines)
		Harare (Air Zimbabwe)
		Kigali (Air Rwanda)
		Kinshasa (Air Zaire)
		Lagos (Nigeria Airways)
		Lusaka (Zambia Airways)
		Monrovia
		Nairobi
		Ouagadougou
		Salisbury
		Springbok Jo'burg (South African Airlines)
		Tunis (Tunis Air)
	CEP-CC-LDOC	Honolulu, San Francisco (ARINC)
	INO-LDOC	Antananarivo (Air Madagascar)
		Mauritius Ops (Air Mauritius)
	MID-LDOC	Beirut (MEA-Cedar Jet)
		Jeddah (Saudi Airlines)
		Manama (Falcon)
		Muscat (Gulf Air)
		Safat (Kuwaiti Airlines)
		Tehran
	NCA-LDOC	Kabul (Ariana Afghan Airlines)
3015.0	EU-RDARA	Greece - Agrinion, Dimokritos, Andravida, Nikos Kazantzakis, Ionnina, Kalamata, Karpathos, Kasos, Kastoria (Arisoteles), Kavala (Amigdhaleon), Kefallinia, Ioannis-Kapodistrias, Chania (Souda), Kos, Kozani (Fillppos), Larissa, Milos, Mitilini, Rodos (Diagoras), Makedonia, Samos, Skiathos, Sparti & Zakinthos Aeradios
3016.0	EA-1 MWARA	Beijing, Canton, Hailar, Irkutsk, Jinan, Kunming, Lanzhou, Pyongyang, Shanghai, Shenyang, Taegu, Ulaanbaatar, Urumqi, Wuhan, Zhengzhou
	EA-RDARA	China - several ACC's
	NAT-A MWARA	Canarias, Gander, New York, Paramaribo, Piarco, Santa Maria, Shanwick
	NCA-RDARA	CIS - Cheropovets , Velikye Luki and several other ACC's
	SAM-RDARA	Argentina - Buenos Aires ACC Ezeiza Control
3019.0	NCA-1 MWARA	Ivdel, Khanty Mansiysk, Moscow, Syktyvkar, Sverdlovsk, Vologda
	OD-RDARA	Offshore Drilling Rigs & Helicopters
3023.0	EU-RDARA	Greenland - Gronnedal Aeradio
		Madeira - Funchal Aeradio
		Norway - Stavanger, Svalbard (Longyear) & Trondheim ACC's
	SP-RDARA	Noumea (La Tontouta) Aeradio
	USCG-AIR	Search and Rescue
	USN	Air/Ground/Ship
3023.5	AFI-RDARA	Canary Islands - Puerto del Rosario (Fuerteventura), La Palma, & Tenerife Aeradios
	CAM-RDARA	Honduras - San Pedro Sula Aeradio
		Nicaragua - Managua (Augusto Cesar Sandino) Aeradio
	MID-RDARA	India - Bikaner Aeradio
	SAM-RDARA	Bolivia - Concepcion, Puerto Suarez & San José Aeradios
		Uruguay - Colonia (Aerp. Deptal) Aeradio
	SAT-RDARA	Sal Island - Sal Aeradio
	SEA-RDARA	Malaysia - Belaga FIS, Lifou (Wanaham) Aeradio
3024.0	NASA	Cape Radio
3026.0	RAF	UKADGE "Whiskey Mike"
3032.0	RAAF	Air Force Darwin
	USAF-ACC	Air Combat Command, Secondary
	USAF-CEN	Commando Escort Net - Hawaii
	USAF-USSTRATCOM	Former SAC "Giant Talk" Network "Whiskey 100"
3036.0	USN	Air/Ground/Ship
3039.0	RAF	UKADGE "Alpha Kilo"
	U.S. Flight Test	United Technologies
	USN	Air/Ground/Ship
3046.0	CANFORCE	MAG - Halifax Military "Delta One Golf"
	NCA-RDARA	CIS - Krasnoyarsk, Yeniseysk & several other ACC's
3047.0	CAR-RDARA	Cuba - Santiago de Cuba Aeradio
3048.0	USAF-USSTRATCOM	"X-ray 206"

FREQ.	SERVICE	STATION/LOCATION
3050.0	RAF	Finningley Air
	USN	Air/Ground
3051.0	RAF	UKADGE "Alpha Mike"
3052.0	USN	Navy Air ASW
3053.0	CAR-RDARA	Cuba - San Julian (Escuela de Aviacion) Aeradio
3060.0	USAF-ACC	Air Combat Command
3061.0	OP-Haiti	Operation Able Manner (Haiti Embargo)
3069.0	FAF	Villacoublay (French Air Force Air/Ground)
3071.0	NORAD	NORAD
3085.0	RAF	Akrotiri AFB, "Cyprus Flight Watch"
3087.0	USN	Navy Air ASW
3088.0	USN	Navy Air ASW
3092.0	CANFORCE	ATG - Trenton Military, MACS - Edmonton Military, St. John's Military, Lahr Military
3095.0	CANFORCE	ATG - Trenton Military
	MID-RDARA	Saudi Arabia - Al Jouf, Bisha, Dhahran, Gizan, Khamis Mushait, Madinah (Prince Moh. bin Abdulaziz), Nejran, Sulayel, Taif & Wejh Aeradios
	SAUDI-AF	Saudi Air Force, Dhahran (Hotel 1), Taif (Hotel 4)
3100.5	USAF-AMC-OP	Operation Restore Hope (Accuse Bravo - Tanker), Lajes
3102.0	NCA-RDARA	CIS - Khabarovsk, Juzno, Sakhalinsk & Yeniseysk ACC's
	RAF	UKADGE "Foxtrot Alpha"
3104.0	US-JCS	United States Joint Chiefs of Staff Net/USN Tactical
3109.0	CEP-RDARA	Hawaii - Barber's Point (John Rodgers), Kanoehe Bay & other ACC's
	US-Flight Test	Seagull Control working Curtis Wilbur Test Seagull
	USN	Air/Ground Gulf of Mexico (secondary)
3110.0	RAF	UKADGE
3112.0	RAF	UKADGE "Alpha" or "Echo", Bampton
3113.0	USAF-USSTRATCOM	Former SAC "Giant Talk" Network "Sierra 302"
3116.0	NA-RDARA	Mexico - Mexico City & Oaxaca ACC's
	RAF	UKADGE - Buchan
	SAF-AF	Langebaanweg, Waterkloof & Ysterplaat Military Radios (South African Air Force)
	USAF-SAM	Mystic Star SAM Series D (Air Force 2)
3120.0	NASA	Cape Radio
	RAF	UKADGE "Whiskey Golf"
	USCG-AIR	Air/Ground
3123.0	US-Customs	Drug Enforcement Air Patrols
	USCG-AIR	Air/Ground
3126.0	RAF	UKADGE - Boulmer AFB, "Juliet November"
3127.0	USN	Air Ground (secondary)
3130.0	RAF	UKADGE "Bravo Foxtrot"
	US-JTF-4	Joint Task Force on Drug Enforcement - US Navy
	USN	Tactical, FACSFAC Jacksonville
3132.0	USCG	Coast Guard Air/Ground
3137.0	SPAF	Palma De Mallorca RCC (Spanish Air Force)
	USAF-CEN	Commando Escort Net - Hawaii
3144.0	GAF	DHM 91 Munster (German Air Force Air/Ground)
3151.0	CANFORCE	MAG - Halifax Military, MACS - St. John's Military
	EU-LDOC	Burgas, Sofia (LAZ - Balkan Bulgarian Airlines)
	USN	USN tracking net with AWACS support
3185.0	SEA-LDOC	Melbourne (Ansett Airways)
3187.0	NASA	Cape Radio
3218.0	RAF	UKADGE "Mike Sierra"
3231.0	USAF-ACC	Air Combat Command
3261.0	USN	Air/Ground/Ship
3279.5	U.S. Flight Test	Grumman Aerospace
3281.0	U.S. Flight Test	Boeing Company
		Grumman Aerospace
		United Technologies
3295.0	NORAD	NORAD
	USAF-USSTRATCOM	Former SAC "Giant Talk" Network "Sierra 303"
3299.0	USAF-ACC	Air Combat Command
3306.0	NORAD	NORAD
3312.0	SAM-RDARA	Paraguay - General Artigas Aeradio
3331.0	US-FAA	U. S. Federal Aviation Administration

Master Frequency List

FREQ.	SERVICE	STATION/LOCATION
3340.0	SAM-RDARA	Uruguay - Montevideo (Carrasco) Aeradio
3341.0	EU-LDOC	Stockholm Radio
3343.0	AFI-RDARA	Ghana - Accra FIS
	U.S. Flight Test	Boeing Company, Seattle
3344.0	NCA-RDARA	CIS, Mid region several ACC's
3345.0	RAF	UKADGE "Tango Quebec"
3346.0	SAM-RDARA	Argentina - several ACC's
3364.0	USAF-ACC	Air Combat Command, Primary
3365.0	NASA	Cape Radio
3369.0	US-DOD	Counterdrug Network "Victor Kilo"
3378.0	NA-CC-LDOC	Tors Cove (Rainbow Radio)
3380.0	RAF	UKADGE "Kilo Alpha"
3383.0	USAF-ACC	Air Combat Command, Primary - East
3394.0	USAF-ACC	Air Combat Command, Primary - West
3404.0	MID-RDARA	Iraq - Baghdad Aeradio
	MID-VOL	Kuwait Volmet
	NA-RDARA	Mexico - Mexico City
3407.0	CAR-RDARA	Cuba - Boyeros, Camaguey, Ciego de Avila, Tunas & Varadero ACC's
	NCA-VOL	Russian Network B, Tbilisi, Georgia (H+00,30), Aktyubinsk, Kazakhstan (H+05,35), Krasnodar, Azerbaijan (H+10,40), Alma Ata, Kazakhstan (H+15,45), Tashkent, Uzbekistan (H+20,50), Baku, Azerbaijan (H+25,55)
	US-NOAA	Hurricane Hunters - KJY74 Miami Air/Ground
3411.0	AFI-RDARA	Angola - Luanda ACC
3411.5	AFI-RDARA	Tunisia - Tunis ACC
3413.0	AFI-LDOC	Lusaka (Zambia Airways)
	CEP-1/2 MWARA	Honolulu, San Francisco
	EU-VOL	Shannon VOLMET (H+00, 25, 30, 55)
	NA-CC-LDOC	New York (ARINC)
3416.0	SEA-RDARA	Indonesia - Banjarmasin, Jakarta & several other aeradios
3419.0	AFI-2 MWARA	Algiers, Brazzaville, Kano, Gao, Niamey, N'djamena, Tamanrasset, Timimoun, Tripoli, Tunis
	CWP-RDARA	Papua New Guinea - Madang, Nadzab, Port Moresby & Wewak Aeradios
3422.0	NCA-RDARA	CIS, Northern region - several ACC's
3425.0	AFI-RDARA	East Africa/Indian Ocean - Cape Town ACC
		Malawi - Lilongwe FIS
	CWP-RDARA	Papua New Guinea - Madang, Nadzab, Port Moresby & Wewak Aeradios
	NCA-RDARA	CIS, Eastern region - Bodaybo, Chita, Irkutsk & Ulan-Ude ACC's
	SAM-RDARA	Brazil - Santa Cruz Aeradio & others
	SP-RDARA	SP-9 RDARA - Faleolo [Samoa], Butaritari [Kiribati], Christmas Island, Fua'Amotu [Tonga], Funafuti [Kiribati], Honiara [Solomon Islands], Nandi [Fiji], Port Moresby [PPN], Port-Vila (Bauerfield) [Vanuatu], Rarotonga [Cook Is], SP-9 RDARA - Santo & Wewak ACC's [PPN]
3428.0	US-DOD	Counterdrug Network "Yankee Alpha"
	US-FAA	U. S. Federal Aviation Administration
3432.0	AFI-RDARA	Guinea
	AFI-RDARA	Guinea, Guinea Bissau & Morocco - several aeradios
	AFI-RDARA	Morocco
	MID-VOL	Karachi Volmet (H+15,45)
3434.0	OD-RDARA	Offshore Drilling Rigs & Helicopters
3440.0	NCA-RDARA	CIS - Aktyubinsk, Kuybyshev, Penza, Severouralsk & Sverdlovsk Aeradios
3443.0	U.S. Flight Test	Boeing Company
		Lockheed Corporation
		McDonnel Douglas
		Rockwell International
3446.0	MID-RDARA	India - several aeradios
	NA-CC-LDOC	Tors Cove (Rainbow Radio)
	SAM-RDARA	Brazil - Carolina & Tucurui Aeradios
		Colombia - Arauca (Santiago Perez), Armedia (El Elden), Barrancabermeja (Yariguies), Bucaramanga (Palonegro), Buenaventura, Cali (Alfonso Bonilla Aragon), Cartagena (Rafael Nuñez), Corozal (Las Brujas), Cucuta (Camilo Daza), Colombia - El Banco (Los Flores), Florencio (Capitolio), Giradot (Santiago Vila), Guapi, Ibague (Perales), Ipiales (San Luis), Magangue (Baracoa), Medellin (Olaya Herrera), Mitu, Monteria (Los Garzines), Nieva (La Manguita), *(cont'd next page)*

FREQ.	SERVICE	STATION/LOCATION
		Ocana (Aguas Claras), Otu, Pasto (Antonio Narino), Pereira (Matecana), Popayan (Guillermo Leon Valencia), Puerto Asis (Tres de Mayo), Puerto Carreno, Quibdo (El Carano), Rio Hacha (Almirante Padilla), San José del Guaviare, San Vincente del Caguan, Santa Marta (Simon Bolivar), Tamé, Trinidad, Tumaco (La Florida), Turbo (Gonzalo Mejia) & Villavicencio (Vanguardia) Aeradios
		Uruguay - Velasquez (Calderon)
3448.0	SAM-RDARA	Colombia - several aeradios
3449.0	NA-RDARA	Alaska - all regions
	OD-RDARA	KYY2 - Amoco Production Company - Offshore Drilling Operations
	U.S. Flight Test	Northern Technical
3452.0	AFI-1 MWARA	Abidjan, Bamako, Bissau, Bobo Dioulasso, Bouake, Casablanca, Conakry, Canarias, Freetown, Kano, Niamey, Nouadhibou, Nouakchott, Ouagadougou, Roberts (Monrovia))
	OD-RDARA	Offshore Drilling Rigs & Helicopters
	SAM-RDARA	Brazil - Recife FIR, Rio de Janeiro Aeradio
	SAT-1 MWARA	Brasilia, Canarias, Cayenne, Dakar, Manaus, Paramaribo, Recife, Rio de Janeiro, Sal Island, Salvador
	SEA-RDARA	Australia HF Network - Northeast, North Central and Central East regions - Alice Springs, Cairns, Charleville, Darwin, Gove, Longreach, Mount Isa, Rockhampton, Tennant Creek, Townsville & Weipa Aeradios
	SP-RDARA	Maldive Islands - Gan FIS (Addu Atoll)
3453.0	EU-RDARA	Norway - Stavanger FIS
	MID-RDARA	Jordan - Amman ACC
		Saudi Arabia - Jeddah, Taif & other Aeradios
		UAE - Abu Dhabi ACC
	OD-RDARA	North Sea Oil Rig Helicopters (Yarmouth Aeradio)
3455.0	CAR-B MWARA	Barranquilla, Boyeros, Cayenne, Georgetown, Maiquetia, New York, Panama, Paramaribo, Piarco, San Andres Is
3458.0	EA-VOL	Beijing (H+15,45), Guangzhou (H+10,40)
	NA-LDOC	Tors Cove (Rainbow Radio)
3459.0	NA-LDOC	Toronto (Elite-Canada 3000)
3460.0	NA-RDARA	Mexico - Mexico City
	SEA-RDARA	Kiribati/Tuvalu - Tabiteuea (North) & Tarawa (Betio) Aeradios
3461.0	NCA-RDARA	CIS, Eastern region - Ekimchan, Samarkand & several other ACC's
	SEA-RDARA	Australia HF Network - Northwest, South Central, Southwest regions - Alice Springs, Broken Hill, Ceduna, Darwin, Derby, Geraldton, Kalgoorlie, Leigh Creek South, Meekatharra, Perth, & Port Hedland FIS's
3466.0	SAM-RDARA	Colombia - Valledupar (Alfonso Lopez) Aeradio
3467.0	AFI-3 MWARA	Addis Ababa, Aden, Asmara, Bahrain, Benghazi, Bujumbura, Cairo, Dar es Salaam, Entebbe, Hargesia, Djibouti, Jeddah, Khartoum, Kigali, Kisimayu, Male, Mogadishu, Nairobi, N'djamena, Sana'a, Seychelles, Triopli
	EA-RDARA	China - Urumqi ACC
	EU-TEST	Pailton, UK (Civil Aviation Radio Measuring Station)
	MID-2 MWARA	Abadan, Alma Ata, Bombay, Delhi, Dushanbe, Frunze, Kabul, Karachi, Kathmandu, Kuwait, Lahore, Male, Muscat, Odessa, Samarkand, Seychelles, Tashkent, Tehran, Tbilisi, Urumqi, Yerevan
	MID-RDARA	Yemen - Riyan Radio
	NCA-RDARA	CIS - Tashkent & Dushanbe ACC's, Uzbekistan
	SP-6/7 MWARA	Auckland, Honolulu, Nandi, Pascua (Easter Is.), Rarotonga, Sydney, Tahiti
	SP-RDARA	New Zealand
3470.0	EA-RDARA	China - Guangzhou & Kunming ACC's
	EU-RDARA	Norway - Stavanger FIS
	MID-RDARA	India - several aeradios
	NA-RDARA	Alaska - Central and Southeast
	SEA-1 MWARA	Bali, Bangkok, Colombo, Calcutta, Dhaka, Guangzhou, Jakarta, Kathmandu, Kuala Lumpur, Kunming, Madras, Male, Singapore, Yangon
	SEA-3 MWARA	Bali, Cocos Is, Darwin, Jakarta, Male, Perth, Singapore, Ujung Pandang
	SEA-RDARA	Indonesia - several aeradios
	SP- RDARA	Christmas Island (proprietary)
3474.0	U.S. Flight Test	Rockwell International
3474.5	SAM-RDARA	Uruguay - Durazno Aeradio (PLUNA Meteo H+00)

Master Frequency List

FREQ.	SERVICE	STATION/LOCATION
3476.0	INO-1 MWARA	Antananarivo, Beira, Blantyre, Bombay, Cocos Is., Colombo, Dar es Salaam, Harare, Jeddah, Johannesburg, Kigali, Lilongwe, Lusaka, Madras, Mahajanga, Male, Mauritius, Moroni, Nairobi, Perth, Seychelles, St. Denis, Toamasina
	INO-RDARA	Madagascar - several aeradios
	NAT-F MWARA	Gander & Shanwick Aeradios
3479.0	EUR-A MWARA	Arkhangelsk, Beirut, Kiev, Lvov, Minsk, Moscow, Murmansk, Odessa, Riga, Simferopol, St. Petersburg, Syktyvkar, Tunis, Valetta, Velikiye, Vitebsk, Vilnius, Vologda
	SAM-C MWARA	Belem, Bogota, Brasilia, Leticia, Manaus, Maiquetia, Porto Velho, Rio de Janeiro
	SAM-NE MWARA	Belem, Cayenne, Georgetown, Maiquetia, Paramaribo, Piarco, Recife
	SAM-RDARA	Brazil - Belem, Brasilia, Campo Grande, Curitiba, Manaus, Porto Velho FIR's
	SAM-SE MWARA	Asuncion, Belem, Brasilia, Buenos Aires, Campo Grande, Curtiba, La Paz, Montevideo, Porto Alegre, Porto Velho, Recife, Salvador Dois De Julho, Santa Cruz
3479.5	MID-RDARA	India - Gauhati Radio
3481.0	RAF	Hong Kong Air
	RNZAF	Wigram AFB
3482.0	EU-CC-LDOC	Somerset (Portishead Radio)
3485.0	EA-2 MWARA	Canton, Irkutsk, Pyongyang, Ulaanbaatar
	NAT-VOL	Gander (H+20, 50), New York (H+00,30)
	SEA-2 MWARA	Bali, Bangkok, Denpasar, Guangzhou, Hanoi, Ho Chi Minh, Hong Kong, Jakarta, Kuala Lumpur, Kota Kinabalu, Manila, Singapore, Vientiane
3488.0	OD-RDARA	North Sea Oil Rig Helicopters (Beccles Aeradio/Great Yarmouth)
	SAM-RDARA	Colombia - Barranquilla & several other aeradios
3491.0	MID-RDARA	India - Calcutta ATC
3494.0	EU-LDOC	Stockholm Radio
	NA-CC-LDOC	New York (ARINC)
3495.0	NCA-RDARA	CIS - Mineralyne-Vody Aeradio
3497.0	EU-LDOC	Bucharest (TAROM - Romanian Air Transport)
		Luqa (Air Malta)
		Prague (Czechoslovak Airlines)
		Speedbird London (British Airways)
	MID-RDARA	India - Mohanbari Aeradio
3497.5	MID-RDARA	India - Agartala, Baghdogra & Mohanbari Aeradios
3499.0	MID-RDARA	India - Agartala, Baghdogra, Gauhati & Mohanbari Aeradios
3512.0	RAF	UKADGE "Quebec Bravo"
3747.0	EU-CC-LDOC	Somerset (Portishead Radio)
3787.5	SAM-VOL	Puerto Montt Volmet (H+20)
3800.0	MID-RDARA	Iraq - Baghdad ACC
3821.0	U.S. Flight Test	Lockheed Corporation
3836.0	INO-LDOC	Port Moresby (Air Niugini)
3840.0	NASA	Johnson Space Center - Shuttle Rebroadcast - LSB
3845.0	NA-CC-LDOC	Tors Cove (Rainbow Radio)
3855.0	MID-RDARA	India - Putussibau Aeradio & others
3860.0	NASA	Goddard Space Center - Shuttle Rebroadcast - LSB
3864.0	RAF	UKADGE "Papa Romeo"
3867.0	RAF	UKADGE "Kilo Delta"
3878.0	USAF-AMC-OP	Operation Restore Hope (Absolution - Mogadishu, Somalia)
3880.0	RAF	UKADGE "Whiskey India"
3885.0	RNAVY	RNAS Culdrose Air
3893.0	RAF	UKADGE "Hotel Echo"
3896.0	FAF	Toulon Air (French Air Force Air/Ground)
3903.5	SAM-LDOC	several South American stations (TASA)
3916.0	RAF	UKADGE "Alpha Hotel" , Buchan
3921.0	EU-LDOC	Amsterdam (KLM-Royal Dutch Airlines)
3932.0	SAF-AF	South African Air Force
3939.0	RAF	UKADGE "Alpha Echo"
3947.0	RAF	UKADGE "Bravo Kilo"
4010.0	AUS-RFDS	Royal Flying Doctor Service
4014.0	USN	Air Ground (Atlantic)
4015.0	USN	Air/Ground/Ship
4030.0	AUS-RFDS	Royal Flying Doctor Service
4038.6	OP-Haiti	Operation Able Manner (Haiti Embargo)
4041.0	EU-LDOC	Stockholm Radio

FREQ.	SERVICE	STATION/LOCATION
4043.0	RAF	UKADGE "Alpha Whiskey"
	USN	Air/Ground/Ship
4045.0	AUS-RFDS	Royal Flying Doctor Service
4055.0	AUS-RFDS	Royal Flying Doctor Service
	US-FAA	U. S. Federal Aviation Administration
4058.0	AFI-RDARA	Lesotho - several aeradios
4125.0	USCG-AIR	Distress - Cutters/Commstas/Aircraft
4273.0	US-CAP	Civil Air Patrol
4277.0	USAF-CI	U.S. Air Force Crash Investigation
4350.0	AUS-RFDS	Royal Flying Doctor Service, Alice Springs
4372.0	USN	Air/Ground/Ship
4373.0	USN	FACSFAC - Giant Killer - Virginia Capes
4376.0	NASA	Cape Radio
	USCG-AIR	Law Enforcement - Air/Ground/Ship
4390.0	EA-RDARA	North Korea - Pyongyang ACC
4397.0	RAF	UKADGE "Quebec Victor"
4416.0	USN	HICOM WESTPAC (COM7THFLT) - E/N NAVCOMSTA UK
4435.0	NORAD	NORAD
4443.0	NORAD	NORAD
4444.0	USAF-SAM	Mystic Star SAM Series B
4445.0	USAF-SAM	Mystic Star SAM Series A
4448.0	RNZAF	Royal New Zealand Air Force
4449.0	USAF-ACC	Air Combat Command
4451.0	CAR-RDARA	Cuba - Baracoa (Oriente), Bayamo, Guantanamo, Holguin, Maisi, Manzanilo, Moa, Nicaro & Santiago De Cuba Aeradios
4455.0	USAF-SAM	Mystic Star SAM Series J
4464.5	US-CAP	"Pico" - Vermont, "Empire" - NY, "Keystone" - PN, "Freedom" - MA
4466.0	US-CAP	Northeast Region, Primary, Southeast Region, Secondary
4467.5	US-CAP	"Low Land" - WV
4469.0	US-CAP	Southeast Region, Primary, Northeast Region, Secondary
4474.0	USAF-ACC	Air Combat Command, Primary - East
4484.0	RAF	UKADGE "Kilo Romeo"
4487.0	USAF-SAM	Mystic Star SAM Series B
4495.0	NORAD	NORAD
	SEA-RDARA	Indonesia - Tapaktuan Aeradio
	USAF-USSTRATCOM	Former SAC "Giant Talk" Network "Sierra 304"
4500.0	NASA	Cape Radio
	US-DOD	Counterdrug Network "Zulu Alpha"
	USAF-ACC	Air Combat Command
4505.0	USAF-SAM	Mystic Star SAM Series C
4506.0	US-CAP	North Central Region, Primary
4507.5	US-CAP	"Bluebird" - MO, "Starfish" - MN, "Jayhawk" - KS
4509.0	US-CAP	North Central Region, Secondary
4510.0	NASA	Cape Radio
4521.0	EU-CC-LDOC	Somerset (Portishead Radio)
4540.0	RAF	UKADGE "Uniform Tango"
4550.0	NA-CC-LDOC	Gulf of Mexico (ARINC)
4560.0	CANFORCE	MAG - Halifax Military
4582.0	US-CAP	National Emergency and Calling Frequency, Middle East Region, Secondary Pacific Region, Secondary
4585.0	US-CAP	"Plant" - MD, "Kiddie Car" - SC, "Red Dog" - NC, "Low Land" - WV, Middle East Middle East Region, Primary - "Plant" - MD, "Kiddie Car" - SC, "Red Dog" - NC, "Low Land" - WV, Middle East, Pacific Region, Primary
4595.0	EU-LDOC	Stockholm Radio
4601.0	US-CAP	Rocky Mountain Region, Primary, Great Lakes Region, Secondary
4602.5	US-CAP	"Blackhawk" - OH, "Badger" - WI, "Great Lakes", "Red Fox" - NC, "Low Land" - WV
4604.0	US-CAP	Great Lakes Region, Primary, Rocky Mountain Region, Secondary
4606.0	AUS-RFDS	Royal Flying Doctor Service
4611.0	AFI-AFTN	AFTN - traffic, Antananarivo & Mahe
4627.0	US-CAP	"Eagle Nest" - TX, "Sooner" - OK Southwest Region, Primary
4630.0	US-CAP	Southwest Region, Secondary - "Eagle Nest" - TX
	USAF-ACC	Air Combat Command, Primary - East

Master Frequency List

FREQ.	SERVICE	STATION/LOCATION
4645.0	OD-RDARA	KXC62 - Amoco Production Company - Offshore Drilling Operations
4654.0	EU-LDOC	Berne ("Berna") Radio
		Madrid (Iberia)
		Stockholm Radio
4657.0	AFI-RDARA	Malawi - Lilongwe & several other aeradios
	INO-RDARA	Comoros Is. - Moroni (Hahaia) Aeradio
	INO-RDARA	Madagascar - Mahajanga (Amborovy) & Toamasina Aeradios
4663.0	DNMK-NAVY	Drederikshavn Naval Air
	NCA-VOL	CIS English Language Network, Khabarovsk, Russia (H+05,35), Tashkent, Uzbekistan (H+10,40), Kiev, Ukraine (H+15,45), Moscow, Russia (H+25,55), Novosibirsk, Russia (H+20,50)
	SAM-RDARA	Paraguay - Asuncion Aeradio
4666.0	CWP-1/2 MWARA	Guam, Honolulu, Manila, Naha, Port Moresby, Seoul, Taipei, Tokyo
	EU-RDARA	Norway - Svalbard Aeradio (Longyear), Spitzbergen
	SAM-LDOC	Sao Paulo (VASP - Viacao Aerea Sao Paulo)
	SEA-CC-LDOC	Sydney SkyComms
	SEA-LDOC	Sydney (Qantas)
4667.0	NA-LDOC	Toronto (Elite-Canada 3000)
4669.0	MID-1 MWARA	Aden, Amman, Ankara, Baghdad, Basrah, Beirut, Cairo, Damascus, Jeddah, Kuwait, Manama, Odessa, Sana'a, Simferopol, Tehran, Tbilisi, Yerevan
	MID-3 MWARA	Aktyubinsk, Alma Ata, Dushanbe, Frunze, Kuybyshev, Kzyl-Orda, Moscow, Samarkand, Tashkent, Uralsk, Yevevan
	NCA-RDARA	CIS, Mid region - several aeradios
	SAM-NW MWARA	Barranquilla, Bogota, Caracas (Maiquetia), Lima, Quito
	SAM-SW MWARA	Antofagasta, Asuncion, Buenos Aires, Cordoba, Easter Is (Pascua), La Paz, Lima, Mendoza, Puerto Montt, Punta Arenas, Resistencia, Salta, Santa Cruz, Santiago, Talara
4670.0	EU-LDOC	Berne ("Berna") Radio
4672.0	NCA-RDARA	CIS, Western region - Syktyvkar & several other aeradios
	OD-RDARA	Offshore Drilling Rigs & Helicopters
4675.0	NAT-D MWARA	Bodo, Cambridge Bay, Churchill, Iqaluit (Frobisher Bay), Gander, Iceland (Reykjavik), Sondrestrom
	SAM-RDARA	Argentina - several ACC's
	SAM-VOL	Comodoro Rivadavia (H+30,40), Resistencia (H+20,50)
	U.S. Flight Test	Rockwell International
	US-FAA	U. S. Federal Aviation Administration
4678.0	NCA-2 MWARA	Barnaul, Irkutsk, Khanty Mansiysk, Kirensk, Kolpashevo, Krasnoyarsk, Novosibirsk, Podkamennaya, Surgut, Yeniseysk
	SEA-RDARA	Australia HF Network - South Eastern region - Dubbo, Melbourne, Midura & Sydney
4682.0	U.S. Flight Test	Rockwell International
4684.0	SAM-LDOC	several Brazilian stations (TransBrazil)
	SEA-RDARA	Australia HF Network - Southwest region - Carnarvon, Kalgoorlie, Perth, Port Hedland
4687.0	CWP-LDOC	Seoul (KAL-Korean Airlines)
		Tokyo (JAL-Japan Airlines)
	EU-LDOC	Amsterdam (KLM-Royal Dutch Airlines)
		Bucharest (TAROM - Romanian Air Transport)
		Frankfurt (Lufthansa)
		Luqa (Air Malta)
		Rome (Alitalia)
		Scheveningen Radio
		Warsaw (LOT - Polskie Linie)
	SEA-CC-LDOC	Sydney SkyComms
	SEA-LDOC	Bangkok (Thai Airways)
		Colombo (Air Lanka)
		Perth, Sydney (Qantas)
		Yangon (Myanma Airways)
4688.0	NCA-RDARA	CIS, Kyrgyzstan - Frunze ACC
4689.0	AFI-RDARA	Tunisia - Tunisia
4690.0	EU-LDOC	Stockholm Radio
4693.0	NCA-RDARA	CIS - Alma Ata Aeradio
	SEA-RDARA	Australia HF Network - South Central region - Alice Springs, Broken Hill, Ceduna, Leigh Creek

FREQ.	SERVICE	STATION/LOCATION
4696.0	SAM-RDARA	Ecuador - Quito Aeradio
4700.0	CANFORCE	MAG - Halifax Military
	USN	Navy Air ASW Pacific (Habitat ASW Command Center)
4701.0	US-NOAA	Hurricane Hunters - KJY74 Miami Air/Ground
	USAF-HH	USAF "Hurricane Hunters", Keesler AFB ("TEAL")
4702.0	EU-LDOC	Berne ("Berna") Radio
	USN	Navy Air ASW Atlantic
4702.5	USAF-AMC-OP	Operation Restore Hope (Accuse Bravo - Tanker), Lajes
4703.0	RNZAF	Whenuapai, Ohakea & Wigram AFB's
	SAF-AF	Waterkloof Military (South African Air Force)
	USN	Air/Ground/Ship
4704.0	CANFORCE	ATG - Trenton Military, MAG - Halifax Military , MACS - Edmonton Military, St. John's Military, Sinai Base
	NASA	Cape Radio
	USN	Air/Ground/Ship
4706.0	USN	Navy Air ASW
4707.0	RAF	UKADGE - Buchan, Bampton "Delta"
	USN	Navy Air ASW Pacific
4709.0	USN	Air/Ground/Ship
4710.0	CAR-VOL	Tegucigalpa Volmet (H+50)
	RAF	UKADGE "Tango Whiskey"
4710.5	USN	Air/Ground (Atlantic)
4711.0	USN	Sealord, Air/Ground (secondary)
4712.0	NCA-RDARA	CIS - Kiev, Kolpashevo, Kuybyshev, Mineralyne-Vody, Novosibirsk, Novy Vasyugan, Odessa, Penza, Rostov-na-Donu, Severouralsk, Simferopol, Sochi, Sverdlovsk, Syktyvkar, Tbilisi, Vitebsk, & Yerevan ACC's
4714.0	NASA	Cape Radio
	USN	Air/Ground/Ship
4716.0	RAF	UKADGE "Echo Tango"
	USN	Air/Ground/Ship
4718.0	SP-RDARA	New Zealand - McMurdo Sector Routes (Antarctic)
	USN	Air/Ground/Ship
4719.0	RAF	UKADGE "Kilo Juliet"
4721.0	USAF-ACC	Air Combat Command
	USAF-SAM	Mystic Star SAM Series K
4722.0	RAF	RAF VOLMET - MVU West Drayton (Bampton)
4725.0	USAF-GHFS	Croughton, Elmendorf, Incirlik, McClellan, Thule, Yakota
	USAF-USSTRATCOM	Former SAC "Giant Talk" Network "Sierra 390"
4728.0	NCA-RDARA	CIS - Bodaybo, Chita, Chulman, Irkutsk, Leningrad, Ulan-Ude, Velikiye Luki, Vitim & Vologda Aeradios
4730.0	CANFORCE	MAG - Halifax Military
	RAF	Cyprus Flight Watch, Hong Kong Air, Pitreavie Air
	USN	Navy Air ASW Atlantic
4732.0	USAF-ACC	Air Combat Command, Secondary (Data) - West
	USN	Navy Air ASW Atlantic, FACSFAC Virginia
4735.0	NORAD	NORAD - "Channel Charlie 32"
	US-JTF-4	Joint Task Force on Drug Enforcement - "Alpha Alpha"
4737.0	USN	Air/Ground/Ship "Hershey Control"
4738.0	NCA-RDARA	CIS - Cheropovets Aeradio
	USN	Air/Ground/Ship
4739.0	CANFORCE	Halifax Military, St. John's Military
	RAF	UKADGE "Quebec Victor"
4742.0	RAF	STCICS - "Foxtrot Sierra" - Architect wx (H+00, H+30), Gibraltar, Uphavon, Ascension (Haven) (H+45), Mt. Pleasant (Viper) (H+15)
	USAF-ACC	Air Combat Command
	USAF-USSTRATCOM	"Xray 209"
4745.0	EU-LDOC	Berlin/Schoenfield (Interflug)
4745.5	EU-RDARA	Greenland - Julianehab & Upernavik Aeradios
	SAM-RDARA	Chile - Quintero Aeradio
4746.0	CANFORCE	St. John's Military
	RAF	UKADGE
	USAF-ACC	Air Combat Command, Secondary
4752.0	CANFORCE	MAG - Halifax Military, St. John's Military

Master Frequency List

FREQ.	SERVICE	STATION/LOCATION
4755.0	NASA	Cape Radio
4760.0	US-ANG	ANG - Air National Guard
	USAF-ACC	Air Combat Command
	USAF-SAM	Mystic Star SAM Series H
		Mystic Star SAM Series Q
4768.0	NETH-AF	Valkenburg Air (Dutch Air Force)
4772.0	USAF-ACC	Air Combat Command, Secondary (Data) - East
4775.0	RNAVY	RNAS Culdrose Air
4790.0	RAF	RAF Flight Training - Finningley
4807.0	EU-CC-LDOC	Somerset (Portishead Radio)
4810.0	EU-CC-LDOC	Somerset (Portishead Radio)
4822.0	RAF	UKADGE "Alpha Golf"
4825.0	NASA	Cape Radio
4830.0	RAF	RAF Flight Training - Finningley
4845.0	RAF	UKADGE "Tango Sierra"
	USAF	"Billboard" wkg "Mellow" in LSB
4856.0	NASA	Cape Radio
4860.0	NASA	Cape Radio
4865.0	USAF-ACC	Air Combat Command, Primary - East
	USAF-SAM	Mystic Star SAM Series C
4872.0	NORAD	NORAD
	USAF-ACC	Air Combat Command, Secondary (Data) - East
4874.0	USAF-ACC	Air Combat Command
4880.0	AUS-RFDS	Royal Flying Doctor Service, Cairns (duplex 4926.0)
4885.0	CAR-LDOC	Boyeros (Cubana Airlines)
4896.0	USAF-ACC	Air Combat Command, Primary - West
4900.0	NASA	Cape Radio
4905.0	SP-AFTN	AFTN Traffic, Auckland, Norfolk Is., Rarotonga (Cook Is.)
4925.0	USAF-SAM	Mystic Star SAM Series C
4926.0	AUS-RFDS	Royal Flying Doctor Service, Cairns (duplex 4880.0)
4935.0	AUS-RFDS	Royal Flying Doctor Service
4938.0	USAF-SAM	Mystic Star SAM Series J
4940.0	AUS-RFDS	Royal Flying Doctor Service
	RNZAF	Royal New Zealand Air Force
4980.0	AUS-RFDS	Royal Flying Doctor Service
4982.0	USAF-SAM	Mystic Star SAM Series Q
		Mystic Star SAM Series R
4986.0	USAF-ACC	Air Combat Command, Primary - East
4991.0	US-DOD	Counterdrug Network "Xray Bravo"
4992.0	NASA	Cape Radio
5026.0	USAF-SAM	Mystic Star SAM Series J
5058.5	US-DOD	Counterdrug Network "Xray Charlie"
5060.0	NASA	Cape Radio
5068.0	NORAD	NORAD - Secondary Nights (Tie-in to US CAP)
	USAF-ACC	Air Combat Command, Backup - East
5076.0	USN	Air/Ground/Ship
5078.0	USAF-SAM	Mystic Star SAM Series C
5095.0	RAF	UKADGE "Papa Kilo"
5110.0	AUS-RFDS	Royal Flying Doctor Service
5120.0	SAM-LDOC	Tegucigalpa (SASHA)
5122.5	SAM-RDARA	Uruguay - Montevideo Aeradio
5145.0	AUS-RFDS	Royal Flying Doctor Service
5152.0	USAF-SAM	Mystic Star SAM Series A
5171.0	USAF-ACC	Air Combat Command, Secondary (Data) - East
5178.0	RAF	UKADGE "Romeo Echo"
5180.0	NASA	Cape Radio
5185.5	USAF-AMC-OP	Operation Restore Hope (Accuse Bravo - Tanker), Lajes
5187.0	NASA	Cape Radio
5190.0	NASA	Cape Radio
5197.0	USAF-AMC	Air Mobility Command
5205.0	CWP-RDARA	Philippines
	SEA-RDARA	Koror, Majuro, Ponape Is., Truk & Yap Aeradios
	SP-RDARA	Caroline Is. - Ulithi Aeradio

FREQ.	SERVICE	STATION/LOCATION
5211.0	RAF	UKADGE
5215.0	CAR-RDARA	Cuba - Boyeros, Camaguey (Ignacio Agramonte) & Santiago de Cuba (Antonio Maceo)) Aeradios
5235.0	NASA	Cape Radio
5246.0	NASA	Cape Radio
5270.0	RAF	UKADGE
	USAF-SAM	Mystic Star SAM Series C
5272.0	USCG-AIR	Air/Ground, San Juan
5277.0	US-DEA	OTH Radio System "Alpha"
5297.0	NORAD	NORAD - Secondary Nights
5300.0	AUS-RFDS	Royal Flying Doctor Service
5305.0	USAF-SAM	Mystic Star SAM Series P
5320.0	USCG-AIR	Air/Ground/Ship
5340.0	SEA-RDARA	Indonesia - several aeradios
	USAF-SAM	Mystic Star SAM Series B
		Mystic Star SAM Series H
5350.0	NASA	Cape Radio
5355.0	AUS-RFDS	Royal Flying Doctor Service
5356.0	RNZAF	Royal New Zealand Air Force
5361.0	RAF	UKADGE "Alpha Bravo"
5395.0	USAF-SAM	Mystic Star SAM Series C
5398.0	USAF-SAM	Mystic Star SAM Series B
5399.5	OP-Haiti	Operation Able Manner (Haiti Embargo)
	US-JTF-4	Joint Task Force on Drug Enforcement - "Three Charlie Five"
5400.0	OP-Haiti	Operation Able Manner (Haiti Embargo)
5403.0	OP-Haiti	Operation Able Manner (Haiti Embargo)
	RAF	UKADGE "Xray Alpha"
5410.0	AUS-RFDS	Royal Flying Doctor Service, Alice Springs
5412.0	USAF-SAM	Mystic Star SAM Series H
5420.0	RAF	UKADGE "Kilo Tango"
5425.0	CAR-LDOC	Westbury Control, Santo Domingo
	MID-RDARA	UAE - Quasiawira Aeradio
5429.0	RAF	UKADGE
5430.0	RAF	UKADGE
5432.0	USAF-SAM	Mystic Star SAM Series A
5434.0	USAF-SAM	Mystic Star SAM Series Q
5436.0	NASA	Cape Radio
	RAF	UKADGE "Delta Alpha"
5437.0	USAF-SAM	Mystic Star SAM Series H
5441.0	RAF	Pitreavie Air
5446.0	RAF	UKADGE
5447.0	RAF	UKADGE "Lima"
5450.0	MID-RDARA	Yemen - Hodeidah Aeradio
	RNAVY	RNAS Yeovilton Air
5451.0	U.S. Flight Test	Aerospatiale Helicopter
		Boeing Company
		McDonnel Douglas
		Rockwell International
5454.0	SAM-RDARA	Chile - Balmaceda & Puerto Montt Aeradios
		Peru - Anta (Comdte. FAP German Arias Grazziani), Arequipa (Rodriguez Ballon), Ayacucho (Coronel FAP Alfredo Mendivil Duarte), Cajamarca (General FAP Armando Revoredo Iglesias), Chiclayo (Cap. Jose Abelardo Quinones Gonzalez), Chimbote, Juliaca, Puerto Maldonado (Padre Aldamiz), Quincemil, Trujillo (Capitan Carlos Martinez de Pinillos - Huanchaco) & Tumbes (Pedro Canga) Aeradios
5458.0	SAM-RDARA	Brazil - Aracatuba Aeradio
5459.0	SAM-RDARA	Bolivia - Rurrenabaque Aeradio
5461.0	CAR-RDARA	Cuba - Guantanamo, Manzanillo, Nicaro & Santa Clara Aeradios
5462.0	RAF	UKADGE "Romeo Mike"
5463.0	OD-RDARA	Offshore Drilling Rigs & Helicopters
5469.0	SAM-RDARA	Bolivia - Camiri, Cochabamba (Jorge Wilsterman), Sucre, Trinidad & Yacuiba Aeradios
	U.S. Flight Test	Boeing Company
		Lockheed Corporation

FREQ.	SERVICE	STATION/LOCATION
5469.0	U.S. Flight Test	McDonnel Douglas
		Rockwell International
5471.0	RAF	UKADGE "Uniform Alpha"
5472.0	NA-RDARA	Alaska, all regions
	OD-RDARA	KYY2 - Amoco Production Company - Offshore Drilling Operations
	U.S. Flight Test	Northern Technical
5475.0	NA-LDOC	Toronto Ops (Elite/Canada 3000)
	SAM-VOL	Salta Aeradio (H+15), Cordoba Aeradio (H+25)
5480.0	INO-RDARA	Comoros Is - Anjouan (Ouani) & Moroni (Iconi) Aeradios
		Madagascar- Ambatondrazaka, Antalaha, Antsiranana (Arrachart), Fianarantsoa, Maintirano, Manakara, Mananjary, Miandrivazo, Morondava, Morombe, Nosy-Be (Fascene), Sambava, Tolagnaro & Toliara Aeradios
	OD-RDARA	North Sea Oil Rig Helicopters (Gt. Yarmouth)
5484.0	MID-RDARA	India - several aeradios
	NA-RDARA	Alaska - Central and Southeast
5487.0	NCA-RDARA	CIS - Sukhumi Aeradio
		CIS, Southern region - Mineralyne-Vody, Rostov-na-Donu, Sochi & Tbilisi Aeradios
5490.0	CAR-LDOC	Antigua (LIAT)
	NA-LDOC	Sault Ste. Marie (Ontair)
	NA-RDARA	Alaska - all regions
	SEA-RDARA	Thailand - Songkhla (Hat Yai), Narathiwat, Pattani, Phuket, Surat Thani & Trang Aeradios
5491.0	NA-FSS	Inuvik Aeradio (NWT)
	SAM-RDARA	Argentina - Monte Caseros & Resistencia ACC's
5491.5	SEA-RDARA	Thailand - Nakhon Sawan Aeradio
5493.0	AFI-4 MWARA	Accra, Bangui, Brazzaville, Bulawayo, Contonou, Douala, Entebbe, Franceville, Francistown, Garoua, Goma, Johannesburg, Kamina-Base, Kano, Kinshasa, Kisangani, Kitona-Base, Lagos, Libreville, Lomé, Luanda, Lumbumbashi, Lusaka, Maroua, Maseru, Nairobi, N'djamena, N'djili, Niamey, Niamtougou, Port Gentil, Salisbury, Sao Tomé (Salazar), Seychelles, Windhoek, Yaounde
5496.0	NA-RDARA	Alaska - Aleutians
	SAM-RDARA	Uruguay - Melo (Aerop. Deptal de Maldonado), Montevideo (Carrasco Int'l), Salto (Serop. Deptal) & Vichadero Aeradios
	SP-RDARA	Fiji Islands
5498.0	AFI-RDARA	Zaire - Kisangani (Bangoka) Aeradio
	SP-RDARA	Nauru Is. Aeradio (Fiji)
5499.0	AFI-VOL	Brazzaville VOLMET (H+10,+25,+30,+55)
5505.0	AFI-RDARA	Djibouti Aeradio
	CWP-RDARA	Japan - Naha ACC (Okinawa)
	EU-VOL	Shannon Aeradio (H+00,+25,+30,+55)
5508.0	OD-RDARA	Offshore Drilling Rigs & Helicopters
	SAM-RDARA	Colombia - Bogota & several other aeradios
5512.0	MID-RDARA	Pakistan - several aeradios
	SEA-RDARA	Nepal - Kathmandu Aeradio
5514.0	SEA-RDARA	Pakistan - Madras & Sargodha Aeradios
5519.0	AFI-RDARA	Central Africa & Tunisia, several ACC's
5520.0	CAR-B MWARA	Barranquilla, Boyeros, Cayenne, Georgetown, Maiquetia, New York, Panama, Paramaribo, Piarco, San Andres Is
	SEA-RDARA	Thailand - Chiang Mai, Prachuap Khiri Khan (Hua Hin), Lampang, Mae Hong Son, Tak (Mae Sot), Nan, Phitsanulok & Phrae Aeradios
5521.5	CAM-RDARA	Nicaragua - Bonanza Aeradio
5526.0	NAT-RDARA	Greenland - Nerlit linatt Constable Pynt, Godthab, Gronnedal, Julianehab, Maarmorlick & Sondre Stromfjord aeradios
	NCA-RDARA	CIS - Yeniseysk Aeradio
	SAM-C MWARA	Belem, Bogota, Brasilia, Leticia, Manaus, Maiquetia, Porto Velho, Rio de Janeiro
	SAM-NE MWARA	Belem, Cayenne, Georgetown, Maiquetia, Paramaribo, Piarco, Recife
	SAM-RDARA	Bolivia - Santa Cruz Aeradio
		Brazil - Belem, Brasilia, Campo Grande Curitiba , Manaus, Porto Velho FIR's
		Colombia - Arauca (Santiago Perez), Cucuta (Camilo Daza), Mitu, Puerto Carreno, San José del Guaviare, Tame, Trinidad & Villavicencio (Vanguardia) Aeradios
		Uruguay - Velasquez (Calderon)
	SAM-SE MWARA	Asuncion, Belem, Brasilia, Buenos Aires, Campo Grande, Curtiba, La Paz, Montevideo, Porto Alegre, Porto Velho, Recife, Salvador Dois De Julho, Santa Cruz

FREQ.	SERVICE	STATION/LOCATION
5526.0	SAUDI-AF	Saudi Air Force, Riyadh (Hotel 2), Tabuk (Hotel 8)
	SEA-LDOC	Singapore (Singapore Airlines)
	SEA-RDARA	Australia HF Network - South Eastern region - Dubbo, Melbourne, Midura & Sydney Aeradios
		Myanmar - Heho, Hommalin, Kengtung, Kawthoung, Kyauktu, Loikaw, Mong-Hsat, Mong-Tong, Magwey, Hpa-An, Hpapun, Sittwe, Thandwe, Tachilek, Tanai & Yangon Aeradios
5529.0	CAR-LDOC	Boyeros (Aeroflot)
		Santo Domingo (Iberia)
	EU-LDOC	Brussels (Sabena)
		Las Palmas (Lineas Aereas Canarias)
		Las Palmas, Madrid (Iberia)
	NA-CC-LDOC	Houston Radio (Universal Aviation)
	NCA-LDOC	Khabarovsk, Moscow (Aeroflot)
5530.0	CAR-RDARA	Guatemala - Camelita & Coban Aeradios
5532.0	AFI-LDOC	Algiers (Air Algerie)
		Harare (Air Zimbabwe)
		Lagos (Nigeria Airways)
		Salisbury
		Springbok Jo'burg (South African Airways)
	EU-LDOC	Amsterdam (KLM-Royal Dutch Airlines)
		Belgrade (Serbia Aerotransport)
		Budapest (MALEV - Hungarian Airlines)
		Dublin (Aer Lingus)
		Lisbon (TAP-Air Portugal)
		Prague (Czechoslovak Airlines)
		Rome (Alitalia)
	MID-LDOC	Abu Dhabi
		Tehran
5533.0	NA-RDARA	Mexico - Mexico City
	NCA-RDARA	CIS, Kyrgyzstan - Frunze ACC
5535.0	EU-LDOC	Speedbird London (British Airways)
	SAM-LDOC	Lima (American Airlines)
		Montevideo (PLUNA)
		Piarco (West Indian)
	SAM-RDARA	Uruguay - Montevideo ACC
5536.0	AFI-RDARA	Ethiopia - Asmara (Yohannes IV Int'l), Bahar Dar, Dire Dawa (Aba Tenna Dejazmatch Yilma) & Jimma Aeradios
5538.0	AFI-LDOC	Abidjan
		Addis Ababa, Asmara (Ethiopian Airlines - Holloway)
		Kinshasa (Air Zaire)
	INO-LDOC	Antananarivo (Air Madagascar)
		St. Louis (Air Mauritius)
	MID-LDOC	Beirut (MEA-Cedar Jet)
		Manama (Falcon)
		Muscat (Gulf Air)
5540.0	INO-RDARA	Comoros Is. - Moroni (Hahaia) ACC
	NCA-RDARA	CIS - Khabarovsk ACC
		CIS - Yedinka Aeradio
5541.0	EU-LDOC	Burgas, Sofia (LAZ - Balkan Bulgarian Airlines)
		Stockholm Radio (SAS)
	SAM-LDOC	Rio de Janeiro (VARIG)
5544.0	AFI-LDOC	Blantyre (Air Malawi)
		Djibouti (Air Djibouti)
		Luanda (TAAG)
		Ouagadougou
	CAR-LDOC	Boyeros (Cubana Airlines)
		Matamoros
		Merida, Mexico City, Tijuana (AeroMexico)
		Willemstad (ALM Antillean)
	EU-LDOC	Scheveningen Radio
	MID-LDOC	Jeddah (Saudi Airlines)
	MID-RDARA	Saudi Arabia - several aeradios

Master Frequency List

FREQ.	SERVICE	STATION/LOCATION
5547.0	CEP-1/2 MWARA	Honolulu, San Francisco
	MID-RDARA	India - Ahmadabad, Amritsar, Bangalore, Bhubaneswar, Bombay, Calcutta, Coimbatore, Delhi, Hyderbad, Lucknow, Nagpur, Patna, Port Blair, Varanasi, & Vishakhapatnam Aeradios
	SAM-RDARA	Argentina - Bahia Blanca (Commandante Espora), Buenos Aires Ezeiza Control, Commodoro Rivadavia, Rio Gallegos, San Carlos de Bariloche, Santa Rosa & Trelew (Almirante Zar) Aeradios
5550.0	CAR-A MWARA	Boyeros, Cayenne, Guatemala City, Merida, New York, Panama, Paramaribo, Piarco, San Andres Is, San Jose, Tegucigalpa
	SEA-RDARA	Indonesia - Ambon Sector, Menado Sector & Ujung Pandang ACC's
5552.0	SAM-LDOC	several South American stations (TASA)
5552.5	MID-RDARA	India- Gauhati Aeradio
5553.0	SAM-LDOC	Belem, Brasilia, Recife, Rio de Janeiro (VARIG)
5554.0	AFI-RDARA	Morocco - Casablanca ACC
5556.0	SAM-RDARA	Colombia - Bogota & several other aeradios
	SEA-RDARA	Myanmar - Sittwe Aeradio
5557.0	NCA-RDARA	CIS - Khabarovsk ACC
5559.0	SAM-LDOC	Porto Alegre, Rio de Janeiro (RIO SUL - Serviços Aéreos Regionais)
5561.0	MID-VOL	Beirut Volmet (H+15,45)
	NCA-RDARA	CIS - Commonwealth of Independent States (former Soviet Union)
5562.0	CAR-LDOC	Boyeros (Cubana Airlines)
	CAR-RDARA	Cuba - Boyeros, Camaguey, Ciego De Avila, Las Tunas, Veradero & several other aeradios
	US-NOAA	Hurricane Hunters - KJY74 Miami Air/Ground
5565.0	AFI-RDARA	Guinea Bissau - Bissau (Oswaldo Vieira Intl) Aeradio
	AFI-RDARA	Johannesburg Aeradio
	CWP-RDARA	Papua New Guinea - Nadzab, Port Moresby & Wewak ACC's
	SAM-RDARA	Brazil - Recife FIR
	SAT-2 MWARA	Canarias, Cayenne, Dakar, Manaus, Paramaribo, Recife, Rio de Janeiro, Sal Island, Salvador (Dois de Julho) FIS
5566.0	CAR-FSS	Cuba - Boyeros, Cayo
5568.0	CAR-LDOC	Antigua (LIAT)
	CAR-RDARA	Cuba - Alajela (San José/Juan Santamaria Int'l) Guatemala - Guatemala City Int'l Aeradio
	MID-RDARA	India - Agartala, Baghdogra, Calcutta, Gauhati, Imphal, Mohanbari & Silchar (Kumbhirgram) Aeradios
	NA-RDARA	Mexico - Mazatlan Aeradio
	NCA-RDARA	CIS - Chulman & several other Russian ACC's
	OD-RDARA	North Sea Oil Rig Helicopters (Aberdeen)
	SAM-RDARA	Brazil -Navegantes Aeradio
5571.0	U.S. Flight Test	Aero Corporation Boeing Company McDonnel Douglas Rockwell International
	US-DOD	Counterdrug Network "Yankee Bravo"
	US-FAA	U. S. Federal Aviation Administration
5574.0	CEP-1/2 MWARA	Honolulu, San Francisco
	NA-CC-LDOC	HF Ramp Check (ARINC)
	SAM-RDARA	Argentina - Buenos Aeries Ezeiza Control, Resistencia & several other aeradios
	SEA-RDARA	Indonesia - Banjamarsin, Biak & Jayapura Aeradios
5575.0	SAM-RDARA	Ecuador - Quito Aeradio
5580.0	MID-RDARA	India - Agartala, Baghogra & several other aeradios
	SEA-RDARA	Indonesia - Biak and several other aeradios
5582.0	MID-RDARA	India - Baghdogra, Mohanbari & Jorhat Aeradios
5582.5	MID-RDARA	India - Agartala Aeradio
5583.0	SAM-RDARA	Chile - Isla Rey Jorge Marsh Approach Chile - Punta Arenas & Santiago Aeradios
	SP-RDARA	Maldive Islands - Gan FIS (Addu Atoll)
5584.0	MID-RDARA	India - Gauhati Aeradio
5586.0	NCA-RDARA	CIS - Kubyshev, Penza, Severouralsk & Sverdlovsk Aeradios
5589.0	EU-LDOC	Stockholm Radio
	MID-LDOC	Tel Aviv (El Al)

FREQ.	SERVICE	STATION/LOCATION
5589.0	SAM-RDARA	Colombia - Armedia (El Elden), Buenaventura, Cali (Alfonso Bonilla Aragon), Cucuta (Camilo Daqza), Florencio (Capitolio), Girardot (Santiago Vila), Ibague (Perales), Ipiales (San Luis), Neiva (La Manguita), Pasto (Antonio Narino), Pereira (Matecana), Popayan (Guillermo Leon Valencia), Puerto Asis, San Vincente del Caguan, Santa Maria (Simon Bolivar) & Tres Esquinas Aeradios
5592.0	SP-RDARA	Australia - Invercargill, Milford Sound, Napier & Queenstown Aeradios
5595.0	CANFORCE	Lahr AB
	EU-RDARA	Norway - Stavanger ACC
5596.0	NCA-RDARA	CIS, Northern region - several ACC's
	SEA-RDARA	Myanmar - Banmaw, Gangtaw, Hommalin, Htilin, Kalemyo, Kyaukta, Lashio, Mandalay, Momeik, Myitkyina, Nyaung, Pauk, Putao, Putussibau &Sinkaling Khamto
	U.S. Flight Test	Rockwell International
5598.0	NA-CC-LDOC	HF Ramp Check (ARINC)
	NAT-A MWARA	Canarias, Gander, New York, Paramaribo, Piarco, Santa Maria, Shanwick
5601.0	MID-RDARA	India - Gilgit, Karachi, Lahore, Multan, Pasni, Peshawar, Ouetta (Samungli), Islamabad (Chaklala), Skardu & Turbat Aeradios
	SAM-VOL	Asuncion VOLMET (H+05), Ezeiza VOLMET (H+15)
5601.5	SAM-RDARA	Venezuela - Upata Aeradio
5603.0	MID-RDARA	Iraq - Baghdad ACC
	MID-VOL	Kuwait Volmet
	NA-CC-LDOC	HF Ramp Check (ARINC)
5604.0	NA-CC-LDOC	Tors Cove (Rainbow Radio)
	SAM-LDOC	several South American stations (Transportes Aereos Marilia)
	SAM-RDARA	Chile - Antofagasta &Iquique Aeradios
5609.0	SAM-LDOC	Sao Paulo (Transportes Aereos Regionales)
5610.0	EU-CC-LDOC	Somerset (Portishead Radio)
	NA-LDOC	Toronto (Elite-Canada 3000)
	RAF	Hong Kong Air
5616.0	NAT-B MWARA	Gander, Iceland (Reykjavik), New York, Santa Maria, Shannon (Shanwick)
5617.0	NA-RDARA	Mexico - Mexico City & Oxaca ACC's
5619.0	CAR-RDARA	Belize International Aeradio
		San Salvador (Ilopango Int'l) Aeradio
5622.0	EU-LDOC	Burgas, Sofia (LAZ - Balkan Bulgarian Airlines)
	NCA-RDARA	CIS - Dushanbe Aeradio
5624.0	SEA-RDARA	Malaysia - Kota Kinabalu Aeradio
5628.0	NP-3/4 MWARA	Honolulu, Tokyo
5630.0	SAM-RDARA	Venezuela - Isla de Coche (Teniente Coronel Andres), Bruzal & Maracay (El Libertador AB) Aeradios
5631.0	Alaska-FSS	Anchorage, Barrow, Cold Bay, Cordova, Ketchikan, Kotzebue, McGrath, Point Barrow & Yakutat FSS
	SAM-RDARA	Colombia - Barrancabermeja (Yariguies), Bucaramanga (Palonegro), Cucuta (Camilo Daza), Manizales (La Nubia), Medellin (Olaya Herrera), Otu, Pereira (Matecana), Quibdo (El Carano) & Turbo (Gonzalo Mejia) Aeradios
	SEA-RDARA	Indonesia - Jakarta, Madang, Medan Sector, Palembang & Pontianak Aeradios
	SEA-RDARA	Thailand - Khon Kaen, Loei, Ubon Ratchathani & Udon Thani Aeradios
5634.0	INO-1 MWARA	Antananarivo, Beira, Blantyre, Bombay, Cocos Is., Colombo, Dar es Salaam, Harare, Jeddah, Johannesburg, Kigali, Lilongwe, Lusaka, Madras, Mahajanga, Male, Mauritius, Moroni, Nairobi, Perth, Seychelles, St. Denis, Toamasina
5637.0	EU-RDARA	Greece - Agrinion, Alexandroupolis, Andravida, Heraklion, Ionnina, Kalamata, Karpathos, Kasos, Kastoria, Kavala, Kefallinia, Kerkyra, Khania, Kos, Kozani, Larisa, Milos, Mitilini, Rhodes, Salonika, Samos, Skiathos, Sparti & Zakinthos ACC's
5640.0	EU-VOL	Shannon Aeradio (H+00,25,30,55)
5642.0	NCA-RDARA	CIS - Moscow ACC
5643.0	SP-6/7 MWARA	Auckland, Honolulu, Nandi, Pascua (Easter Is.), Rarotonga, Sydney, Tahiti
	SP-RDARA	Australia & New Zealand, several aeradios
5645.0	EU-LDOC	Amsterdam (KLM-Royal Dutch Airlines)
		Brussels (Sabena)
	EU-LDOC	Frankfurt (Lufthansa)
	NCA-RDARA	CIS - Samarkand, Tashkent & Termez Aeradios
	OD-RDARA	North Sea Oil Rig Helicopters (Gt. Yarmouth Aeradio, Stavanger Aeradio, Amsterdam Heliport)
5646.0	NCA-1 MWARA	Ivdel, Khanty Mansiysk, Moscow, Syktyvkar, Sverdlovsk, Vologda
5649.0	EA-2 MWARA	Canton, Irkutsk, Pyongyang, Ulaanbaatar

Master Frequency List

FREQ.	SERVICE	STATION/LOCATION
5649.0	NAT-C MWARA	Gander, Iceland (Reykjavik), Shannon (Shanwick)
	SEA-2 MWARA	Bali, Bangkok, Denpasar, Guangzhou, Hanoi, Ho Chi Minh, Hong Kong, Jakarta, Kuala Lumpur, Kota Kinabalu, Manila, Singapore, Vientiane
5652.0	AFI-2 MWARA	Algiers, Brazzaville, Kano, Gao, Niamey, N'djamena, Tamanrasset, Timimoun, Tripoli, Tunis
	AFI-RDARA	AFI-2 RDARA - Algiers, Ghardaia, Kano, Niamey, Tamanrasset & Tripoli ACC's
5655.0	EA-2 MWARA	Canton, Irkutsk, Pyongyang, Ulaanbaatar
	SEA-2 MWARA	Bali, Bangkok, Denpasar, Guangzhou, Hanoi, Ho Chi Minh, Hong Kong, Jakarta, Kuala Lumpur, Kota Kinabalu, Manila, Singapore, Vientiane
5658.0	AFI-3 MWARA	Addis Ababa, Aden, Asmara, Bahrain, Benghazi, Bujumbura, Cairo, Dar es Salaam, Entebbe, Hargesia, Djibouti, Jeddah, Khartoum, Kigali, Kisimayu, Male, Mogadishu, \`Nairobi, N'djamena, Sana'a, Seychelles, Triopli
	AFI-RDARA	Asmara (Yohannes IV Int'l) ACC
	CAR-LDOC	Antigua, Adams/Barbados (LIAT)
	EA-RDARA	China - Urumqi ACC & several other aeradios
	MID-2 MWARA	Abadan, Alma Ata, Bombay, Delhi, Dushanbe, Frunze, Kabul, Karachi, Kathmandu, Kuwait, Lahore, Male, Muscat, Odessa, Samarkand, Seychelles, Tashkent, Tehran, Tbilisi, Urumqi, Yerevan
	MID-RDARA	India - several aeradios
		Riyan [Yemen] & Shiraz [Iran] Aeradios
	NCA-RDARA	CIS - Dushanbe & Tashkent ACC's
	SEA-RDARA	Lumpen Aero, Bombay, Karachi
5659.0	AFI-RDARA	Djibouti Aeradio
	EU-LDOC	Amsterdam (KLM-Royal Dutch Airlines)
	SAM-RDARA	Uruguay - Maldonado (Capitan Carlos A. Curbelo) Naval Aeradio & Punta del Este Aeradio
	SEA-RDARA	Indonesia - Jayapura & Timika (Tembagapura) Aeradios
5659.5	SAM-RDARA	Venezuela - Isla de Coche (Teniente Coronel Andres)
5661.0	EUR-A MWARA	Arkhangelsk, Beirut, Berlin, Kiev, Lvov, Malta, Minsk, Moscow, Murmansk, Odessa, Riga, Simferopol, Sofia, St. Petersburg, Syktyvkar, Tunis, Valetta, Velikiye, Vitebsk, Vilnius, Vologda
5662.0	AFI-RDARA	Lomé (Tokoin) & N'Djamena FIS
5664.0	NCA-3 MWARA	Chita, Chulman, Ekimchan, Irkutsk, Kirensk, Khabarovsk, Pyongyang, Ulaanbaatar, Ulan Ude
5666.0	NA-RDARA	Mexico - Mexico City
5667.0	MID-1 MWARA	Aden, Amman, Ankara, Baghdad, Basrah, Beirut, Cairo, Damascus, Jeddah, Kuwait, Manama, Odessa, Sana'a, Simferopol, Tehran, Tbilisi, Yerevan
	MID-VOL	Damascus Volmet (H+00)
	NP	Honolulu
5670.0	EU-CC-LDOC	Somerset (Portishead Radio)
	NCA-RDARA	CIS - Cheropevets Center ACC
	USAF	Tactical
5673.0	EA-VOL	Beijing (H+05,45), Guangzhou (H+10,50)
5674.0	AFI-RDARA	Algeria - Sebha ACC
5676.0	NCA-VOL	CIS English Language Network, Khabarovsk, Russia (H+05,35), Tashkent, Uzbekistan (H+10,40), Kiev, Ukraine (H+15,45), Moscow, Russia (H+25,55), Novosibirsk, Russia (H+20,50)
5677.0	NP-3/4 MWARA	Honolulu , Tokyo
5677.5	CAM-RDARA	Honduras - Juticalpa & Tela Aeradios
5680.0	AFI-RDARA	Angola - Cabinda & Lobito Aeradios
		Burkina Faso - Bobo-Dioulasso & Ouagadougou Aeradios
		Gambia - Banjul Aeradio
		Ghana - Accra (Kotoka Int'l)
		Guinea - Conakry & Kamsar (Kawass) Aeradios
		Lesotho - Maseru (Moshoeshoe Int'l) & Qachas'Nek Aeradios
		Madagascar - Maroantsetra Aeradio
		Mali - Gao, Kayes, Mopti (Barbe), Nara (Keibane), Nioro, Tessalit and Tombouctou Aeradios
		Mauritania - Aioun El Atrouss, Akjoujt, Atar, Bir Moghrein & Kiffa Aeradios
		Mozambique - Beira, Inhambane, Lichinga, Maputo & Quelimane Aeradios
		Sao Tomé & Principe - Principe (Jorge Gorgulho) & Sao Tomé (Salazar) Aeradios
		Senegal - Cap Skiring, Saint Louis, Tambacounda & Ziguinchor Aeradios

FREQ.	SERVICE	STATION/LOCATION
5680.0	AFI-RDARA	South Africa - Alexander Bay, Grootfontein, Phalaborwa (Hendrik van Eck) & Keetmanshoop Aeradios
		Swaziland - Manzini (Matsapa), Mhlume & Mokhotlong Aeradios
	CANADA-FSS	Baker Lake, Churchill, Coppermine, Fort Nelson, Goose Bay, Inuvik, Lynn Lake, Kapuskasing, Kujjuuaq, Kuujjuarapik, Mayo, Watson Lake & Yellowknife FSS'
	CAR-RDARA	Santo Domingo Aeradio
	EU-RDARA	Norway - Stavanger, Svalbard (Longyear) & Trondheim Aeradios
	NASA	Cape Radio
	SAF-AF	South African Air Force (SAR)
	SAM-RDARA	Venezuela - Maracay (El Libertador)
	SEA-RDARA	Malaysia - Penang ACC
		Vanuatu - Port-Vila (Bauerfield) ACC
	SP-RDARA	New Caledonia - Noumea ACC
		Polynesia - Bora Bora, Huahine (Fare), Manihi, Mururoa, Nuka Hiva, Raiatea (Uturoa), Rangiroa, Rurutu, Tahiti, Tubuai (Mataura) & Ua Huka Aeradios
	UK-RCC	Edinburgh Rescue, Plymouth Rescue
	USCG-AIR	Search and Rescue
	USN	Air/Ground
5682.0	SAM-LDOC	Duranzo Aeradio (PLUNA Meteo H+00)
5684.0	CANFORCE	MAG - Halifax Military
5685.0	ITALY-AF	Italian Air Force Air/Ground
	RAF	Doncaster, Finningley - RAF helicopter training
5686.5	USN	1RK wkg 60Q (naval exercises)
5688.0	EU-LDOC	Belgrade (Serbia Aerotransport)
	RAAF	Air Force Perth
	RNZAF	Whenuapi, Ohakea & Wigram AFB's
5690.0	CANFORCE	Lahr Military, Germany (Wx H +18), Sinai Base
	EU-CC-LDOC	Somerset (Portishead Radio)
	ITALY-AF	Italian Air Force Air/Ground
	MID-RDARA	Iran - Aghajari, Ahwaz, Gachsaran, Khark Is. & Masjed Soleiman Aeradios
	NETH-AF	Valkenburg Air (Dutch Air Force)
5691.0	GAF	DHM91 Munster, DHO23 Landsberg (German Air Force Air/Ground)
	NCA-VOL	Russian Network D, Kirensk, Russia (H+00,30), Yakutsk, Russia (H+10,40), Khabarovsk, Russia (H+15,45), Magadan, Russia (H+20,50), Irkutsk, Russia (H+25,55)
5691.5	GAF	DHM91 Munster (Wx H+55) (German Air Force Air/Ground)
5692.0	USCG-AIR	Air/Ground - helicopters (primary)
5694.0	USN	Air/Ground/Ship
5695.0	RAAF	Air Force Townsville (Distress Channel)
	SAF-AF	Langebaanweg, Waterkloof & Ysterplaat Military (South African Air Force secondary interior channel)
	SAM-RDARA	Bolivia - several aeradios
	SEA-RDARA	Indonesia - Tanjung Harapan Aeradio
	UK-RCC	Edinburgh Rescue, Plymouth Rescue (secondary)
5695.5	CAR-RDARA	Santo Domingo Aeradio
	SAM-RDARA	Bolivia - Todos Los Santos Aeradio
		Venezuela - Maracay (El Libertador), Caracas (Generalisimo Francisco de Miranada AB) Aeradios
5696.0	FAF	FAF Volmet (Bordeaux 0145 UTC)
	US-NOAA	Hurricane Hunters - KJY74 Miami Air/Ground
	USCG-AIR	Air/Ground - primary SAR
	USN	Air/Ground & SAR
5700.0	EU-VOL	unid French Volmet
	USAF-ACC	Air Combat Command, AWACS Aircraft
	USAF-SAM	Mystic Star SAM Series Unassigned
	USAF-USSTRATCOM	Former SAC "Giant Talk" Network "Papa 381"
5702.0	SWD-AF	Stockholm Air (Swedish Air Force)
5703.0	CANFORCE	
	NCA-RDARA	Albania -Tirana Aeradio
	US-ANG	ANG - Air National Guard
	USAF-ACC	Air Combat Command, Secondary, Croughton ECC
5705.0	NETH-AF	Valkenburg Air (Dutch Air Force)
5707.0	RNZAF	Whenuapai AFB

Master Frequency List

FREQ.	SERVICE	STATION/LOCATION
5708.0	FAF	Orleans (French Air Force Air/Ground)
5710.0	CAR-LDOC	Boyeros (Aeroflot)
	NCA-LDOC	Moscow (Aeroflot)
	SAM-RDARA	Colombia - Cali & Tres Esquinas Aeradios
		Peru - Arequipa, Cuzco, & Lima Aeradios
	USAF	EAM (H+47)
5710.5	CHILE-AF	Quintero Aeradio - Chilean Air Force
	MID-RDARA	Iraq - Ain Zalah & Haditha Aeradios
		Qatar - Dham Aeradio
5712.0	RAF	UKADGE "Zulu Alpha"
5713.0	GAF	DHM91 Munster (German Air Force Air/Ground)
	RAAF	Air Force Sydney
	RAF	STCICS - Architect wx (H+00, H+30), Uphavon
5717.0	RAF	UKADGE "Juliet Papa"
5718.0	AFI-RDARA	Botswana - Jwaneng Aeradio
	CANFORCE	Air/Ground (SAR) - Edmonton Military, Halifax Military, St. John's Military, Trenton Military, Lahr Military
	NASA	Cape Radio
	RAAF	Air Force Darwin, Perth
	RNZAF	Air Force Auckland
	SAM-RDARA	Argentina - San Julian Aeradio
	USN	Air/Ground/Ship
5720.0	USN	Air/Ground/Ship
5721.0	ITALY-AF	Italian Air Force Air/Ground
	RAF	UKADGE "Foxtrot Whiskey"
5724.0	USN	Air/Ground/Ship
5725.0	FAF	Orleans (French Air Force Air/Ground)
5725.5	SAM-RDARA	Chile - Llanada Grande Aeradio
5726.0	SP-RDARA	New Zealand - McMurdo Sector Routes (Antarctic Region)
	USN	Air/Ground/Ship
5728.0	US-JCS	United States Joint Chiefs of Staff Net
	USN	USN AWACS SECOM "This is Juliet" KFT wkg PFT
5729.0	RAF	STCICS - Romeo Delta - Architect wx (H+00, H+30)
5732.0	US-DOD	US-DOD (Hotel 702 (Selscan tone))
5733.0	SEA-3 MWARA	Bali, Cocos Is, Darwin, Jakarta, Male, Perth, Singapore, Ujung Pandang
5745.0	US-ANG	ANG - Air National Guard
5747.0	RAF	UKADGE
5760.0	USAF-SAM	Mystic Star SAM Series P
5766.0	USAF-ACC	Air Combat Command
5766.5	CAM-RDARA	Honduras - Orlanchito Aeradio
5775.0	NASA	Cape Radio
	USAF-SAM	Mystic Star SAM Series R
5800.0	USAF-ACC	Air Combat Command
	USAF-SAM	Mystic Star SAM Series C
	USAF-USSTRATCOM	Former SAC "Giant Talk" Network "Whiskey 101"
5803.0	SAM-VOL	Montevideo Volmet (H+15)
5805.0	US-ANG	ANG - Air National Guard
5810.0	NASA	Cape Radio
5812.0	NORAD	NORAD - Air Defense Exercises
5820.0	USAF-SAM	Mystic Star SAM Series H
		Mystic Star SAM Series J
		Mystic Star SAM Series Q
5822.0	NASA	Cape Radio
	USAF-SAM	Mystic Star SAM Series R
5826.0	USAF-USSTRATCOM	Former SAC "Giant Talk" Network "Papa 382"
5827.0	US-ANG	ANG - Air National Guard
5830.0	AFI-RDARA	Egypt - Cairo ACC
5833.0	SEA-SES+	Hawker Williston SES Rescue (Australia)
5841.0	US-DEA	OTH Radio System "Bravo"
5850.0	CANFORCE	MAG - Halifax Military "Delta One Bravo"
5859.0	AFI-RDARA	Egypt - Cairo ACC
5860.0	US-FAA	U. S. Federal Aviation Administration
5895.0	USAF-AMC-OP	Operation Restore Hope (Accuse Delta - Tanker), Moron

FREQ.	SERVICE	STATION/LOCATION
5910.0	USAF-SAM	Mystic Star SAM Series P
5912.0	US-DOD	Counterdrug Network "Whiskey Charlie"
5937.0	USAF-SAM	Mystic Star SAM Series J
5960.0	NORAD	NORAD - Air Defense Exercises
5992.0	USAF-AMC-OP	Operation Restore Hope (Accuse Bravo - Tanker), Lajes
6100.0	US-ANG	ANG - Air National Guard
6121.0	USAF-ACC	Air Combat Command, Primary -East
6136.0	USAF-ACC	Air Combat Command, Primary -East
6141.0	USAF-ACC	Air Combat Command
6224.0	RAN	Royal Australian Navy, Jarvis Bay, Air/ground
6230.0	USCG-AIR	Coast Guard air to vessel
6236.0	OP-Haiti	Operation Able Manner (Haiti Embargo)
6388.0	US-JCS	United States Joint Chiefs of Staff Net/USN Tactical
6513.0	CAN-CG*	Canadian Coast Guard - Air/Vessel
	USCG-AIR	USCG-Air/Ground/Vessel
6525.0	PHIL-AF	Philippine Air Force air/ground
6526.0	AFI-LDOC	Mahe (Air Seychelles)
	CAR-LDOC	Bridgetown Operations (Caribbean Airways)
		Kingston Dispatch (Air Jamaica)
	EU-LDOC	Berne ("Berna") Radio
		Paris Radio (Air France)
	NA-CC-LDOC	New York (ARINC)
	RAF	Hong Kong Air
	SEA-LDOC	Sydney (Qantas)
6529.0	EU-LDOC	Madrid (Iberia)
6532.0	CWP-1/2 MWARA	Guam, Hong Kong, Honolulu, Manila, Naha, Port Moresby, Seoul, Taipei, Tokyo
	SAM-RDARA	Colombia - Barranquilla & several other aeradios
	SEA-CC-LDOC	Sydney SkyComms
6532.5	AFI-RDARA	Nigeria - Lagos Radio
6533.0	MID-RDARA	India - Bangalore, Bhubaneswar, Bombay, Calcutta, Cochin, Coimbatore, Madurai, Nagpur, Tiruchirapalli, Trivandrum , Vijayawada & Vishakhapatnam Aeradios
	SAM-RDARA	Ecuador - Pastaza Aeradio
	SEA-RDARA	Andaman Is. - Port Blair Aeradio
6535.0	AFI-1 MWARA	Abidjan, Bamako, Bangui, Bissau, Bobo Dioulasso, Bouake, Casablanca, Conakry, Canarias, Freetown, Kano, Niamey, Nouadhibou, Nouakchott, Ouagadougou, Roberts (Monrovia))
	AFI-RDARA	Guinea Bissau - Bissau (Oswaldo Vieira Intl) Aeradio
	SAT-1 MWARA	Brasilia, Canarias, Cayenne, Dakar, Manaus, Paramaribo, Recife, Rio de Janeiro, Sal Island, Salvador
6536.0	NCA-RDARA	CIS - Samarkand Aeradio
6537.0	AFI-RDARA	Equatorial Guinea - Bata Aeradio
6540.0	CAR-RDARA	Santo Domingo (De Las Americas) Aeradio
6541.0	SEA-RDARA	Australia HF Network - North Central region - Alice Springs, Darwin, Gove, & Tennant Creek FIS
6544.0	EU-RDARA	Norway - Bodo ACC
	SEA-RDARA	Indonesia - Ujung Pandang & several other aeradios
	SP-RDARA	Maldive Islands - Gan FIS (Addu Atoll)
6547.0	MID-RDARA	Iran - several aeradios
	NCA-RDARA	Bandar Abbass, Kabul, Ramsar, Rasht, & Shiraz Aeradios
	SAM-LDOC	Sao Paulo, Rio de Janeiro (VARIG)
6549.0	SAM-NW MWARA	Barranquilla, Bogota, Caracas (Maiquetia), Lima, Quito
	SAM-SW MWARA	Antofagasta, Asuncion, Buenos Aires, Cordoba, Easter Is (Pascua), La Paz, Lima, Mendoza, Puerto Montt, Punta Arenas, Resistencia, Salta, Santa Cruz, Santiago, Talara
6550.0	SAM-LDOC	several South American stations (Transportes Aereos Marilia)
	SAM-RDARA	Brazil - Maringa Aeradio
	U.S. Flight Test	Aero Corporation
		Boeing Company
		Lockheed Corporation
		McDonnel Douglas
		Rockwell International
6553.0	SAM-RDARA	Colombia - Bogota & several other aeradios
		Peru - several aeradios

Master Frequency List

FREQ.	SERVICE	STATION/LOCATION
6553.0	SP-RDARA	SP-9 RDARA, Apia, Butaritari, Christmas Is., Fua'Amotu, Funafuti, Honiara, Nandi, Nausori, Niue, Port Vila, Rarotonga, Santo & Wallis Aeradios
6554.0	SAM-RDARA	Argentina - Cordoba, Salta & Tucuman Aeradios
6556.0	EA-RDARA	China - Kunming & Guangzhou Aeradios
	EU-CC-LDOC	Somerset (Portishead Radio)
	EU-LDOC	Luton (Britannia Airlines)
		Luton (Monarch Airlines)
	MID-RDARA	India - several aeradios
	SEA-1 MWARA	Bali, Bangkok, Colombo, Calcutta, Dhaka, Guangzhou, Jakarta, Kathmandu, Kuala Lumpur, Kunming, Madras, Male, Singapore & Yangon Aeradios
	SEA-3 MWARA	Bali, Cocos Is, Darwin, Jakarta, Male, Perth, Singapore, Ujung Pandang
	SEA-RDARA	Indonesia - several aeradios
	SP- RDARA	Christmas Island (proprietary)
6557.0	EA-RDARA	China - Haiphong Aeradio
6558.0	AFI-RDARA	Botswana - several aeradios
6559.0	AFI-RDARA	Beira, Brazzaville, Douala, Franceville, Garoua, Johannesburg, Kamina-Base, Kinshasa, Kitona, Libreville, Luanda, Nairobi, N'Gaoundre, Port Gentil & Yaounde Aeradios
6562.0	CWP-1/2 MWARA	Guam, Honolulu, Manila, Naha, Port Moresby, Seoul, Taipei, Tokyo
	SAM-LDOC	several Brazilian stations (TransBrazil)
6565.0	SEA-RDARA	Australia HF Network - Southwest region - Carnarvon, Geraldton, Kalgoorlie, Meekatharra, Perth & Port Hedland FIS
6567.0	CAR-LDOC	St. Thomas (Caribair)
	CAR-RDARA	Belize International Aeradio, San José Int'l Aeradio & San Salvador Aeradio
6568.0	CAR-RDARA	Guatemala - Guatemala City Aeradio
6569.0	SEA-RDARA	Myanmar - Hommalin Aeradio
6571.0	EA-1 MWARA	Beijing, Canton, Hailar, Irkutsk, Jinan, Kunming, Lanzhou, Pyongyang, Shanghai, Shenyang, Taegu, Ulaanbaatar, Urumqi, Wuhan, Zhengzhou
6574.0	AFI-RDARA	Addis Ababa, Asmara, Cairo, Hargesia, Kisimayu
6575.0	SP-RDARA	Tabiteuea North Flight Service (Tawara Atoll) & Tarawa Aeradio (Tuvalu)
6577.0	CAR-A MWARA	Boyeros, Guatemala City, Merida, New York, Panama, Piarco, San Andres Is, San Jose, Tegucigalpa
	SEA-RDARA	Indonesia - Banjamarsin & several other aeradios
		Thailand - Hat Yai, Narathiwat, Pattani, Phuket, Surat Thani & Trang Aeradios
6578.0	SAM-RDARA	Brazil - Aracatuba Aeradio
6580.0	AFI-RDARA	South Africa - Cape Town ACC
	NA-RDARA	Alaska - Central and Southeast
	SAM-LDOC	several South American stations (TASA)
	SEA-RDARA	Australia HF Network - South Central region - Alice Springs, Broken Hill, Ceduna & Leigh Creek ACC's
6582.0	SAM-RDARA	Argentina - Mercedes, San Gregorio & Teniente Parallada Aeradios
6583.0	MID-RDARA	India - several aeradios
6585.0	SAM-RDARA	Argentina - Buenos Aires ACC Ezeiza Control
6586.0	AFI-RDARA	AFI-4 RDARA, Abidjan, Accra, Cotonou, Dakar, Francistown, Gaborone, Kano, Lusaka, Niamtougou, Ouagadougou, Parakou
	CAR-B MWARA	Barranquilla, Boyeros, Cayenne, Georgetown, Maiquetia, New York, Panama, Paramaribo, Piarco, San Andres Is
	SAM-AGS	Colombia - San Andres (Sesquicentenario) Radio
	SAM-RDARA	Argentina - Cordoba ACC
6589.0	AFI-RDARA	Gabon - Franceville Aeradio
		Guinea - Banankoro, Boke, Kasmar, Kankan, Kissidougou, Labe, Macenta, N'Zerekore, Sambailo, Sangaredi & Siguri Aeradios
	NA-RDARA	Mexico - Mexico City
	NCA-RDARA	CIS, Eastern region - several ACC's (Alma Ata, Ekimchan & Khabarovsk ACC's)
	SEA-RDARA	Malaysia - Kota Kinabalu, Padang Sidempuan & Tapaktuan Aeradios
		Myanmar - Heho, Kawthaung, Kyauktu, Loikaw, Magwey, Mong-Hsat, Mong-Tong, Pakokku, Hpapun, Hpa-An, Thandwe, Sittwe, Tachilek, Tangyang & Yangon Aeradios
6592.0	NCA-2 MWARA	Barnaul, Irkutsk, Khanty Mansiysk, Kirensk, Kolpashevo, Krasnoyarsk, Novosibirsk, Podkamennaya, Surgut, Yeniseysk
6595.0	SEA-RDARA	Indonesia - Jakarta, Khon Kaen, Loei, Ubon-Ratchathani & Udon Thani Aeradios
		Thailand - Khon Kaen, Loei, Ubon-Ratchathani & Udon Thani ACC's
6598.0	CWP-RDARA	Papua New Guinea - Madang & Wewak Aeradios

FREQ.	SERVICE	STATION/LOCATION
6598.0	EUR-A MWARA	Arkhangelsk, Beirut, Kiev, Lvov, Minsk, Moscow, Murmansk, Odessa, Riga, Simferopol, St. Petersburg, Syktyvkar, Tunis, Valetta, Velikiye, Vitebsk, Vilnius, Vologda
	NA-LDOC	Air Wemindji
6603.0	AFI-RDARA	Swaziland - Manzini/Manzapa Aeradio
	SAM-VOL	Belem, Brasilia , Galeao, Manaus, Recife Volmets
6604.0	NA-RDARA	Alaska - Central and Southeast
	NAT-VOL	Gander (H+20,50), New York (continuous)
	SEA-RDARA	Australia HF Network - Northwest region - Darwin, Derby, Kununurra & Port Hedland FIS
6610.0	AFI-RDARA	Morocco - Casablanca ACC
	MID-RDARA	Amman, Jeddah, Madinah, Riyadh, Tabuk & Taif Aeradios
	SEA-RDARA	Australia HF Network - Central Eastern region -Charleville, Longreach, Rockhampton
6616.0	SEA-RDARA	Australia HF Network - North East region - Cairns, Mount Isa, Townsville & Weipa
6617.0	CWP-RDARA	Philippines - Davao Radio (Francisco Bangoy Int'l)
	NCA-VOL	Russian Network A, Riga, Latvia (H+00,30), St. Petersburg, Russia (H+05,35), Moscow, Russia H+10,15,40,45), Kiev, Ukraine (H+20,50), Rostov, Ukraine (H+25,55)
	SAM-RDARA	Peru - Chachapoyas, Chiclayo, Iquitos, Moyobamba, Pucallpa, Puerto Maldonado, Tingo Maria, Truljio, Yurimaguas, Aeradios
	SEA-RDARA	Indonesia - Jayapura, Mulia & Timika Aeradios
6619.5	SAM-RDARA	Bolivia - Todos Los Santos Aeradio
6622.0	CWP-RDARA	Papua New Guinea - Madang, Nadzab & Port Moresby Aeradios
	NAT-F MWARA	Gander & Shanwick Aeradios
6624.0	MID-RDARA	CIS - Abadan Aeradio
		India - several aeradios
	MID-VOL	Kuwait Volmet
6628.0	NAT-E MWARA	New York, Santa Maria
6631.0	MID-1 MWARA	Aden, Amman, Ankara, Baghdad, Basrah, Beirut, Cairo, Damascus, Jeddah, Kuwait, Manama, Odessa, Sana'a, Simferopol, Tehran, Tbilisi, Yerevan
	MID-3 MWARA	Aktyubinsk, Alma Ata, Dushanbe, Frunze, Kuybyshev, Kzyl-Orda, Moscow, Samarkand, Tashkent, Uralsk, Yevevan
	SEA-RDARA	Indonesia - Biak & Jayapura ACC's
6632.0	SEA-LDOC	Perth (Qantas)
6633.0	MID-RDARA	India - several aeradios
6634.0	EU-CC-LDOC	Somerset (Portishead Radio)
6636.0	USN	Air/Ground/Ship
6637.0	CWP-LDOC	Hong Kong (Dragonair)
		Manila (Philippines Air)
		Tokyo (JAL-Japan Airlines)
	EA-LDOC	Beijing
		Athens (Olympic Airlines)
		Frankfurt (Lufthansa)
		Larnaca (Cyprus Airways)
		Paris Radio (Air France)
	MID-LDOC	Bombay (Air India)
		Kathmandu (Royal Nepal Airlines)
		Tel Aviv (El Al)
	NA-CC-LDOC	Houston Radio (Universal Aviation)
	SEA-LDOC	Colombo (Air Lanka)
		Jakarta
		Perth, Sydney (Qantas)
		Singapore (Singapore Airlines)
		Singapore (Singapore Airlines)
	SP-LDOC	Auckland (Air New Zealand)
		Nauru Island (Air Nauru)
6638.0	AFI-RDARA	Algeria - Agades, Banjul, Bechar, Biskra, Bo, Cotonou, Djanet, El Golea, El Oued, Hassi-Messaoud, Kemna, Ouargla, Sunyani, Takoradi, Touggourt, Zarzaitine, Zinder
	SAM-RDARA	Bolivia - Abopo, Ascension de Guarayos, Camiri, Cobija, Cochabamba, Guayaramerin, Magdalena, Oruro, Potosi, Reyes, Riberalta, Robore, Rurrenabaque, San Borja, San Ignacio de Moxos, San Javier, San Joaquin, Santa Ana de Yacuma, Sucre, Trinidad & Yacuiba Aeradios

Master Frequency List

FREQ.	SERVICE	STATION/LOCATION
6640.0	AFI-LDOC	Cairo (Egypt Air)
		Dar es Salaam (Air Tanzania)
		Entebbe (Uganda Airlines)
		Kigali (Air Rwanda)
		Lusaka (Zambia Airways)
		Nairobi
		Ouagadougou
		Tunis (Tunis Air)
	CEP-CC-LDOC	Honolulu, San Francisco (ARINC)
	MID-LDOC	Safat (Kuwaiti Airlines)
	NA-CC-LDOC	New York (ARINC)
	NCA-LDOC	Kabul (Ariana Afghan Airlines)
6642.0	SAM-RDARA	Venezuela - Upata Aeradio
6643.0	AFI-RDARA	Algeria - Algiers ACC
	EU-LDOC	Berne ("Berna") Radio
		Dusseldorf (LTU)
		Hanover (Hapag Lloyd Fluggesellschaft)
	SAM-LDOC	Buenos Aires (Aerolineas Argentinas)
		Caracas (AVENSA)
		Maiquetia (VIASA)
		San Salvador
		Santiago
6645.0	AFI-RDARA	Ethiopia - Dire Dawa Aeradio
	SAM-RDARA	Argentina - Mendoza Aeradio
6646.0	AFI-LDOC	Algiers (Air Algerie)
	AFI-LDOC	Roberts/Monrovia
	CAR-LDOC	Grand Cayman (Cayman Air)
6649.5	SEA-RDARA	Myanmar - Toungoo Aeradio
6652.0	SEA-RDARA	Thailand - Nakon Si Thammarat Aeradio
6653.0	SP-RDARA	SP-9(R) - Nandi
6655.0	MID-RDARA	India - several aeradios
	NP-3/4	Honolulu, Tokyo
6656.0	NCA-RDARA	CIS - Mineralyne-Vody Aeradio
6659.0	SEA-RDARA	Myanmar - Banmaw, Gangtaw, Hommalin, Htilin, Kalemyo, Kyaukta, Lashio, Mandalay, Momeik, Myitkyina, Nyaung, Pauk, Putao, Putussibau & Sinkaling Khamto Aeradios
	U.S. Flight Test	Rockwell International
6664.0	AFI-RDARA	Equatorial Guinea - Bata Aeradio
6665.0	CWP-RDARA	South Korea - Taegu Aeradio
	NP-3/4 MWARA	Honolulu , Tokyo
6666.0	SAM-RDARA	Bolivia - La Paz & Quito Aeradios
6667.0	SEA-RDARA	Thailand - Bangkok ACC, Chiang Mai, Hua Hin, Lampang, Mae Hongson, Mae Sot, Nan, Pai, Phitsanoluk & Phrae Aeradios
6670.0	NCA-RDARA	CIS, Eastern region - several ACC's (Bodaybo, Chita, Irkutsk & Ulan-Ude ACC's)
6672.0	SEA-RDARA	Thailand - Nakhon Sawan & Uttaradit Aeradios
6673.0	AFI-RDARA	AFI-1 RDARA, Abidjan, Bamako, Bangui, Bobo-Dioulasso, Bouake, Dakar, Daloa, Freetown, In Salah, Korhogo, Man, Nouadhibou, Nouakchott, Odienne, Ouagadougou, Roberts, San Pedro, Sassandra, Tabou & Tamanrasset Aeradios
		Ivory Coast - Yamoussourko Aeradio
	CEP-5	Honolulu, San Francisco
	SAM-RDARA	Colombia - Cartagena (Rafael Nunez), Corozal (Las Brujas), Cucuta (Camilo Daza), El Banco (Las Flores), Magangue (Baracoa), Medellin (Olaya Herrera), Monteria (Los Garzones), Puerto Bolivar (Riohacha) & Valledupar (Alfonso Lopez) Aeradios
	US-NOAA	Hurricane Hunters - Delta - KJY74 Miami Air/Ground
6674.0	CWP-RDARA	South Korea - Taegu Aeradio
6675.0	AFI-RDARA	Somalia - Mogadishu ACC
6676.0	SEA-VOL*	Sydney (H+00,+30), Calcutta (H+05,35), Bangkok (H+10,+40), Karachi (H+15,+45), Singapore (H+20,+50), Bombay (H+25,55)
6677.0	MID-LDOC	Tel Aviv (El Al)
6679.0	PAC-VOL	Honolulu (H+00,30), Tokyo (H+10,40), Hong Kong (H+15,45), Auckland (H+20,50)
6680.0	MID-VOL	Karachi Volmet (H+15,45)
6681.0	USN	Air/Ground/Ship
6683.0	USAF-SAM	Mystic Star SAM Series K "SAM 203", (Air Force 1 & 2)

FREQ.	SERVICE	STATION/LOCATION
	USAF-USSTRATCOM	Former SAC "Giant Talk" Network "Whiskey 102"
	USN	Air/Ground
6685.0	MID-LDOC	Jeddah (Saudi Airlines)
6686.0	OP-Haiti	Operation Able Manner (Haiti Embargo)
	USN	Fleet HICOM - Atlantic/Caribbean
6687.0	SAF-AF	Langenbaanweg, Waterkloof & Ysterplaat Military (South African Air Force)
6688.0	AFI-LDOC	Tunis (Tunis Air)
6689.0	NETH-AF	Valkenburg Air (Dutch Air Force)
6690.0	RAF	UKADGE "Juliet Tango"
	USN	Air/Ground/Ship
6691.5	USAF-AMC-OP	Operation Restore Hope (Accuse Bravo - Tanker), Lajes
6692.0	NCA-RDARA	CIS - Khabarovsk & Juzno-Sakhalinsk ACC's
6693.0	CANFORCE	Air/Ground - Halifax, St. John's, Vancouver Military "Delta One Gulf"
	GAF	DHM91 Munster (German Air Force Air/Ground)
	MEX-AF	Mexican Air Force
	NCA-VOL	Russian Network C, Syktyvkar, Russia (H+00,30), Sverdlovsk, Russia (H+05,35), Novosibirsk, Russia (H+10,40), Kuybyshev, Russia (H+15,45), Tyuman, Russia (H+20,50)
	RAF	UKADGE "Delta Sierra"
	SEA-RDARA	Indonesia - Sebha Aeradio
	USAF-SAM	Mystic Star SAM Series A
6694.5	U.S. Flight Test	Grumman Aerospace
6697.0	RAF	Pitreavie Air
	US-JCS	United States Joint Chiefs of Staff Net
	USN	Air/Ground primary - LANT/CARIB (CINCLANTFLT)
6699.0	USN	Air/Ground/Ship
6701.0	MID-RDARA	Saudi Arabia - Al Jouf, Arar, Hail & Tabuk Aeradios
	USAF-AMC-OP	Operation Restore Hope (Accuse Bravo - Tanker), Lajes
	USN	Air/Ground/Ship
6703.0	US-JCS	United States Joint Chiefs of Staff Net/USN Tactical
6704.0	NCA-RDARA	CIS, Northern region - several ACC's (Krasnoyarsk & Yeniseysk ACC's)
	SAM-RDARA	Brazil - Altamira, Cruzeiro do Sul, Juiz de Fora, Porto das Caixas, Porto Velho & Salvador Dois De Julho ACC's
6705.0	CANFORCE	Air/Ground - Edmonton Military, Lahr Military, Trenton Military, Vancouver Military
	EU-LDOC	Berne ("Berna") Radio (Swiss Air)
	USAF	Thule AB
	USN	Air/Ground/Ship
6708.0	BRZ-AF	Brazilian Air Force
	CANFORCE	MACS - Edmonton Military
	CAR-RDARA	Cuba
	NORAD	SAGE/NORAD
	USAF-ACC	Air Combat Command, Secondary (Data) - East/AWACS Aircraft
	USN	Navy Air ASW Atlantic, Pacific
6712.0	CANFORCE	Pipeline/MOC wkg aircraft
	EU-LDOC	Paris Radio (Air France)
	FAF	Villacoublay (French Air Force Air/Ground)
	USAF-ARRS	Air Rescue Service
	USAF-CEN	Commando Escort Net - Hawaii "Alpha 2"
6713.5	US-ANG	ANG - Air National Guard 161st Air Refuelling Group, Sky Habor AZ
6714.0	US-ANG	ANG - Air National Guard
	USAF-ARRS	Air Rescue Service, Selfridge ANGB, NAS Moffett
6715.0	ITALY-AF	Italian Air Force - LDOC
	RAF	UKADGE - Boulmer "Papa Oscar"
	USAF-ARRS	Air Rescue Service, formerly Homestead AFB
6716.0	CANFORCE	Halifax, Vancouver Military air/ground "D3H"
	USAF-SAM	Mystic Star SAM Series T
6718.0	GAF	DHM91 Munster (German Air Force Air/Ground)
6720.0	NASA	Cape Radio
	US-JCS	United States Joint Chiefs of Staff Net
	USN	Fleet HICOM E/N Atlantic/W Pacific - Tactical, ASW
6721.0	USN	Navy Air ASW Atlantic
6723.0	CAR-RDARA	Bermuda & Guantanamo Bay NAS Aeradios
	CEP-RDARA	Hawaii - Barber's Point (John Rogers) & Kanoehe Bay (Silverdale) Aeradios

Master Frequency List

FREQ.	SERVICE	STATION/LOCATION
	USN	FACSFAC - "Sea Lord" - Jacksonville FL, "Beaver" - San Diego CA
6724.0	EU-LDOC	Belgrade (Serbia Aerotransport)
	NCA-RDARA	CIS - Cheropovets Center ACC
6726.0	NETH-AF	Valkenburg Air (Dutch Air Force)
6727.0	USAF-ACC	Air Combat Command, AWACS Aircraft
6728.0	USAF-SAM	Mystic Star SAM Series F
6729.0	NETH-AF	Valkenburg Air (Dutch Air Force)
6730.0	NCA-VOL	Russian Network B, Tbilisi, Georgia (H+00,30), Aktyubinsk, Kazakhstan (H+05,35), Krasnodar, Azerbaijan (H+10,40), Alma Ata, Kazakhstan (H+15,45), Tashkent, Uzbekistan (H+20,50), Baku, Azerbaijan (H+25,55)
	RAF	UKADGE, Neatishead "Foxtrot Charlie"
	SAM-LDOC	Canaima (AVENSA)
	U.S. Flight Test	Lockheed Flight Path wkg UA1
	USAF-ACC	Air Combat Command, Andrews, Thule
	USAF-SAM	Mystic Star SAM Series E (Air Force 2)
	USAF-USSTRATCOM	Former SAC "Giant Talk" Network "Xray 903"
6731.0	USAF-SAM	Mystic Star SAM Series F
6732.0	DNMK-AF	Karup Air (Danish Air Force)
	USAF	USAF aircraft "transmitting in the blind"
6734.0	RAF	UKADGE "Delta Kilo"
6735.0	NORAD	NORAD/AWACS "Channel Charlie 2"
	USAF-ACC	Air Combat Command, Backup - West/AWACS "Charlie 2"
6738.0	FAF	Orleans (French Air Force Air/Ground)
	RAAF	Royal Australian Air Force
	RAF	STCICS - Bravo - Architect wx (H+00, H+30), Uphavon
	RNZAF	Air Force Auckland
	USAF-GHFS	Albrook, Anderson, Andrews, Ascension, Croughton, Elmendorf, Hickham, Incirlik, Lajes, Loring, MacDill, McClellan, Offutt, Thule, Yokota
6740.0	ITALY-AF	Air/ground Pisa, Rome
6742.0	EU-LDOC	Berne ("Berna") Radio
	RAF	UKADGE - Boulmer, Buchan, "Hotel Mike"
6743.0	GAF	Flensburg AB (German Air Force Air/Ground)
	ITALY-AF	Air/ground Pisa, Rome
6745.0	CAR-LDOC	Boyeros (Aeroflot)
	NCA-LDOC	Moscow (Aeroflot)
	NCA-RDARA	CIS - Khabarovsk ACC
6745.5	SAM-VOL	Puerto Montt Volmet (H+20)
6746.0	CANFORCE	St. John's Military (EAM H+03,Wx H+20), Halifax Military (EAM H+01,Wx H+20)
	EU-LDOC	Paris Radio (Air France)
6747.0	FAF	Orleans (French Air Force Air/Ground)
	GAF	Flensburg AB (German Air Force Air/Ground)
6748.0	CAR-LDOC	Boyeros (Aeroflot)
	NCA-LDOC	Moscow (Aeroflot)
	NCA-RDARA	CIS - Khabarovsk ACC
	RAF	UKADGE "Alpha Lima"
6750.0	NASA	Cape Radio
	NORAD	NORAD "Channel Charlie 3"
	USAF-CEN	Commando Escort Net - Hawaii
	USAF-SAM	Mystic Star SAM Series Unassigned, Andrews, Croughton, Offutt
	USN	USN Foxtrot Tango Net
6751.0	RAF	Akrotiri "Cyprus Flight Watch"
6752.0	FAF	Orleans (French Air Force Air/Ground)
6753.0	CANFORCE	MAG/MACS - Aviation Wx - Edmonton (H+20), Trenton (H+30), St. John's (H+40)
	EU-LDOC	Berlin/Schoenfield (Interflug)
	NASA	Cape Radio
	USAF-ACC	Air Combat Command, Primary
6754.0	AFI-RDARA	Djibouti Aeradio
6756.0	USAF-SAM	Mystic Star SAM Series I "SAM 440" (Air Force 1)
	USAF-SAM	Mystic Star SAM Series K
6757.0	NORAD	NORAD
	RAF	UKADGE - Buchan "Papa Echo"
	USAF-ACC	Air Combat Command, Backup - East
	USAF-SAM	Mystic Star SAM Series Unassigned "Whiskey 103"

FREQ.	SERVICE	STATION/LOCATION
6723.0	RNZAF	Whenuapai, Ohakea & Wigram AFB
	USAF-USSTRATCOM	Former SAC "Giant Talk" Network "Whiskey 103"
6760.0	ITALY-AF	Air/ground Pisa, Rome
	RAF	UKADGE "Alpha November" - Neatishead, Portreath
	RNZAF	Air Force Auckland
	USAF-SAM	Mystic Star SAM Series Unassigned
6760.5	MID-RDARA	India - Udhampur ACC
6761.0	RNZAF	Whenuapai AFB (phone patches)
	USAF-USSTRATCOM	Former SAC "Giant Talk" Network "Sierra 391"
6762.0	GAF	DHM91 Munster (German Air Force Air/Ground)
6764.0	CANFORCE	Halifax Military
6765.0	RAF	UKADGE "Tango Golf"
6769.0	US-ANG	ANG - Air National Guard
6775.0	NCA-RDARA	Albania -Tirana Aeradio
6780.0	USAF-SAM	Mystic Star SAM Series Unassigned
6785.0	AUS-RFDS	Royal Flying Doctor Service, Cairns (duplex 6866.0)
6788.0	US-JTF-4	Joint Task Force on Drug Enforcement - "Alpha Charlie"
	USN	Hershey - air/ground
6790.0	USAF-SAM	Mystic Star SAM Series P
6793.0	USAF-SAM	Mystic Star SAM Series J
6800.0	US-ANG	ANG - Air National Guard
6805.0	USAF	Andrews working SAM flights
6810.0	NASA	Cape Radio
	SAM-ATC	Venezuela - San Tomé Aeradio
6812.0	USAF-SAM	Mystic Star SAM Series C (Air Force 1 & 2) "Foxtrot 888"
6813.0	USAF-SAM	Mystic Star SAM Series Unassigned, Andrews wkg "Executive One Foxtrot"
6813.5	AFI-AFTN	AFTN - Tripoli
6814.0	USAF-SAM	Mystic Star SAM Series Unassigned, Andrews wkg SAM flights
6815.6	OP-Haiti	Operation Able Manner (Haiti Embargo)
6817.0	USAF-SAM	Mystic Star SAM Series Q (Air Force 1)
6820.0	NA-CC-LDOC	Gulf of Mexico (ARINC)
6821.3	AFI-AFTN	AFTN - Antananarivo
6821.4	AFI-AFTN	AFTN - Port Louis, traffic to Antananarivo & Mahe
6825.0	AUS-RFDS	Royal Flying Doctor Service
6832.0	GAF	DHJ61 (German Air Force Air/Ground)
6835.0	SP-RDARA	New Zealand -McMurdo Sector Routes (Antarctic Region)
6837.0	NASA	Cape Radio
6840.0	AUS-RFDS	Royal Flying Doctor Service, Darwin
6845.0	AUS-RFDS	Royal Flying Doctor Service, Charleville
6854.0	EU-CC-LDOC	Somerset (Portishead Radio)
6866.0	AUS-RFDS	Royal Flying Doctor Service, Cairns (duplex 6785.0)
6870.0	US-FAA	U. S. Federal Aviation Administration (Selscan Ch# 5)
6879.0	AFI-RDARA	Nigeria - Kano Aeradio
6880.0	AUS-RFDS	Royal Flying Doctor Service, Meekatharra WA
	NASA	Cape Radio
6890.0	AUS-RFDS	Royal Flying Doctor Service, Carnarvon WA, Port Augusta SA
	US-ANG	ANG - Air National Guard
6895.0	US-ANG	ANG - Air National Guard
6896.0	NASA	Cape Radio
6897.0	NASA	DOD Cape Radio
6904.0	USAF-ACC	Air Combat Command, Primary - East
6919.0	NASA	Cape Radio
6920.0	AUS-RFDS	Royal Flying Doctor Service, Broken Hill NSW
6925.0	AUS-RFDS	Royal Flying Doctor Service, Derby WA
6927.0	USAF-SAM	Mystic Star SAM Series M
6940.0	US-ANG	ANG - Air National Guard
	USAF-ACC	Air Combat Command, Primary - East
6942.0	USAF-ACC	Air Combat Command, Primary - East
6944.0	USAF-CEN	Commando Escort Net - Hawaii "Sierra"
6945.0	AUS-RFDS	Royal Flying Doctor Service, Wyndham WA
6947.0	USAF-ACC	Air Combat Command, Primary - East
6950.0	AUS-RFDS	Royal Flying Doctor Service, Alice Springs NT
6960.0	AUS-RFDS	Royal Flying Doctor Service, Port Hedland WA

Master Frequency List

FREQ.	SERVICE	STATION/LOCATION
6965.0	AUS-RFDS	Royal Flying Doctor Service, Mount Isa QLD
6969.0	USAF	USAF Tactical
6975.0	AUS-RFDS	Royal Flying Doctor Service
6989.0	USAF-SAM	Mystic Star SAM Series M
6993.0	USAF-SAM	Mystic Star SAM Series B
		Mystic Star SAM Series H
7185.0	NASA	Goddard Space Center - Shuttle Rebroadcast - LSB
7300.0	SAUDI-AF	Saudi Air Force, Riyadh (Hotel 2), Taif (Hotel 4), Tabuk (Hotel 8)
	US-DEA	OTH Radio System "Charlie"
7305.0	USAF-SAM	Mystic Star SAM Series G
7307.0	AUS-RFDS	Royal Flying Doctor Service, Charleville (duplex 7410.0)
7313.0	NASA	Cape Radio
7316.0	USAF-SAM	Mystic Star SAM Series P
7330.0	USAF-USSTRATCOM	Former SAC "Giant Talk" Network "Sierra 307"
7350.0	INO-LDOC	Port Moresby (Air Niugini)
7357.5	CHILE-AF	Los Cerillos AB (Chilean Air Force)
7392.0	AUS-RFDS	Royal Flying Doctor Service
7397.0	USAF-ACC	Air Combat Command, Primary - West
7400.0	SAM-LDOC	La Ceiba (SOSA)
7410.0	AUS-RFDS	Royal Flying Doctor Service, Charleville (duplex 7307.0)
7412.0	NASA	Cape Radio
7415.0	USAF-CEN	Commando Escort Net - Hawaii "Hotel"
7433.0	EU-LDOC	Stockholm Radio
7450.0	US-ANG	ANG - Air National Guard - Arizona Training Net
7453.0	EU-LDOC	Stockholm Radio
7460.0	US-ANG	ANG - Air National Guard
	USAF-ACC	Air Combat Command, AWACS Aircraft
7461.0	NASA	Cape Radio
7465.0	AUS-RFDS	Royal Flying Doctor Service, Cairns QLD
7466.0	USAF-SAM	Mystic Star SAM Series M
7469.0	USAF-SAM	Mystic Star SAM Series G
7475.0	AUS-RFDS	Royal Flying Doctor Service, Mt. Isa QLD
	US-DOD	Counterdrug Network "Victor Delta"
	US-FAA	U. S. Federal Aviation Administration (Selscan Ch# 6)
	USAF-USSTRATCOM	Former SAC "Giant Talk" Network "Whiskey 104"
7497.0	USAF-SAM	Mystic Star SAM Series J
7517.0	AUS-RFDS	Royal Flying Doctor Service
7525.0	NASA	Cape Radio
7527.0	US-Customs	COTHERN "Zulu Bravo" - Selscan 1
	US-DOD	Counterdrug Network "Zulu Bravo"
	USAF	Training Exercise (Delmar Hotel)
7535.0	USN	Ballbearing wkg USS Hampshire
7541.0	AFI-LDOC	Addis Ababa (Ethiopian Airlines - Holloway)
7550.0	AUS-RFDS	Royal Flying Doctor Service, Kalgoorlie WA
7552.0	INO-RDARA	Madagascar - Antananarivo Radio
7595.0	AFI-RDARA	Addis Ababa Air Traffic Control, Asmara ACC
	USN	Air/Ground/Ship
7605.0	NASA	Cape Radio
	USAF-SAM	Mystic Star SAM Series R
7611.0	US-FAA	U. S. Federal Aviation Administration (Selscan Ch# 7)
7632.0	USAF-ACC	Air Combat Command
7635.0	US-CAP	National Command Net, CAP-USAF Frequency
7657.0	US-DEA	OTH Radio System "Foxtrot"
7660.0	USAF-SAM	Mystic Star SAM Series P
7675.0	USAF-ACC	Air Combat Command
7676.0	NASA	Cape Radio
7690.0	USAF-SAM	Mystic Star SAM Series A
		Mystic Star SAM Series J
7693.0	USAF-SAM	Mystic Star SAM Series Unassigned (Air Force 1)
7697.0	NASA	Cape Radio
7713.0	USAF-AMC-OP	Operation Restore Hope (Accuse Delta - Tanker), Moron
7735.0	USAF-SAM	Mystic Star SAM Series C
7740.0	SP-AFTN	Auckland, Chatham Island & Rarotonga AFTN stations

FREQ.	SERVICE	STATION/LOCATION
7741.0	OP-Haiti	Operation Able Manner (Haiti Embargo) Primary Air/Ship
7742.0	NASA	Cape Radio
7765.0	NASA	Cape Radio
	USAF-SAM	Mystic Star SAM Series R
7771.0	CAR-RDARA	Cuba - Boyeros, Camaguey & Santiago de Cuba Aeradios
7778.5	US-DOD	Counterdrug Network "Xray Delta"
7782.0	BRZ-AF	Brazilian Air Force
7804.0	NASA	Cape Radio
7807.0	NASA	Cape Radio
7811.0	NORAD	NORAD (Tie-in to US CAP)
	USAF-ACC	Air Combat Command, Backup - West
7813.0	USAF-ARRS	Air Rescue Service
	USAF-SAM	Mystic Star SAM Series P (Air Force 1)
7827.0	USAF-SAM	Mystic Star SAM Series J
7831.0	USAF-USSTRATCOM	Former SAC "Giant Talk" Network "Whiskey 105"
7833.0	NASA	Cape Radio
7844.0	USAF-AMC-OP	Operation Restore Hope (Absolution - Mogadishu, Somalia)
7853.0	US-ANG	ANG - Air National Guard
7860.0	NASA	Cape Radio
7870.0	EU-CC-LDOC	Somerset (Portishead Radio)
7873.0	USAF-SAM	Mystic Star SAM Series A
7883.0	USN	Navy Air ASW Atlantic
7893.0	USN	Navy Air ASW Atlantic
7907.0	USAF-SAM	Mystic Star SAM Series C
7910.0	NASA	Cape Radio
	USAF-SAM	Mystic Star SAM Series R
7912.5	SAM-LDOC	several South American stations (TASA)
7919.0	NASA	Cape Radio
7920.0	US-CAP	Civil Air Patrol
7922.0	USAF-SAM	Mystic Star SAM Series A
7930.0	USAF-SAM	Mystic Star SAM Series P
7940.0	SAT-AFTN	Recife & Dakar AFTN stations
7975.0	AUS-RFDS	Royal Flying Doctor Service, Darwin NT
	USAF-SAM	Mystic Star SAM Series M
7982.0	USAF-SAM	Mystic Star SAM Series C
7985.0	NASA	Cape Radio
7997.0	USAF-SAM	Mystic Star SAM Series Q
8014.0	SAM-LDOC	several South American stations (Transportes Aereos Marilia)
8029.0	USAF-SAM	Mystic Star SAM Series A
8039.0	USAF-SAM	Mystic Star SAM Series Q
8045.0	USAF-SAM	Mystic Star SAM Series C
8047.0	USAF-SAM	Mystic Star SAM Series G
8050.0	USAF-SAM	Mystic Star SAM Series Q
8055.0	RNZAF	Ohakea AFB
	USAF-SAM	Mystic Star SAM Series H
8060.0	USAF-SAM	Mystic Star SAM Series J
8070.0	NA-CC-LDOC	Gulf of Mexico (ARINC)
8077.0	NASA	Cape Radio
8080.0	USAF-SAM	Mystic Star SAM Series N
8081.5	SEA-RDARA	Indonesia - several aeradios
8086.0	USAF-SAM	Mystic Star SAM Series C
8100.0	US-Customs	"Thunderbolt" working unid aircraft
8125.0	US-FAA	U. S. Federal Aviation Administration (Selscan Ch# 8)
8140.0	SEA-CC-LDOC	Sydney SkyComms
8144.0	AUS-RFDS	Royal Flying Doctor Service, Kalgoorlie WA
8147.0	AUS-RFDS	Royal Flying Doctor Service
8156.0	RAF	UKADGE
8162.0	USAF-SAM	Mystic Star SAM Series G
		Mystic Star SAM Series H
		Mystic Star SAM Series N
8165.0	AUS-RFDS	Royal Flying Doctor Service, Port Augusta SA
8170.0	EU-CC-LDOC	Somerset (Portishead Radio)
	USAF-SAM	Mystic Star SAM Series A

Master Frequency List

FREQ.	SERVICE	STATION/LOCATION
8176.0	USAF-SAM	Mystic Star SAM Series H
8180.0	EU-CC-LDOC	Somerset (Portishead Radio)
8185.0	EU-CC-LDOC	Somerset (Portishead Radio)
8190.0	RAF	RAF Air/Ground
8192.0	USAF-AMC-OP	Operation Restore Hope (Absolution - Mogadishu, Somalia)
8586.0	SAM-RDARA	Argentina - Mendoza ACC
8711.0	USAF-ACC	Air Combat Command, Primary
8731.0	US-ANG	ANG - Air National Guard
8778.0	USN	HICOM - Eastern/Mid Pacific (COM3RDFLT)
8790.0	RAF	UKADGE "Quebec Romeo"
8816.0	SAM-LDOC	Porto Alegre, Rio de Janeiro (RIO SUL - Serviços Aéreos Regionais)
8819.0	MID-VOL	Beirut Volmet (H+15,45)
	NA-CC-LDOC	Tors Cove (Rainbow Radio)
	NCA-VOL	Russian Network B, Tbilisi, Georgia (H+00,30), Aktyubinsk, Kazakhstan (H+05,35), Krasnodar, Azerbaijan (H+10,40), Alma Ata, Kazakhstan (H+15,45), Tashkent, Uzbekistan (H+20,50), Baku, Azerbaijan (H+25,55)
	SAM-LDOC	several Brazilian stations (TransBrazil)
8822.0	MID-LDOC	Jeddah (Saudi Airlines)
	SEA-RDARA	Australia HF Network - Southwest region - Carnarvon, Kalgoorlie, Meekatharra, Perth & Port Hedland FIS
	SP-RDARA	Maldive Islands - Gan FIS (Addu Atoll)
	U.S. Flight Test	Aero Corporation
		Boeing Company, Witchita KS
		Falcon Jet Corp
		Lockheed Corporation
		McDonnel Douglas
		Rockwell International, Cedar Rapids IA
8825.0	NAT-E MWARA	New York, Santa Maria
8826.0	AFI-RDARA	Sao Tomé & Principe - Sao Tomé Aeradio
		Tunisia - Tunisia
	SAM-RDARA	Ecuador - Quito Aeradio
8828.0	PAC-VOL	Honolulu (H+00,+30), Tokyo (H+10,+40), Hong Kong (H+15,+45), Auckland (H+20,50)
8831.0	NAT-F MWARA	Gander & Shanwick Aeradios
	SEA-RDARA	Australia HF Network - Central Eastern region - Charleville, Longreach & Rockhampton FIS
		Thailand - Bangkok ACC
8833.0	SEA-RDARA	Indonesia - Timika (Tembagapura) FIS
8834.0	BRZ-AF	Brazilian Air Force
	SEA-RDARA	Indonesia - Biak & Jayapura ACC's
8837.0	CWP-RDARA	Papua New Guinea - Port Moresby, Madang & Nadzab ACC's
	MID-LDOC	Tel Aviv (El AL)
8840.0	AFI-RDARA	Zaire - Goma Radio, Kinsangani (Bangoka) FIS
	EU-RDARA	Norway - Svalbard (Longyear) Aeradio
8842.0	CAR-LDOC	Boyeros (Aeroflot)
	NCA-LDOC	Moscow (Aeroflot)
8843.0	AFI-LDOC	Lusaka (Zambia Airways)
	CEP-1/2 MWARA	Honolulu, San Francisco (ARINC)
	NA-CC-LDOC	New York (ARINC)
	SAM-RDARA	Brazil -several aeradios
		Colombia - Bogota ACC
	SEA-RDARA	Australia HF Network - North Central region - Alice Springs, Darwin, Gove & Tennant Creek Aeradios
8846.0	CAR-B MWARA	Barranquilla, Boyeros, Cayenne, Georgetown, Maiquetia, New York, Panama, Paramaribo, Piarco, San Andres Is.
	SEA-RDARA	Kiribati/Tuvalu - Kiribati
	SP-RDARA	SP-9 RDARA - Apia, Butaritari, Christmas Is., Fua'Amotu (Tonga), Honiara, Nandi, Niue, Port Vila, Rarotonga, Santo (Pekoa) & Wallis Aeradios
8847.0	MID-RDARA	Lebanon - Basrah & Beirut Aeradios
	MID-VOL	Kuwait Volmet
8849.0	AFI-LDOC	Mahe (Air Seychelles)
	EA-VOL	Beijing (H+05,45), Guangzhou (H+10,50)

FREQ.	SERVICE	STATION/LOCATION
8849.0	SAM-LDOC	Sao Paulo (Brazil Central - Linha Aérea Regional)
		several South American stations (Transportes Aereos Marilia)
8852.0	NCA-VOL	Russian Network E, Pevek, Russia (H+10,40), Katanga, Russia (H+15,45)
8855.0	SAM-C MWARA	Belem, Bogota, Brasilia, Iquitos, Leticia, Manaus, Maiquetia, Porto Velho, Rio de Janeiro
	SAM-NE MWARA	Belem, Cayenne, Georgetown, Maiquetia, Paramaribo, Piarco, Recife
	SAM-RDARA	Brazil - Belem, Brasilia, Campo Grande, Curitiba , Manaus, Porto Velho, Recife FIR's
	SAM-SE MWARA	Asuncion, Belem, Brasilia, Buenos Aires, Campo Grande, Curtiba, La Paz, Montevideo, Lima, Pascua, Porto Alegre, Porto Velho, Recife, Resistencia, Salvador Dois De Julho, Santa Cruz
8856.0	SAM-RDARA	Brazil - Rio de Janeiro Int'l (Galeao) Aeradio
8858.0	SEA-RDARA	Australia HF Network - South Central region - Alice Springs, Broken Hill, Ceduna & Leigh Creek FIS
8861.0	AFI-1 MWARA	Abidjan, Bamako, Bissau, Bobo Dioulasso, Bouake, Casablanca, Conakry, Canarias, Freetown, Kano, Niamey, Nouadhibou, Nouakchott, Ouagadougou, Roberts (Monrovia)
	AFI-RDARA	Johannesburg & Windhoek ACC's
	MID-RDARA	India - several aeradios
	NCA-VOL	Russian Network D, Kirensk, Russia (H+00,30), Yakutsk, Russia (H+10,40), Khabarovsk, Russia (H+15,45), Magadan, Russia (H+20,50), Irkutsk, Russia (H+25,55)
	SAM-RDARA	Brazil - Recife, Rio de Janeiro & Salvador Dois De Julho Aeradios
	SAT-1 MWARA	Brasilia, Canarias, Cayenne, Dakar, Manaus, Paramaribo, Recife, Rio de Janeiro, Sal Island, Salvador
	SP-RDARA	Nadzab, Lae, Port Moresby & Wewak ACC's
8862.0	AFI-LDOC	Dakar (Air Senegal)
8864.0	NAT-B MWARA	Gander, Iceland (Reykjavik), New York, Santa Maria, Shannon (Shanwick)
	SAM-RDARA	Chile - Isla Rey Jorge Marsh Approach
8867.0	SP-6/7 MWARA	Auckland, Honolulu, Nandi, Pascua (Easter Is.), Port Vila, Rarotonga, Sydney, Tahiti, Wallis
	SP-RDARA	Auckland, Christmas Is., Lord Howe Is. & Tahiti ACC's
8868.0	SEA-RDARA	Vietnam - Hanoi ACC
8870.0	AFI-RDARA	AFI-3 RDARA, Addis Ababa, Dar-es-Salaam
8873.0	AFI-RDARA	AFI-4 RDARA, Algiers, Brazzaville, Dakar, Douala, Franceville, Garoua, In Salah, Libreville, N'djamena Tamanrasset ACC's
	CANFORCE	MAG - Halifax Military
	USN	Air/Ground/Ship
8875.0	CWP-RDARA	Papua New Guinea - Madang Aeradio
	SAM-RDARA	Colombia - Arauca, Mitu, Puerto Carrena, San José del Guaviare, Tame, Trinidad & Villavencencio Aeradios
8875.8	NCA-RDARA	Albania -Tirana Aeradio
8876.0	CAR-LDOC	Boyeros, Camaguey, Ciego De Avila, Santiago de Cuba & Veradero Aeradios
	NA-RDARA	Alaska - Central and Southeast
	SEA-RDARA	Australia HF Network - South Eastern region, Dubbo, Melbourne, Midura, Sydney
	US-NOAA	Hurricane Hunters - Echo - KJY74 Miami Air/Ground
8879.0	AFI-RDARA	East Africa/Indian Ocean
	INO-1 MWARA	Antananarivo, Beira, Blantyre, Bombay, Cocos Is., Colombo, Dar es Salaam, Harare, Jeddah, Johannesburg, Kigali, Lilongwe, Lusaka, Madras, Mahajanga, Male, Mauritius, Moroni, Nairobi, Perth, Seychelles, St. Denis, Toamasina
	INO-RDARA	Madagascar - several aeradios
	NAT-C MWARA	Gander, Iceland (Reykjavik), Shannon (Shanwick)
8880.0	AFI-RDARA	Botswana - Francistown, Selebi-Phikwe* & several other aeradios
	AFI-RDARA	Morocco - Casablanca ACC
8882.0	SEA-RDARA	Indonesia - Banjarmasin, Kupang, & several other aeradios
8884.0	USN	Air/Ground/Ship
8885.0	SAM-LDOC	Lima (American Airlines)
8888.0	AFI-RDARA	AFI-4 RDARA, Beria, Bujumbura, Cape Town, Dar es Salaam, Gaborone, Kamina-Base, Kinshasa, Kitona Base, Luanda & Nairobi ACC's
	CAR-LDOC	Boyeros (Cubana Airlines)
	NCA-VOL	Russian Network C, Syktyvkar, Russia (H+00,30), Sverdlovsk, Russia (H+05,35), Novosibirsk, Russia (H+10,40), Kuybyshev, Russia (H+15,45), Tyuman, Russia (H+20,50)

Master Frequency List

FREQ.	SERVICE	STATION/LOCATION
8888.0	USAF	Satcom wkg Mill Star
8889.0	MID-RDARA	India - Delhi ACC
8890.0	SAM-LDOC	Cochabamba (LAB - Lloyd Aéreo Boliviano)
8891.0	MID-RDARA	India - several aeradios
	NAT-D MWARA	Bodo, Cambridge Bay, Churchill, Iqaluit (Frobisher Bay), Gander, Iceland (Reykjavik), Sondrestrom
	SAM-LDOC	unid Panama xx wkg "Referaria"
	SEA-RDARA	Australia HF Network - North Eastern region - Cairns. Mt. Isa, Townsville & Weipa
8894.0	AFI-2 MWARA	Algiers, Brazzaville, Kano, Gao, Niamey, N'djamena, Tamanrasset, Timimoun, Tripoli, Tunis
	AFI-RDARA	AFI-2 RDARA, Gao, Kano, Niamey & several other aeradios
		Algeria - Adrar, Algiers, Biskra, Bordj Mokhtar, Djanet, El Golea, El Oued, Ghardaia, Hassi-Messaoud, In Salah, Ouargla, Touggourt, & Zarzaitine Aeradios
	SAM-RDARA	Colombia - Cali, Leticia, Villavicencio & several other aeradios
8895.0	AFI-LDOC	Algiers (Air Algerie)
8896.0	NA-LDOC	Float Plane "Frogman" (on Rupert River, Labrador) wkg Kingfisher
	SAM-LDOC	Lima (American Airlines)
8896.5	SAM-RDARA	Peru - Iquitos, Lima & Pucalpa Aeradios
8897.0	EA-1 MWARA	Beijing, Canton, Hailar, Irkutsk, Jinan, Kunming, Lanzhou, Pyongyang, Shanghai, Shenyang, Taegu, Ulaanbaatar, Urumqi, Wuhan, Zhengzhou
	EA-RDARA	China - several ACC's
8900.0	NA-LDOC	Toronto Ops (Elite/Canada 3000)
	SEA-RDARA	Australia HF Network - Northwest region - Darwin, Derby, Kununurra, Port Hedland Aeradios
	USN	unid exercises "All weapons deployed - FL310"
8903.0	AFI-4 MWARA	Accra, Bangui, Brazzaville, Bujumbura, Bulawayo, Contonou, Douala, Entebbe, Franceville, Francistown, Garoua, Goma, Johannesburg, Kamina Base, Kano, Kinshasa, Kisangani, Kitona Base, Lagos, Libreville, Lomé, Luanda, Lumbumbashi, Lusaka, Maroua, Maseru, Nairobi, N'djamena, N'djili, Niamey, Niamtougou, Port Gentil, Salisbury, Salazar, Sao Tomé, Seychelles, Windhoek, Yaounde
	AFI-RDARA	Zaire - Gbadolite Aeradio
	CWP-1/2 MWARA	Guam, Hong Kong, Honolulu, Manila, Naha, Port Moresby, Seoul, Taipei, Tokyo
	SEA-CC-LDOC	Sydney SkyComms
	SEA-LDOC	Sydney (Qantas)
8906.0	CWP-RDARA	Papua New Guinea - Madang & Wewak Aeradios
	MID-RDARA	India - Delhi, Bombay & several other aeradios
	NAT-A MWARA	Canarias, Gander, New York, Paramaribo, Piarco, Santa Maria, Shanwick
8907.0	RNZAF	Whenuapai AFB
8909.0	MID-RDARA	India - several aeradios
8910.0	EU-LDOC	Reykjavik (Iceland Aeradio)
	SAM-RDARA	Trinidad - Piarco ACC
	USAF-GHFS	Offutt AFB Global - discrete frequency
8912.0	US-Customs	COTHERN "Yankee Charlie" - Selscan 2
	US-DOD	Counterdrug Network "Yankee Charlie"
	US-FAA	U. S. Federal Aviation Administration
8913.0	AFI-RDARA	AFI-4 RDARA - Kinshasa, Lubumbashi
	ZAIRE-AF	Kinshasa (Zairian Air Force)
8915.0	NP-3/4 MWARA	Honolulu , Tokyo
8917.0	MID-RDARA	India - Andaman Is., Bombay, Calcutta, Mangolore, Port Blair & Trivandrtum Aeradios
8918.0	CAR-A MWARA	Barranquilla, Boyeros, Cayenne, Cenamer, Guatemala, Maiquetia, Merida, New York, Panama, Paramaribo, San Andres Is, San José
	MID-RDARA	Kuwait, Jeddah & Riyan ACC's
		Yemen - several aeradios
	MID-VOL	Damascus Volmet
	NA-LDOC	Mexico City (AeroMexico)
	NCA-RDARA	CIS, Armenia - Yerevan ACC
	SEA-RDARA	Indonesia - Ambon, Manado, Ujung Pandang & several other aeradios
	U.S. Flight Test	Boeing Company
		McDonnel Douglas
		Rockwell International
	USN	Air/Ground/Ship

FREQ.	SERVICE	STATION/LOCATION
8921.0	CWP-LDOC	Hong Kong (Dragonair)
	EU-LDOC	Dusseldorf (LTU)
		Frankfurt (Lufthansa)
		Speedbird London (British Airways)
	RAF	Hong Kong Air
	SEA-LDOC	Colombo (Air Lanka)
		Jakarta
		Sydney (Qantas)
8924.0	AFI-RDARA	Equatorial Guinea - Bata Aeradio
	CAR-LDOC	Boyeros (Aeroflot)
	EU-LDOC	Amsterdam (KLM-Royal Dutch Airlines)
		Brussels (Sabena)
		Dublin (Aer Lingus)
		Lisbon (TAP/VARIG)
		Prague (Czechoslovak Airlines)
		Warsaw (LOT - Polskie Linie)
	MID-LDOC	Tel Aviv (El Al)
	MID-RDARA	India - Agartala, Baghdogra, Bechar*, Calcutta, Dibrugarh, El Oued*, Gauhati, Imphal & Silchar Aeradios
	NCA-LDOC	Khabarovsk, Moscow (Aeroflot)
	SAM-LDOC	Caracas (AVENSA)
		Maiquetia (VIASA)
		Montevideo (PLUNA)
		Piarco (West Indian)
		Rio de Janeiro (VARIG)
	SAM-RDARA	Uruguay - Montevideo ACC
	SP-RDARA	Fernando Po, Nauru, Tabiteuea & Tarawa Aeradios
8927.0	AFI-LDOC	Abidjan
		Addis Ababa, Asmara (Ethiopian Airlines - Holloway)
		Dar es Salaam (Air Tanzania)
		Entebbe (Uganda Airlines)
		Lagos (Nigeria Airways)
		Luanda (TAAG)
		Nairobi
	AFI-RDARA	Dire Dawa, Asmara & Franceville Aeradios
	CAR-LDOC	Boyeros (Cubana Airlines)
	NA-LDOC	Matamoros
		Merida, Mexico City, Tijuana (AeroMexico)
	INO-LDOC	Antananarivo (Air Madagascar)
	MID-LDOC	Jeddah & Riyadh (Saudi Airlines)
8929.0	SAM-RDARA	Brazil - several aeradios
8930.0	EA-LDOC	Beijing
		Budapest (MALEV - Hungarian Airlines)
		Stockholm Radio (SAS)
	MID-LDOC	Bombay (Air India)
		Karachi (PIA-Pakistani International Airlines)
		Tel Aviv (El Al)
	MID-RDARA	India - several aeradios
	SEA-CC-LDOC	Sydney SkyComms
	SEA-LDOC	Bangkok (Thai Airways)
		Singapore (Singapore Airlines)
8931.0	CWP-RDARA	Papua New Guinea - Madang Aeradio
	EU-LDOC	Rome (Alitalia)
8933.0	AFI-LDOC	Algiers (Air Algerie)
		Blantyre, Lilongwe (Air Malawi)
		Cairo (Egypt Air)
		Djibouti (Air Djibouti)
		Springbok Jo'burg (South African Airways) shared by Mauritius Ops (Air Mauritius)
	EU-LDOC	Scheveningen Radio
	NA-CC-LDOC	New York (ARINC)
8936.0	CAR-LDOC	Grand Cayman (Cayman Air)
		Santo Domingo
		Willemstad (ALM Antillean)

Master Frequency List

FREQ.	SERVICE	STATION/LOCATION
8936.0	EU-LDOC	Berne ("Berna") Radio (Swiss Air)
		Las Palmas (Lineas Aereas Canarias)
		Madrid (Iberia)
	SAM-LDOC	Belem, Rio de Janeiro (VARIG)
		Cartagena (Aero Condor)
	SEA-CC-LDOC	Sydney SkyComms
8938.0	MID-RDARA	India - Ahmadabab, Amritsar, Bhopal, Bombay, Calcutta, Delhi, Hyderabad, Lucknow, Nagpur, Patna, Srinagar & Varanasi Aeradios
	SAM-VOL	Comodoro Rivadavia (H+30)
8939.0	NCA-VOL	Russian Network A, Riga, Latvia (H+00,30), St. Petersburg, Russia (H+05,35), Moscow, Russia H+10,15,40,45), Kiev, Ukraine (H+20,50), Rostov, Ukraine (H+25,55)
	SAM-LDOC	Belem, Rio de Janeiro, Sao Paulo (VARIG)
	SAM-RDARA	Brazil -Navegantes Aeradio
	USAF-SAM	Mystic Star SAM Series Unassigned
8942.0	EA-2 MWARA	Canton, Irkutsk, Pyongyang, Ulaanbaatar
	SEA-2 MWARA	Bali, Bangkok, Denpasar, Guangzhou, Hanoi, Ho Chi Minh, Hong Kong, Jakarta, Kuala Lumpur, Kota Kinabalu, Manila, Seoul, Singapore, Tokyo & Vientiane
8943.0	USN	Air/Ground/Ship
8945.0	CAR-LDOC	Bridgetown Operations (Caribbean Airways)
	SAM-LDOC	Salvador & several other stations (NLA - Nordeste Linhas Aéreas Regionais)
	USAF	Sondre Stromfjord FIC (Greenland)
8947.0	SAM-RDARA	Venezuela - Upata Aeradio
8948.0	MID-RDARA	India - several aeradios
8949.0	AFI-LDOC	Harare (Air Zimbabwe)
8951.0	MID-1 MWARA	Aden, Amman, Ankara, Baghdad, Basrah, Beirut, Cairo, Damascus, Jeddah, Kuwait, Manama, Odessa, Sana'a, Simferopol, Tehran, Tbilisi, Yerevan
	MID-3 MWARA	Aktyubinsk, Alma Ata, Dushanbe, Frunze, Kuybyshev, Kzyl-Orda, Moscow, Samarkand, Tashkent, Uralsk, Yevevan
	NP-RDARA	Honolulu & Tokyo ACC
	EU-LDOC	Amsterdam (KLM-Royal Dutch Airlines)
	SAM-RDARA	Argentina - several aeradios
8952.0	SAM-VOL	Cordoba Volmet (H+25)
8957.0	EU-VOL	Shannon Aeradio (H+00,+25,+30,+55)
	SAM-RDARA	Peru - Cochabamba Aeradio
	SEA-RDARA	Indonesia - Jakarta, Medan, Palembang, & Pontianak ACC's
8959.0	AFI-RDARA	Djibouti, Dongola, Hargeisa, Juba, Kassala & Port Sudan Aeradios
	CAR-RDARA	Santo Domingo (De Las Americas) Aeradio
	MID-LDOC	Jeddah (Saudi Airlines)
8960.0	EU-CC-LDOC	Somerset (Portishead Radio)
	NA-LDOC	Toronto (Elite-Canada 3000)
8963.0	AFI-LDOC	Lagos (Nigeria Airways)
8964.0	FAF	Orleans (French Air Force Air/Ground)
	USAF-ACC	Air Combat Command
	USAF-GHFS	Ascension AB Discrete Frequency
8965.0	RAF	UKADGE "Charlie Alpha"
8967.0	AFI-LDOC	Mahe (Air Seychelles)
	EU-LDOC	Belgrade (Serbia Aerotransport)
	GAF	DHM91 Munster (German Air Force Air/Ground)
	MID-RDARA	Saudi Arabia - Al Jouf, Bisha, Gassim, Gizan, Madinah, Nejran, Sulayel, Taif & Wejh Aeradios
	RAF	UKADGE "Papa Hotel"
	RNZAF	Auckland AB
	SAUDI-AF	Dhahran "Hotel 1", Taif "Hotel 4", King Khalid Air Base (Khamis Mushait)
	USAF-GHFS	Anderson, Andrews, Elmendorf, Hickham, Lajes, McClellan, Offutt, Thule, Yokota
	USN	USN "Foxtrot Tango" Net
8970.0	MID-LDOC	Safat (Kuwaiti Airlines)
	NETH-AF	Valkenburg AB, Dutch Naval Air, Holland
8971.0	MID-RDARA	India - Bangalore Aeradio
	RAF	UKADGE
8972.0	EU-LDOC	Paris Radio (Air France)
		Stockholm Radio
	OP-Haiti	Operation Able Manner (Haiti Embargo)

FREQ.	SERVICE	STATION/LOCATION
8972.0	SEA-CC-LDOC	Sydney SkyComms
	US-JTF-4	Joint Task Force on Drug Enforcement - US Navy
	USN	Atlantic Safety of Flight "Kilo"
8973.5	US-JCS	United States Joint Chiefs of Staff Net/USN Tactical
8975.0	SAF-AF	Langenbaanweg, Waterkloof & Ysterplaat Military (South African Air Force primary interior channel)
8975.5	RAF	UKADGE
8976.0	RAAF	Air Force Butterworth (Malaysia), Darwin, Pearce, Richmond, Sydney, Townsville
	RNZAF	Whenuapai & Wigram AFB's "SRA262"
	USN	Navy Air ASW Atlantic
8977.0	RNAVY	Royal Naval Air Station Yeovilton
8980.0	RAF	RAF Bases in Germany "Bravo Hotel"
	USCG-AIR	Air/ground (helicopters - secondary)
8981.0	FAF	Orleans (French Air Force Air/Ground)
8981.5	USN	Air/Ground/Ship
8983.0	EU-LDOC	Frankfurt (Lufthansa)
8984.0	AFI-RDARA	Mauritania - Nouadhibou ACC
	EU-LDOC	Berlin/Schoenfield (Interflug)
		Madrid (Iberia)
	RAF	UKADGE/STCICS "Hotel Juliet", RAF Training - Finningley AF
	RNZAF	Whenuapai AFB
	SAF-AF	South African Air Force
	USCG-AIR	Air/Ground (secondary)
8985.0	GAF	DHM91 Munster (German Air Force Air/Ground)
8987.0	FAF	Orleans (French Air Force Air/Ground)
	RAF	Pitreavie Air "November Juliet"
8988.0	USN	Air/Ground/Ship
8989.0	BEL-AF	Rouveroy Radio (Belgian Air Force Air/Ground)
	CANFORCE	Edmonton Military air/ground
8990.0	RAAF	Air Force Sydney
	RAF	UKADGE
	SAUDI-AF	Saudi Air Force, Dhahran "Hotel 1", Riyadh "Hotel 2"
8991.0	ITALY-AF	Pisa, Rome (Italian Air Force Air/Ground)
8992.0	PRT-AF	Portuguese Air Force, Lisbon
	RAF	UKADGE - Boulmer
	RNZAF	Whenuapai, Wigram & Ohakea AFB's
	SAF-AF	Waterkloof Military (South African Air Force primary overseas channel)
	USAF-SAM	Mystic Star SAM Series Unassigned
8993.0	EU-LDOC	Dresden
	NASA	Cape Radio
	RAF	Portland
	RNAVY	Royal Naval Air Station Portland
	USAF-AMC	Air Mobility Command
	USAF-GHFS	Ascension AB Discrete Frequency, Bayonne
	USAF-SAM	Mystic Star SAM Series Unassigned
8996.0	RAF	UKADGE "Delta Mike"
8997.0	RNZAF	Flights to Antarctica
	SP-RDARA	Christchurch Radio, McMurdo Sector Routes (Antarctic Region)
	USN	USN 5 Antarctic Primary Air/Ground - McMurdo Base
9000.0	GAF	DHM91 Munster (German Air Force Air/Ground)
9001.0	BRZ-AF	Brazilian Air Force
	US-JCS	United States Joint Chiefs of Staff Net/USN Tactical
	USN	Air/Ground/Ship
9002.0	USN	Air/Ground/Ship
9003.0	MID-LDOC	Amman, (ALIA/Royal Jordanian Airlines)
9006.0	CANFORCE	ATG/MACS Air/Ground - Edmonton, Trenton, St. John's, Lahr Military, Sinai Base
	CAR-LDOC	Mexico City (AeroMexico)
	RAAF	Air Force Sydney
	USAF-SAM	Mystic Star SAM Series S , Andrews AFB wkg E1F in LSB
	USN	Air/Ground/Ship
9007.0	USAF-SAM	Mystic Star SAM Series G
9008.0	USN	Air/Ground/Ship
9009.0	BRZ-AF	Brazilian Air Force Air/Ground

Master Frequency List

FREQ.	SERVICE	STATION/LOCATION
9010.0	CANFORCE	MAG - Halifax Military (Wx H+20), St. John's Military (EAM H+01), Vancouver Military "Delta One Hotel"
	USN	Air/Ground/Ship
9010.5	U.S. Flight Test	Grumman Aerospace
9011.0	GAF	DHM91 Munster (German Air Force Air/Ground)
	RAF	UKADGE "Alpha Delta"
9011.5	U.S. Flight Test	United Technologies
9012.0	USN	Air/Ground/Ship
9013.0	ITALY-AF	Italian Air Force Air/Ground
	SAM-LDOC	Buenos Aires (Aerolineas Argentinas)
	U.S. Flight Test	United Technologies
9014.0	RAF	UKADGE
	RNAVY	Royal Naval Air Station Prestwick
	USAF-ACC	Air Combat Command
9015.0	FAF	Paris Radio (French Air Force)
9016.0	RNZAF	Air Force Auckland
9017.0	U.S. Flight Test	Boeing Flight Test (Seattle)
	USAF-ACC	Former SAC "Giant Talk" Network (EAM + 42) "Xray 904"
	USAF-SAM	Mystic Star SAM Series E "Xray 904" (Air Force 1)
		Mystic Star SAM Series F
9018.0	CUBA-AF	Cuban Air Force
	NASA	Cape Radio
	RNZAF	Auckland Air
	SAM-RDARA	Argentina - San Julian Aeradio
	USAF	SAM - Andrews AFB
	USAF-SAM	Mystic Star SAM Series Unassigned (Air Force 1)
9020.0	US-NOAA	Hurricane Hunters - KJY74 Miami Air/Ground
	USAF	MacDill AFB
9022.0	NASA	Cape Radio
	RAF	UKADGE "Alpha Foxtrot", Bampton
9023.0	CANFORCE	Trenton Military
	NORAD	NORAD SOCC to AWACS, Secondary (NORAD HQ - Ringmaster) "Channel Delta" or "Charlie Channel 5"
	RAAF	Air Force Darwin
	USAF-SAM	Mystic Star SAM Series Unassigned
	USAF-USSTRATCOM	Former SAC "Giant Talk" Network "Whiskey 106"
	USN	USN "Foxtrot Tango" Net
9024.0	NCA-RDARA	CIS - St. Petersburg FIR
	RAF	RAF Training, Finningley AF
9025.0	GAF	DHM91 Munster (German Air Force Air/Ground)
9026.0	SP-LDOC	Suava (Air Pacific)
9027.0	CANFORCE	MAG - Halifax Military
	NORAD	NORAD - Tactical
	RAAF	Air Force Sydney, Townsville
	RNZAF	Wigram AFB
	USAF-USSTRATCOM	Former SAC "Giant Talk" Network "Sierra 392"
9032.0	RAF	STCICS - "Delta Whiskey" - Architect (Wx H+00, H+30), Akrotiri (Cyprus Flight Watch), Gibraltar, Uphavon, Ascension (Haven), Mt. Pleasant (Viper)
	SAM-LDOC	Cartagena (Aero Condor)
	unid-LDOC	a/c bound for Miami in Spanish, Barranquilla, Miami
	USN	Air/Ground/Ship
9035.0	USN	Air/Ground/Ship
9036.0	RAF	Pitreavie Air
	USN	Air/ground
9037.0	USN	Air/ground (Atlantic secondary)
9040.0	SEA-CC-LDOC	Sydney SkyComms
9043.0	NASA	Cape Radio
	USAF-SAM	Mystic Star SAM Series R
9057.0	USAF-SAM	Mystic Star SAM Series Unassigned
	USAF-USSTRATCOM	Former SAC "Giant Talk" Network "Sierra 309"
9093.0	BRZ-AF	Brazilian Air Force
9106.0	UK-RESEARCH	British Antarctic Research Stations
9115.0	NASA	Cape Radio

FREQ.	SERVICE	STATION/LOCATION
9116.0	SP-AFTN	Papeete (Tahiti) AFTN Net Control
9129.0	USAF-CEN	Commando Escort Net - Hawaii "Golf"
9130.0	SAUDI-AF	Saudi Air Force, Dhahran ("Hotel 1"), Taif ("Hotel 4")
9132.0	NASA	Cape Radio
9138.0	NASA	Cape Radio
9170.0	NASA	Cape Radio
9175.0	USAF-AMC-OP	Operation Restore Hope (Absolution - Mogadishu, Somalia)
9180.0	USAF-SAM	Mystic Star SAM Series S
9188.0	USAF-SAM	Mystic Star SAM Series P
9191.0	USN	Air/Ground/Ship
9211.0	EU-LDOC	Berne ("Berna") Radio (Swiss Air)
9215.0	USAF-SAM	Mystic Star SAM Series N
9232.0	NORAD	NORAD (Tie-in to US CAP)
9234.0	USAF-ACC	Air Combat Command, Backup - East
9235.0	NORAD	NORAD
9238.5	US-DOD	Counterdrug Network "Xray Echo"
9270.0	USAF-SAM	Mystic Star SAM Series H
9315.0	NORAD	NORAD
9320.0	USAF-SAM	Mystic Star SAM Series C
		Mystic Star SAM Series N
		Mystic Star SAM Series Q
9336.0	SP-AFTN	Port Moresby AFTN station
9414.0	USAF-SAM	Mystic Star SAM Series H
9424.5	AFI-AFTN	AFTN - Antananarivo traffic to Nairobi and Dar es Salaam
9425.0	USAF-SAM	Mystic Star SAM Series C
9474.0	USAF-ACC	Air Combat Command, Secondary (Data) - West
9475.0	USAF-SAM	Mystic Star SAM Series M
9495.0	AFI-RDARA	Nigeria - Kano & Lagos ACC's
9497.0	US-DEA	OTH Radio System "Delta"
9500.0	NORAD	NORAD - Air Defense Exercises
9510.0	NORAD	NORAD - Air Defense Exercises
9568.0	USAF-ACC	Air Combat Command, AWACS Aircraft
9586.0	NORAD	NORAD - Air Defense Exercises
9650.0	NORAD	NORAD - Air Defense Exercises
9723.0	NORAD	NORAD
9793.0	NORAD	NORAD - Air Defense Exercises, (Secondary Tie-in to US CAP)
9802.0	US-DOD	Counterdrug Network "Zulu Charlie"
9806.0	USAF-USSTRATCOM	Former SAC "Giant Talk" Network "Whiskey 107"
9809.0	USAF-USSTRATCOM	"Whiskey 106"
9866.0	USAF-SAM	Mystic Star SAM Series M
9885.0	USAF-SAM	Mystic Star SAM Series C
9892.0	USN	Air/Ground/Ship
9910.0	NASA	Cape Radio
9914.0	US-FAA	U. S. Federal Aviation Administration (Selscan Ch# 11)
9921.0	USAF-SAM	Mystic Star SAM Series M
9958.0	USAF-SAM	Mystic Star SAM Series H
9987.0	USAF-AMC-OP	Operation Restore Hope (Accuse Delta - Tanker), Moron
9991.0	USAF-SAM	Mystic Star SAM Series G
9993.0	NORAD	NORAD
10006.0	SAM-RDARA	Argentina - Cordoba, Buenos Aires ACC Ezeiza Control & Resistencia Aeradios
10009.0	MID-RDARA	India - New Delhi
	MID-VOL	Kuwait Volmet
10015.0	unid-LDOC	unid location, New England
	US-NOAA	Hurricane Hunters - KJY74 Miami Air/Ground
10017.0	CAM-RDARA	Guatemala City Int'l (La Aurora) Aeradio, Mazatlan Aeradio
	MID-VOL	Karachi Volmet (H+15,45)
10018.0	AFI-3 MWARA	Addis Ababa, Aden, Asmara, Bahrain, Benghazi, Bujumbura, Cairo, Dar es Salaam, Entebbe, Hargesia, Djibouti, Jeddah, Khartoum, Kigali, Kisimayu, Male, Mogadishu, Nairobi, N'djamena, Sana'a, Seychelles, Triopli
	EU-LDOC	Frankfurt (Lufthansa)
	MID-2 MWARA	Abadan, Alma Ata, Bombay, Delhi, Dushanbe, Frunze, Kabul, Karachi, Kathmandu, Kuwait, Lahore, Male, Muscat, Odessa, Samarkand, Seychelles, Tashkent, Tehran, Tbilisi, Urumqi, Yerevan

Master Frequency List

FREQ.	SERVICE	STATION/LOCATION
10018.0	MID-RDARA	Iran - Shiraz and several other aeradios
10021.0	CAM-RDARA	El Salvador (Ilopango) Aeradio
	EU-LDOC	Bucharest (TAROM - Romanian Air Transport)
		Luton (Britannia Airlines)
		Luton (Monarch Airlines)
		Madrid (Iberia)
10024.0	SAM-NW MWARA	Barranquilla, Bogota, Caracas (Maiquetia), Lima, Quito
	SAM-RDARA	Paraguay -Asuncion & Isla Rey Jorge Marsh Approach [Chile] Aeradios
	SAM-SW MWARA	Antofagasta, Asuncion, Buenos Aires, Comodoro Rivadavia, Cordoba, Easter Is (Pascua), Guayaquil, La Paz, Lima, Mendoza, Puerto Montt, Punta Arenas, Resistencia, Salta, Santa Cruz, Santiago, Talara
10025.0	CAR-LDOC	Boyeros (Aeroflot)
	EU-LDOC	Prague (Czechoslovak Airlines)
	MID-LDOC	Bombay (Air India)
	NCA-LDOC	Kabul, Moscow (Aeroflot)
		Moscow (Aeroflot)
	SAM-RDARA	Argentina - Cordoba, Monte Caseros, Resistencia, Salta & Tucuman Aeradios
10027.0	CAR-LDOC	Santo Domingo (Iberia)
	EU-LDOC	Bucharest (TAROM - Romanian Air Transport)
		Las Palmas (Lineas Aereas Canarias)
		Las Palmas, Madrid (Iberia)
		Prague (Czechoslovak Airlines)
		Rome (Alitalia)
	MID-LDOC	Amman, (ALIA/Royal Jordanian Airlines)
10030.0	CAR-LDOC	Boyeros (Aeroflot)
	EU-LDOC	Berlin/Schoenfield (Interflug)
		Dusseldorf (LTU)
	NCA-LDOC	Khabarovsk, Moscow (Aeroflot)
	SAM-LDOC	Buenos Aires (Aerolineas Argentinas)
		San Salvador, Santiago
	SEA-LDOC	Australian HF channel
10033.0	AFI-LDOC	Kinshasa (Air Zaire)
	AFI-LDOC	Ouagadougou
		Tunis (Tunis Air)
	CEP-CC-LDOC	Honolulu (ARINC)
	MID-LDOC	Abu Dhabi
		Muscat (Gulf Air)
		Safat (Kuwaiti Airlines)
	NA-LDOC	Mexico City (AeroMexico/Iberia)
10034.0	SAM-LDOC	Lima Radio
10036.0	SAM-LDOC	Santiago (LADECO - Linea Aérea del Cobre)
10039.0	NCA-3 MWARA	Chita, Chulman, Ekimchan, Irkutsk, Kirensk, Khabarovsk, Pyongyang, Ulaanbaatar, Ulan Ude
10042.0	EA-1 MWARA	Beijing, Canton, Hailar, Irkutsk, Jinan, Kunming, Lanzhou, Pyongyang, Shanghai, Shenyang, Taegu, Ulaanbaatar, Urumqi, Wuhan, Zhengzhou
	SAM-LDOC	several South American stations (TASA)
	SAM-RDARA	Brazil - Campo Grande FIR & several other ACC's
10045.0	U.S. Flight Test	Boeing Company, Seattle
		Lockheed Corporation
		McDonnel Douglas
10047.0	unid-LDOC	unid a/c in English (also tried 13339.0 and 15022.0 - possibly Jeddah)
10048.0	NCA-RDARA	CIS - Khabarovsk ACC
	NP-3/4 MWARA	Honolulu, Tokyo
10049.0	IAF	Indian Air Force
10051.0	NAT-VOL	Gander (H+20,+50), New York (continuous)
10057.0	AFI-VOL	Brazzaville (H+10,+25,+30,+55)
	CEP-5	Honolulu, San Francisco
	SAM-VOL	Belem, Brasilia, Guarulhos, Recife, Rio de Janeiro Volmets
10060.0	EU-LDOC	Burgas, Sofia (LAZ - Balkan Bulgarian Airlines)
	SAM-RDARA	Brazil -Navegantes Aeradio
10065.0	EU-LDOC	Frankfurt (Lufthansa)
10066.0	MID-RDARA	India - Trivandrum and several other aeradios
	NA-RDARA	Alaska, Aleutians

FREQ.	SERVICE	STATION/LOCATION
10066.0	SAM-RDARA	Peru - several ACC's
	SEA-1 MWARA	Bali, Bangkok, Colombo, Calcutta, Dhaka, Jakarta, Kathmandu, Kuala Lumpur, Madras, Male, Singapore, Yangon
	SEA-3 MWARA	Bali, Cocos Is, Darwin, Jakarta, Male, Perth, Singapore, Ujung Pandang
	SEA-RDARA	China - Guangzhou & Kunming ACC's
10067.0	SAM-VOL	Asuncion Volmet (H+15)
10069.0	EU-LDOC	Berne ("Berna") Radio (Swiss Air)
		Frankfurt (Hapag Lloyd Fluggesellschaft)
	SAM-LDOC	Rio de Janeiro (VARIG)
10072.0	CWP-LDOC	Seoul (KAL-Korean Airlines)
	EU-LDOC	Frankfurt, Main (Lufthansa)
		Speedbird London (British Airways)
	MID-LDOC	Bombay, Delhi (Air India)
	SEA-CC-LDOC	Sydney SkyComms
	SEA-LDOC	Jakarta
		Singapore (Singapore Airlines)
	SP-LDOC	Auckland (Air New Zealand)
10075.0	AFI-LDOC	Algiers (Air Algerie)
		Harare (Air Zimbabwe)
		Kigali (Air Rwanda)
		Salisbury
	MID-LDOC	Beirut (MEA-Cedar Jet)
		Dubai
	NA-CC-LDOC	Houston Radio (Universal Aviation)
	NCA-LDOC	Kabul (Ariana Afghan Airlines)
	SEA-LDOC	Sydney (Qantas)
10078.0	EU-LDOC	Athens (Olympic Airlines)
		Brussels (Sabena)
		Dusseldorf (LTU)
		Frankfurt (Lufthansa)
		Larnaca (Cyprus Airways)
		Luqa (Air Malta)
		Prague (Czechoslovak Airlines)
	SEA-LDOC	Perth, Sydney (Qantas)
		Singapore (Singapore Airlines)
10081.0	EA-RDARA	China - Kunming ACC
	SAM-RDARA	Argentina - Bahia Blanca Naval, Comodoro Rivadavia, Rio Gallegos, San Carlos de Bariloche & Santa Rosa Aeradios
		Brazil - Rio Gallegos Aeradio
10084.0	EU-LDOC	Luqa (Air Malta)
	EUR-A MWARA	Arkhangelsk, Beirut, Kiev, Lvov, Minsk, Moscow, Murmansk, Odessa, Riga, Simferopol, St. Petersburg, Syktyvkar, Tunis, Valetta, Velikiye, Vitebsk, Vilnius, Vologda
10089.0	NCA-RDARA	CIS - Sverdlovsk Aeradio
10090.0	NCA-VOL	CIS English Language Network, Khabarovsk, Russia (H+05,35), Tashkent, Uzbekistan (H+10,40), Kiev, Ukraine (H+15,45), Moscow, Russia (H+25,55), Novosibirsk, Russia (H+20,50)
10093.0	CAR-LDOC	Kingston Dispatch (Air Jamaica)
	CWP-LDOC	Tokyo (JAL-Japan Airlines)
	EU-LDOC	Paris Radio (Air France)
	MID-LDOC	Beirut (MEA-Cedar Jet)
		Manama (Falcon)
	RAF	Hong Kong Air
	SEA-LDOC	Sydney (Qantas)
10096.0	NCA-2 MWARA	Barnaul, Irkutsk, Khanty Mansiysk, Kirensk, Kolpashevo, Krasnoyarsk, Novosibirsk, Podkamennaya, Surgut, Yeniseysk
	SAM-C MWARA	Belem, Bogota, Brasilia, Leticia, Manaus, Maiquetia, Porto Velho, Rio de Janeiro
	SAM-NE MWARA	Belem, Cayenne, Georgetown, Maiquetia, Paramaribo, Piarco, Recife
	SAM-RDARA	Brazil - Belem, Brasilia, Campo Grande Curitiba , Manaus, Porto Alegre, Porto Velho, Recife FIR's
	SAM-SE MWARA	Asuncion, Belem, Brasilia, Buenos Aires, Campo Grande, Curtiba, Iquitos, La Paz, Lima, Montevideo, Porto Alegre, Porto Velho, Recife, Salvador Dois De Julho, Santa Cruz, Santiago

Master Frequency List

FREQ.	SERVICE	STATION/LOCATION
10097.0	EU-LDOC	unid (possibly Prague)
10099.0	U.S. Flight Test	Rockwell International
10112.0	USAF-SAM	Mystic Star SAM Series Q
10153.0	USAF-SAM	Mystic Star SAM Series P
10159.0	NASA	Cape Radio
10165.0	EU-LDOC	Stockholm Radio
10194.0	NORAD	NORAD
	RAF	UKADGE
10202.0	USAF-SAM	Mystic Star SAM Series A
10208.0	SAM-AFTN	Belem AFTN tfc to Paramaribo
10215.0	NASA	Cape Radio
10230.0	NASA	Cape Radio
10242.0	US-Customs	COTHERN "Victor Echo" - Selscan 3
	US-DOD	Counterdrug Network "Victor Echo"
10246.0	USN	Navy Air ASW Pacific (Habitat ASW Command Center)
10247.0	USAF-SAM	Mystic Star SAM Series C
10258.0	USN	Air/Ground/Ship
10264.0	NA-LDOC	Tors Cove (Rainbow Radio phone patches)
10267.0	USAF-ACC	Air Combat Command, Primary - West
10270.0	NASA	Cape Radio
10291.0	EU-CC-LDOC	Somerset (Portishead Radio)
10301.0	NASA	Cape Radio
10305.0	NASA	Cape Radio
	USAF-PMR	Pacific Missile Range, Wheeler AFB wkg AGAR aircraft
10310.0	NASA	Cape Radio
10327.0	NASA	Cape Radio
10330.0	SEA-RDARA	Papua New Guinea - Port Moresby Radio
10357.0	USAF-SAM	Mystic Star SAM Series P
10427.0	USAF-SAM	Mystic Star SAM Series H
10452.0	NORAD	NORAD
	USAF-CEN	Commando Escort Net - Hawaii "Oscar"
10475.0	NASA	Cape Radio - duplex for pp with 10780.0
10510.0	USAF-CEN	Commando Escort Net - Hawaii "Charlie"
10530.0	USAF-SAM	Mystic Star SAM Series P
10550.0	USAF-SAM	Mystic Star SAM Series P
10575.0	EU-LDOC	Stockholm Radio
10583.0	USAF-SAM	Mystic Star SAM Series N
10586.0	USAF-SAM	Mystic Star SAM Series H
10590.0	USAF-SAM	Mystic Star SAM Series C
10603.0	USAF-SAM	Mystic Star SAM Series M
10665.0	USAF-ACC	Air Combat Command, Primary - West
10720.0	USAF-SAM	Mystic Star SAM Series N
10765.0	USAF-SAM	Mystic Star SAM Series C
10780.0	NASA	Ascension Radio, Cape Radio - Shuttle Missions
	USAF-SAM	Mystic Star SAM Series C
10805.0	EU-LDOC	Stockholm Radio
	USN	Air/Ground/Ship
10846.0	AFI-AFTN	AFTN - Niamey
10850.0	NASA	Cape Radio
10880.0	NASA	Cape Radio
	USAF-SAM	Mystic Star SAM Series N, "Foxtrot 277"
10881.0	USAF-SAM	Mystic Star SAM Series M
10884.0	EU-CC-LDOC	Somerset (Portishead Radio)
	EU-LDOC	Stockholm Radio
10895.0	USAF-ACC	Air Combat Command, Primary - East
10905.0	NASA	Cape Radio
10930.0	USAF-AMC-OP	Operation Restore Hope (Absolution, Accuse)
10937.0	RAF	UKADGE
10949.0	NASA	Cape Radio
10960.0	EU-CC-LDOC	Somerset (Portishead Radio)
10975.0	SAM-LDOC	several South American stations (TASA)
10987.0	USAF-ACC	Air Combat Command, Primary - West

FREQ.	SERVICE	STATION/LOCATION
11007.0	NORAD	NORAD
	USAF-ACC	Air Combat Command, Primary - West
11016.0	USAF-ACC	Air Combat Command, Primary - East/AWACS Communications Channel
11035.0	USAF-SAM	Mystic Star SAM Series Unassigned (Air Force 1)
11052.0	USAF-SAM	Mystic Star SAM Series Unassigned
11053.0	USAF-SAM	Mystic Star SAM Series Unassigned
11055.0	USAF-SAM	Mystic Star SAM Series M Mystic Star SAM Series N
11056.0	USAF-SAM	Mystic Star SAM Series A Mystic Star SAM Series L
11058.0	USAF-SAM	Mystic Star SAM Series Q
11071.0	US-DOD	Counterdrug Network
11073.5	US-DOD	Counterdrug Network
11076.0	US-DEA	OTH Radio System "Echo"
11100.0	SAUDI-AF	Saudi Air Force, Dhahran (Hotel 1)
11104.0	NASA	Cape Radio - Shuttle Missions
11110.0	USAF-PMR	Pacific Missile Range, Wheeler AFB wkg AGAR aircraft
11117.0	AFI-LDOC	Tunis (Tunis Air)
11118.0	USAF-SAM	Mystic Star SAM Series P
11122.0	SAM-LDOC	several South American stations (TASA)
11130.0	USAF-ACC	Air Combat Command
11132.0	SEA-CC-LDOC	Sydney SkyComms
11141.0	NORAD	NORAD
11150.0	USAF-GHFS	Lajes Field - Discrete Frequency, WASP wkg 24 Bravo RED (USB & Digital Tfc)
11153.0	USAF-SAM	Mystic Star SAM Series G
11156.0	USAF-SAM	Mystic Star SAM Series N Mystic Star SAM Series Q
11172.0	BRZ-AF	Brazilian Air Force
11176.0	RAF	RAF bases in Germany
	USAF-GHFS	Albrook, Anderson, Andrews, Ascension, Bayonne, Croughton, Elmendorf, Hickham, Incirlik, Loring, MacDill, McClellan, Offutt, Thule
11179.0	GAF	DHM91 Munster (German Air Force Air/Ground)
11180.0	RAF	STCICS "Alpha Papa", Buchan
	RNZAF	Wigram AFB
	USAF-SAM	Mystic Star SAM Series Unassigned (Air Force 1 & 2)
11182.0	EU-LDOC	Madrid (AVIANCO - Aviacion y Comercio, SA)
	EU-LDOC	Madrid (Iberia)
	NETH-AF	Valkenburg Air (Dutch Air Force)
	NWG NAVY	Stavanger Naval (Norway) - air/ground
11184.0	EU-LDOC	Lisbon (TAP-Air Portugal)
11185.0	MID-LDOC	Istanbul (THY-Turkish Airlines)
11186.0	CANFORCE	Halifax Military working SAR aircraft
	USN	Air/Ground/Ship
11187.0	GAF	DHM91 Munster (German Air Force Air/Ground)
11190.0	EU-LDOC	Frankfurt (Lufthansa)
11191.0	US-DOD	Counterdrug Network "Xray Foxtrot" - Foxtrot Tango wkg Roadside
	US-JTF-4	Joint Task Force on Drug Enforcement - "Alpha Bravo"
	USN	Navy Air ASW Atlantic
11193.0	CAR-LDOC	Boyeros (Aeroflot)
	NCA-LDOC	Moscow (Aeroflot)
11195.0	RAAF	Air Force Darwin
	SAM-RDARA	Brazil - Altamira FIS, Cruzeiro do Sul, Juiz de Fora, Porto das Caixas & Porto Velho Aeradios
	US-DOD	Drug Enforcement - Combined Forces
	USCG-AIR	USCG-Air
	USN	Air/Ground/Ship
11198.0	CAR-LDOC	Boyeros (Aeroflot)
	NCA-LDOC	Moscow (Aeroflot)
	US-DOD	Drug Enforcement - Combined Forces
	USN	Air/Ground/Ship
11199.0	USN	Air/Ground/Ship
11200.0	RAF	RAF VOLMET - MVU West Drayton

Master Frequency List

FREQ.	SERVICE	STATION/LOCATION
11201.0	USCG-AIR	Air/Ground (Kodiak)
	USN	Air/Ground/Ship
11204.0	RAF	STCICS - "Alpha" - Architect (Wx H+00,H+30), "Belize Flight Watch", Stanley Field, Belize
11205.0	USN	Air/Ground/Ship
	USN	Tactical
11209.0	CANFORCE	ATG - Trenton Military, MACS - Edmonton Military, St. John's Military, Lahr Military
	RAAF	Royal Australian Air Force Air/Ground
	USAF-SAM	Mystic Star SAM Series Unassigned
	USN	Air/Ground/Ship
11210.0	USAF-SAM	Mystic Star SAM Series Unassigned
11210.5	U.S. Flight Test	Grumman Aerospace
11212.0	RAF	RAF Martello - flight clg MKL (Pitreavie Air)
11214.0	CANFORCE	ATG/MACS - Air/Ground - Edmonton Military, Trenton Military
	ITALY-AF	Italian Air Force Air/Ground
	NORAD	NORAD "Channel Charlie 6"
	RAF	Gibraltar Flight Watch
	USAF-ACC	Air Combat Command, AWACS Aircraft Primary to Raymond 24
	USAF-AMC	Air Mobility Command
	USN	USN "Foxtrot Tango" Net
11215.0	SAM-LDOC	Lima
11216.0	CIS-AF	former Soviet Air Force
11217.0	CANFORCE	MACS - Edmonton Military
	GAF	DHM91 Munster (German Air Force Air/Ground)
	RAF	UKADGE
11220.0	USAF-SAM	Mystic Star SAM Series F
	USAF-USSTRATCOM	Former SAC "Giant Talk" Network "Sierra 310"
11221.0	USN	Air/Ground/Ship
11222.0	EU-LDOC	Stockholm Radio (airphone patches to North America)
11223.0	FAF	Orleans (French Air Force Air/Ground)
11224.0	RNZAF	Auckland Air
11225.0	EU-LDOC	Stockholm Radio (airphone patches to North America)
11226.0	NORAD	NORAD - Tactical
	USAF-AMC	Air Mobility Command
	USAF-GHFS	Ascension AB, Andrews AFB Discrete Frequency
	USAF-SAM	Mystic Star SAM Series E (Air Force 1) "Foxtrot 141"
	USAF-USSTRATCOM	Former SAC "Giant Talk" Network "Xray 905"
11228.0	EU-LDOC	Belgrade (Serbia Aerotransport)
	NA-LDOC	Miami (Eldorado - Bolivia/Colombia)
	USAF-SAM	Mystic Star SAM Series Unassigned
11229.0	USAF-SAM	Mystic Star SAM Series D (Air Force 1)
11233.0	CANFORCE	Air/Ground - Edmonton Military, Lahr Military, Trenton Military
	CANFORCE	MAG - Halifax Military, Sinai Base
11234.0	RAF	STCICS - Upavon, "Haven", Ascension (Wx H+45), "Cyprus Flight Watch" Akrotiri, "Gibraltar Flight Watch", Gibraltar, "Viper", Mt. Pleasant, Falkland Islands, "Hotel Whiskey"
11234.5	SEA-RDARA	Diego Garcia Aeradio
11235.0	RAAF	Air Force Perth
11236.0	CANFORCE	MAG - Halifax Military
	RAAF	Air Force Darwin, Pearce, Sydney
	RNZAF	Wigram & Whenuapai AFB's
	unid-LDOC	Flight from Miami to Guayaquil
11237.0	SAF-AF	Langenbaanweg, Waterkloof & Ysterplaat Military
11237.5	EU-LDOC	Berlin/Schoenfield (Interflug)
11240.0	MID-LDOC	Damascus (Syrian Arab Airlines)
	NORAD	NORAD
	USAF-ACC	Air Combat Command, Backup - West
11240.5	CANFORCE	ATG - Trenton Military
11243.0	RAF	Falmouth VOLMET
	SAM-LDOC	Rio de Janeiro (FURNAS)
	US-JCS	United States Joint Chiefs of Staff Net
	USAF-USSTRATCOM	Former SAC "Giant Talk" Network "Sierra 393"
11245.0	DNMK-AF	Danish Air Force

FREQ.	SERVICE	STATION/LOCATION
11246.0	RNZAF	Whenuapai, Wigram & Ohakea AFB's
11247.0	BRZ-AF	Brazilian Air Force Air/Ground
11249.0	CANFORCE	MAG - Halifax Military (Wx H+20), Vancouver Military
	USAF-SAM	Mystic Star SAM Series Unassigned
11252.0	NASA	Cape Radio
11255.0	SP-RDARA	McMurdo Centre Sector Routes (Antarctic Region)
	US-JCS	United States Joint Chiefs of Staff Net
	USN	Fleet HICOM - East/North Atlantic, West Pacific - Tactical
11256.0	AFI-LDOC	Addis Ababa (Ethiopian Airlines - Holloway)
	AFI-RDARA	Ethiopia - Bahar Dar, Dire Dawa, Jimma, Yohannes IV Int'l (Asmara)
	USN	Air/Ground/Ship
11260.0	US-JCS	United States Joint Chiefs of Staff Net
11263.0	USN	Air/Ground/Ship
11265.0	CANFORCE	ATG - Trenton Military, MACS - Edmonton Military, St. John's Military
	USN	Fleet HICOM - Atlantic/Caribbean - Tactical
11266.0	GAF	DHM91 Munster (German Air Force Air/Ground)
	USN	Air/Ground/Ship
11267.0	RAAF	Royal Australian Air Force
	US-JCS	United States Joint Chiefs of Staff Net
	USN	HICOM - LANT/CARIB
11268.0	BEL-AF	Rouveroy Radio (Belgian Air Force Air/Ground)
11270.0	RAF	UKADGE "November Kilo"
	USMC	Night Hawk, Night Hawk Base (President's Helo's)
	USN	Air/Ground/Ship
11271.0	CANFORCE	Edmonton Military (pp for USAF MAC)
11272.0	CANFORCE	ATG - Trenton Military
	GAF	DHM91 Munster (German Air Force Air/Ground)
	UK-RCC	Edinburgh Rescue, Plymouth Rescue
11273.0	BRZ-AF	Brazilian Air Force
	EU-LDOC	Burgas, Sofia (LAZ - Balkan Bulgarian Airlines)
11275.0	BEL-AF	Belgian Air Force
11279.0	AFI-VOL	Algiers, Kano
	NAT-D MWARA	Bodo, Cambridge Bay, Churchill, Iqaluit (Frobisher Bay), Gander, Iceland (Reykjavik), Sondrestrom
	NCA-VOL	Russian Network B, Tbilisi, Georgia (H+00,30), Aktyubinsk, Kazakhstan (H+05,35), Krasnodar, Azerbaijan (H+10,40), Alma Ata, Kazakhstan (H+15,45), Tashkent, Uzbekistan (H+20,50), Baku, Azerbaijan (H+25,55)
11282.0	CEP-1/2 MWARA	Honolulu, San Francisco
	SAM-RDARA	Argentina - Buenos Aires ACC Ezeiza Control
11284.0	NORAD	NORAD
11285.0	SEA-LDOC	Kuala Lumpur, Colombo
11287.0	GAF	DHM91 Munster (German Air Force Air/Ground)
11288.0	AFI-LDOC	Cairo (Egypt Air)
	MID-LDOC	Jeddah (Saudi Airlines)
	NA-LDOC	Rockwell (Saudi Airlines)
	U.S. Flight Test	Boeing Company McDonnel Douglas Rockwell International
	US-DOD	Counterdrug Network "Yankee Delta"
	US-FAA	U. S. Federal Aviation Administration
11291.0	SAT-2 MWARA	Canarias, Cayenne, Dakar, Manaus, Paramaribo, Recife, Rio de Janeiro, Sal Island, Salvador
11297.0	NCA-VOL	Russian Network A, Riga, Latvia (H+00,30), St. Petersburg, Russia (H+05,35), Moscow, Russia H+10,15,40,45), Kiev, Ukraine (H+20,50), Rostov, Ukraine (H+25,55)
11300.0	AFI-3 MWARA	Addis Ababa, Aden, Asmara, Bahrain, Benghazi, Bujumbura, Cairo, Dar es Salaam, Entebbe, Hargesia, Djibouti, Jeddah, Khartoum, Kigali, Kisimayu, Male, Mogadishu, Nairobi, N'djamena, Sana'a, Seychelles, Triopli
	MID-2 MWARA	Abadan, Alma Ata, Bombay, Delhi, Dushanbe, Frunze, Kabul, Karachi, Kathmandu, Kuwait, Lahore, Male, Muscat, Odessa, Samarkand, Seychelles, Tashkent, Tehran, Tbilisi, Urumqi, Yerevan
	MID-RDARA	India - several aeradios Yemen - Riyan Radio

Master Frequency List

FREQ.	SERVICE	STATION/LOCATION
11305.0	NA-LDOC	Toronto (Elite-Canada 3000)
	SAM-LDOC	Maiquetia (VIASA)
		Rio de Janeiro (VARIG)
11306.0	AFI-RDARA	Tanzania - Dar es Salaam ACC
	EU-CC-LDOC	Somerset (Portishead Radio) - UK Flight Support (formerly Eastern Airlines channel)
	SAM-LDOC	Lima, Panama (American Airlines)
	U.S. Flight Test	Boeing Company
		Lockheed Corporation
		McDonnel Douglas
		Rockwell International (Cedar Rapids, Richardson)
11309.0	NAT-E MWARA	New York, Santa Maria
	SEA-RDARA	Indonesia - Jakarta, Biak, Banjarmasin & Ujung Pandang ACC's
11312.0	CAR-LDOC	Boyeros (Aeroflot/Cubana Airlines)
	NCA-LDOC	Moscow (Aeroflot)
11318.0	EU-LDOC	Madrid (Iberia)
	MID-LDOC	Tel Aviv (El Al)
	NCA-VOL	Russian Network C, Syktyvkar, Russia (H+00,30), Sverdlovsk, Russia (H+05,35), Novosibirsk, Russia (H+10,40), Kuybyshev, Russia (H+15,45), Tyuman, Russia (H+20,50)
11319.0	SP-RDARA	Nauru Is. & Tarawa, Kiribati Aeradios
11324.0	EU-LDOC	Madrid (Iberia)
	MID-LDOC	Bombay (Air India)
		Tel Aviv (El Al)
11325.0	SAM-LDOC	Rio de Janeiro (VARIG)
11327.0	SAM-LDOC	Rio de Janeiro (VARIG)
11330.0	CAR-B MWARA	Barranquilla, Boyeros, Cayenne, Georgetown, Maiquetia, New York, Panama, Paramaribo, Piarco, San Andres Is
11333.0	NCA-RDARA	CIS - Khabarovsk & Yerevan ACC's
11336.0	NAT-F MWARA	Gander & Shanwick Aeradios
11339.0	SAM-LDOC	Sao Paulo
	SP-RDARA	SP-9 RDARA - Kiribati, Apia (Faleolo Int'l), Butaritari, Christmas Is. (Cassidy Int'l), Fua'Amotu (Tonga), Funafuti, Honiara, Nandi, Port Vila (Bauerfield), Rarotonga (Cook Is) & Santo (Pekoa) ACC's
11342.0	AFI-LDOC	Lusaka (Zambia Airways)
	CEP-CC-LDOC	Honolulu, San Francisco (ARINC)
	CWP-LDOC	Tokyo (JAL-Japan Airlines)
	NA-CC-LDOC	Honolulu, New York, San Francisco (ARINC)
	SEA-CC-LDOC	Sydney SkyComms
11343.0	SAM-RDARA	Ecuador - Quito Aeradio
11345.0	EU-LDOC	Budapest (MALEV - Hungarian Airlines)
		Hanover (Hapag Lloyd Fluggesellschaft)
		Paris Radio (Air France)
		Stockholm Radio (SAS)
		Warsaw (LOT - Polskie Linie)
	SAM-LDOC	Cali Radio
		Caracas/Maiquetia (AVENSA)
		Lima, Panama (American Airlines)
		Maiquetia (VIASA)
		Piarco (West Indian)
	SEA-LDOC	Karachi (PIA-Pakistani International Airlines)
11346.0	SAM-LDOC	several Brazilian stations (VARIG)
11348.0	AFI-LDOC	Roberts/Monrovia
	CAR-LDOC	Boyeros (Aeroflot)
	MID-LDOC	Tehran
	NCA-LDOC	Moscow (Aeroflot)
11351.0	CWP-LDOC	Manila (Philippines Air)
	EA-LDOC	Beijing
	EU-LDOC	Belgrade (Serbia Aerotransport)
		Budapest (MALEV - Hungarian Airlines)
		Paris Radio (Air France)
		Warsaw (LOT - Polskie Linie)
	MID-LDOC	Karachi (PIA-Pakistani International Airlines)
	SEA-LDOC	Yangon (Myanma Airways)

FREQ.	SERVICE	STATION/LOCATION
11354.0	AFI-LDOC	Algiers (Air Algerie)
		Luanda (TAAG)
		Springbok Jo'burg (South African Airlines)
	EU-LDOC	Warsaw (LOT - Polskie Linie)
	MID-LDOC	Abu Dubai
		Manama (Falcon)
	NCA-LDOC	unid Russian Radio (Aeroflot)
11357.0	ITALY-AF	Italian Air Force - LDOC
	NA-RDARA	Alaska - Central and Southeast
11359.0	CAR-LDOC	Boyeros (Aeroflot)
	NCA-LDOC	Moscow (Aeroflot)
11360.0	SAM-NW MWARA	Barranquilla, Bogota, Caracas (Maiquetia), Lima, Quito
	SAM-SW MWARA	Antofagasta, Asuncion, Buenos Aires, Cordoba, Easter Is (Pascua), La Paz, Lima, Mendoza, Puerto Montt, Punta Arenas, Resistencia, Salta, Santa Cruz, Santiago, Talara
11363.0	EU-CC-LDOC	Somerset (Portishead Radio)
	EU-LDOC	Bucharest (TAROM - Romanian Air Transport)
		Luton (Britannia Airlines)
		Luton (Monarch Airlines)
	NA-RDARA	Alaska, Aleutians
11366.0	SAM-LDOC	Rio de Janeiro (VARIG) (several aeradios - Brazil)
	SEA-RDARA	Indonesia - Jakarta ACC & several other ACC's
11369.0	SAM-VOL	Ezeiza (Buenos Aires) Volmet (H+15)
11375.0	MID-1 MWARA	Aden, Amman, Ankara, Baghdad, Basrah, Beirut, Cairo, Damascus, Jeddah, Kuwait, Manama, Odessa, Sana'a, Simferopol, Tehran, Tbilisi, Yerevan
	MID-3 MWARA	Aktyubinsk, Alma Ata, Dushanbe, Frunze, Kuybyshev, Kzyl-Orda, Moscow, Samarkand, Tashkent, Uralsk, Yevevan
	SAM-LDOC	Rio de Janeiro, Sao Paulo (VARIG, VASP)
	U.S. Flight Test	Boeing Company
11377.0	USN	Air/Ground/Ship
11378.0	SAM-LDOC	Quito, Lima (AeroPeru)
11384.0	CWP-1/2 MWARA	Guam, Honolulu, Manila, Naha, Port Moresby, Seoul, Taipei, Tokyo
	EU-LDOC	Burgas, Sofia (LAZ - Balkan Bulgarian Airlines)
11387.0	SEA-VOL	Sydney (H+00,+30), Calcutta (H+05,35), Bangkok (H+10,+40), Karachi (H+15,+45), Singapore (H+20,+50), Bombay (H+25,55)
11390.0	AFI-LDOC	Brazzaville (Lignes Congolaises)
	CAR-LDOC	Boyeros (Aeroflot)
	NA-LDOC	Toronto Ops (Elite/Canada 3000)
	NCA-LDOC	Moscow (Aeroflot)
11393.0	SP-RDARA	Honiara FIC (Solomon Is.), Port Moresby & Nadzab Aeradios (PNG)
11396.0	CAR-A MWARA	Boyeros, Guatemala City, Merida, New York, Panama, Piarco, San Andres Is, San Jose, Tegucigalpa
	EA-2 MWARA	Canton, Irkutsk, Pyongyang, Ulaanbaatar
	SEA-1 MWARA	Bali, Bangkok, Colombo, Calcutta, Dhaka, Jakarta, Kathmandu, Kuala Lumpur, Madras, Male, Singapore, Yangon
	SEA-2 MWARA	Bali, Bangkok, Denpasar, Guangzhou, Hanoi, Ho Chi Minh, Hong Kong, Jakarta, Kuala Lumpur, Kota Kinabalu, Manila, Singapore, Vientiane
	SEA-3 MWARA	Bali, Cocos Is, Darwin, Jakarta, Male, Perth, Singapore, Ujung Pandang
	SEA-RDARA	Indonesia - several aeradios
	SP- RDARA	Christmas Island (proprietary)
11397.0	SAM-LDOC	Asuncion (LAP - Lineas Aereas Paraguayas)
11398.0	US-NOAA	Hurricane Hunters - KJY74 Miami Air/Ground
11401.0	US-FAA	U. S. Federal Aviation Administration
11407.0	NASA	Cape Radio
	USAF-SAM	Mystic Star SAM Series R
11408.0	USAF-USSTRATCOM	Former SAC "Giant Talk" Network (EAM H+56) "Papa 382"
11413.0	USAF-GHFS	Andrews AFB Discrete Frequency
	USAF-SAM	Mystic Star SAM Series B
11414.0	NASA	Cape Radio
11430.0	USN	Air/Ground/Ship
11440.0	USAF-ARRS	Air Rescue Service, Elgin AFB
11441.0	NORAD	NORAD - Secondary Day (Tie-in to US CAP)
	USAF-SAM	Mystic Star SAM Series C

FREQ.	SERVICE	STATION/LOCATION
11448.0	USAF-SAM	Mystic Star SAM Series N
11466.0	USAF-SAM	Mystic Star SAM Series A (Air Force 1 & 2)
		Mystic Star SAM Series G
11484.0	USAF-SAM	Mystic Star SAM Series G
11488.0	USAF-SAM	Mystic Star SAM Series Unassigned
11494.0	US-Customs	COTHERN "Victor Foxtrot" - Selscan 4
	US-DOD	Counterdrug Network "Victor Foxtrot"
	USAF-SAM	Mystic Star SAM Series F (Air Force 1)
	USAF-USSTRATCOM	Former SAC "Giant Talk" Network "Sierra 311"
11498.0	USAF-SAM	Mystic Star SAM Series M
11510.0	USAF-ACC	Air Combat Command, Primary - West
11545.0	USAF-SAM	Mystic Star SAM Series M
11548.0	NASA	Cape Radio
11607.0	NORAD	NORAD
11610.0	USAF-ACC	Air Combat Command, AWACS Aircraft
11615.0	NASA	Ascension Radio, Cape Radio - Shuttle Missions
	USAF-SAM	Mystic Star SAM Series C
11621.0	NASA	Cape Radio
11623.0	USAF-ACC	Air Combat Command, Primary - West
11627.0	USAF-SAM	Mystic Star SAM Series N
11634.0	NASA	Cape Radio
	USAF-SAM	Mystic Star SAM Series R
11637.0	US-FAA	U. S. Federal Aviation Administration (Selscan Ch# 12)
11667.0	USAF-SAM	Mystic Star SAM Series P
		Mystic Star SAM Series S
11697.0	USAF-CEN	Commando Escort Net - Hawaii "Foxtrot"
11740.0	USAF-ACC	Air Combat Command
11975.0	US-CAP	CAP-USAF Frequency
11984.0	NASA	Cape Radio
11988.0	NASA	Cape Radio
	USAF-SAM	Mystic Star SAM Series R
11995.0	USAF-SAM	Mystic Star SAM Series A
		Mystic Star SAM Series B
		Mystic Star SAM Series G
		Mystic Star SAM Series H
12029.0	USAF-SAM	Mystic Star SAM Series B
12058.0	USAF-SAM	Mystic Star SAM Series C
12060.0	USAF-SAM	Mystic Star SAM Series G
12070.0	USAF-USSTRATCOM	Former SAC "Giant Talk" Network "Whiskey 108"
12090.0	USAF-SAM	Mystic Star SAM Series H
12105.0	USAF-SAM	Mystic Star SAM Series C
12106.0	USAF-SAM	Mystic Star SAM Series A
		Mystic Star SAM Series G
		Mystic Star SAM Series H
12107.0	NASA	Ascension, Cape Radio
	USAF-SAM	Mystic Star SAM Series R
12112.0	SAUDI-AF	Saudi Air Force, Riyadh (Hotel 2), Taif (Hotel 4), Tabuk (Hotel 8)
12133.0	EU-CC-LDOC	Somerset (Portishead Radio)
12138.5	US-DOD	Counterdrug Network "Whiskey Delta" (may also use 12138.0)
12155.0	USAF-SAM	Mystic Star SAM Series C
12160.0	NASA	Cape Radio
12168.0	EU-CC-LDOC	Somerset (Portishead Radio)
12170.0	USAF-SAM	Mystic Star SAM Series M
12203.0	USAF-ACC	Air Combat Command, Primary - West
12215.0	US-DOD	Counterdrug Network
12222.0	US-DOD	Counterdrug Network "Zulu Delta"
12234.0	USN	Air/Ground/Ship
12237.0	USN	Air/Ground/Ship
12240.0	USAF-SAM	Mystic Star SAM Series H
		Mystic Star SAM Series N
12242.0	USAF-SAM	Mystic Star SAM Series P
12250.0	USAF-SAM	Mystic Star SAM Series G
12254.0	USAF-SAM	Mystic Star SAM Series M

FREQ.	SERVICE	STATION/LOCATION
12258.0	USAF-SAM	Mystic Star SAM Series B
		Mystic Star SAM Series H
12270.0	USAF-SAM	Mystic Star SAM Series C
12277.0	NASA	Cape Radio
	USAF-SAM	Mystic Star SAM Series R
12287.0	NASA	Cape Radio
12290.0	USAF-AMC-OP	Operation Restore Hope (Absolution, Accuse)
12317.0	USAF-SAM	Mystic Star SAM Series A
12324.0	USAF-SAM	Mystic Star SAM Series N
12348.6	NA-CC-LDOC	Tors Cove (Rainbow Radio phone patches)
12876.0	NASA	Cape Radio
13008.0	SEA-RDARA	Papua New Guinea - Madang Aeradio
13119.4	NA-CC-LDOC	Tors Cove (Rainbow Radio phone patches)
13181.0	USN	HICOM - Eastern/Mid Pacific (COM3RDFLT)
13200.0	GAF	DHM91 Wunsdorf Air (German Air Force Air/Ground)
13201.0	USAF-GHFS	Anderson, Croughton, Elmendorf, Hickham, McClellan, Thule, Yokota
13204.0	USAF-ACC	Air Combat Command, Primary - Battlefield Air Interdiction Training Net (JTIDS Aircraft)
	USAF-AMC	Air Mobility Command
	USAF-SAM	Mystic Star SAM Series D
13205.0	AFI-LDOC	Mahe (Air Seychelles)
	CAR-LDOC	Boyeros (Aeroflot)
		Bridgetown Operations (Caribbean Airways)
	EU-LDOC	Berne ("Berna") Radio (Swiss Air)
	NCA-LDOC	Moscow (Aeroflot)
	RAAF	Air Force Darwin, Sydney, Townsville, Butterworth (Malaysia)
	RNZAF	Auckland Air, Christchurch Air, Ohakea Air
	UK-RCC	Edinburgh Rescue, Plymouth Rescue
	USAF-SAM	Mystic Star SAM Series Unassigned
13207.0	CANFORCE	ATG - Trenton Military
	NORAD	NORAD "Channel Charlie 7"
	RAAF	Air Force Darwin, Sydney
	RNZAF	Auckland Air
	USAF-ACC	Air Combat Command, AWACS - Strategic Air Defense Network
	USAF-ARRS	Air Rescue Service
	USN	Ship/Air - USS Alamo
13208.5	unid-LDOC	Pearl 95 working Control, Pearl 81 enroute Minneapolis FL310
13210.0	NASA	Cape Radio
	USAF-SAM	Mystic Star SAM Series Unassigned
13211.0	USAF-SAM	Mystic Star SAM Series F (Air Force 2)
	USAF-USSTRATCOM	Former SAC "Giant Talk" Network "Sierra 312"
13213.0	EU-LDOC	Frankfurt (Lufthansa)
	USAF-USSTRATCOM	Former SAC "Giant Talk" Network "Sierra 321"
	USN	Air/Ground/Ship
13217.0	USAF-SAM	Mystic Star SAM Series E
	USAF-USSTRATCOM	Former SAC "Giant Talk" Network "Xray 906"
13220.0	CAR-LDOC	Boyeros (Aeroflot)
	ITALY-AF	Air/ground Pisa, Rome, Sarajevo Base
	NCA-LDOC	Moscow (Aeroflot)
	NCA-RDARA	CIS - Khabarovsk ACC
13221.0	BRZ-AF	Brazilian Air Force
13222.0	AFI-LDOC	Tunis (Tunis Air)
	USN	Air/Ground/Ship
13223.0	EU-LDOC	Berlin/Schoenfield (Interflug)
13223.5	USN	Air/Ground/Ship
13224.0	USN	Air/Ground/Ship
13225.0	BRZ-AF	Brazilian Air Force
	EU-LDOC	Vienna
	MID-LDOC	Amman, (ALIA/Royal Jordanian Airlines)
	U.S. Flight Test	Grumman Aerospace
13225.5	U.S. Flight Test	Grumman Aerospace
13227.0	NASA	Cape Radio
13227.5	USN	Air/Ground/Ship

Master Frequency List

FREQ.	SERVICE	STATION/LOCATION
13231.0	CANFORCE	Lahr Military, Germany (Wx H+16), Sinai Base
	USN	Air/Ground/Ship
13235.0	EU-LDOC	Berlin/Schoenfield (Interflug)
		Vienna
13237.0	NASA	Cape Radio
	RAF	Pitreavie Air
13239.0	FAF	French Air Force Primary Air/Ground
13240.0	SAM-LDOC	Buenos Aires (Aerolineas Argentinas)
13241.0	EU-LDOC	Belgrade (Serbia Aerotransport)
	MID-LDOC	Amman, (ALIA/Royal Jordanian Airlines)
	USAF-USSTRATCOM	Former SAC "Giant Talk" Network "Sierra 394"
13244.0	NASA	Cape Radio
13245.0	GAF	DHM91 Munster (German Air Force Air/Ground)
	RAF	STCICS "Delta Hotel"
13247.0	CAR-LDOC	Boyeros (Aeroflot)
	NCA-LDOC	Moscow (Aeroflot)
	USAF-SAM	Mystic Star SAM Series J (Air Force 1)
		Mystic Star SAM Series K
		Mystic Star SAM Series Unassigned- "Foxtrot 442"
	USAF-USSTRATCOM	Former SAC "Giant Talk" Network "Whiskey 109"
13248.0	EU-LDOC	Belgrade (Serbia Aerotransport)
	EU-LDOC	Frankfurt (Lufthansa)
	G-NAVY	Air/Ship - German Navy
	GAF	DHM91 Munster "Oscar" (German Air Force Air/Ground)
13250.0	BRZ-AF	Brazilian Air Force
	RAF	Cyprus Flight Watch
	USMC	Night Hawk (President's Helo's)
13251.0	RNZAF	Wigram AFB
	SP-RDARA	Christchurch, McMurdo Centre Sector Routes (Antarctic Region)
	USN	USN 5 Antarctic Secondary Air/Ground - McMurdo Base, Navy Air ASW Pacific
13254.0	CANFORCE	MACS/MAG - Halifax Military (EAM H+04), St John's Military (EAM H+00), Vancouver Military a/g
	USN	Air/Ground/Ship
13257.0	CANFORCE	MACS/ATG - Air/Ground - Edmonton Military, St John's Military (Wx H+45), Trenton Military, Sinai Base
	RAF	STCICS "Foxtrot", Uphavon
	USN	Air/Ground/Ship
13260.0	CAR-LDOC	Bridgetown Operations (Caribbean Airways)
13261.0	AFI-VOL	Brazzaville (H+10,+25,+30,+55)
	CEP-1/2 MWARA	Honolulu, San Francisco
	SP-7	Pascua (Easter Island) ,Tahiti, Nandi, Honolulu
	SP-RDARA	New Zealand
	USN	Air/Ground/Ship
13264.0	AFI-RDARA	Zaire - Kinsangani (Bangoka) Radio FIS
	EU-VOL	Shannon Aeradio (H+00,+25,+30,+55)
13266.0	EU-LDOC	Berne ("Berna") Radio
13267.0	NCA-VOL	Russian Network D, Kirensk, Russia (H+00,30), Yakutsk, Russia (H+10,40), Khabarovsk, Russia (H+15,45), Magadan, Russia (H+20,50), Irkutsk, Russia (H+25,55)
	US-NOAA	Hurricane Hunters - KJY74 Miami Air/Ground "Golf"
13270.0	NAT-VOL	Gander (H+20,+50) New York (continuous)
13273.0	AFI-2 MWARA	Algiers, Brazzaville, Kano, Gao, Niamey, N'djamena, Tamanrasset, Timimoun, Tripoli, Tunis
	SP-6/7 MWARA	Auckland, Honolulu, Nandi, Pascua (Easter Is.), Rarotonga, Sydney, Tahiti
13279.0	NCA-VOL	CIS English Language Network, Khabarovsk, Russia (H+05,35), Tashkent, Uzbekistan (H+10,40), Kiev, Ukraine (H+15,45), Moscow, Russia (H+25,55), Novosibirsk, Russia (H+20,50)
	SAM-VOL	Buenos Aires VOLMET (H+55)
13282.0	SP-RDARA	Honolulu (H+00,+30), Tokyo (H+10,+40), Hong Kong (H+15,+45), Auckland (H+20,50)
13283.0	USAF-SAM	Mystic Star SAM Series K
13285.0	CEP-5	Honolulu, San Francisco
	EA-VOL	Beijing (H+05,45), Guangzhou (H+10,50)

FREQ.	SERVICE	STATION/LOCATION
13285.0	NA-CC-LDOC	Tors Cove (Rainbow Radio)
	NA-LDOC	Calgary, Montreal, Toronto (Canadian Airlines) Ottawa (Bradley First Air)
	USAF-SAM	Mystic Star SAM Series I
13288.0	AFI-3 MWARA	Addis Ababa, Aden, Asmara, Bahrain, Benghazi, Bujumbura, Cairo, Dar es Salaam, Entebbe, Hargesia, Djibouti, Jeddah, Khartoum, Kigali, Kisimayu, Male, Mogadishu, Nairobi, N'djamena, Sana'a, Seychelles, Triopli
	CEP-2	Honolulu
	EU-A MWARA	Arkhangelsk, Beirut, Kiev, Lvov, Minsk, Moscow, Murmansk, Odessa, Riga, Simferopol, St. Petersburg, Syktyvkar, Tunis, Valetta, Velikiye, Vitebsk, Vilnius, Vologda
	MID-2 MWARA	Abadan, Alma Ata, Bombay, Delhi, Dushanbe, Frunze, Kabul, Karachi, Kathmandu, Kuwait, Lahore, Male, Muscat, Odessa, Samarkand, Seychelles, Tashkent, Tehran, Tbilisi, Urumqi, Yerevan
	MID-RDARA	India - several aeradios Yemen - Riyan Radio
13291.0	NAT-B MWARA	Gander, Iceland (Reykjavik), New York, Santa Maria, Shannon (Shanwick)
	NAT-D MWARA	Bodo, Cambridge Bay, Churchill, Iqaluit (Frobisher Bay), Gander, Iceland (Reykjavik), Sondrestrom
	NAT-F MWARA	Gander & Shanwick Aeradios
	NORAD	NORAD
13294.0	AFI-4 MWARA	Accra, Bangui, Brazzaville, Bujumbura, Bulawayo, Contonou, Douala, Entebbe, Franceville, Francistown, Garoua, Goma, Johannesburg, Kano, Kinshasa, Kisangani, Kitona Base, Lagos, Libreville, Lomé, Luanda, Lumbumbashi, Lusaka, Maroua, Maseru, Nairobi, N'djamena, N'djili, Niamey, Niamtougou, Port Gentil, Salisbury, Salazar (Sao Tomé) ,Seychelles, Windhoek, Yaounde
	NP-3/4 MWARA	Honolulu, San Francisco, Tokyo
	RAF	UKADGE - Neatishead, Portreath, Architect
	SP-RDARA	Fernando Po Radio
13294.5	SAM-RDARA	Uruguay - Durazno Aeradio (PLUNA)
13295.0	RNZAF	Ohakea AFB
13297.0	CAR-A MWARA	Boyeros, Guatemala City, Merida, New York, Panama, Piarco, San Andres Is, San Jose, Tegucigalpa
	EA-RDARA	China - Hailar ACC
	SAM-C MWARA	Belem, Bogota, Brasilia, Leticia, Manaus, Maiquetia, Porto Velho, Rio de Janeiro
	SAM-NE MWARA	Belem, Cayenne, Georgetown, Maiquetia, Paramaribo, Piarco, Recife
	SAM-SE MWARA	Asuncion, Belem, Brasilia, Buenos Aires, Campo Grande, Curtiba, La Paz, Montevideo, Porto Alegre, Porto Velho, Recife, Salvador Dois De Julho, Santa Cruz
13300.0	AFI-LDOC	Lusaka (Zambia Airways)
	CWP-1/2 MWARA	Guam, Hong Kong, Honolulu, Manila, Naha, Port Moresby, Seoul, Taipei, Tokyo
	EU-LDOC	Stockholm Radio
	MID-LDOC	Beirut (MEA-Cedar Jet)
	NA-CC-LDOC	New York (ARINC)
	SAM-RDARA	Chile - Santiago ACC
	SP-6/7	Auckland, Honolulu, Nandi, Sydney, Tahiti, Tokyo
	SP-RDARA	Christmas Island FIS
13303.0	NCA-3 MWARA	Chita, Chulman, Ekimchan, Irkutsk, Kirensk, Khabarovsk, Pyongyang, Ulaanbaatar, Ulan Ude
13304.0	AFI-RDAR	West Africa, several ACC's
	MID-LDOC	Tel Aviv (El Al)
13306.0	INO-1 MWARA	Antananarivo, Beira, Blantyre, Bombay, Cocos Is., Colombo, Dar es Salaam, Harare, Jeddah, Johannesburg, Kigali, Lilongwe, Lusaka, Madras, Mahajanga, Male, Mauritius, Moroni, Nairobi, Perth, Seychelles, St. Denis, Toamasina
	NAT-A MWARA	Canarias, Gander, New York, Paramaribo, Piarco, Santa Maria, Shanwick
	NAT-C MWARA	Gander, Iceland (Reykjavik), Shannon (Shanwick)
13309.0	EA-2 MWARA	Canton, Irkutsk, Pyongyang, Ulaanbaatar
	SAM-LDOC	Rio de Janeiro (VARIG)
	SEA-2 MWARA	Bali, Bangkok, Denpasar, Guangzhou, Hanoi, Ho Chi Minh, Hong Kong, Jakarta, Kuala Lumpur, Kota Kinabalu, Manila, Singapore, Vientiane
13312.0	MID-LDOC	Jeddah (Saudi Airlines)
	MID-VOL	Damascus Volmet (H+00)
	NA-LDOC	Rockwell (Saudi Airlines)

Master Frequency List

FREQ.	SERVICE	STATION/LOCATION
13312.0	U.S. Flight Test	Aerospatiale Helicopter
		Boeing Company (Seattle)
		Lockheed Corporation
		McDonnel Douglas
		Rockwell Flight Test (Cedar Rapids)
	US-Customs	"Yankee Echo"
	US-DOD	Counterdrug Network "Yankee Echo"
	US-FAA	U. S. Federal Aviation Administration (Selscan Ch# 13)
13315.0	AFI-RDARA	Johannesburg ACC
	CANFORCE	MAG - Halifax Military
	NCA-1 MWARA	Ivdel, Khanty Mansiysk, Moscow, Syktyvkar, Sverdlovsk, Vologda
	SAT-2 MWARA	Canarias, Cayenne, Dakar, Manaus, Paramaribo, Recife, Rio de Janeiro, Sal Island, Salvador
13318.0	MID-RDARA	India - several aeradios
	SEA-1 MWARA	Bali, Bangkok, Colombo, Calcutta, Dhaka, Jakarta, Kathmandu, Kuala Lumpur, Madras, Male, Singapore, Yangon
	SEA-3 MWARA	Bali, Cocos Is, Darwin, Jakarta, Male, Perth, Singapore, Ujung Pandang
	SP- RDARA	Christmas Island (proprietary)
13320.0	NCA-RDARA	CIS - Moscow/RFNV Radio
13324.0	CWP-LDOC	Tokyo (JAL-Japan Airlines)
	EU-LDOC	Berne ("Berna") Radio
		Dusseldorf (LTU, Lufthansa)
		Frankfurt (Hapag Lloyd Fluggesellschaft)
		Frankfurt (Lufthansa)
	MID-LDOC	Baghdad (Iraqi Airways)
		Cairo, Baghdad (Iraqi Airways)
		Manama (Falcon)
	NA-CC-LDOC	JFK Ramp Check (ARINC)
	SEA-LDOC	Colombo (Air Lanka)
13327.0	AFI-LDOC	Springbok Jo'burg (South African Airlines)
	EU-LDOC	Amsterdam/Schiphol (KLM-Royal Dutch Airlines)
		Athens (Olympic Airlines)
		Frankfurt (Condor)
		Frankfurt (Lufthansa)
		Hanover (Hapag Lloyd Fluggesellschaft)
		Las Palmas (Lineas Aereas Canarias)
		Luqa (Air Malta)
		Madrid (Iberia), (Hapag Lloyd Fluggesellschaft)
		Scheveningen Radio
	SAM-LDOC	Buenos Aires (Aerolineas Argentinas)
		Rio de Janeiro (VARIG)
13330.0	AFI-LDOC	Abidjan
		Harare (Air Zimbabwe)
		Kano (Kano Air)
		Salisbury
		Springbok Jo'Burg (South African Airways)
	CAR-LDOC	Boyeros (Cubana Airlines)
	EU-LDOC	Speedbird London (British Airways)
		Stockholm Radio
	INO-LDOC	Antananarivo (Air Madagascar)
	MID-LDOC	Beirut (MEA-Cedar Jet)
		Muscat (Gulf Air)
	NA-CC-LDOC	Houston Radio (Universal Aviation)
		New York, San Francisco, Honolulu (ARINC)
	NCA-LDOC	Kabul (Ariana Afghan Airlines)
	SEA-CC-LDOC	Sydney SkyComms
13333.0	CWP-LDOC	Hong Kong (Cathay Pacific)
		Hong Kong (Dragonair)
		Seoul (KAL-Korean Airlines)
	EU-LDOC	Speedbird London (British Airways)
	MID-LDOC	Bombay (Air India)
		Manama (Falcon)
	SEA-LDOC	Singapore (Singapore Airlines)

FREQ.	SERVICE	STATION/LOCATION
13333.0	SP-LDOC	Auckland (Air New Zealand)
13335.0	MID-RDARA	Lebanon - Basrah/Beirut ACC
	SAM-RDARA	Uruguay - Montevideo Control
13336.0	EU-LDOC	Amsterdam (KLM-Royal Dutch Airlines)
		Belgrade (Serbia Aerotransport)
		Budapest (MALEV - Hungarian Airlines)
		Lisbon (TAP-Air Portugal)
		Rome (Alitalia)
		Warsaw (LOT - Polskie Linie)
	MID-LDOC	Bombay (Air India)
	MID-VOL	Kuwait Volmet
	SAM-LDOC	Montevideo (PLUNA)
		Piarco (West Indian)
13339.0	AFI-LDOC	Addis Ababa, Asmara (Ethiopian Airlines - Holloway)
		Blantyre (Air Malawi)
		Dar es Salaam (Air Tanzania)
		Djibouti (Air Djibouti)
		Entebbe (Uganda Airlines)
		Kigali (Air Rwanda)
		Kinshasa (Air Zaire)
		Lagos (Nigeria Airways)
		Lilongwe (Air Malawi)
		Nairobi
		Tunis (Tunis Air)
	CAR-LDOC	Boyeros, Holguin (Cubana Airlines)
		Grand Cayman (Cayman Air)
		Willemstad (ALM Antillean)
	MID-LDOC	Jeddah (Saudi Airlines)
		Manama (Falcon)
	NA-LDOC	Matamoros
		Merida, Mexico City, Tijuana (AeroMexico)
	NP-3/4 MWARA	Honolulu , Tokyo
13342.0	EU-LDOC	Amsterdam (KLM-Royal Dutch Airlines)
		Las Palmas (Lineas Aereas Canarias)
		Stockholm Radio (SAS)
	MID-LDOC	Jeddah (Saudi Airlines)
		Karachi (PIA-Pakistani International Airlines)
		Kathmandu (Royal Nepal Airlines)
	RAF	Hong Kong Air
	SEA-LDOC	Perth, Sydney (Qantas)
		Yangon (Myanma Airways)
13345.0	CAR-LDOC	Boyeros (Aeroflot)
	EU-LDOC	Bucharest (TAROM - Romanian Air Transport)
		Rome (Alitalia)
		Warsaw (LOT - Polskie Linie)
	NCA-LDOC	Khabarovsk, Moscow (Aeroflot)
	SAM-LDOC	San Salvador
		Santiago
	SEA-LDOC	Sydney (Qantas)
	SP-LDOC	Auckland (Air New Zealand)
		Easter Island
13348.0	AFI-LDOC	Algiers (Air Algerie)
		Lusaka (Zambia Airways)
		Roberts/Monrovia
	CAR-LDOC	Santo Domingo (Iberia)
	CEP-CC-LDOC	Honolulu San Francisco (ARINC)
	EU-LDOC	Madrid (Iberia)
	INO-LDOC	Mauritius Ops (Air Mauritius)
	MID-LDOC	Abu Dhabi
		Dubai
		Tehran

Master Frequency List

FREQ.	SERVICE	STATION/LOCATION
13351.0	CWP-LDOC	Manila (Philippines Air)
	EA-LDOC	Beijing
	EU-LDOC	Brussels (Sabena)
		Dublin (Aer Lingus)
		Larnaca (Cyprus Airways)
		Paris Radio (Air France)
		Prague (Czechoslovak Airlines)
	MID-LDOC	Bombay (Air India)
		Tel Aviv (El Al)
	SEA-LDOC	Bangkok (Thai Airways)
		Jakarta
	SP-LDOC	Nauru Island (Air Nauru)
13352.0	SAM-VOL	Belem, Brasilia, Galeao, Guarulhos, Manaus, Porto Alegre, Recife VOLMETs
13354.0	AFI-LDOC	Lusaka (Zambia Airways)
	CEP-CC-LDOC	Honolulu, San Francisco (ARINC)
	NA-CC-LDOC	New York
	NAT-E MWARA	New York, Santa Maria
	SAM-RDARA	Venezuela - Upata Aeradio
	SP-RDARA	Cook Islands - Rarotonga ACC
	US-NOAA	Hurricane Hunters - KJY74 Miami Air/Ground
13356.0	AFI-LDOC	Cairo (Egypt Air)
		Lagos (Nigeria Airways)
	CAR-LDOC	Kingston Dispatch (Air Jamaica)
	MID-LDOC	Beirut (MEA-Cedar Jet)
		Manama (Falcon)
13356.5	NA-LDOC	Tors Cove (Rainbow Radio phone patches)
13357.0	AFI-1 MWARA	Abidjan, Bamako, Bissau, Bobo Dioulasso, Bouake, Casablanca, Conakry, Freetown, Kano, Niamey, Nouadhibou, Nouakchott, Ouagadougou, Roberts (Monrovia)
	SAM-RDARA	Brazil - Recife FIR
	SAT-1 MWARA	Brasilia, Canarias, Cayenne, Dakar, Manaus, Paramaribo, Recife, Rio de Janeiro, Sal Island, Salvador
13373.0	INO-AFTN	Antananarivo, Mahe & Port Louis AFTN stations
13373.5	NA-CC-LDOC	Tors Cove (Rainbow Radio phone patches)
13380.0	NASA	Cape Radio
	USN	Air/Ground/Ship
13384.0	CWP-2	Honolulu
13412.0	USAF-SAM	Mystic Star SAM Series C
		Mystic Star SAM Series Unassigned, Andrews AFB, USB/LSB
13420.0	NA-CC-LDOC	Tors Cove (Rainbow Radio phone patches)
13426.0	USAF-ACC	Air Combat Command, Secondary (Data) - West
13440.0	USAF-SAM	Mystic Star SAM Series H (Air Force 1)
		Mystic Star SAM Series I
13442.0	EU-LDOC	Amsterdam (KLM - Royal Dutch Airlines)
	unid-LDOC	a/c wkg Control in Spanish
13445.0	USAF-SAM	Mystic Star SAM Series P
13457.0	US-DOD	Counterdrug Network
	US-FAA	U. S. Federal Aviation Administration (SHARES) (Selscan Ch# 14)
	USAF-ACC	Air Combat Command, Backup - East/Air Defense Training
	USAF-SAM	Mystic Star SAM Series M
13468.0	NASA	Cape Radio
13484.0	USAF-SAM	Mystic Star SAM Series M
13485.0	USAF-SAM	Mystic Star SAM Series C
13495.0	NASA	Cape Radio
13520.0	USN	Air/Ground/Ship
13530.0	USN	Air/Ground/Ship
13542.0	USN	Air/Ground/Ship
13545.0	USN	Air/Ground/Ship
13547.0	NORAD	NORAD
13555.0	MID-LDOC	Amman, (ALIA/Royal Jordanian Airlines)
13558.0	USN	Air/Ground/Ship
13565.0	USAF-SAM	Mystic Star SAM Series G
13576.0	EU-LDOC	Stockholm Radio (pp)

FREQ.	SERVICE	STATION/LOCATION
13582.0	USAF-SAM	Mystic Star SAM Series P
13585.0	USAF-SAM	Mystic Star SAM Series M
13593.0	EU-LDOC	Berne ("Berna") Radio
13600.0	NASA	Cape Radio
13604.0	USAF-SAM	Mystic Star SAM Series N
13630.0	US-FAA	U. S. Federal Aviation Administration (Selscan Ch# 16)
13658.5	US-DOD	Counterdrug Network "Whiskey Echo"
13670.0	USAF-ACC	Air Combat Command, Primary - East/AWACS Communications Channel
13676.0	NASA	Cape Radio
13700.0	SAM-AFTN	Brasilia AFTN
13710.0	USAF-SAM	Mystic Star SAM Series N
13735.0	NASA	Cape Radio
13742.0	NASA	Cape Radio
13752.0	USAF-SAM	Mystic Star SAM Series A
13760.0	USAF-SAM	Mystic Star SAM Series P
13765.0	USAF-SAM	Mystic Star SAM Series N
13812.0	SP-AFTN	Caroline Is. AFTN
13825.0	USAF-SAM	Mystic Star SAM Series J
		Mystic Star SAM Series P
13865.0	EU-CC-LDOC	Somerset (Portishead Radio)
13878.0	NASA	Cape Radio - Shuttle Missions
	USAF-SAM	Mystic Star SAM Series R (Air Force 2)
13907.0	US-Customs	COTHERN "Victor Golf" - Selscan 5
	US-DOD	Counterdrug Network "Victor Golf"
13924.0	RAF	Architect
13942.0	NASA	Ascension Radio, Cape Radio - Shuttle Missions
13942.5	EU-LDOC	Stockholm Radio
14280.0	NASA	Johnson Space Center, Jet Propulsion Labs - Shuttle Rebroadcast
14295.0	NASA	Goddard Space Center - Shuttle Rebroadcast
14350.0	US-DEA	OTH Radio System "Lima"
14364.0	NORAD	NORAD
	USAF-SAM	Mystic Star SAM Series G
14400.0	USN	Air/Ground/Ship
14412.0	USAF-SAM	Mystic Star SAM Series C
		Mystic Star SAM Series I
14417.0	USAF-SAM	Mystic Star SAM Series A
14448.0	USAF-SAM	Mystic Star SAM Series J
14497.0	NASA	Cape Radio
	USAF-SAM	Mystic Star SAM Series R
14500.0	SP-AFTN	Rarotonga AFTN
14516.0	SAM-LDOC	several South American stations (Transportes Aereos Marilia)
14545.0	NA-CC-LDOC	Tors Cove (Rainbow Radio phone patches)
14572.0	USAF-SAM	Mystic Star SAM Series N
14576.0	USAF-SAM	Mystic Star SAM Series K
14585.0	NASA	Cape Radio
14615.0	NASA	Cape Radio
14645.0	EU-LDOC	Stockholm Radio (phone patches)
14650.0	NASA	Cape Radio
	US-ANG	ANG - Air National Guard
	USAF-ACC	Air Combat Command, Battlefield Air Interdiction Training Net
14655.0	USAF-AMC-OP	Operation Restore Hope (Absolution, Accuse)
14670.0	USAF-SAM	Mystic Star SAM Series B
14686.0	US-DEA	OTH Radio System "Papa"
14690.0	US-DEA	OTH Radio System "Golf"
14715.0	USAF-SAM	Mystic Star SAM Series C
14766.0	USAF-SAM	Mystic Star SAM Series N
14829.0	USAF-SAM	Mystic Star SAM Series N
14863.0	USAF-SAM	Mystic Star SAM Series A
14867.0	USAF-SAM	Mystic Star SAM Series B
14876.0	USAF-SAM	Mystic Star SAM Series K
14887.0	USAF-SAM	Mystic Star SAM Series N
14890.0	EU-CC-LDOC	Somerset (Portishead Radio)
14894.0	NORAD	NORAD - Primary channel (Tie-in to US CAP)

FREQ.	SERVICE	STATION/LOCATION
14896.0	NASA	Cape Radio
	USAF-SAM	Mystic Star SAM Series I
		Mystic Star SAM Series R
14897.0	USAF-SAM	Mystic Star SAM Series C
14900.0	SP-AFTN	Rarotonga AFTN
14902.0	US-CAP	National Command Net, CAP-USAF Frequency
	USAF-SAM	Mystic Star SAM Series P
14905.0	USAF-ACC	Air Combat Command
14913.0	USAF-SAM	Mystic Star SAM Series M (Air Force 2)
14937.0	NASA	Cape Radio
14957.0	USAF-SAM	Mystic Star SAM Series C
		Mystic Star SAM Series M
14967.0	NASA	Cape Radio
15011.0	USAF-ARRS	Air Rescue Service
15015.0	USAF-GHFS	Albrook, Ascension, Bayonne, Croughton, Elmendorf, Incirlik, Lajes, Loring, MacDill, McClellan, Yokota
15018.0	USAF-SAM	Mystic Star SAM Series T
15021.0	EU-LDOC	Stockholm Radio
	USN	Air/Ground/Ship
15022.0	unid LDOC	unid
15024.0	CAR-LDOC	Boyeros (Aeroflot)
	NCA-LDOC	Moscow (Aeroflot)
	USN	Air/Ground/Ship
15026.0	ITALY-AF	Italian Air Force
	MID-LDOC	Jeddah (Saudi Airlines)
	USN	Air/Ground/Ship
15027.0	USN	Air/Ground/Ship
15027.5	U.S. Flight Test	Grumman Aerospace
15028.0	USN	Air/Ground/Ship
15031.0	CANFORCE	ATG - Trenton Military, MACS - Edmonton Military
	RAF	STCICS "Architect"
15035.0	CANFORCE	Aviation Wx - Edmonton (H+20), Trenton (H+30), St John's (H+40) "Charlie"
15036.0	USAF-SAM	Mystic Star SAM Series J
	USN	Air/Ground/Ship
15038.0	CANFORCE	MAG - Halifax Military - Wx (H+20/EAM H+01) "X211"
	USAF-USSTRATCOM	Former SAC "Giant Talk" Network "Xray 211", now "Sierra 211"
15040.0	RAF	Royal Air Force Air/ground
15041.0	USAF-SAM	Mystic Star SAM Series J
15044.0	RNZAF	Wigram AFB
	USAF-USSTRATCOM	Former SAC "Giant Talk" Network "Papa 383", Lajes
15046.0	EU-LDOC	Berlin/Schoenfield (Interflug)
		Berne ("Berna") Radio
		Stockholm Radio
15048.0	USAF-SAM	Mystic Star SAM Series Unassigned
15050.0	EU-LDOC	Berne ("Berna") Radio
15051.0	USN	Air/Ground/Ship
15053.0	RNZAF	Air Force Auckland
15054.0	USN	Air/Ground/Ship
15056.0	SAF-AF	South African Air Force
15057.0	USN	Air/Ground/Ship
15058.0	USAF-SAM	Mystic Star SAM Series Unassigned
	USN	Air/Ground/Ship
15061.0	USN	Air/Ground/Ship
15064.0	USN	Air/Ground/Ship
15066.0	USN	Air/Ground/Ship
15067.0	USN	Navy Air ASW
15071.0	USN	Air/Ground/Ship
15074.0	USN	Air/Ground/Ship
15076.0	USN	Air/Ground/Ship
15078.0	USN	Air/Ground/Ship
15081.0	US-Customs	Drug Enforcement Air Patrols
	USCG-AIR	Air/Ground
	USN	Air/Ground/Ship

FREQ.	SERVICE	STATION/LOCATION
15084.0	US-Customs	Drug Enforcement Air Patrols
	US-DOD	Drug Enforcement - Combined Forces
	USCG-AIR	Air/Ground
	USN	Air/Ground/Ship
15086.0	USN	Air/Ground/Ship
15087.0	USCG-AIR	Air/Ground
	USN	Navy Air ASW Pacific
15091.0	USAF-ACC	Air Combat Command, Secondary
15500.0	USN	Air/Ground/Ship
15522.0	USN	Air/Ground/Ship
15535.0	USN	Air/Ground/Ship
15550.0	USAF-SAM	Mystic Star SAM Series P
15555.0	USAF-SAM	Mystic Star SAM Series H
		Mystic Star SAM Series M
15595.0	USAF-SAM	Mystic Star SAM Series A
15664.0	USAF-SAM	Mystic Star SAM Series N
15672.0	USAF-SAM	Mystic Star SAM Series H
15685.0	EU-LDOC	Stockholm Radio
15687.0	USAF-SAM	Mystic Star SAM Series B
15698.0	NASA	Cape Radio
15710.0	USAF-SAM	Mystic Star SAM Series H
		Mystic Star SAM Series M
15724.0	USAF-SAM	Mystic Star SAM Series N
15733.0	USAF-SAM	Mystic Star SAM Series A
15742.0	USAF-SAM	Mystic Star SAM Series H
15760.0	USAF-SAM	Mystic Star SAM Series M
15776.0	USAF-SAM	Mystic Star SAM Series P
15793.0	USAF-PMR	Pacific Missile Range, Wheeler AFB wkg AGAR aircraft
15821.0	USAF-SAM	Mystic Star SAM Series P, "Foxtrot 988" (Air Force 2)
15835.0	EU-LDOC	Berne ("Berna") Radio
15851.0	US-FAA	U. S. Federal Aviation Administration (Selscan Ch# 17)
15860.0	USAF-SAM	Mystic Star SAM Series M
15867.0	US-Customs	COTHERN "Zulu Echo" - Selscan 6
	US-DOD	Counterdrug Network "Zulu Echo"
15908.0	USAF-SAM	Mystic Star SAM Series P
15953.5	US-DOD	Counterdrug Network "Xray Golf"
15962.0	USAF-USSTRATCOM	Former SAC "Giant Talk" Network "Sierra 315"
15964.0	EU-CC-LDOC	Somerset (Portishead Radio)
	US-DOD	Counterdrug Network "Whiskey Foxtrot"
16003.0	EU-CC-LDOC	Somerset (Portishead Radio)
16011.0	USAF-SAM	Mystic Star SAM Series G
16041.0	USAF-SAM	Mystic Star SAM Series P
		Mystic Star SAM Series S
16070.0	USAF-SAM	Mystic Star SAM Series H
16077.0	USAF-SAM	Mystic Star SAM Series G
16080.0	USAF-SAM	Mystic Star SAM Series N
16100.0	USAF-SAM	Mystic Star SAM Series H
16117.0	USAF-SAM	Mystic Star SAM Series L
16120.0	USAF-SAM	Mystic Star SAM Series A
16121.0	USAF-SAM	Mystic Star SAM Series B
		Mystic Star SAM Series M
16160.0	USAF-SAM	Mystic Star SAM Series N
16186.0	USAF-SAM	Mystic Star SAM Series N
16191.0	USAF-AMC-OP	Operation Restore Hope (Accuse Delta - Tanker), Moron
16207.0	EU-LDOC	Stockholm Radio
16216.0	NASA	Cape Radio
16230.0	USAF-SAM	Mystic Star SAM Series G
16246.0	NASA	Cape Radio - Shuttle Missions
	USAF-SAM	Mystic Star SAM Series I
		Mystic Star SAM Series R
16320.0	USAF-SAM	Mystic Star SAM Series A
		Mystic Star SAM Series M
16348.0	US-FAA	U. S. Federal Aviation Administration

Master Frequency List

FREQ.	SERVICE	STATION/LOCATION
16362.0	USAF-ACC	Air Combat Command, Backup - West
16363.0	NORAD	NORAD
16370.0	EU-CC-LDOC	Somerset (Portishead Radio)
16385.0	USAF-SAM	Mystic Star SAM Series G
16407.0	USAF-SAM	Mystic Star SAM Series H
		Mystic Star SAM Series M
16443.0	EU-CC-LDOC	Somerset (Portishead Radio)
17282.5	NA-CC-LDOC	Tors Cove (Rainbow Radio phone patches)
17386.0	USAF-SAM	Mystic Star SAM Series M
17405.0	EU-CC-LDOC	Somerset (Portishead Radio)
17414.0	USAF-CEN	Commando Escort Net - Hawaii "November"
17427.0	USAF-SAM	Mystic Star SAM Series M
17433.0	USAF-SAM	Mystic Star SAM Series A
17440.0	SEA-CC-LDOC	Sydney SkyComms
17457.0	USAF-SAM	Mystic Star SAM Series K
17460.0	USAF-SAM	Mystic Star SAM Series G
		Mystic Star SAM Series N
17464.0	USAF-CEN	Commando Escort Net - Hawaii "Papa"
17470.0	NASA	Cape Radio
17480.0	USAF-SAM	Mystic Star SAM Series A
		Mystic Star SAM Series H
		Mystic Star SAM Series M
		Mystic Star SAM Series N
		Mystic Star SAM Series P
17485.0	CAR-LDOC	Bridgetown Operations (Caribbean Airways)
17496.0	USAF-SAM	Mystic Star SAM Series B
17547.0	USAF-SAM	Mystic Star SAM Series P
17554.0	NASA	Cape Radio
		Mystic Star SAM Series I
		Mystic Star SAM Series R
17562.0	USAF-SAM	Mystic Star SAM Series N
17565.0	USAF-SAM	Mystic Star SAM Series G
17601.0	US-DOD	Counterdrug Network "Xray Hotel"
17625.0	USAF-SAM	Mystic Star SAM Series H
17668.0	NASA	Cape Radio
17679.0	USAF-SAM	Mystic Star SAM Series N
17840.0	USAF-SAM	Mystic Star SAM Series K
17901.0	US-NOAA	Hurricane Hunters - KJY74 Miami Air/Ground
17904.0	CWP-1/2 MWARA	Guam, Honolulu, Manila, Naha, Port Moresby, Seoul, Taipei, Tokyo
	NP-3/4 MWARA	Honolulu , Tokyo
	SP-6/7 MWARA	Auckland, Honolulu, Nandi, Pascua (Easter Is.), Rarotonga, Sydney, Tahiti
	SP-RDARA	New Zealand - Auckland ACC
	USN	Navy Air ASW
17907.0	CAR-A MWARA	Boyeros, Guatemala City, Merida, New York, Panama, Piarco, San Andres Is, San Jose, Tegucigalpa
	CAR-B MWARA	Barranquilla, Boyeros, Cayenne, Georgetown, Maiquetia, New York, Panama, Paramaribo, Piarco, San Andres Is
	EA-2 MWARA	Canton, Irkutsk, Pyongyang, Ulaanbaatar
	SAM-C MWARA	Belem, Bogota, Brasilia, Leticia, Manaus, Maiquetia, Porto Velho, Rio de Janeiro
	SAM-NE MWARA	Belem, Cayenne, Georgetown, Maiquetia, Paramaribo, Piarco, Recife
	SAM-NW MWARA	Barranquilla, Bogota, Caracas (Maiquetia), Lima, Quito
	SAM-RDARA	Chile - Isla Rey Jorge Marsh Approach
	SAM-SE MWARA	Asuncion, Belem, Brasilia, Buenos Aires, Campo Grande, Curtiba, La Paz, Montevideo, Porto Alegre, Porto Velho, Recife, Salvador Dois De Julho, Santa Cruz
	SAM-SW MWARA	Antofagasta, Asuncion, Buenos Aires, Cordoba, Easter Is (Pascua), La Paz, Lima, Mendoza, Puerto Montt, Punta Arenas, Resistencia, Salta, Santa Cruz, Santiago, Talara
	SEA-1 MWARA	Bali, Bangkok, Colombo, Calcutta, Dhaka, Jakarta, Kathmandu, Kuala Lumpur, Madras, Male, Singapore, Yangon
	SEA-2 MWARA	Bali, Bangkok, Denpasar, Guangzhou, Hanoi, Ho Chi Minh, Hong Kong, Jakarta, Kuala Lumpur, Kota Kinabalu, Manila, Singapore, Vientiane
	SEA-3 MWARA	Bali, Cocos Is, Darwin, Jakarta, Male, Perth, Singapore, Ujung Pandang
	SP- RDARA	Christmas Island (proprietary)

FREQ.	SERVICE	STATION/LOCATION
17909.0	SAM-RDARA	Paraguay - Asuncion ACC
17910.0	CAR-LDOC	Bridgetown Operations (Caribbean Airways)
	NA-CC-LDOC	Tors Cove (Rainbow Radio)
	NA-LDOC	Toronto Ops (Elite/Canada 3000)
17913.0	SAM-LDOC	Rio de Janeiro, Sao Paulo (VARIG)
17916.0	CWP-LDOC	Manila (Philippines Air)
		Seoul (KAL-Korean Airlines)
	EU-LDOC	Athens (Olympic Airlines)
		Belgrade (Serbia Aerotransport)
		Dublin (Aer Lingus)
		Frankfurt (Hapag Lloyd Fluggesellschaft)
		Paris Radio (Air France)
		Stockholm Radio
	MID-LDOC	Bombay (Air India)
	SEA-LDOC	Jakarta
	SP-LDOC	Nauru Island (Air Nauru)
17919.0	CAR-LDOC	Willemstad (ALM Antillean)
	NA-LDOC	Matamoros
		Merida, Mexico City, Tijuana (AeroMexico)
	SAM-LDOC	Buenos Aires (Aerolineas Argentinas)
		Montevideo (PLUNA)
		Rio de Janeiro (VARIG)
17922.0	EU-LDOC	Speedbird London (British Airways)
	SEA-LDOC	Bangkok (Thai Airways)
		Colombo (Air Lanka)
		Perth, Sydney (Qantas)
17925.0	AFI-LDOC	Djibouti (Air Djibouti)
		Lusaka (Zambia Airways)
		Springbok Jo'burg (South African Airlines)
		Tunis (Tunis Air)
17925.0	CAR-LDOC	Mexico City, Tijuana (AeroMexico)
	CEP-CC-LDOC	Honolulu, San Francisco (ARINC)
	CWP-LDOC	Tokyo (JAL-Japan Airlines)
	EU-LDOC	Berlin/Schoenfield (Interflug)
		Scheveningen Radio
	MID-LDOC	Jeddah (Saudi Airlines)
	NA-CC-LDOC	New York, Honolulu, San Francisco (ARINC)
	NCA-LDOC	Kabul (Ariana Afghan Airlines)
17928.0	CWP-LDOC	Tokyo (JAL-Japan Airlines)
	SAM-LDOC	Buenos Aires (Aerolineas Argentinas)
		Piarco (West Indian)
17931.0	AFI-LDOC	Addis Ababa, Asmara (Ethiopian Airlines - Holloway)
		Blantyre (Air Malawi)
		Cairo (Egypt Air)
		Dar es Salaam (Air Tanzania)
		Kigali (Air Rwanda)
		Kinshasa (Air Zaire)
		Lagos (Nigeria Airways)
		Nairobi
	EU-LDOC	Berne ("Berna") Radio
		Bucharest (TAROM - Romanian Air Transport)
		Dusseldorf (LTU)
		Frankfurt (Lufthansa)
		Hanover (Hapag Lloyd Fluggesellschaft)
		Larnaca (Cyprus Airways)
		Luqa (Air Malta)
		Stuttgart (Deutsche Rettungsflugwacht)
	INO-LDOC	Antananarivo (Air Madagascar)
	MID-LDOC	Abu Dhabi
		Beirut (MEA-Cedar Jet)
		Manama (Falcon)
		Muscat (Gulf Air)
		Safat (Kuwaiti Airlines)

FREQ.	SERVICE	STATION/LOCATION
17931.0	SAM-LDOC	Rio de Janeiro (VARIG)
17934.0	CAR-LDOC	Boyeros (Cubana Airlines/Aeroflot)
		Santo Domingo
	EA-LDOC	Beijing
	NCA-LDOC	Moscow (Aeroflot)
	SEA-CC-LDOC	Sydney SkyComms
	SEA-LDOC	Singapore (Singapore Airlines)
		Yangon (Myanma Airways)
17936.0	CAR-LDOC	Boyeros (Aeroflot, Cubana)
	NCA-LDOC	Moscow (Aeroflot, Cubana)
17937.0	AFI-LDOC	Harare (Air Zimbabwe)
		Roberts/Monrovia
		Salisbury
	CAR-LDOC	Kingston Dispatch (Air Jamaica)
	INO-LDOC	Port Louis (Air Mauritius)
	MID-LDOC	Tehran
	SAM-LDOC	Caracas/Maiquetia (AVENSA)
		Lima (American Airlines)
		Maiquetia (VIASA)
		San Salvador
		Santiago
17940.0	CAR-LDOC	Boyeros (Aeroflot)
	CWP-LDOC	Hong Kong (Dragonair)
	EU-LDOC	Amsterdam (KLM-Royal Dutch Airlines)
		Brussels (Sabena)
		Budapest (MALEV - Hungarian Airlines)
		Las Palmas (Lineas Aereas Canarias)
		Las Palmas, Madrid (Iberia)
		Lisbon (TAP-Air Portugal)
		Prague (Czechoslovak Airlines)
		Rome (Alitalia)
		Warsaw (LOT - Polskie Linie)
	MID-LDOC	Karachi (PIA-Pakistani International Airlines)
		Tel Aviv (El Al)
	NA-CC-LDOC	Houston Radio (Universal Aviation)
	NASA	Cape Radio
	NCA-LDOC	Khabarovsk, Moscow (Aeroflot)
	SEA-CC-LDOC	Sydney SkyComms
	SP-LDOC	Auckland (Air New Zealand)
17941.0	EU-LDOC	Paris Radio (Air France)
17943.0	SAM-LDOC	Sao Paulo (VASP - Viacao Aerea Sao Paulo)
17944.0	AFI-LDOC	Harare (Air Zimbabwe)
17946.0	NAT-A MWARA	Canarias, Gander, New York, Paramaribo, Piarco, Santa Maria, Shanwick
	NAT-B MWARA	Gander, Iceland (Reykjavik), New York, Santa Maria, Shannon (Shanwick)
	NAT-C MWARA	Gander, Iceland (Reykjavik), Shannon (Shanwick)
	NAT-D MWARA	Bodo, Cambridge Bay, Churchill, Iqaluit (Frobisher Bay), Gander, Iceland (Reykjavik), Sondrestrom
	NP-3/4 MWARA	Honolulu , Tokyo
17948.0	EU-LDOC	Warsaw (LOT - Polskie Linie)
17949.0	EU-LDOC	Madrid (Iberia)
	SEA-LDOC	Sydney (Qantas)
17952.0	US-DOD	Counterdrug Network "Yankee Foxtrot"
	US-FAA	U. S. Federal Aviation Administration
17955.0	AFI-1 MWARA	Abidjan, Bamako, Bissau, Bobo Dioulasso, Bouake, Casablanca, Conakry, Freetown, Kano, Niamey, Nouadhibou, Nouakchott, Ouagadougou, Roberts (Monrovia)
	AFI-RDARA	Johannesburg Aeradio
	EU-LDOC	Berlin/Schoenfield (Interflug)
	SAT-1 MWARA	Brasilia, Canarias, Cayenne, Dakar, Manaus, Paramaribo, Recife, Rio de Janeiro, Sal Island, Salvador
	SAT-2 MWARA	Canarias, Cayenne, Dakar, Manaus, Paramaribo, Recife, Rio de Janeiro, Sal Island, Salvador
17957.0	BRZ-AF	Brazilian Air Force, Manaus

FREQ.	SERVICE	STATION/LOCATION
17958.0	EA-1 MWARA	Beijing, Canton, Hailar, Irkutsk, Jinan, Kunming, Lanzhou, Pyongyang, Shanghai, Shenyang, Taegu, Ulaanbaatar, Urumqi, Wuhan, Zhengzhou
	NCA-1 MWARA	Ivdel, Khanty Mansiysk, Moscow, Syktyvkar, Sverdlovsk, Vologda
	NCA-2 MWARA	Barnaul, Irkutsk, Khanty Mansiysk, Kirensk, Kolpashevo, Krasnoyarsk, Novosibirsk, Podkamennaya, Surgut, Yeniseysk
	NCA-3 MWARA	Chita, Chulman, Ekimchan, Irkutsk, Kirensk, Khabarovsk, Pyongyang, Ulaanbaatar, Ulan Ude
17961.0	AFI-2 MWARA	Algiers, Brazzaville, Kano, Gao, Niamey, N'djamena, Tamanrasset, Timimoun, Tripoli, Tunis
	AFI-3 MWARA	Addis Ababa, Aden, Asmara, Bahrain, Benghazi, Bujumbura, Cairo, Dar es Salaam, Entebbe, Hargesia, Djibouti, Jeddah, Khartoum, Kigali, Kisimayu, Male, Mogadishu, Nairobi, N'djamena, Sana'a, Seychelles, Triopli
	AFI-4 MWARA	Accra, Bangui, Brazzaville, Bulawayo, Contonou, Douala, Entebbe, Franceville, Francistown, Garoua, Goma, Johannesburg, Kano, Kinshasa, Kisangani, Lagos, Libreville, Lomé, Luanda, Lumbumbashi, Lusaka, Maroua, Maseru, Nairobi, N'djamena, N'djili Niamey, Niamtougou, Port Gentil, Salisbury, Salazar, Seychelles, Windhoek, Yaounde
	EUR-A MWARA	Arkhangelsk, Beirut, Kiev, Lvov, Minsk, Moscow, Murmansk, Odessa, Riga, Simferopol, St. Petersburg, Syktyvkar, Tunis, Valetta, Velikiye, Vitebsk, Vilnius, Vologda
	INO-1 MWARA	Antananarivo, Beira, Blantyre, Bombay, Cocos Is., Colombo, Dar es Salaam, Harare, Jeddah, Johannesburg, Kigali, Lilongwe, Lusaka, Madras, Mahajanga, Male, Mauritius, Moroni, Nairobi, Perth, Seychelles, St. Denis, Toamasina
	MID-1 MWARA	Aden, Amman, Ankara, Baghdad, Basrah, Beirut, Cairo, Damascus, Jeddah, Kuwait, Manama, Odessa, Sana'a, Simferopol, Tehran, Tbilisi, Yerevan
	MID-2 MWARA	Abadan, Alma Ata, Bombay, Delhi, Dushanbe, Frunze, Kabul, Karachi, Kathmandu, Kuwait, Lahore, Male, Muscat, Odessa, Samarkand, Seychelles, Tashkent, Tehran, Tbilisi, Urumqi, Yerevan
	MID-3 MWARA	Aktyubinsk, Alma Ata, Dushanbe, Frunze, Kuybyshev, Kzyl-Orda, Moscow, Samarkand, Tashkent, Uralsk, Yevevan
17964.0	U.S. Flight Test	Boeing Company
		Falcon Jet Corp
		Lockheed Corporation
		McDonnel Douglas
		Rockwell Flight Test
17965.0	MID-LDOC	Beirut (MEA-Cedar Jet)
17970.0	AFI-LDOC	Lagos (Nigeria Airways)
17972.0	USAF-SAM	Mystic Star SAM Series Unassigned "Whiskey 111"
	USAF-USSTRATCOM	Former SAC "Giant Talk" Network "Whiskey 111"
17974.0	CAR-LDOC	Boyeros (Cubana Airlines)
17975.0	EU-LDOC	Berlin/Schoenfield (Interflug)
	US-ANG	ANG - Air National Guard
	USAF-GHFS	Andrews, Croughton, Elmendorf, Incirlik, McClellan, Offutt, Thule, Yokota
	USAF-USSTRATCOM	Former SAC "Giant Talk" Network "Sierra 395"
17977.0	unid-LDOC	JVL clg Operations
17979.0	USN	Air/Ground/Ship
17982.0	EU-LDOC	Stockholm Radio
	RAF	Royal Air Force
	RNZAF	Air Force Auckland
	USN	Tactical - (Mongoose wkg Radiator)
17983.0	BRZ-AF	Brazilian Air Force
	MID-LDOC	Jeddah (Saudi Airlines)
	U.S. Flight Test	United Technologies
17985.0	USAF-SAM	Mystic Star SAM Series N
	USN	Air/Ground/Ship
17992.0	GAF	DHM91 Munster "Whiskey" (German Air Force Air/Ground)
	USAF-USSTRATCOM	Former SAC "Giant Talk" Network "Xray 908"
17993.0	SAF-AF	South African Air Force (Secondary Overseas)
17995.0	AFI-ASECNA	ASECNA - Dakar, Lomé
	CANFORCE	ATG - Trenton Military, MACS - Edmonton Military
17999.0	CANFORCE	MAG - Halifax Military (Joint USAF exercises)
	NORAD	Joint USAF/CANFORCE NORAD exercises - Canadian Far North

Master Frequency List

FREQ.	SERVICE	STATION/LOCATION
18002.0	BEL-AF	Rouveroy Radio (Belgian Air Force Air/Ground)
	USAF-ACC	Air Combat Command, AWACS Aircraft
18005.0	USAF-CEN	Commando Escort Net - Hawaii "Tango"
18006.0	GAF	DHM91 Munster (German Air Force Air/Ground)
18009.0	NASA	Cape Radio
	USN	HICOM WESTPAC (COM7THFLT)
18012.0	CANFORCE	ATG - Trenton Military, MACS - Edmonton Military
	RNZAF	Whenuapai AFB
	USN	Air/Ground/Ship
18014.0	USN	Air/Ground/Ship
18015.0	USN	Air/Ground/Ship
18018.0	RAF	STCICS - Architect (Wx H+00, H+30), Uphavon, Cyprus Flight Watch
18019.0	SAUDI-AF	Dhahran Air "Hotel One" (Saudi Air Force)
	USAF-ACC	Air Combat Command, Primary, Ascension
18022.0	NASA	Cape Radio
18023.0	EU-LDOC	Berne ("Berna") Radio (Swiss Air)
	RAAF	Royal Australian Air Force
	USAF	USAF Tactical
	USAF-SAM	Mystic Star SAM Series D "SAM 401"
18025.0	US-CAP	Alaska - Primary
18027.0	CANFORCE	MACS - Halifax Military, Edmonton Military
	NORAD	NORAD "Channel Charlie 8"
	USAF-ACC	Air Combat Command, Backup -East
	USAF-AMC	Air Mobility Command
18036.0	USN	Air/Ground/Ship
18046.0	USAF	"Papa 384"
18051.0	NASA	Cape Radio
18060.0	USAF-SAM	Mystic Star SAM Series B (Air Force 1)
18080.0	USN	Air/Ground/Ship
18095.0	USAF-SAM	Mystic Star SAM Series H
18100.0	USAF-SAM	Mystic Star SAM Series G
	USN	Air/Ground/Ship
18125.0	USN	Air/Ground/Ship
18128.0	USN	Air/Ground/Ship
18146.0	USAF-SAM	Mystic Star SAM Series N
18171.0	US-DEA	OTH Radio System "Sierra India"
18175.0	USAF-SAM	Mystic Star SAM Series H
18196.0	NASA	Cape Radio
18210.0	EU-CC-LDOC	Somerset (Portishead Radio)
18218.0	USAF-SAM	Mystic Star SAM Series P
18230.0	USAF-SAM	Mystic Star SAM Series K
18240.0	USAF-AMC-OP	Operation Restore Hope (Accuse Delta - Tanker), Moron
18270.0	USAF-SAM	Mystic Star SAM Series M
18310.0	NASA	Cape Radio
18320.0	USAF-SAM	Mystic Star SAM Series A
		Mystic Star SAM Series B
18331.0	NASA	Cape Radio
	USAF-SAM	Mystic Star SAM Series I
		Mystic Star SAM Series R
18354.0	NASA	Cape Radio
18397.0	USAF	"Whiskey 112"
18399.0	USAF-AMC-OP	Operation Restore Hope (Absolution, Accuse)
18400.0	USAF-SAM	Mystic Star SAM Series N
18434.0	NASA	Cape Radio
18478.0	USAF-SAM	Mystic Star SAM Series H
18480.0	EU-LDOC	Berne ("Berna") Radio (Swiss Air)
18490.0	USAF-SAM	Mystic Star SAM Series M
18532.0	USAF-SAM	Mystic Star SAM Series G
18590.0	USAF-SAM	Mystic Star SAM Series P
18594.0	US-Customs	COTHERN "Victor Charlie" - Selscan 7
	US-DOD	Counterdrug Network "Victor Charlie"
18624.5	USN	Air/Ground/Ship
18629.0	USAF-SAM	Mystic Star SAM Series N

FREQ.	SERVICE	STATION/LOCATION
18666.0	US-DEA	OTH Radio System "Hotel"
18675.0	USAF-SAM	Mystic Star SAM Series B
18700.0	NASA	Cape Radio
18769.0	NASA	Cape Radio
18790.0	USAF-SAM	Mystic Star SAM Series N
18795.0	USAF-SAM	Mystic Star SAM Series K
18800.0	USN	Air/Ground/Ship
18801.0	NASA	Cape Radio
18937.0	USAF-USSTRATCOM	Former SAC "Giant Talk" Network
18980.0	USAF-SAM	Mystic Star SAM Series H
18990.0	NASA	Cape Radio
19005.0	USAF-SAM	Mystic Star SAM Series A
19008.0	USAF-SAM	Mystic Star SAM Series G
19047.0	USAF-SAM	Mystic Star SAM Series N
19050.0	USAF-SAM	Mystic Star SAM Series A
19060.0	USAF-SAM	Mystic Star SAM Series M
19092.0	USAF-SAM	Mystic Star SAM Series N
19126.0	NASA	Cape Radio
19131.0	US-DEA	OTH Radio System "Sierra Juliet"
	US-DOD	Counterdrug Network "Xray India"
19143.0	NASA	Cape Radio
19149.5	NASA	Cape Radio
19160.0	USAF-SAM	Mystic Star SAM Series K
19180.0	USAF-SAM	Mystic Star SAM Series H
19237.0	USAF-SAM	Mystic Star SAM Series P
19270.0	USAF-SAM	Mystic Star SAM Series N
19303.0	NASA	Cape Radio
19340.0	USAF-SAM	Mystic Star SAM Series N
19371.0	NASA	Cape Radio
19373.0	USAF-SAM	Mystic Star SAM Series M
19390.0	NASA	Cape Radio
19410.0	US-FAA	U. S. Federal Aviation Administration
19447.0	USAF-SAM	Mystic Star SAM Series H
19500.0	SAM-AFTN	Brasilia AFTN
19510.0	EU-CC-LDOC	Somerset (Portishead Radio)
19513.0	USAF-SAM	Mystic Star SAM Series B
19554.0	EU-LDOC	Berne ("Berna") Radio
19640.0	NASA	Cape Radio
19653.0	USAF-SAM	Mystic Star SAM Series A
19758.0	USAF-SAM	Mystic Star SAM Series B
19800.0	USAF-SAM	Mystic Star SAM Series P
19895.0	USAF-SAM	Mystic Star SAM Series O
19904.0	CAR-LDOC	Boyeros (Aeroflot)
	NCA-LDOC	Moscow (Aeroflot)
19928.0	NASA	Cape Radio
19943.0	SAM-LDOC	Sao Paulo (VASP - Viacao Aerea Sao Paulo)
19963.0	NASA	Cape Radio
19966.0	NASA	Cape Radio
20016.0	USAF-SAM	Mystic Star SAM Series O
20019.0	USAF-ACC	Air Combat Command, Forward Air Control Network
20035.0	EU-LDOC	Berne ("Berna") Radio
20042.0	NORAD	NORAD
20053.0	USAF-SAM	Mystic Star SAM Series A (Air Force 1)
20065.0	EU-CC-LDOC	Somerset (Portishead Radio)
20124.0	USAF-SAM	Mystic Star SAM Series B
	USAF-USSTRATCOM	Former SAC "Giant Talk" Network "Whiskey 115"
20150.0	USAF-SAM	Mystic Star SAM Series N
20154.0	USAF-SAM	Mystic Star SAM Series K
20160.0	SEA-CC-LDOC	Sydney SkyComms
20165.0	USAF-SAM	Mystic Star SAM Series H
20167.0	USAF-USSTRATCOM	Former SAC "Giant Talk" Network "Whiskey "116"
20185.0	NASA	Cape Radio - Shuttle Communications (USB)
20186.0	NASA	Cape Radio

Master Frequency List

FREQ.	SERVICE	STATION/LOCATION
20192.0	ESA	Khourou Control, Cayenne Launch (European Space Agency)
	NASA	Cape Radio - Shuttle Communications (LSB)
20195.0	USAF-SAM	Mystic Star SAM Series I
		Mystic Star SAM Series R
20198.0	NASA	Antigua, Cape Radio - Shuttle Communications (LSB)
20266.0	NASA	Cape Radio
20272.0	NASA	Cape Radio
20313.0	USAF-SAM	Mystic Star SAM Series P
20321.0	USAF-SAM	Mystic Star SAM Series N
20340.0	USAF-SAM	Mystic Star SAM Series I
		Mystic Star SAM Series R
20390.0	NASA	Ascension Radio, Cape Radio - Shuttle Missions
20395.0	USAF-SAM	Mystic Star SAM Series O
20400.0	USAF-SAM	Mystic Star SAM Series A
		Mystic Star SAM Series H
		Mystic Star SAM Series K
20406.0	USAF-ACC	Air Combat Command, Okie Sam RTTY Channel
20407.0	USAF-USSTRATCOM	Former SAC "Giant Talk" Network "Whiskey "117"
20415.0	USAF-SAM	Mystic Star SAM Series P
20420.0	NORAD	NORAD
20425.0	USAF-SAM	Mystic Star SAM Series N
20433.0	NORAD	NORAD
20452.0	USAF-SAM	Mystic Star SAM Series G
20475.0	NASA	Cape Radio
	USAF-SAM	Mystic Star SAM Series I
		Mystic Star SAM Series R
20535.0	USAF-SAM	Mystic Star SAM Series P
20631.0	US-DOD	Counterdrug Network "Victor Bravo"
20640.0	USAF-SAM	Mystic Star SAM Series P
20650.0	USAF-SAM	Mystic Star SAM Series G
20665.0	EU-CC-LDOC	Somerset (Portishead Radio)
	USAF-SAM	Mystic Star SAM Series O
20690.0	NASA	Cape Radio
20737.0	USAF-CEN	Commando Escort Net - Hawaii
20740.0	USAF-CEN	Commando Escort Net - Hawaii "Lima"
20758.0	USAF-SAM	Mystic Star SAM Series N
20770.0	EU-LDOC	Stockholm Radio
	MID-LDOC	Beirut (MEA-Cedar Jet)
20855.0	NORAD	NORAD - Secondary Day (Tie-in to US CAP)
20870.0	EU-LDOC	Berne ("Berna") Radio
20873.0	US-CAP	CAP-USAF Frequency
20890.0	US-Customs	COTHERN "Yankee Golf" - Selscan 8
	US-DOD	Counterdrug Network "Yankee Golf"
20943.0	US-Customs	Counterdrug Network
20953.0	USAF-SAM	Mystic Star SAM Series B
20972.0	USAF-SAM	Mystic Star SAM Series H
21280.0	NASA	Jet Propulsion Labs - Shuttle Rebroadcast
21395.0	NASA	Goddard Space Center - Shuttle Rebroadcast
21754.0	USAF-CEN	Commando Escort Net - Hawaii "Uniform"
21765.0	EU-CC-LDOC	Somerset (Portishead Radio)
21770.0	USAF-SAM	Mystic Star SAM Series H
21810.0	NASA	Cape Radio
21843.0	USAF-SAM	Mystic Star SAM Series H
21860.0	SAF-AF	Waterkloof Radio, Ysterplaat Radio (South African Air Force)
21866.0	USAF-ACC	Air Combat Command, AWACS Aircraft Channel
21880.0	MID-LDOC	Tel Aviv (El Al)
21886.0	AFI-LDOC	Mahe (Air Seychelles)
	MID-LDOC	Tel Aviv (El Al)
	SEA-LDOC	Sydney (Qantas)
21925.0	EU-LDOC	Amsterdam (KLM-Royal Dutch Airlines)
	NP-3/4 MWARA	Honolulu , Tokyo
21926.0	AFI-RDARA	Johannesburg ACC

FREQ.	SERVICE	STATION/LOCATION
21931.0	U.S. Flight Test	Boeing Company
		Lockheed Corporation
		McDonnel Douglas
		Rockwell International
21933.0	EU-LDOC	Berne ("Berna") Radio (Swiss Air)
	MID-LDOC	Damascus (Syrian)
21937.0	US-NOAA	Hurricane Hunters - KJY74 Miami Air/Ground
21940.0	EU-LDOC	Belgrade (Serbia Aerotransport)
		Paris Radio (Air France)
21942.0	AFI-LDOC	Algiers (Air Algerie)
21943.0	AFI-LDOC	Ouagadougou
		Springbok Jo'burg (South African Airways)
	MID-LDOC	Abu Dhabi
		Beirut (MEA-Cedar Jet)
		Bombay (Air India)
		Manama (Falcon)
		Muscat (Gulf Air)
21944.0	AFI-LDOC	Djibouti (Air Djibouti)
	EU-LDOC	Paris Radio (Air France)
	MID-LDOC	Jeddah (Saudi Airlines)
21946.0	EU-LDOC	Speedbird London (British Airways)
21949.0	CWP-LDOC	Manila (Philippines Air)
		Seoul (KAL-Korean Airlines)
		Tokyo (JAL-Japan Airlines)
	MID-LDOC	Bombay (Air India)
	SEA-LDOC	Colombo (Air Lanka)
		Singapore (Singapore Airlines)
		Yangon (Myanma Airways)
	SP-LDOC	Nauru Island (Air Nauru)
21952.0	EU-LDOC	Bucharest (TAROM - Romanian Air Transport)
		Dublin (Aer Lingus)
		Lisbon (TAP-Air Portugal)
		Rome (Alitalia)
	MID-LDOC	Tel Aviv (El Al)
21955.0	SAM-LDOC	Buenos Aires (Aerolineas Argentinas)
		Piarco (West Indian)
		Rio de Janeiro (VARIG)
21958.0	CAR-LDOC	Boyeros (Aeroflot)
	EU-LDOC	Frankfurt (Hapag Lloyd Fluggesellschaft)
	NCA-LDOC	Khabarovsk, Moscow (Aeroflot)
21961.0	AFI-LDOC	Roberts/Monrovia
	MID-LDOC	Tehran
21964.0	AFI-LDOC	Lusaka (Zambia Airways)
	CEP-CC-LDOC	Honolulu, San Francisco (ARINC)
	NA-CC-LDOC	Houston Radio (Universal Aviation)
		New York (ARINC)
21967.0	EU-LDOC	Frankfurt (Lufthansa)
		Las Palmas (Lineas Aereas Canarias)
		Luqa (Air Malta)
		Madrid (Iberia)
		Prague (Czechoslovak Airlines)
		Scheveningen Radio
		Warsaw (LOT - Polskie Linie)
21970.0	CWP-LDOC	Hong Kong (Dragonair)
		Seoul (KAL-Korean Airlines)
	MID-LDOC	Karachi (PIA-Pakistani International Airlines)
	SEA-LDOC	Bangkok (Thai Airways)
		Jakarta
		Perth, Sydney (Qantas)
	SP-LDOC	Auckland (Air New Zealand)
21973.0	EU-LDOC	Amsterdam (KLM-Royal Dutch Airlines)
		Budapest (MALEV - Hungarian Airlines)

Master Frequency List

FREQ.	SERVICE	STATION/LOCATION
21976.0	SAM-LDOC	Caracas/Maiquetia (AVENSA)
		Lima (American Airlines)
		Montevideo (PLUNA)
		San Salvador
21977.0	EU-LDOC	Stockholm Radio
21979.0	EU-LDOC	Athens (Olympic Airlines)
	EU-LDOC	Frankfurt (Lufthansa)
	EU-LDOC	Larnaca (Cyprus Airways)
	MID-LDOC	Bombay (Air India)
21982.0	AFI-LDOC	Blantyre (Air Malawi)
		Cairo (Egypt Air)
		Dar es Salaam (Air Tanzania)
		Entebbe (Uganda Airlines)
		Kigali (Air Rwanda)
		Kinshasa (Air Zaire)
		Lagos (Nigeria Airways)
		Nairobi
	INO-LDOC	Antananarivo (Air Madagascar)
		Mauritius Ops (Air Mauritius)
	NCA-LDOC	Kabul (Ariana Afghan Airlines)
21985.0	CAR-LDOC	Boyeros (Cubana Airlines)
		Santo Domingo
		Willemstad (ALM Antillean)
	CWP-1/2 MWARA	Guam, Honolulu, Manila, Naha, Port Moresby, Seoul, Taipei, Tokyo
21988.0	AFI-LDOC	Lagos (Nigeria Airways)
	EU-LDOC	Berne ("Berna") Radio
21991.0	SAM-LDOC	Rio de Janeiro (VARIG)
		Santiago
21993.0	MID-LDOC	Damascus (Syrian Arab Airlines)
21994.0	AFI-LDOC	Tunis (Tunis Air)
	BRZ-AF	Brazilian Air Force
	MID-LDOC	Jeddah (Saudi Airlines)
		Safat (Kuwaiti Airlines)
21997.0	EU-LDOC	Stockholm Radio
22683.0	NASA	Cape Radio
22723.0	USAF-SAM	Mystic Star SAM Series B
22755.0	NASA	Cape Radio
22913.0	USAF-SAM	Mystic Star SAM Series A
22940.0	USAF-SAM	Mystic Star SAM Series G
22990.0	NASA	Cape Radio
23035.0	NASA	Ascension Radio, Cape Radio - Shuttle Missions
	USAF-SAM	Mystic Star SAM Series I
		Mystic Star SAM Series R
23040.0	EU-LDOC	Stockholm Radio
23070.0	SEA-CC-LDOC	Sydney SkyComms
23132.0	USAF-SAM	Mystic Star SAM Series O
23134.0	ITALY-AF	Italian Air Force - LDOC
23142.0	EU-CC-LDOC	Somerset (Portishead Radio)
23150.0	RNZAF	Whenuapai AFB
23177.0	USN	Air/Ground/Ship
23206.0	USAF-ACC	Air Combat Command, Secondary
23210.0	EU-CC-LDOC	Somerset (Portishead Radio)
	EU-LDOC	Stockholm Radio
	RNZAF	Whenuapai AFB
23214.0	US-Customs	COTHERN "Yankee Hotel " -Selscan 9
	US-DOD	Counterdrug Network "Yankee Hotel"
23220.0	RAF	Architect (Wx H+00, H+30), Cyprus Flight Watch
23221.0	USN	Air/Ground/Ship
23224.0	USN	Air/Ground/Ship
23225.0	EU-LDOC	Berlin/Schoenfield (Interflug)
23227.0	USN	Air/Ground/Ship
23230.0	MID-LDOC	Karachi (PIA-Pakistani International Airlines)
23242.0	USN	Air/Ground/Ship

FREQ.	SERVICE	STATION/LOCATION
23243.0	USAF-SAM	Mystic Star SAM Series G
23249.0	FAF	French Air Force Air/Ground
23250.0	CANFORCE	ATG - Edmonton Military, Trenton Military
23254.0	FAF	Eveux (French Air Force Air/Ground)
23264.0	USAF-ACC	Air Combat Command, Backup - West
23265.0	NORAD	NORAD
	USAF-USSTRATCOM	Former SAC "Giant Talk" Network "Xray 909"
23281.0	NASA	Cape Radio
	USN	Air/Ground/Ship
23284.0	USN	Air/Ground/Ship
23285.0	EU-LDOC	Berne ("Berna") Radio
23287.0	SAF-AF	South African Air Force
	US-JCS	United States Joint Chiefs of Staff Net
	USN	HICOM - Atlantic/Caribbean - Air/Ground/Ship
23290.0	USN	Air/Ground/Ship
23293.0	USN	Air/Ground/Ship
23303.0	USN	Air/Ground/Ship
23306.0	USN	Air/Ground/Ship
23307.0	MID-LDOC	Jeddah (Saudi Airlines)
23312.0	USN	Air/Ground/Ship
23315.0	USN	Air/Ground/Ship
23325.0	NASA	Cape Radio
23331.0	U.S. Flight Test	Grumman Aerospace
23332.5	U.S. Flight Test	Grumman Aerospace
23342.0	GAF	DHM91 Munster (German Air Force Air/Ground)
23397.0	USAF-SAM	Mystic Star SAM Series N
23402.5	US-DEA	OTH Radio System "Romeo"
23412.0	EU-CC-LDOC	Somerset (Portishead Radio)
23413.0	NASA	Cape Radio
23419.0	NORAD	NORAD
	USAF-ACC	Air Combat Command, Backup - East
23441.0	USAF-CEN	Commando Escort Net - Hawaii "Victor"
23442.0	USN	Air/Ground/Ship
23479.0	NASA	Cape Radio
23485.0	NASA	Cape Radio
23500.0	USN	Air/Ground/Ship
23643.0	USAF-SAM	Mystic Star SAM Series B
23661.0	NASA	Cape Radio
23675.0	US-DEA	OTH Radio System "India"
23687.0	USAF-SAM	Mystic Star SAM Series A
		Mystic Star SAM Series K
23689.0	USAF-CEN	Commando Escort Net - Hawaii "Whiskey"
23692.0	EU-LDOC	Brussels (Sabena)
23840.0	NASA	Cape Radio
23940.0	NASA	Cape Radio
24127.0	USAF-SAM	Mystic Star SAM Series Unassigned
24240.0	NASA	Cape Radio
24274.0	USAF-SAM	Mystic Star SAM Series B
24430.0	USN	Air/Ground/Ship
24483.0	USAF-SAM	Mystic Star SAM Series Q
24512.0	NASA	Cape Radio
24530.0	NASA	Cape Radio
24655.0	EU-CC-LDOC	Somerset (Portishead Radio)
24780.0	NASA	Cape Radio
24914.0	NASA	Cape Radio
24933.0	USAF-SAM	Mystic Star SAM Series G
25035.0	EU-LDOC	Stockholm Radio
25109.0	EU-CC-LDOC	Somerset (Portishead Radio)
25130.0	NASA	Cape Radio
	USAF-SAM	Mystic Star SAM Series I
		Mystic Star SAM Series R
25161.0	NASA	Cape Radio
25198.0	NASA	Cape Radio

Master Frequency List

FREQ.	SERVICE	STATION/LOCATION
25227.0	USAF-SAM	Mystic Star SAM Series O
25245.0	NASA	Cape Radio
25340.0	NORAD	NORAD
	USAF-ACC	Air Combat Command, Backup -West
25350.0	US-Customs	COTHERN "Yankee India" - Selscan 10
	US-DOD	Counterdrug Network "Yankee India"
25385.0	EU-LDOC	Stockholm Radio
25433.0	USAF-SAM	Mystic Star SAM Series G
25500.0	EU-LDOC	Berne ("Berna") Radio
25597.0	NASA	Cape Radio
26356.0	NASA	Cape Radio
26389.0	NASA	Cape Radio
26515.0	NASA	Cape Radio
	USAF-CEN	Commando Escort Net - Hawaii
26610.0	USN	Air/Ground/Ship
26615.0	USN	Air/Ground/Ship
26617.0	US-CAP	Civil Air Patrol
26620.0	US-CAP	CAP-USAF Frequency
26684.0	NASA	Cape Radio
26722.0	USN	Air/Ground/Ship
26725.0	USN	Air/Ground/Ship
26965.0	USN	Air/Ground/Ship
27065.0	NASA	Cape Radio
27218.0	EU-CC-LDOC	Somerset (Portishead Radio)
27575.0	US-FAA	U. S. Federal Aviation Administration
27585.0	US-FAA	U. S. Federal Aviation Administration
27625.0	US-FAA	U. S. Federal Aviation Administration
27665.0	US-FAA	U. S. Federal Aviation Administration
27720.0	NASA	Cape Radio
27870.0	US-DOD	Counterdrug Network "Victor Alpha"
28650.0	NASA	Goddard Space Center - Shuttle Rebroadcast

MWARA - Major World Air Route Areas

ICAO HF Enroute Networks

For the purposes of aeronautical radio communications, the world has been divided into specific regions known as Major World Air Route Areas (MWARA).

This section details the frequencies and stations to be found in each of the areas.

For the sake of clarity, stations that share a common geographical area have been grouped together.

The data and maps in this section are organized as follows:

North America	NAT-A NAT-B NAT-C NAT-D NAT-E NAT-F	**Indian Ocean**	INO-1
Caribbean	CAR-A CAR-B	**Middle East**	MID-1 MID-2 MID-3
South America	SAM-C SAM-NE SAM-NW SAM-SE SAM-SW	**North Central Asia**	EUR-A NCA-1 NCA-2 NCA-3
South Atlantic	SAT-1 SAT-2	**East Asia**	EA-1 EA2
Africa	AFI-1 AFI-2 AFI-3 AFI-4	**South East Asia**	SEA-1 SEA-2 SEA-3
		Pacific	CEP-1/2 CWP-1/2 NP-3/4 SP-6/7

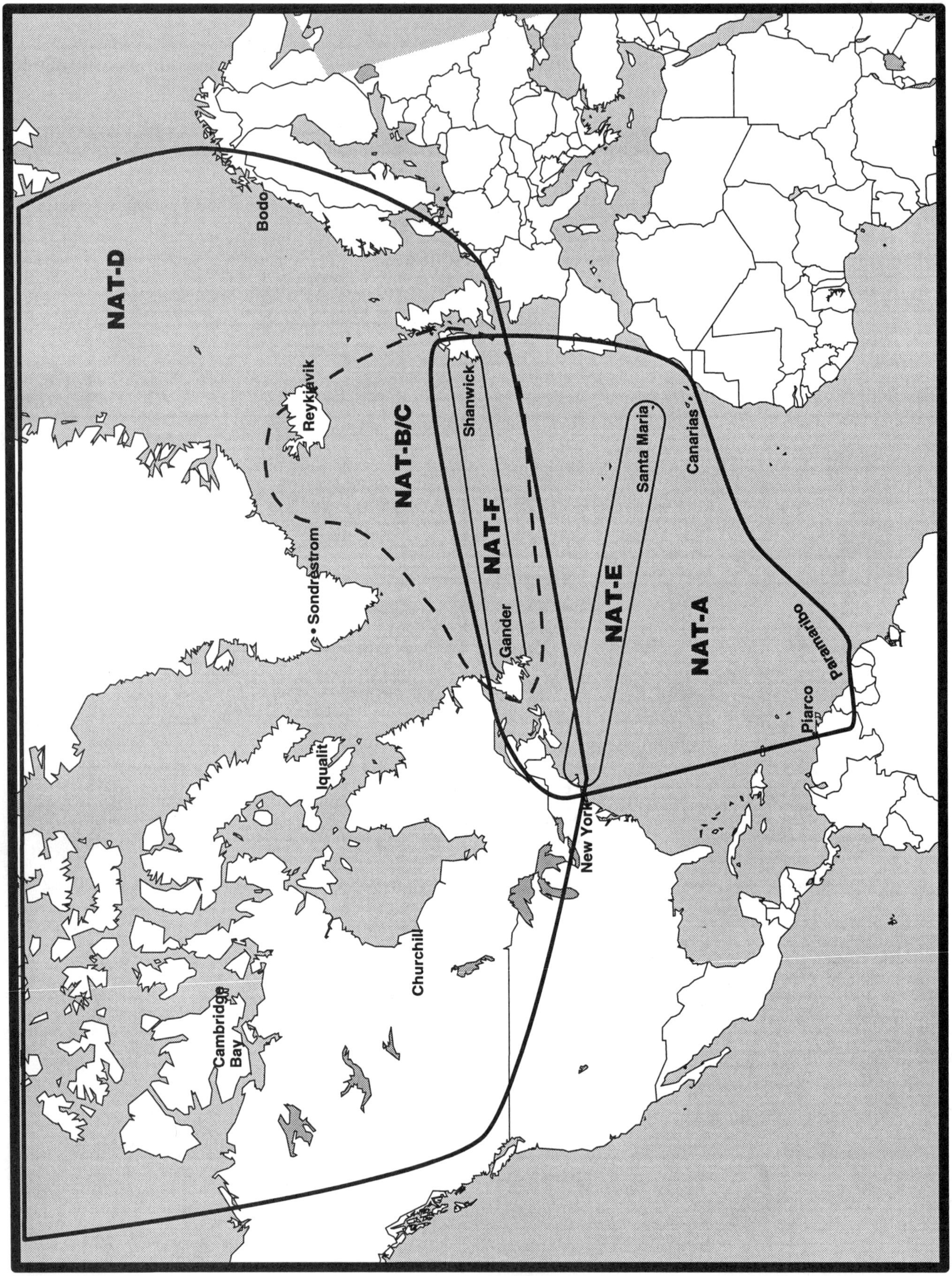
NAT-D
Bodo
Reykjavik
NAT-B/C
Shanwick
NAT-F
Sondrestrom
Gander
NAT-E
Santa Maria
Canarias
NAT-A
Paramaribo
Piarco
New York
Iqualit
Churchill
Cambridge Bay

NAT-A MWARA **North Atlantic Family A**

Ground stations and aircraft inflight across the south central part of the North Atlantic Ocean. Covers a vast, almost rectangular area of the North Atlantic bounded by Paramaribo, New York, Reykjavik and Canarias. Overlaps portions of all other NAT families.

3016.0 5598.0 8906.0 13306.0 17946.0

Canarias, Gander, New York, Paramaribo, Piarco, Santa Maria, Shanwick

NAT-B MWARA **North Atlantic Family B**

Ground stations and aircraft inflight across the North Atlantic Ocean for all aircraft registered west of 30 degrees west. (This includes all aircraft with North, Central and South American registry). Overlaps portions of the NAT-A, NAT-C and NAT-D areas.

2899.0 5616.0 8864.0 13291.0 17946.0

Gander, Iceland (Reykjavik), New York, Santa Maria, Shannon (Shanwick)

NAT-C MWARA **North Atlantic Family C**

Ground stations and aircraft inflight across the North Atlantic Ocean for all aircraft registered east of 30 degrees west. (This includes all aircraft with European, African and Middle Eastern registry). Overlaps portions of the NAT-A, NAT-B and NAT-D areas.

2862.0 5649.0 8879.0 13306.0 17946.0

Gander, Iceland (Reykjavik), Shannon (Shanwick)

NAT-D MWARA **North Atlantic Family D**

Ground stations and aircraft inflight across the most northern part of the North Atlantic Ocean including the north polar region. Overlaps portions of the NAT-A, NAT-B and NAT-C areas.

2971.0 4675.0 8891.0 11279.0 13291.0 17946.0

Bodo, Cambridge Bay, Churchill, Iqaluit (Frobisher Bay), Gander, Iceland (Reykjavik), Sondrestrom

NAT-E MWARA **North Atlantic Family E**

Ground stations and aircraft inflight in the corridor between New York and Santa Maria. This family was created as a result of USAF tactical support traffic during the Gulf War. This area falls within the larger NAT-A area.

2962.0 6628.0 8825.0 11309.0 13354.0

New York, Santa Maria

NAT-F MWARA **North Atlantic Family F**

Ground stations and aircraft inflight in the corridor between Gander and Shanwick. This area falls within the larger NAT-A and NAT-B/C areas.

3476.0 6622.0 8831.0 11336.0 13291.0

Gander, Shanwick

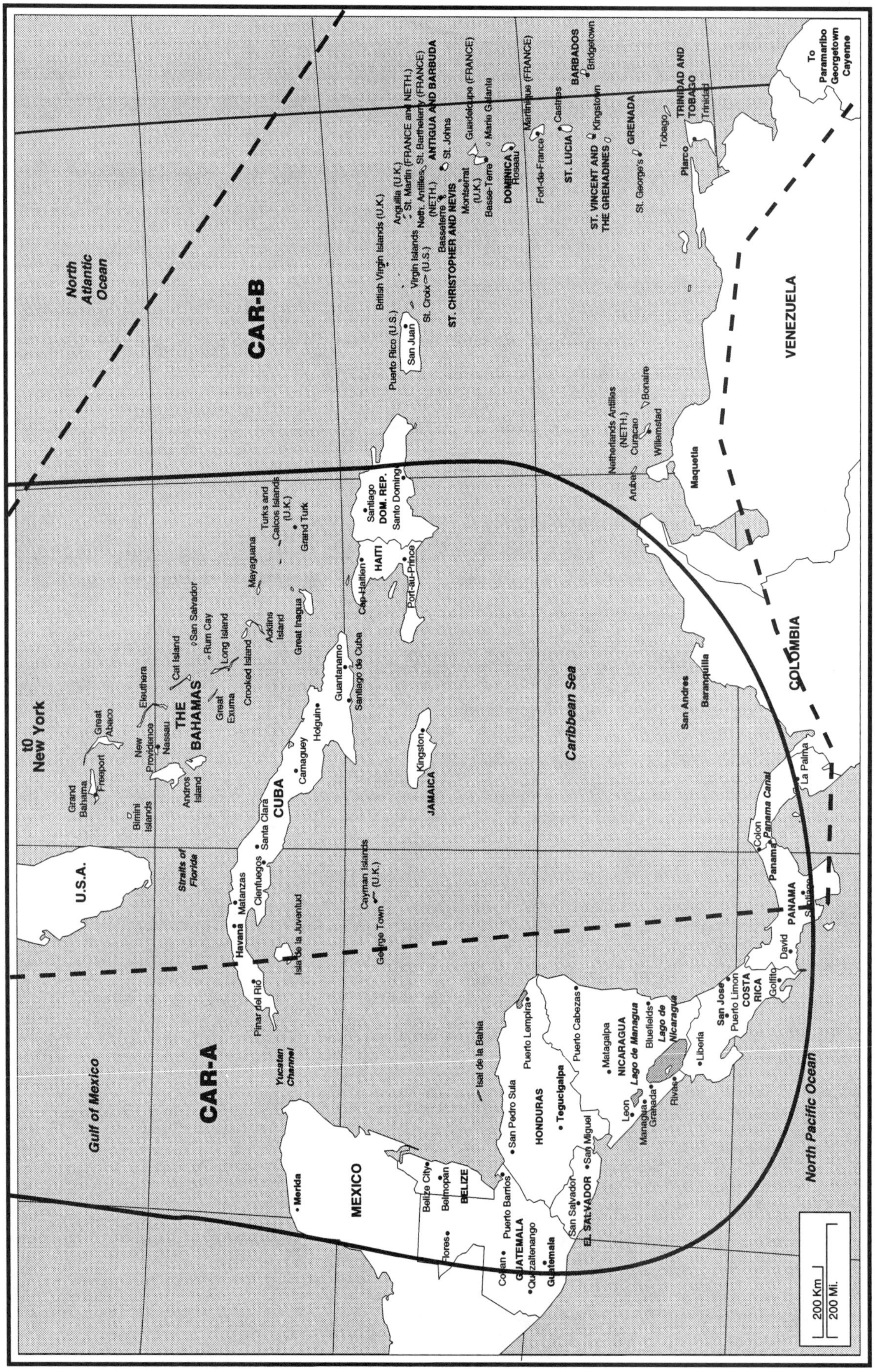
CAR-A
CAR-B
North Atlantic Ocean
Gulf of Mexico
Caribbean Sea
North Pacific Ocean
to New York
U.S.A.
Straits of Florida
Yucatan Channel
MEXICO
Merida
BELIZE
Belize City
Belmopan
Flores
GUATEMALA
Coban
Puerto Barrios
Quezaltenango
Guatemala
EL SALVADOR
San Salvador
San Miguel
HONDURAS
San Pedro Sula
Tegucigalpa
Puerto Lempira
Isla de la Bahia
NICARAGUA
Puerto Cabezas
Matagalpa
Leon
Managua
Granada
Rivas
Bluefields
Lago de Managua
Lago de Nicaragua
COSTA RICA
Liberia
San Jose
Puerto Limon
Golfito
PANAMA
David
Santiago
Panama
Colon
Panama Canal
La Palma
COLOMBIA
Barranquilla
San Andres
VENEZUELA
Maquetia
CUBA
Havana
Matanzas
Pinar del Rio
Cienfuegos
Santa Clara
Camaguey
Holguin
Guantanamo
Santiago de Cuba
Isla de la Juventud
Cayman Islands (U.K.)
George Town
JAMAICA
Kingston
THE BAHAMAS
Grand Bahama
Freeport
Great Abaco
Bimini Islands
Andros Island
New Providence
Nassau
Eleuthera
Cat Island
San Salvador
Rum Cay
Great Exuma
Long Island
Crooked Island
Adkins Island
Mayaguana
Great Inagua
Turks and Caicos Islands (U.K.)
Grand Turk
HAITI
Cap-Haitien
Port-au-Prince
DOM. REP.
Santiago
Santo Domingo
Puerto Rico (U.S.)
San Juan
British Virgin Islands (U.K.)
Virgin Islands
St. Croix (U.S.)
Anguilla (U.K.)
St. Martin (FRANCE and NETH.)
Neth. Antilles, St. Barthelemy (FRANCE)
(NETH.)
ANTIGUA AND BARBUDA
St. Johns
Basseterre
ST. CHRISTOPHER AND NEVIS
Montserrat (U.K.)
Guadeloupe (FRANCE)
Basse-Terre
Marie Galante
DOMINICA
Roseau
Martinique (FRANCE)
Fort-de-France
ST. LUCIA
Castries
BARBADOS
Bridgetown
ST. VINCENT AND THE GRENADINES
Kingstown
GRENADA
St. George's
Tobago
TRINIDAD AND TOBAGO
Trinidad
Piarco
Netherlands Antilles (NETH.)
Aruba
Curacao
Willemstad
Bonaire
To Paramaribo Georgetown Cayenne
200 Km
200 Mi.

CAR-A MWARA **Caribbean Area A**

Ground stations and aircraft inflight across southern Mexico, Central America and the north western Caribbean region of South America. Overlaps parts of the NAT-E and CAR-B areas.

2887.0 5550.0 6577.0 8918.0 11396.0 13297.0 17907.0

Barranquilla, Boyeros, Guatemala City, Merida, New York, Panama, Piarco, San Andres Is (Sesquicentenario), San José, Tegucigalpa (Toncontin Int'l)

CAR-B MWARA **Caribbean Area B**

Ground stations and aircraft inflight across the north west, central and eastern Caribbean regions of South America, including the north eastern part of South America. Overlaps parts of CAR-A, NAT-A and SAT-1 areas.

3455.0 5520.0 6586.0 8846.0 11330.0 17907.0

Barranquilla, Boyeros, Cayenne, Georgetown, Maiquetia, New York, Panama, Paramaribo, Piarco, San Andres Is

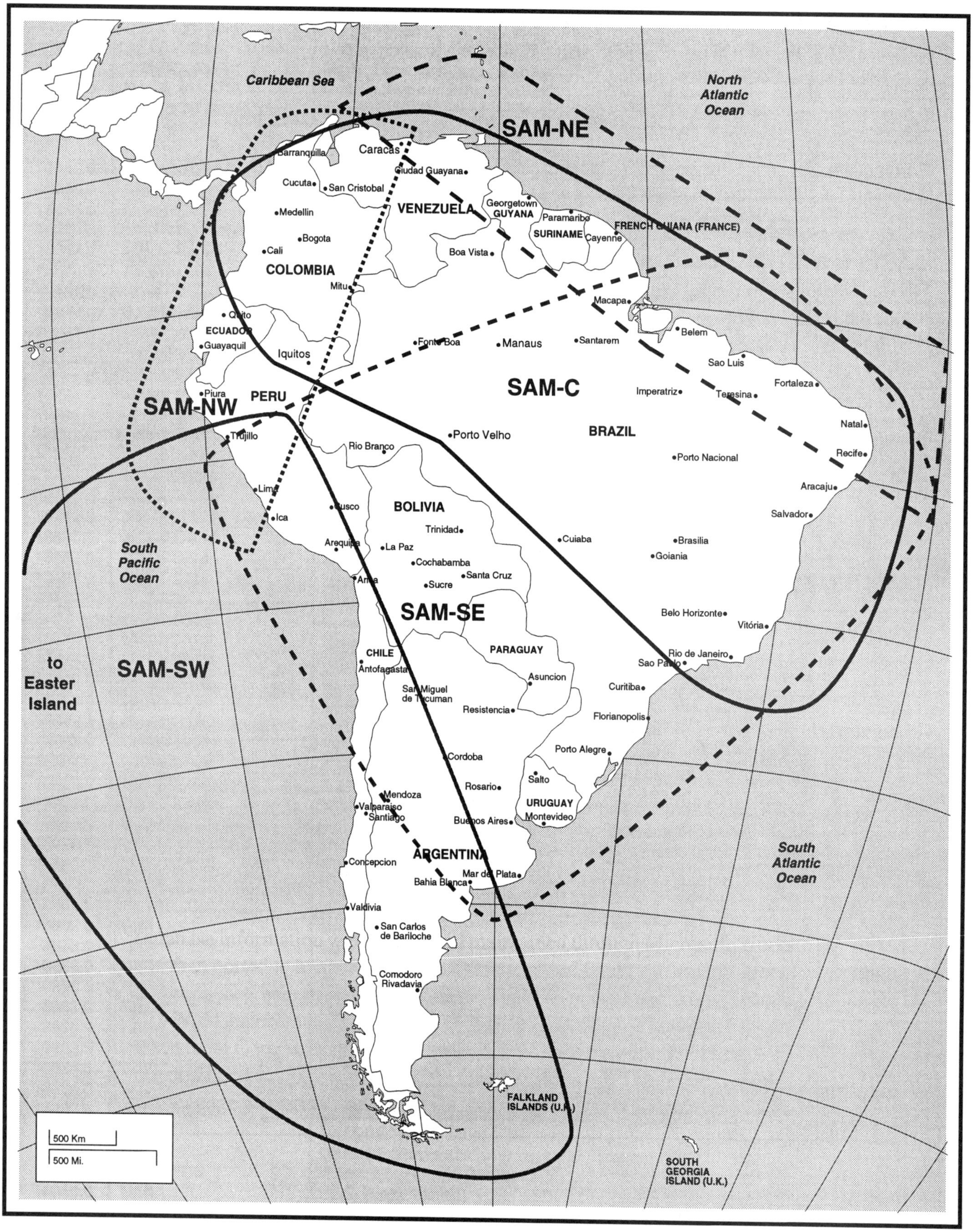
Caribbean Sea
North Atlantic Ocean
SAM-NE
SAM-C
SAM-NW
SAM-SE
SAM-SW
South Pacific Ocean
South Atlantic Ocean
to Easter Island
Barranquilla
Caracas
Ciudad Guayana
Cucuta
San Cristobal
Medellin
Bogota
Cali
COLOMBIA
Mitu
VENEZUELA
Georgetown
GUYANA
Paramaribo
SURINAME
Cayenne
FRENCH GUIANA (FRANCE)
Boa Vista
Macapa
Quito
ECUADOR
Guayaquil
Iquitos
Fonte Boa
Manaus
Santarem
Belem
Sao Luis
Fortaleza
Imperatriz
Teresina
Piura
PERU
Trujillo
Porto Velho
BRAZIL
Natal
Recife
Rio Branco
Porto Nacional
Aracaju
Lima
Cusco
BOLIVIA
Salvador
Ica
Trinidad
Cuiaba
Brasilia
Arequipa
La Paz
Goiania
Cochabamba
Santa Cruz
Arica
Sucre
Belo Horizonte
Vitória
PARAGUAY
Rio de Janeiro
CHILE
Sao Paulo
Antofagasta
Asuncion
San Miguel de Tucuman
Curitiba
Resistencia
Florianopolis
Porto Alegre
Cordoba
Salto
Rosario
Mendoza
URUGUAY
Valparaiso
Santiago
Buenos Aires
Montevideo
ARGENTINA
Concepcion
Mar del Plata
Bahia Blanca
Valdivia
San Carlos de Bariloche
Comodoro Rivadavia
FALKLAND ISLANDS (U.K.)
SOUTH GEORGIA ISLAND (U.K.)
500 Km
500 Mi.

SAM-C MWARA **South America Central Area**

Ground stations and aircraft inflight across the north central part of South America, including parts of Colombia, Peru, Venezuela and much of north central Brazil. Overlaps other SAM areas.

3479.0 5526.0 8855.0 10096.0 13297.0 17907.0

Belem, Bogota, Brasilia, Iquitos, Leticia, Manaus, Maiquetia, Porto Velho, Rio de Janeiro

SAM-NE MWARA **South America North Eastern Area**

Ground stations and aircraft inflight across the north eastern coastal regions of South America, including the coastal waters of Venezuela, French Guiana, Guyana, Surinam, Trinidad and Brazil. Overlaps other SAM areas.

3479.0 5526.0 8855.0 10096.0 13297.0 17907.0

Belem, Cayenne, Georgetown, Maiquetia, Paramaribo, Piarco, Recife

SAM-NW MWARA **South America North Western Area**

Ground stations and aircraft inflight across the north western section of South America. Overlaps other SAM areas.

2944.0 4669.0 6549.0 10024.0 11360.0 17907.0

Barranquilla, Bogota, Caracas (Maiquetia), Lima, Quito

SAM-SE MWARA **South America South Eastern Area**

Ground stations and aircraft inflight across the south eastern section of South America. Overlaps other SAM areas as well as SAT-1.

3479.0 5526.0 8855.0 10096.0 13297.0 17907.0

Asuncion, Belem, Brasilia, Buenos Aires, Campo Grande, Curtiba, La Paz, Montevideo, Lima, Porto Alegre, Porto Velho, Recife, Resistencia, Salvador (Dois De Julho), Santa Cruz

SAM-SW MWARA **South America South Western Area**

Ground stations and aircraft inflight across the south western portion of the South American continent. The western boundary encompasses Easter Island in the South Pacific.

2944.0 4669.0 6549.0 10024.0 11360.0 17907.0

Antofagasta, Asuncion, Bariloche, Buenos Aires (Ezeiza), Comodoro Rivadavia, Cordoba, Easter Is (Pascua), La Paz, Lima, Mendoza, Puerto Montt, Punta Arenas, Resistencia, Salta, Santa Cruz (El Trompillo), Santiago, Talara, Ushuaia

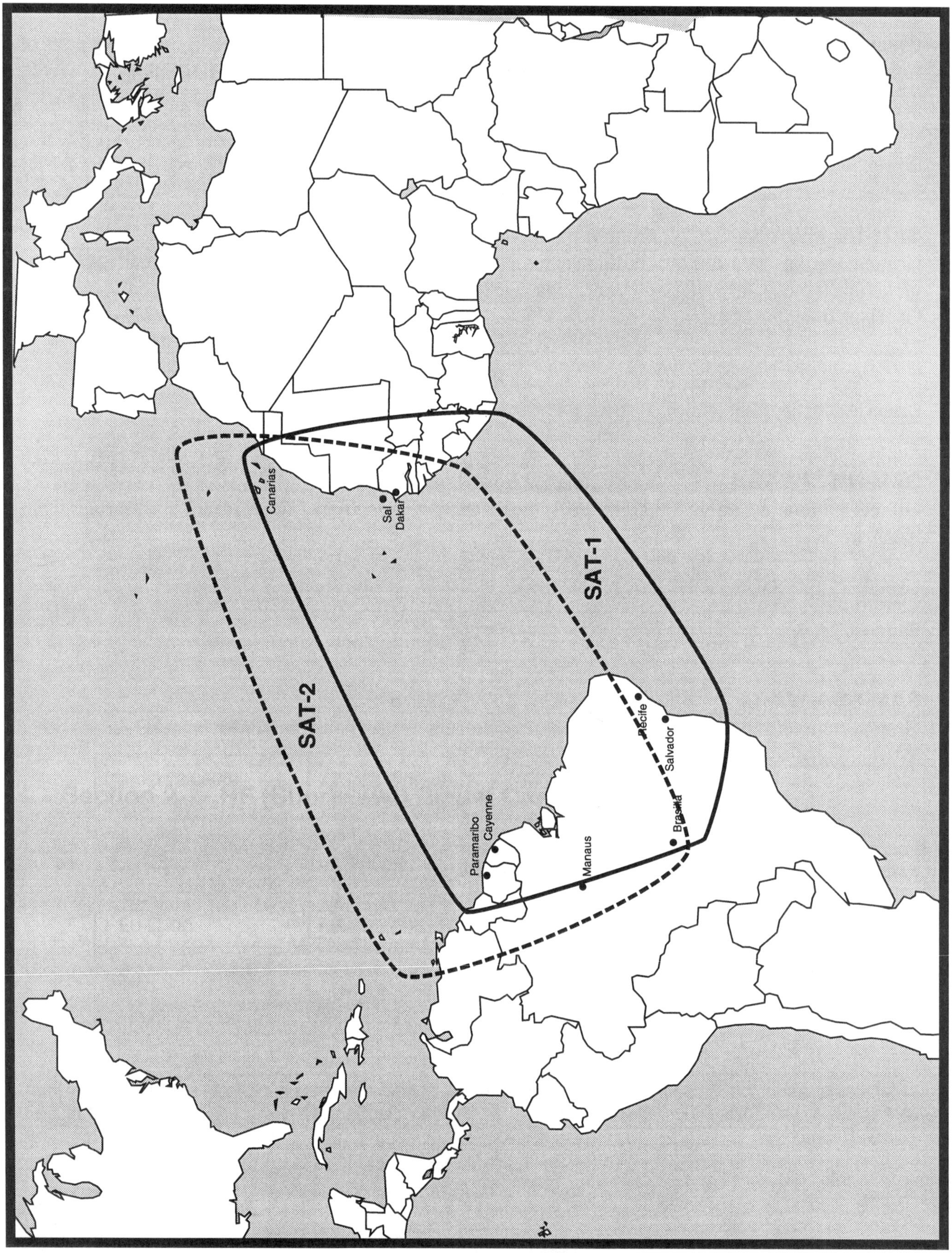
SAT-1
SAT-2
Canarias
Sal
Dakar
Recife
Salvador
Brasilia
Paramaribo
Cayenne
Manaus

SAT-1 MWARA — South Atlantic Area 1

Ground stations and aircraft inflight across the southern portion of the South Atlantic Ocean, from the coast of Brazil to the north west coast of Africa. Overlaps portions of the AFI-1, SAT-2 and SAM-SE areas.

3452.0 6535.0 8861.0 13357.0 17955.0

Brasilia, Canarias, Cayenne, Dakar, Manaus, Paramaribo, Recife, Rio de Janeiro, Sal Island, Salvador (Dois de Julho)

SAT-2 MWARA — South Atlantic Area 2

Ground stations and aircraft inflight across the northern portion of the South Atlantic Ocean, from the north eastern coast of South America to the north west coast of Africa. Overlaps portions of the AFI-1, SAT-1 and SAM-SE areas.

2854.0 5565.0 11291.0 13315.0 17955.0

Canarias, Cayenne, Dakar, Manaus, Paramaribo, Recife, Rio de Janeiro, Sal Island, Salvador (Dois de Julho)

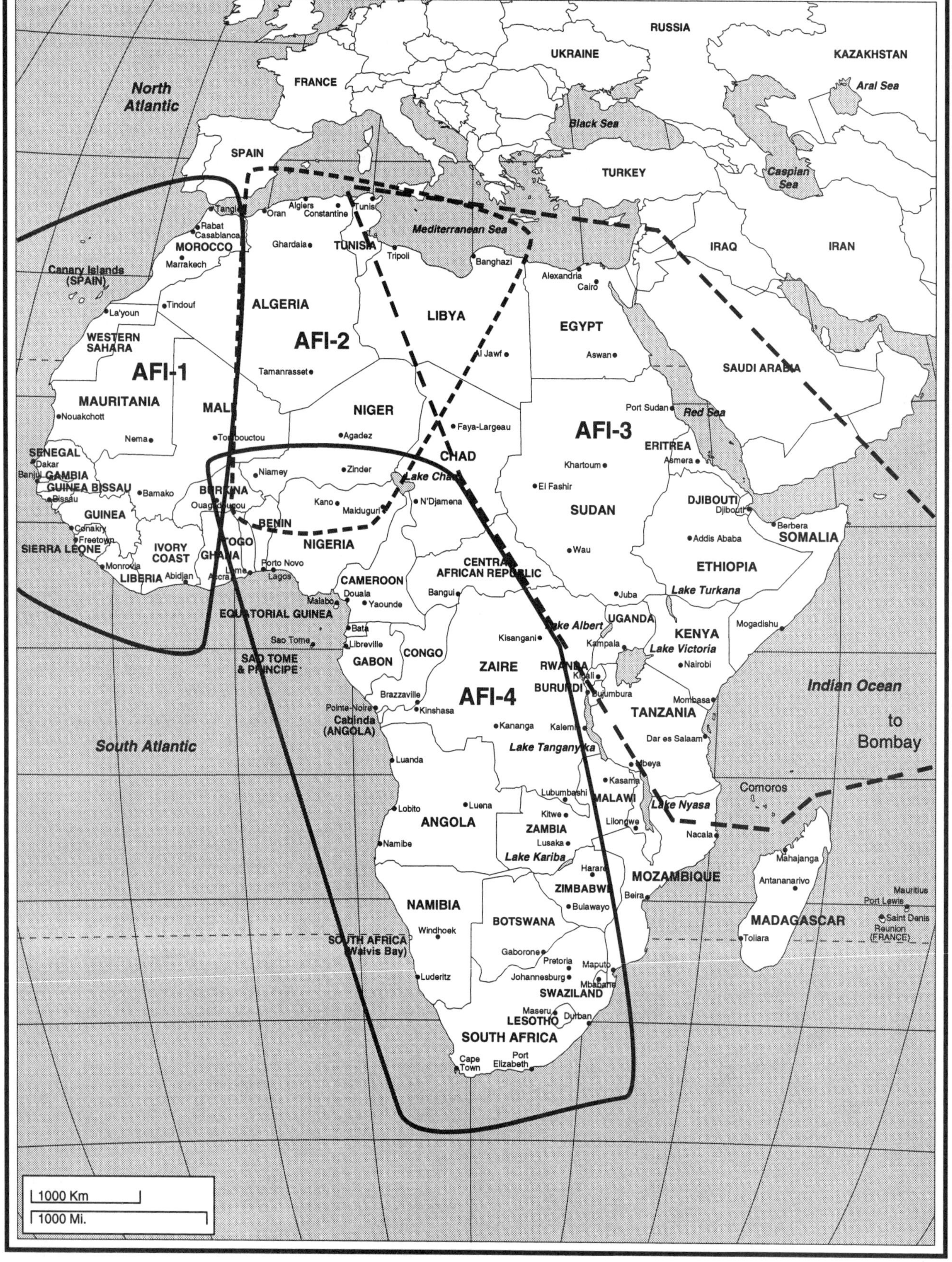
RUSSIA
UKRAINE
KAZAKHSTAN
Aral Sea
FRANCE
North Atlantic
Black Sea
SPAIN
TURKEY
Caspian Sea
Mediterranean Sea
IRAQ
IRAN
MOROCCO
ALGERIA
TUNISIA
LIBYA
EGYPT
SAUDI ARABIA
AFI-1
AFI-2
AFI-3
AFI-4
WESTERN SAHARA
MAURITANIA
MALI
NIGER
CHAD
SUDAN
ERITREA
Red Sea
SENEGAL
GAMBIA
GUINEA BISSAU
GUINEA
SIERRA LEONE
LIBERIA
IVORY COAST
GHANA
TOGO
BENIN
NIGERIA
CAMEROON
CENTRAL AFRICAN REPUBLIC
DJIBOUTI
SOMALIA
ETHIOPIA
Lake Turkana
UGANDA
KENYA
Lake Victoria
Lake Albert
EQUATORIAL GUINEA
SAO TOME & PRINCIPE
GABON
CONGO
ZAIRE
RWANDA
BURUNDI
TANZANIA
Lake Tanganyika
Indian Ocean
to Bombay
Cabinda (ANGOLA)
South Atlantic
ANGOLA
ZAMBIA
MALAWI
Lake Nyasa
Lake Kariba
Comoros
ZIMBABWE
MOZAMBIQUE
MADAGASCAR
NAMIBIA
BOTSWANA
SOUTH AFRICA (Walvis Bay)
SWAZILAND
LESOTHO
SOUTH AFRICA
Canary Islands (SPAIN)
Mauritius
Port Lewis
Saint Denis
Reunion (FRANCE)
1000 Km
1000 Mi.

AFI-1 MWARA **Africa Area 1**

Ground stations and aircraft inflight across the north eastern part of Africa. Overlaps parts of the AFI-2 and SAT-1 areas.

3452.0 6535.0 8861.0 13357.0 17955.0

Abidjan, Bamako, Bangui, Bissau, Bobo Dioulasso, Bouake, Casablanca, Conakry, Canarias, Dakar, Freetown, Kano, Niamey, Nouadhibou, Nouakchott, Ouagadougou, Roberts (Monrovia)

AFI-2 MWARA **Africa Area 2**

Ground stations and aircraft inflight across the north central portion of Africa. Overlaps parts of the AFI-3 and AFI-4 areas.

3419.0 5652.0 8894.0 13273.0 17961.0

Algiers, Brazzaville, Kano, Gao, Niamey, N'djamena, Tamanrasset, Timimoun, Tripoli, Tunis

AFI-3 MWARA **Africa Area 3**

Ground stations and aircraft inflight across the north and central western part of Africa including the eastern section of the Middle East, down to the Comoros and Seychelle islands in the Indian Ocean and across to Bombay. Overlaps parts of the MID-1 and INO-1 areas.

3467.0 5658.0 10018.0 11300.0 13288.0 17961.0

Addis Ababa, Aden, Asmara, Bahrain, Benghazi, Bombay, Bujumbura, Cairo, Comoros Is., Dar es Salaam, Entebbe, Hargesia, Djibouti, Jeddah, Khartoum, Kigali, Kisimayu, Male, Mogadishu, Nairobi, N'djamena, Sana'a, Seychelles, Triopli

AFI-4 MWARA **Africa Area 4**

Ground stations and aircraft inflight across the central and south eastern part of Africa. Overlaps parts of the SAT-1, AFI-2, AFI-3 and INO-1 areas.

2878.0 5493.0 8903.0 13294.0 17961.0

Accra, Bangui, Brazzaville, Bulawayo, Contonou, Douala, Entebbe, Franceville, Francistown, Garoua, Goma, Johannesburg, Kano, Kinshasa, Kisangani, Lagos, Libreville, Lome, Luanda, Lumbumbashi, Lusaka, Maroua, Maseru, Nairobi, N'djamena, N'djili, Niamey, Niamtougou, Port Gentil, Roberts (Monrovia), Salisbury, Salazar, Seychelles, Windhoek, Yaounde

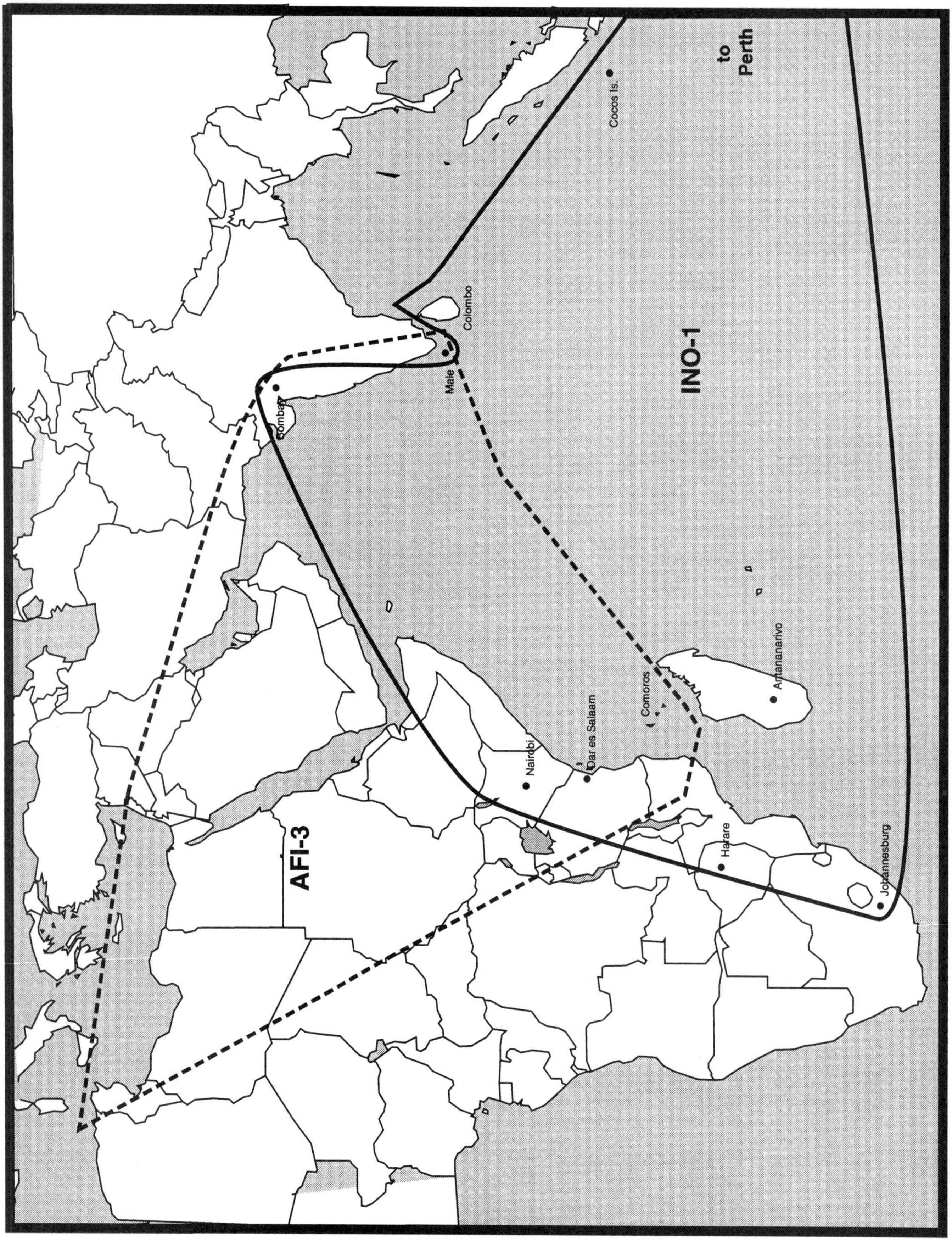
to
Perth
Cocos Is.
Colombo
Male
Bombay
INO-1
Antananarivo
Comoros
Dar es Salaam
Nairobi
Harare
Johannesburg
AFI-3

INO-1 MWARA **Indian Ocean Area 1**

Ground stations and aircraft inflight across the broad expanse of the Indian Ocean, stretching from the central and south eastern coast of Africa across to the western coasts of India and Australia. Overlaps portions of the AFI-3 and SEA-1 areas.

3476.0 5634.0 8879.0 13306.0 17961.0

Antananarivo, Beira, Blantyre, Bombay, Cocos Is., Colombo, Dar es Salaam, Harare, Jeddah, Johannesburg, Kigali, Lilongwe, Lusaka, Madras, Mahajanga, Male, Mauritius, Moroni, Nairobi, Perth, Seychelles, St. Denis, Toamasina

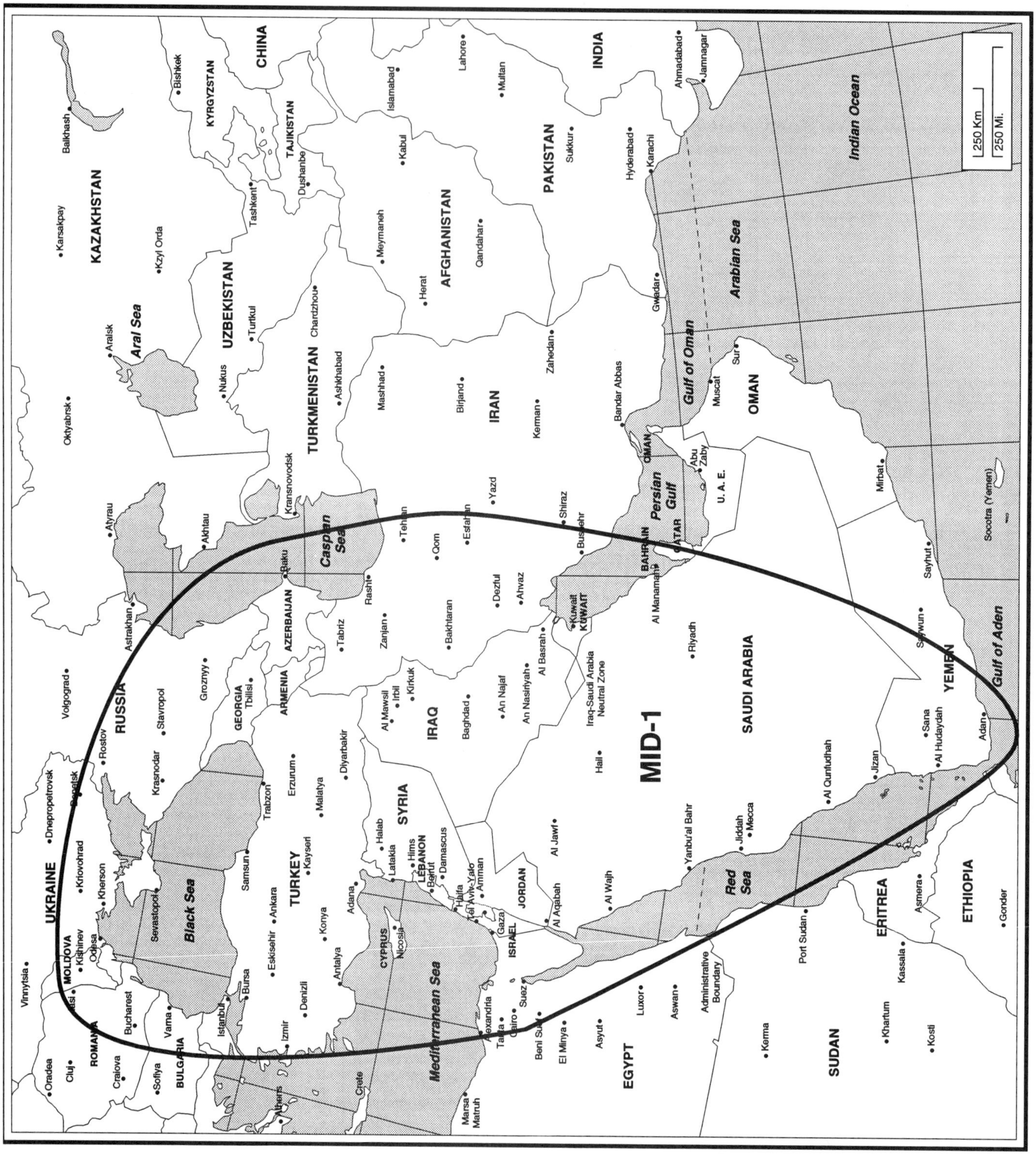
MID-1
KAZAKHSTAN
UZBEKISTAN
TURKMENISTAN
KYRGYZSTAN
TAJIKISTAN
CHINA
AFGHANISTAN
PAKISTAN
INDIA
IRAN
IRAQ
SYRIA
LEBANON
JORDAN
ISRAEL
TURKEY
GEORGIA
ARMENIA
AZERBAIJAN
RUSSIA
UKRAINE
MOLDOVA
ROMANIA
BULGARIA
CYPRUS
EGYPT
SUDAN
ERITREA
ETHIOPIA
SAUDI ARABIA
YEMEN
OMAN
U. A. E.
QATAR
BAHRAIN
KUWAIT
Aral Sea
Caspian Sea
Black Sea
Mediterranean Sea
Red Sea
Persian Gulf
Gulf of Oman
Arabian Sea
Gulf of Aden
Indian Ocean
Iraq-Saudi Arabia Neutral Zone
Administrative Boundary
Socotra (Yemen)
250 Km
250 Mi.
Balkhash
Karsakpay
Oktyabrsk
Aralsk
Atyrau
Akhtau
Kzyl Orda
Bishkek
Tashkent
Dushanbe
Nukus
Turtkul
Chardzhou
Ashkhabad
Kransnovodsk
Baku
Astrakhan
Volgograd
Rostov
Donetsk
Dnepropetrovsk
Krivohrad
Kherson
Odesa
Kishinev
Vinnytsia
Iasi
Bucharest
Varna
Cluj
Oradea
Craiova
Sofiya
Sevastopol
Krasnodar
Stavropol
Groznyy
Tbilisi
Trabzon
Samsun
Erzurum
Malatya
Diyarbakir
Kayseri
Ankara
Eskisehir
Bursa
Istanbul
Izmir
Denizli
Antalya
Konya
Adana
Halab
Latakia
Hims
Beirut
Damascus
Haifa
Tel Aviv-Yafo
Amman
Gaza
Nicosia
Athens
Crete
Marsa Matruh
Alexandria
Tanta
Cairo
Suez
Beni Suef
El Minya
Asyut
Luxor
Aswan
Kerma
Khartum
Kosti
Kassala
Asmera
Gonder
Port Sudan
Al Aqabah
Al Wajh
Al Jawf
Hail
Yanbu'al Bahr
Jiddah
Mecca
Al Qunfudhah
Jizan
Sana
Al Hudaydah
Adan
Sayhut
Saywun
Mirbat
Riyadh
Al Manamah
Abu Zaby
Muscat
Sur
Tabriz
Zanjan
Rasht
Tehran
Qom
Esfahan
Bakhtaran
Dezful
Ahvaz
Yazd
Shiraz
Bushehr
Kerman
Birjand
Mashhad
Zahedan
Bandar Abbas
Al Mawsil
Irbil
Kirkuk
Baghdad
An Najaf
An Nasiriyah
Al Basrah
Kuwait
Herat
Meymaneh
Kabul
Qandahar
Islamabad
Lahore
Multan
Sukkur
Hyderabad
Karachi
Gwadar
Ahmadabad
Jamnagar

MID-1 MWARA **Middle East Area 1**

Ground stations and aircraft inflight across the north eastern part of Africa and the Saudi Arabian peninsula, including portions of the Ukraine. Overlaps part of the AFI-3 area.

2992.0 4669.0 5667.0 6631.0 8951.0 11375.0 17961.0

Aden, Amman, Ankara, Baghdad, Basrah, Beirut, Cairo, Damascus, Jeddah, Kuwait, Manama, Odessa, Sanaa, Simferopol, Tehran, Tbilisi, Yerevan

See next page for MID-2 and MID-3

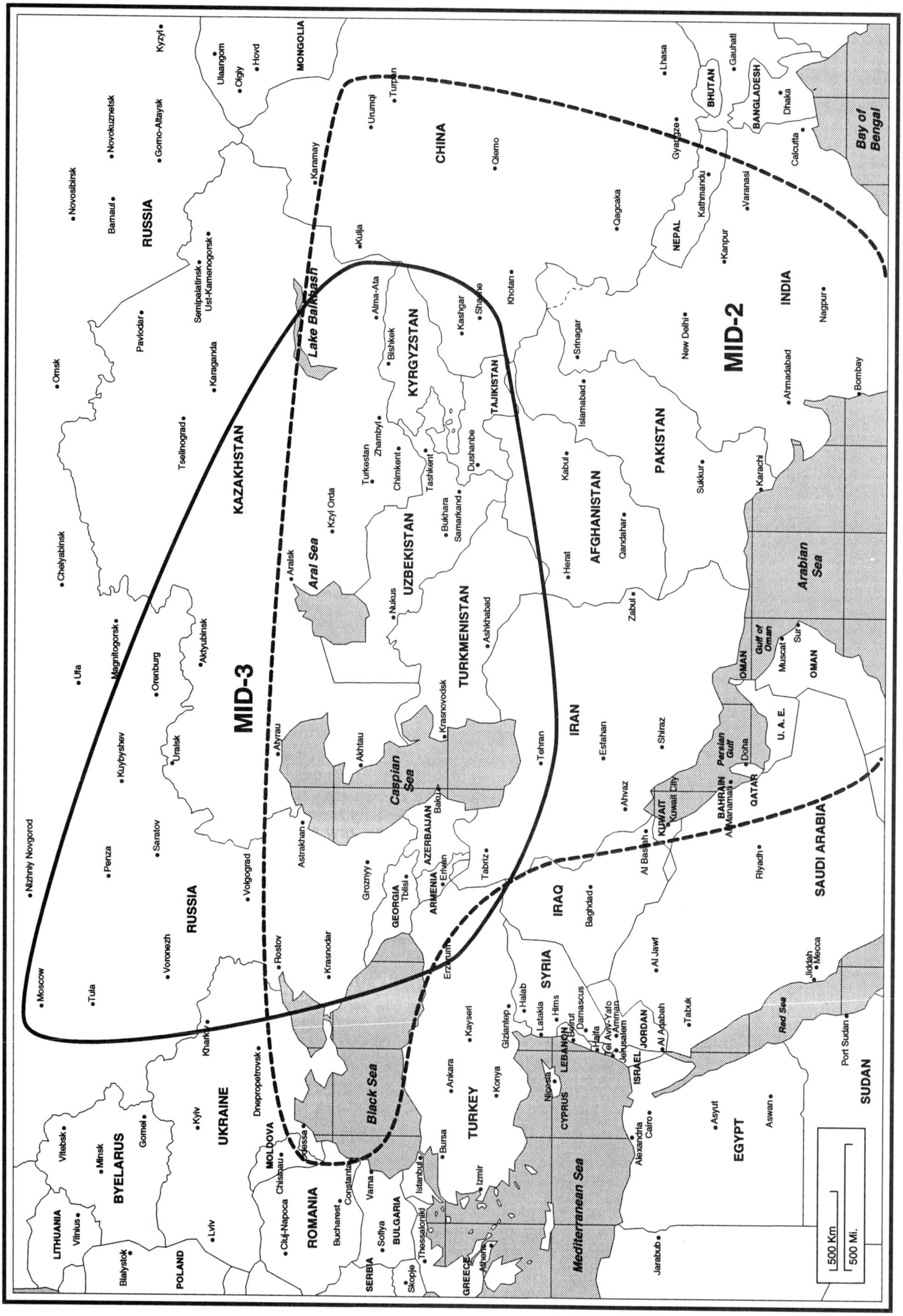
MID-3
MID-2
RUSSIA
KAZAKHSTAN
UZBEKISTAN
TURKMENISTAN
KYRGYZSTAN
TAJIKISTAN
CHINA
MONGOLIA
AFGHANISTAN
PAKISTAN
INDIA
NEPAL
BHUTAN
BANGLADESH
IRAN
IRAQ
SYRIA
LEBANON
ISRAEL
JORDAN
KUWAIT
BAHRAIN
QATAR
U. A. E.
OMAN
SAUDI ARABIA
EGYPT
SUDAN
TURKEY
CYPRUS
GREECE
BULGARIA
ROMANIA
MOLDOVA
UKRAINE
BYELARUS
LITHUANIA
POLAND
SERBIA
GEORGIA
ARMENIA
AZERBAIJAN
Caspian Sea
Aral Sea
Lake Balkhash
Black Sea
Mediterranean Sea
Red Sea
Persian Gulf
Gulf of Oman
Arabian Sea
Bay of Bengal
Moscow
Tula
Voronezh
Nizhniy Novgorod
Penza
Saratov
Volgograd
Rostov
Krasnodar
Astrakhan
Grozny
Kuybyshev
Uralsk
Ufa
Orenburg
Magnitogorsk
Aktyubinsk
Chelyabinsk
Tselinograd
Omsk
Karaganda
Pavlodar
Semipalatinsk
Ust-Kamenogorsk
Novosibirsk
Barnaul
Novokuznetsk
Gorno-Altaysk
Kyzyl
Ulaangom
Olgiy
Hovd
Karamay
Urumqi
Turpan
Qiemo
Kulja
Alma-Ata
Bishkek
Zhambyl
Turkestan
Chimkent
Tashkent
Dushanbe
Kashgar
Shache
Khotan
Kzyl Orda
Aralsk
Nukus
Bukhara
Samarkand
Ashkhabad
Krasnovodsk
Atyrau
Akhtau
Baku
Tbilisi
Erivan
Tabriz
Tehran
Esfahan
Shiraz
Ahvaz
Herat
Kabul
Qandahar
Zabul
Islamabad
Srinagar
Sukkur
Karachi
New Delhi
Ahmadabad
Bombay
Nagpur
Kanpur
Varanasi
Kathmandu
Qagcaka
Gyangze
Lhasa
Gauhati
Dhaka
Calcutta
Muscat
Sur
Doha
Manama
Kuwait City
Al Basrah
Riyadh
Baghdad
Al Jawf
Jiddah
Mecca
Tabuk
Al Aqabah
Amman
Jerusalem
Tel Aviv-Yafo
Haifa
Beirut
Damascus
Hims
Latakia
Halab
Gaziantep
Kayseri
Erzurum
Ankara
Konya
Bursa
Izmir
Istanbul
Nicosia
Alexandria
Cairo
Asyut
Aswan
Port Sudan
Jarabub
Athens
Thessaloniki
Skopje
Sofiya
Varna
Constanta
Bucharest
Cluj-Napoca
Chisinau
Odessa
Dnepropetrovsk
Kharkov
Kyiv
Gomel
Minsk
Vitebsk
Vilnius
Bialystok
Lviv
500 Km
500 Mi.

MID-2 MWARA **Middle East Area 2**

Ground stations and aircraft inflight across the north eastern part of the Middle East, including Iran , Nepal, southern parts of the former Soviet Union, and the north eastern portions of China, India and Pakistan. Boundary changes made in 1993 now encompass Male and the Seychelles in the south. Overlaps portions of the SEA-1 and AFI-3 areas.

3467.0 5658.0 10018.0 11300.0 13288.0 17961.0

Abadan, Alma Ata, Bombay, Delhi, Dushanbe, Frunze, Kabul, Karachi, Kathmandu, Kuwait, Lahore, Male, Muscat, Odessa, Samarkand, Seychelles, Tashkent, Tehran, Tbilisi, Urumqi, Yerevan

MID-3 MWARA **Middle East Area 3**

Ground stations and aircraft inflight across the north eastern part of Russia, bounded by Moscow in the north, Alma Ata in the east and Kabul in the south. Overlaps portions of the NCA-1 and MID-2 areas.

2944.0 4669.0 6631.0 8951.0 11375.0 17961.0

Aktyubinsk, Alma Ata, Dushanbe, Frunze, Kuybyshev, Kzyl-Orda, Moscow, Samarkand, Tashkent, Uralsk, Yerevan

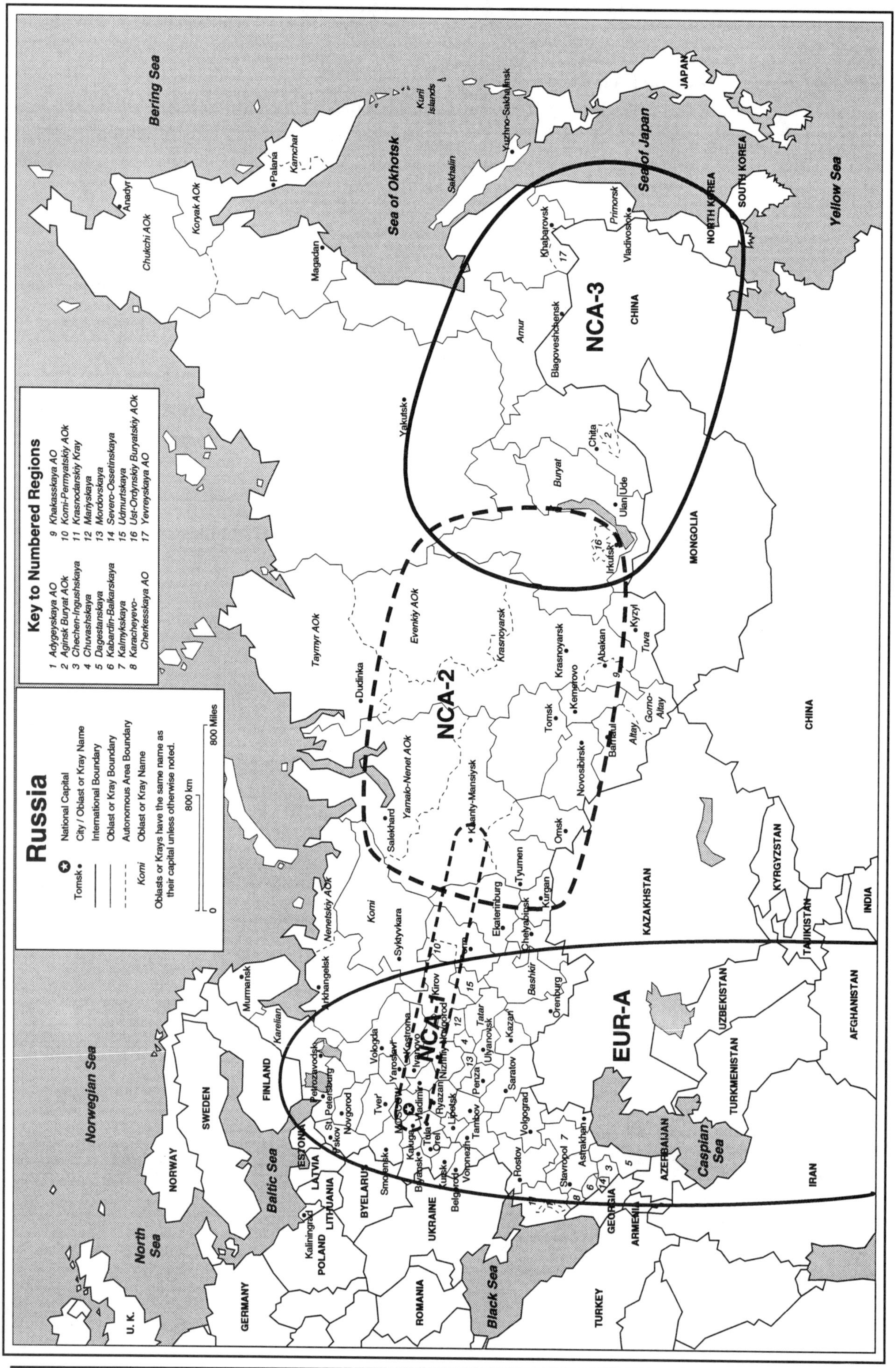
Russia
National Capital
Tomsk • City / Oblast or Kray Name
International Boundary
Oblast or Kray Boundary
Autonomous Area Boundary
Komi Oblast or Kray Name
Oblasts or Krays have the same name as their capital unless otherwise noted.
0
800 km
800 Miles
Key to Numbered Regions
1 Adygeyskaya AO
2 Aginsk Buryat AOk
3 Chechen-Ingushskaya
4 Chuvashskaya
5 Dagestanskaya
6 Kabardin-Balkarskaya
7 Kalmykskaya
8 Karacheyevo-Cherkesskaya AO
9 Khakasskaya AO
10 Komi-Permyatskiy AOk
11 Krasnodarskiy Kray
12 Mariyskaya
13 Mordovskaya
14 Severo-Osetinskaya
15 Udmurtskaya
16 Ust-Ordynskiy Buryatskiy AOk
17 Yevreyskaya AO
NCA-1
NCA-2
NCA-3
EUR-A
Bering Sea
Sea of Okhotsk
Sea of Japan
Yellow Sea
Norwegian Sea
North Sea
Baltic Sea
Black Sea
Caspian Sea
JAPAN
NORTH KOREA
SOUTH KOREA
CHINA
MONGOLIA
KAZAKHSTAN
KYRGYZSTAN
TAJIKISTAN
INDIA
UZBEKISTAN
TURKMENISTAN
AFGHANISTAN
IRAN
AZERBAIJAN
ARMENIA
GEORGIA
TURKEY
UKRAINE
BYELARUS
ROMANIA
POLAND
LITHUANIA
LATVIA
ESTONIA
FINLAND
SWEDEN
NORWAY
GERMANY
U. K.
Chukchi AOk
Koryak AOk
Magadan
Anadyr
Palana
Kamchat
Kuril Islands
Sakhalin
Yuzhno-Sakhalinsk
Khabarovsk
Primorsk
Vladivostok
Amur
Blagoveshchensk
Yakutsk
Chita
Buryat
Ulan Ude
Irkutsk
Kyzyl
Tuva
Abakan
Krasnoyarsk
Evenkiy AOk
Taymyr AOk
Dudinka
Kemerovo
Tomsk
Novosibirsk
Barnaul
Altay
Gorno-Altay
Omsk
Yamalo-Nenet AOk
Salekhard
Khanty-Mansiysk
Tyumen
Kurgan
Ekaterinburg
Chelyabinsk
Nenetskiy AOk
Komi
Syktyvkara
Arkhangelsk
Murmansk
Karelian
Petrozavodsk
St. Petersburg
Novgorod
Pskov
Tver'
Vologda
Yaroslavl'
Kostroma
Ivanovo
Vladimir
Moscow
Kirov
Nizhniy Novgorod
Tatar
Kazan'
Ulyanovsk
Bashkir
Orenburg
Saratov
Penza
Ryazan
Tula
Kaluga
Orel
Lipetsk
Tambov
Smolensk
Bryansk
Kursk
Belgorod
Voronezh
Volgograd
Rostov
Astrakhan
Stavropol
Kaliningrad

MWARA - Major World Air Route Areas

EUR-A MWARA **Europe Area A**

Ground stations and aircraft inflight across the eastern portions of the former Soviet Union stretching down into the Middle East region. Note that due to their geographical proximity, the countries of western and central Europe (commonly referred to as "the continent") use only VHF for aeronautical traffic control. Overlaps portions of the NCA-1, MID-1 and MID-2 regions

3479.0 5661.0 6598.0 10084.0 13288.0 17961.0

Arkhangelsk, Beirut, Berlin, Kiev, Lvov, Minsk, Moscow, Murmansk, Odessa, Riga, Simferopol, Sofia, St. Petersburg, Syktyvkar, Tunis, Valetta, Velikiye, Vitebsk, Vilnius, Vologda

NCA-1 MWARA **North Central Asia Area 1**

Ground stations and aircraft inflight across the narrow corridor between Moscow and Khanty Mansiysk in north eastern Russia. Overlaps portions of the NCA-2 and NCA-3 areas.

3019.0 5646.0 13315.0 17958.0

Ivdel, Khanty Mansiysk, Moscow, Syktyvkar, Sverdlovsk, Vologda

NCA-2 MWARA **North Central Asia Area 2**

Ground stations and aircraft inflight across the north central part of Russia. Overlaps portions of the NCA-1 and NCA-3 areas.

2851.0 4678.0 6592.0 10096.0 17958.0

Barnaul, Irkutsk, Khanty Mansiysk, Kirensk, Kolpashevo, Krasnoyarsk, Novosibirsk, Podkamennaya, Surgut, Yeniseysk

NCA-3 MWARA **North Central Asia Area 3**

Ground stations and aircraft inflight across the north eastern part of Russia and China, Korea and Mongolia. Overlaps portions of the NCA-2 and EA-1 areas.

3004.0 5664.0 10039.0 13303.0 17958.0

Chita, Chulman, Ekimchan, Irkutsk, Kirensk, Khabarovsk, Pyongyang, Ulaanbaatar, Ulan Ude

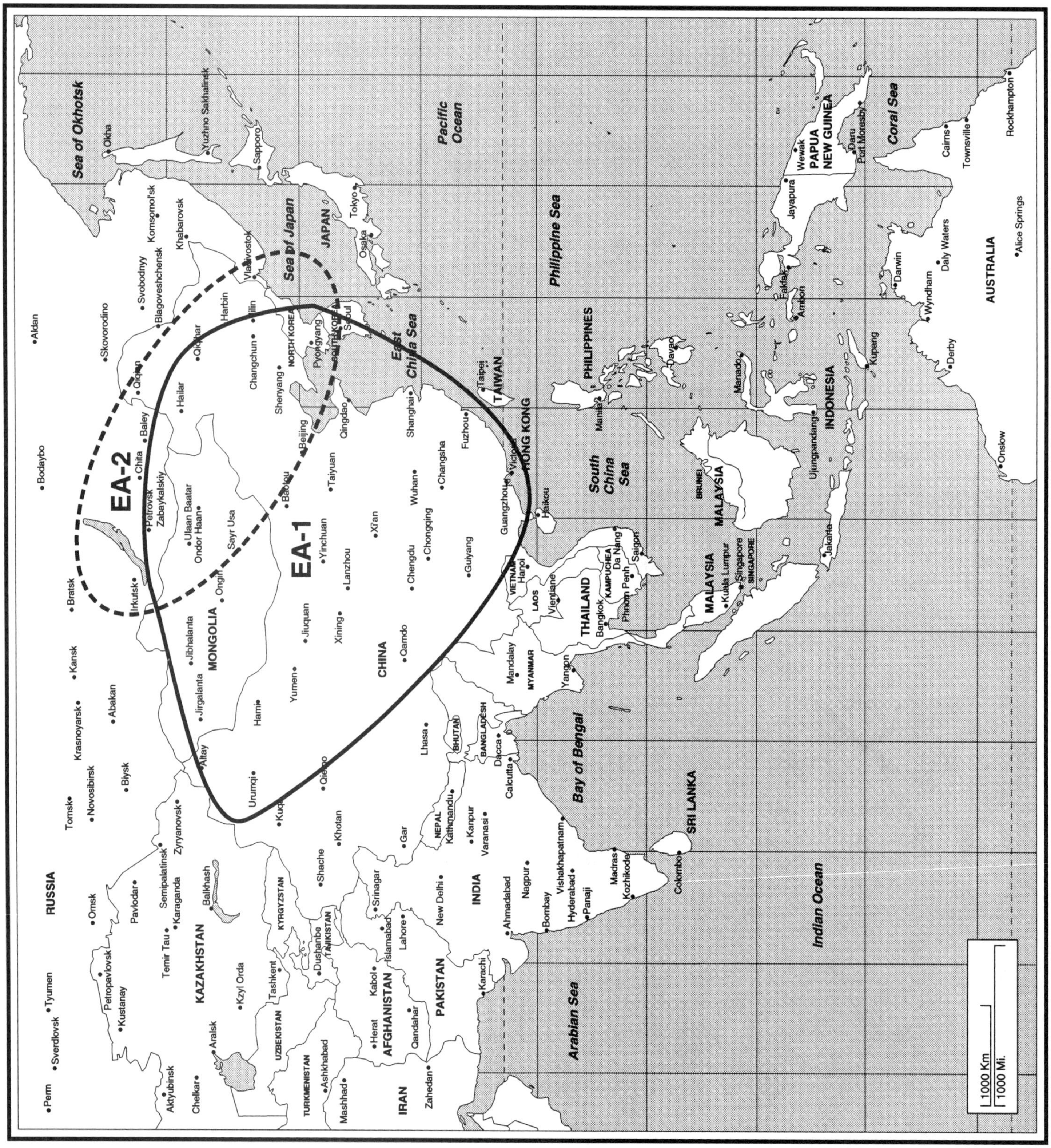
EA-1
EA-2
RUSSIA
KAZAKHSTAN
MONGOLIA
CHINA
JAPAN
NORTH KOREA
SOUTH KOREA
TAIWAN
HONG KONG
PHILIPPINES
VIETNAM
LAOS
KAMPUCHEA
THAILAND
MYANMAR
MALAYSIA
BRUNEI
SINGAPORE
INDONESIA
PAPUA NEW GUINEA
AUSTRALIA
INDIA
NEPAL
BHUTAN
BANGLADESH
SRI LANKA
PAKISTAN
AFGHANISTAN
IRAN
TURKMENISTAN
UZBEKISTAN
KYRGYZSTAN
TAJIKISTAN
Sea of Okhotsk
Sea of Japan
East China Sea
South China Sea
Philippine Sea
Pacific Ocean
Coral Sea
Bay of Bengal
Arabian Sea
Indian Ocean
1000 Km
1000 Mi.

MWARA - Major World Air Route Areas

EA-1 MWARA **East Asia Area 1**

Ground stations and aircraft inflight across the eastern portions of Mongolia and mainland China, Korea and Hong Kong. Overlaps parts of the EA-2, NCA-2 and NCA-3 areas.

3016.0 6571.0 8897.0 10042.0 17958.0

Beijing, Canton, Hailar, Irkutsk, Jinan, Kunming, Lanzhou, Pyongyang, Shanghai, Shenyang, Taegu, Ulaanbaatar, Urumqi, Wuhan, Zhengzhou

EA-2 MWARA **East Asia Area 2**

Ground stations and aircraft inflight across the narrow corridor between Irkutsk and Pyongyang. Overlaps portions of the EA-1 and NCA-3 areas.

3485.0 5649.0 5655.0 8942.0 11396.0 13309.0 17907.0

Canton, Irkutsk, Pyongyang, Ulaanbaatar

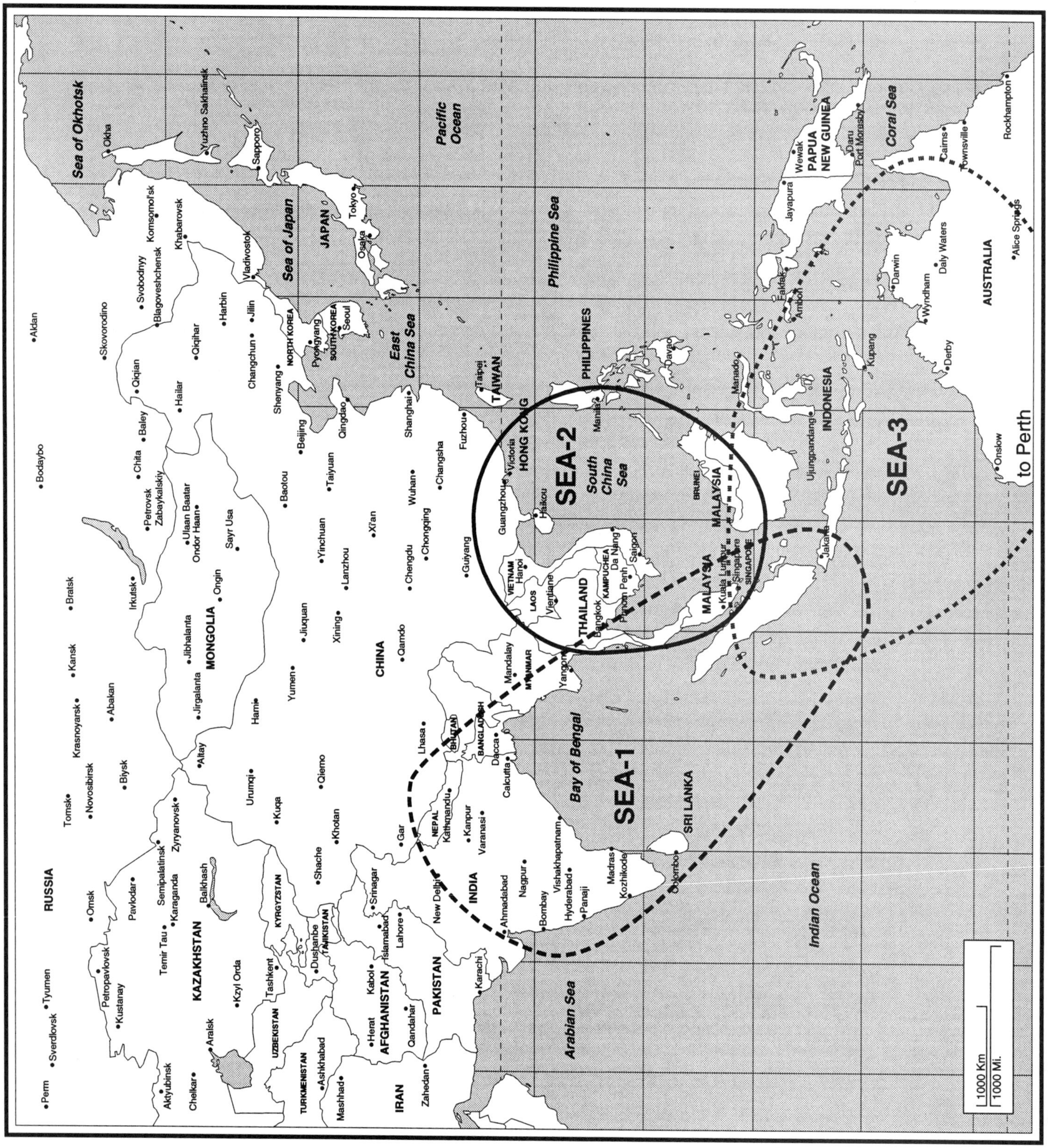
SEA-1
SEA-2
SEA-3
to Perth
Sea of Okhotsk
Pacific Ocean
Sea of Japan
East China Sea
Philippine Sea
South China Sea
Bay of Bengal
Arabian Sea
Indian Ocean
Coral Sea
RUSSIA
KAZAKHSTAN
MONGOLIA
CHINA
JAPAN
NORTH KOREA
SOUTH KOREA
TAIWAN
HONG KONG
PHILIPPINES
VIETNAM
LAOS
THAILAND
KAMPUCHEA
MYANMAR
MALAYSIA
BRUNEI
SINGAPORE
INDONESIA
PAPUA NEW GUINEA
AUSTRALIA
INDIA
NEPAL
BHUTAN
BANGLADESH
SRI LANKA
PAKISTAN
AFGHANISTAN
IRAN
TURKMENISTAN
UZBEKISTAN
KYRGYZSTAN
TAJIKISTAN
1000 Km
1000 Mi.

SEA-1 MWARA **South East Asia Area 1**

Ground stations and aircraft inflight across the south east Asian region of China, Thailand, Singapore, India, Myanmar and Malaysia. Overlaps portions of the EA-1, SEA-2 and INO-1 areas.

3470.0 6556.0 10066.0 13318.0 17907.0

Bali, Bangkok, Colombo, Calcutta, Dhaka, Guangzhou, Jakarta, Kathmandu, Kuala Lumpur, Kunming, Madras, Male, Singapore & Yangon

SEA-2 MWARA **South East Asia Area 2**

Ground stations and aircraft inflight across the central Indonesian part of south east Asia. Overlaps portions of the SEA-1, SEA-3 and CSP areas.

3485.0 5649.0 5655.0 8942.0 11396.0 13309.0 17907.0

Bali, Bangkok, Denpasar, Guangzhou, Hanoi, Ho Chi Minh, Hong Kong, Jakarta, Kuala Lumpur, Kota Kinabalu, Manila, Seoul, Singapore, Tokyo, Vientiane

SEA-3 MWARA **South East Asia Area 3**

Ground stations and aircraft inflight across much of Indonesia and Australia. Overlaps portions of the INO-1 and SP areas.

3470.0 5733.0 6556.0 10066.0 11396.0 13318.0 17907.0

Bali, Cocos Is, Darwin, Jakarta, Male, Perth, Singapore, Ujung Pandang

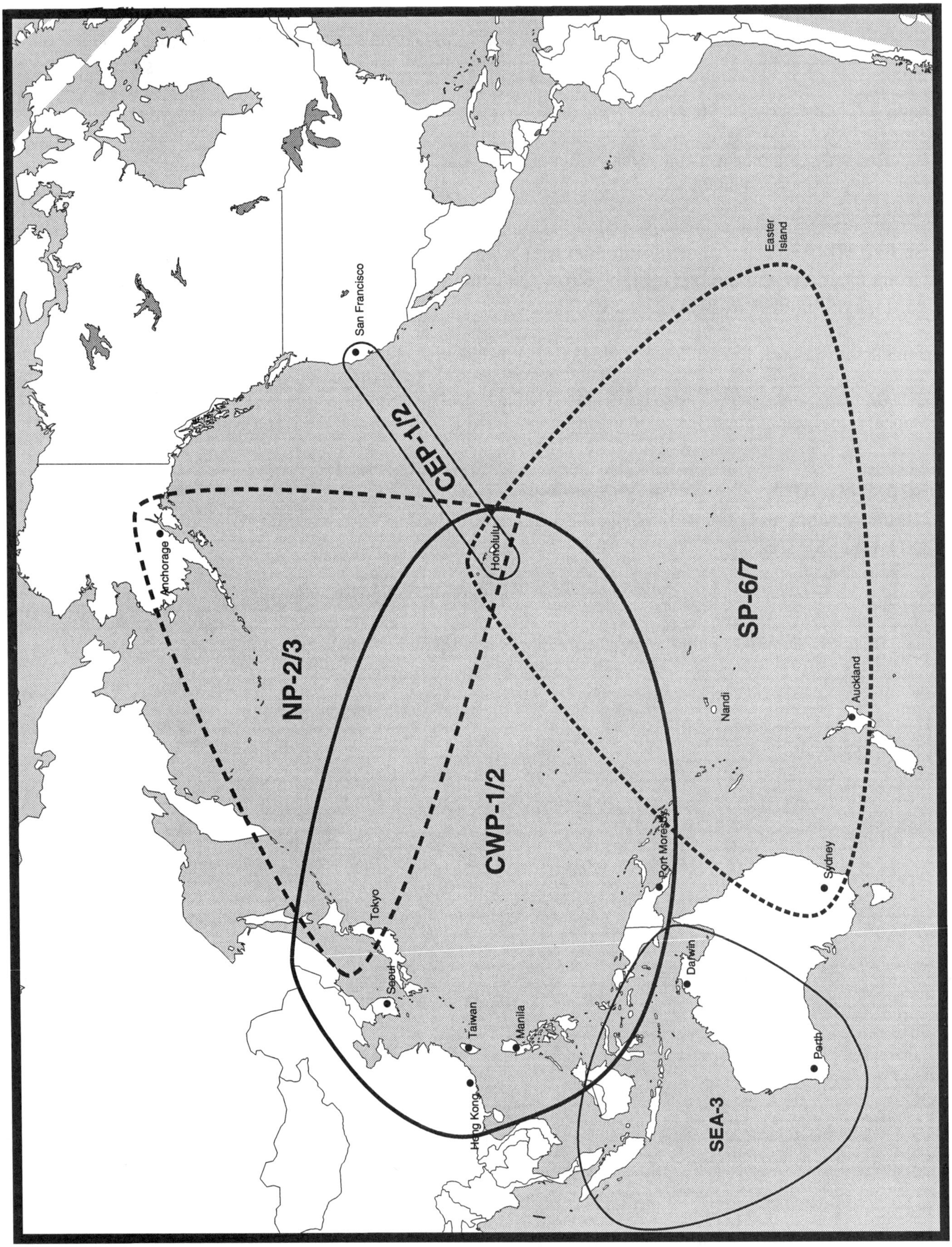
San Francisco
Easter Island
CEP-1/2
Anchorage
Honolulu
SP-6/7
NP-2/3
Nandi
Auckland
CWP-1/2
Port Moresby
Sydney
Tokyo
Darwin
Seoul
Taiwan
Manila
Perth
Hong Kong
SEA-3

CEP-1/2 MWARA **Central East Pacific Areas 1/2**

Ground stations and aircraft inflight in the corridor between San Francisco and Honolulu. Overlaps parts of the NP, CWP and SP areas.

2869.0 3413.0 5547.0 5574.0 8843.0 11282.0 13261.0 17904.0

Honolulu, San Francisco

CWP-1/2 MWARA **Central West Pacific Area 1/2**

Ground stations and aircraft inflight in the central western Pacific area bounded by Honolulu in the east, Seoul in the north, Hong Kong in the east and Port Moresby in the south. Overlaps parts of the EA-1, EA-2, SP, CWP and NP areas.

2998.0 4666.0 6532.0 6562.0 8903.0 11384.0 13300.0 17904.0
21985.0

Guam, Hong Kong, Honolulu, Manila, Naha, Port Moresby, Seoul, Taipei, Tokyo

NP-3/4 MWARA **North Pacific Area 3/4**

Ground stations and aircraft inflight in a triangular area of the North Pacific bounded by Anchorage, Honolulu and Tokyo. Overlaps portions of the CEP and CWP areas.

2932.0 5628.0 5677.0 6665.0 8915.0 10048.0 13294.0 13339.0
17904.0 17946.0 21925.0

Honolulu, San Francisco, Tokyo (Note that San Francisco Radio provides coverage for Anchorage)

SP-6/7 MWARA **South Pacific Area 6/7**

Ground stations and aircraft inflight across the broad expanse of the South Pacific Ocean. Includes New Zealand, eastern Australia, Nandi, Tahiti and Honolulu. Overlaps portions of the SEA-3, CEP and CWP areas.

3467.0 5643.0 8867.0 13273.0 17904.0

Auckland, Honolulu, Nandi, Pascua (Easter Is.), Port Vila, Rarotonga, Sydney, Tahiti, Wallis

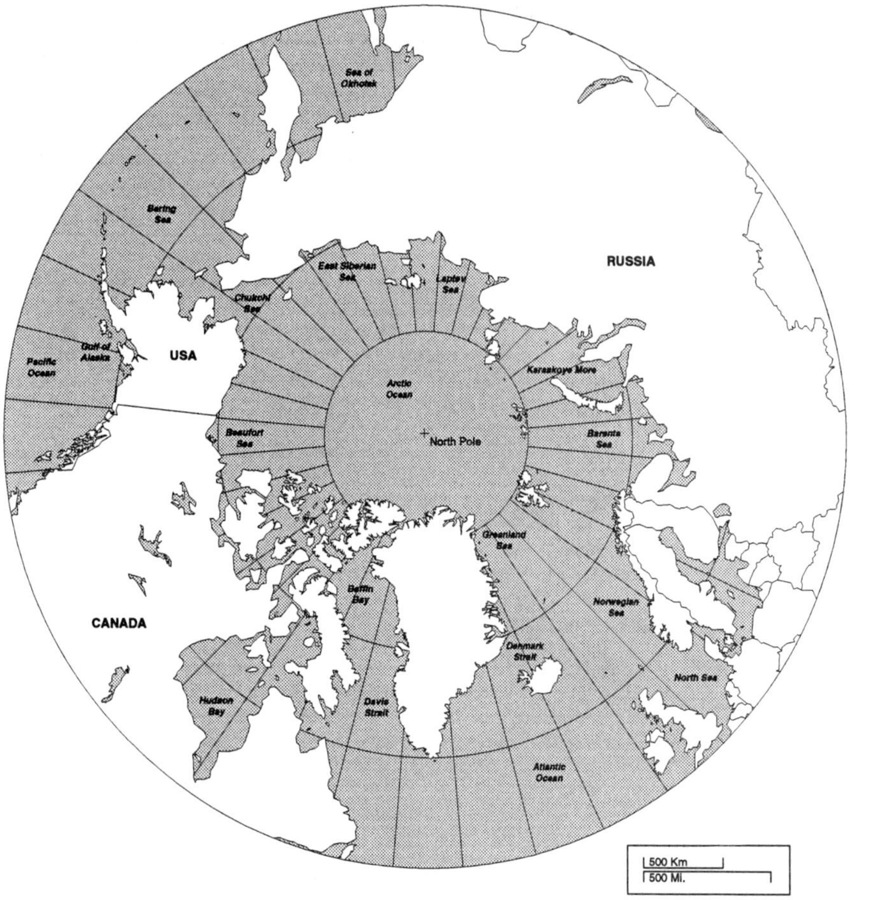
Sea of Okhotsk
Bering Sea
East Siberian Sea
Laptev Sea
RUSSIA
Chukchi Sea
Gulf of Alaska
Pacific Ocean
USA
Arctic Ocean
Karaskoye More
North Pole
Beaufort Sea
Barents Sea
Greenland Sea
Baffin Bay
Norwegian Sea
CANADA
Denmark Strait
North Sea
Hudson Bay
Davis Strait
Atlantic Ocean
500 Km
500 Mi.

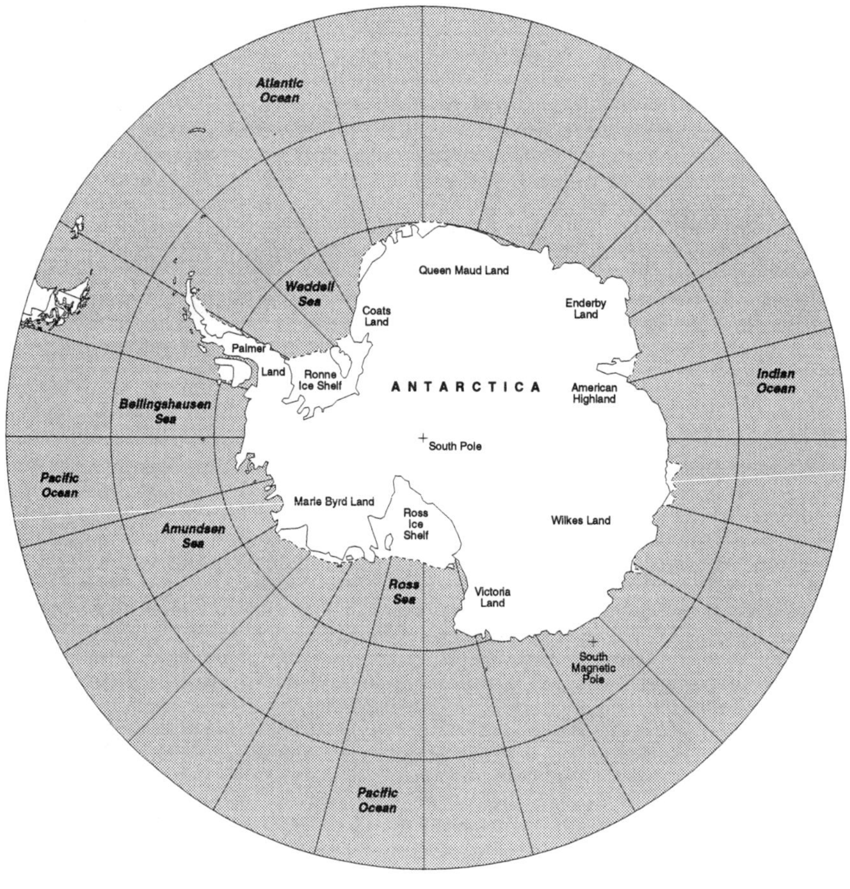
Atlantic Ocean
Queen Maud Land
Weddell Sea
Coats Land
Enderby Land
Palmer Land
Ronne Ice Shelf
ANTARCTICA
American Highland
Indian Ocean
Bellingshausen Sea
South Pole
Pacific Ocean
Marie Byrd Land
Ross Ice Shelf
Wilkes Land
Amundsen Sea
Ross Sea
Victoria Land
South Magnetic Pole
Pacific Ocean

LDOC - Long Distance Operational Control

Carrier	Location	Frequencies			
Aer Lingus	Dublin	3010.0	5532.0	8924.0	13351.0
		17916.0	21952.0		
Aero Condor	Cartagena	8936.0	9032.0		
Aeroflot	Boyeros	2896.0	5529.0	5710.0	6745.0
		6748.0	8842.0	8924.0	10025.0
		10030.0	11193.0	11198.0	11312.0
		11348.0	11359.0	11390.0	13205.0
		13220.0	13247.0	13345.0	15024.0
		17934.0	17936.0	17940.0	19904.0
		21958.0			
	Kabul	10025.0			
	Khabarovsk	5529.0	8924.0	10030.0	13345.0
		17940.0	21958.0		
	Moscow	2896.0	5529.0	5710.0	6745.0
		6748.0	8842.0	8924.0	10025.0
		10030.0	11193.0	11198.0	11312.0
		11348.0	11354.0	11359.0	11390.0
		13205.0	13220.0	13247.0	13345.0
		15024.0	17490.0	17934.0	17936.0
		19904.0	21958.0		
Aerolineas Argentinas	Buenos Aires	3010.0	6643.0	9013.0	10030.0
		13240.0	13327.0	17919.0	17928.0
		21955.0			
AeroMexico	Merida	3007.0	5544.0	8927.0	13339.0
		17919.0			
	Mexico City	3007.0	5544.0	8927.0	8918.0
		9006.0	13339.0	17919.0	17925.0
	Tijuana	3007.0	5544.0	8927.0	13339.0
		17919.0			
AeroPeru	Lima, Quito	11378.0			
Air Algerie	Algiers	3013.0	5532.0	6646.0	8895.0
		8933.0	10075.0	11354.0	13348.0
Air Djibouti	Djibouti	3013.0	5544.0	8933.0	13339.0
		17925.0	21944.0		
Air France	Paris	3010.0	6526.0	6637.0	6712.0
		6746.0	8972.0	10093.0	11345.0
		11351.0	13351.0	17916.0	17941.0
		21940.0	21944.0		
Air India	Bombay	3007.0	6637.0	8930.0	10025.0
		10072.0	11324.0	13333.0	13336.0
		13351.0	17916.0	21943.0	21949.0
		21979.0			
Air Jamaica	Kingston	6526.0	10093.0	13356.0	17937.0

LDOC - Long Distance Operational Control

Carrier	Location	Frequencies			
Air Lanka	Colombo	4687.0	6637.0	8921.0	13324.0
		17922.0	21949.0		
Air Madagascar	Antananarivo	3013.0	5538.0	8927.0	13330.0
		17931.0	21982.0		
Air Malawi	Blantyre, Lilongwe	3013.0	5544.0	8933.0	13339.0
		17931.0	21982.0		
Air Malta	Luqa	3497.0	4687.0	10078.0	10084.0
		13327.0	17931.0	21967.0	
Air Mauritius	Port Louis	3013.0	5538.0	8933.0	13348.0
		17937.0	21982.0		
Air Nauru	Nauru Island	6637.0	13351.0	17916.0	21949.0
Air New Zealand	Auckland	3007.0	6637.0	10072.0	13333.0
		13345.0	17940.0	21970.0	
Air Niugini	Port Moresby	3836.0	7350.0		
Air Pacific	Suava	9026.0			
Air Rwanda	Kigali	3013.0	6640.0	10075.0	13339.0
		17931.0	21982.0		
Air Seychelles	Mahe	6526.0	8849.0	8967.0	13205.0
		21886.0			
Air Tanzania	Dar es Salaam	3013.0	6640.0	8927.0	13339.0
		17931.0	21982.0		
Air Wemindji	Wemindji	6598.0			
Air Zaire	Kinshasa	3013.0	5538.0	10033.0	13339.0
		17931.0	21982.0		
Air Zimbabwe	Harare	3013.0	5532.0	8949.0	10075.0
		13330.0	17937.0	17944.0	
ALIA/Royal Jordanian Airlines	Amman	9003.0	10027.0	13225.0	13241.0
		13555.0			
Alitalia	Rome	4687.0	5532.0	8931.0	10027.0
		13336.0	13345.0	17940.0	21952.0
ALM Antillean	Willemstad	3007.0	5544.0	8936.0	13339.0
		17919.0	21985.0		
American Airlines	Lima	3010.0	5535.0	8885.0	8896.0
		11306.0	11345.0	17937.0	21976.0
Ansett Airways	Melbourne	3185.0			

Carrier	Location	Frequencies			
Ariana Afghan Airlines	Kabul	3013.0	6640.0	10075.0	13330.0
		17925.0	21982.0		
AVENSA	Canaima				
	Caracas	6730.0	3010.0	6643.0	8924.0
		11345.0	17937.0	21976.0	
AVIANCO - Aviacion y Comercio	Madrid	11182.0			
Bradley First Air	Ottawa	13285.0			
Brazil Central - Linha Aérea Regiona	Sao Paulo	8849.0			
Britannia Airlines	Luton	6556.0	10021.0	11363.0	
British Airways (Speedbird)	London	3497.0	5535.0	8921.0	10072.0
		13330.0	13333.0	17922.0	21946.0
Canadian Airlines	Calgary,Toronto	13285.0	*(inactive for some time now)*		
CaribAir	St. Thomas	6567.0			
Caribbean Airways	Bridgetown	6526.0	8945.0	13205.0	13260.0
		17485.0	17910.0		
Cathay Pacific	Hong Kong	13333.0			
Cayman Air	Grand Cayman	6646.0	8936.0	13339.0	
Condor	Frankfurt	13327.0			
Cubana Airlines	Boyeros	3007.0	4885.0	5544.0	5562.0
		8888.0	8927.0	11312.0	13330.0
		13339.0	17934.0	17936.0	17974.0
		21985.0			
	Holguin	13339.0			
	Moscow	17936.0			
Cyprus Airways	Larnaca	6637.0	10078.0	13351.0	17931.0
		21979.0			
Czechoslovak Airlines	Prague	3497.0	5532.0	8924.0	10025.0
		10027.0	10078.0	13351.0	17940.0
		21967.0			
Deutsche Rettungsflugwacht	Stuttgart	17931.0			
DragonAir	Hong Kong	3007.0	6637.0	8921.0	13333.0
		17940.0	21970.0		
Egypt Air	Cairo	3013.0	6640.0	8933.0	11288.0
		13356.0	17931.0	21982.0	

LDOC - Long Distance Operational Control

Carrier	Location	Frequencies			
El Al	Tel Aviv	3010.0	5589.0	6637.0	6677.0
		8837.0	8924.0	8930.0	11318.0
		11324.0	13304.0	13351.0	17940.0
		21880.0	21886.0	21952.0	
Elite - Canada 3000	Toronto	3459.0	4667.0	5475.0	5610.0
		8900.0	8960.0	11305.0	11390.0
		17910.0			
Ethiopian Airlines (Holloway)	Addis Ababa	3013.0	5538.0	7541.0	8927.0
		13339.0	17931.0		
	Asmara	3018.0	5538.0	8927.0	13339.0
		17931.0			
Falcon	Manama	3013.0	5538.0	10093.0	1354.0
		13324.0	13333.0	13339.0	13356.0
		17931.0	21943.0		
FURNAS	Rio de Janeiro	11243.0			
Gulf Air	Muscat	3013.0	5538.0	10033.0	13330.0
		17931.0	21943.0		
Hapag Lloyd Fluggesellschaft	Hanover, Frankfurt	6643.0	10069.0	11345.0	13324.0
		13327.0	17916.0	17931.0	21958.0
Iberia	Las Palmas	5529.0	10027.0	17940.0	
	Madrid	4654.0	5529.0	8936.0	8984.0
		10021.0	10027.0	11182.0	11318.0
		11324.0	13327.0	13348.0	17940.0
		17949.0	21967.0		
	Santo Domingo	5529.0	10027.0	13348.0	
Interflug	Berlin/Schoenfield	4745.0	6753.0	8984.0	10030.0
		11237.0	13223.0	13235.0	15046.0
		17925.0	17955.0	17975.0	23225.0
Iraqi Airways	Baghdad	Cairo	13324.0		
JAL - Japan Airlines	Tokyo	4687.0	6637.0	10093.0	11342.0
		13324.0	17925.0	17928.0	21949.0
KAL - Korean Airlines	Seoul	3007.0	4687.0	10072.0	13333.0
		17916.0	21949.0	21970.0	
Kano Air	Kano	13330.0			
KLM - Royal Dutch Airlines	Amsterdam	3010.0	3921.0	4687.0	5532.0
		5645.0	5659.0	8924.0	8952.0
		13327.0	13336.0	13442.0	17940.0
		21925.0	21973.0		
Kuwaiti Airlines	Safat	3013.0	6640.0	8970.0	10033.0
		17931.0	21994.0		

Carrier	Location	Frequencies			
LAB - Lloyd Aéreo Boliviano	Cochabamba	8890.0			
LADECO - Linea Aérea del Cobre	Santiago	10036.0			
LAP - Lineas Aereas Paraguayas	Asuncion	11397.0			
LAZ - Balkan Bulgarian Airlines	Burgas, Sofia	3151.0	5541.0	5622.0	10060.0
		11273.0	11384.0		
LIAT	Antigua	5490.0	5568.0	5658.0	
	Adams/Barbados	5568.0	5658.0		
Lignes Congolaises	Brazzaville	11390.0			
Lineas Aereas Canarias	Las Palmas	5529.0	8936.0	10027.0	13327.0
		13342.0	17940.0	21967.0	
LOT - Polskie Linie	Warsaw	4687.0	8924.0	11345.0	11351.0
		11354.0	13336.0	13345.0	17940.0
		17948.0	21967.0		
LTU	Dusseldorf	6643.0	8921.0	10030.0	10078.0
		17931.0	13324.0		
Lufthansa	Dusseldorf	13324.0			
	Frankfurt	3010.0	4687.0	5645.0	6637.0
		8921.0	8983.0	10018.0	10065.0
		10072.0	10078.0	11190.0	13213.0
		13248.0	13324.0	13327.0	17931.0
		21967.0	21979.0		
MALEV - Hungarian Airlines	Budapest	5532.0	8930.0	11345.0	11351.0
		13336.0	17940.0	21973.0	
MEA - Cedar Jet	Beirut	3013.0	5538.0	10075.0	10093.0
		13300.0	13330.0	13356.0	17931.0
		17965.0	20770.0	21943.0	
Monarch Airlines	Luton	6556.0	10021.0	11363.0	
Myanma Airways	Yangon	3007.0	4687.0	11351.0	13342.0
		17934.0	21949.0		
Nigeria Airways	Lagos	3013.0	5532.0	8927.0	8963.0
		13339.0	13356.0	17931.0	17970.0
		21982.0	21988.0		
NLA - Nordeste Linhas Aéreas Regionais	Salvador	8945.0			
Olympic Airlines	Athens	3010.0	6637.0	10078.0	13327.0
		17916.0	21979.0		
Ontair	Sault Ste. Marie	5490.0			

LDOC - Long Distance Operational Control

Carrier	Location	Frequencies			
Philippines Air	Manila	3007.0	6637.0	11351.0	13351.0
		17916.0	21949.0		
PIA-Pakistani International Airlines	Karachi	8930.0	11345.0	11351.0	13342.0
		17940.0	21970.0	23230.0	
PLUNA	Montevideo	3010.0	55.25.0	5628.0	8924.0
		13336.0	17919.0	21976.0	
QANTAS	Perth	4687.0	6632.0	10078.0	13342.0
		17922.0	21970.0		
	Sydney	3007.0	4666.0	4687.0	6526.0
		6632.0	6637.0	8903.0	8921.0
		10075.0	10078.0	10093.0	13342.0
		13345.0	17922.0	17949.0	21886.0
		21970.0			
RIO SUL - Serviços Aéreos Regionais	Porto Alegre	5559.0	8816.0		
	Rio de Janeiro	5559.0	8816.0		
Royal Nepal Airlines	Kathmandu	6637.0	13342.0		
Sabena	Brussels	3010.0	5529.0	5645.0	8924.0
		10078.0	13351.0	17940.0	23692.0
SAS	Stockholm	5541.0	8930.0	11345.0	13342.0
SASHA	Tegucigalpa	5120.0			
Saudi Airlines	Jeddah	3013.0	5544.0	6685.0	8822.0
		8927.0	8959.0	11288.0	13312.0
		13339.0	13342.0	15026.0	17925.0
		17983.0	21944.0	21994.0	23307.0
	Riyadh	8927.0			
	Rockwell USA	11288.0	13312.0		
Serbia Aerotransport	Belgrade (Beograd)	3010.0	5532.0	5688.0	6724.0
		8967.0	11228.0	11351.0	13241.0
		13248.0	13336.0	17916.0	21940.0
Singapore Airlines	Singapore	5526.0	6637.0	8930.0	10072.0
		10078.0	13333.0	17934.0	21949.0
SOSA	La Cieba	7400.0			
South African Airways (Springbok)	Johannesburg	3013.0	5532.0	8933.0	11354.0
		13327.0	13330.0	17925.0	21943.0
Swiss Air	Berne	6705.0	8936.0	9211.0	10069.0
		13205.0	18023.0	18480.0	21933.0
Syrian Arab Airlines	Damascus	11240.0	21993.0		
TAAG	Luanda	5544.0	8927.0	11354.0	

Carrier	Location	Frequencies			
TAP - Air Portugal	Lisbon	3010.0	5532.0	8924.0	11184.0
		13336.0	17940.0	21952.0	
TAROM - Romanian Air Transport	Bucharest	3497.0	4687.0	10021.0	10027.0
		11363.0	13345.0	17931.0	21952.0
TASA	Peru	3903.5	5552.0	6580.0	7912.0
		10042.0	10975.0	11122.0	
Thai Aiways	Bangkok	3007.0	4687.0	8930.0	13351.0
		17922.0	21970.0		
THY-Turkish Airlines	Istanbul	11185.0			
TransBrazil	Brazil	4684.0	6562.0	8819.0	
Transportes Aereos Marilia	Brazil	5604.0	6550.0	8014.0	8849.0
		14516.0			
Transportes Aereos Regionales	Sao Paulo	5609.0			
Tunis Air	Tunis	3013.0	6640.0	6688.0	10033.0
		11117.0	13222.0	13339.0	17925.0
		21994.0			
Uganda Airlines	Entebbe	3013.0	6640.0	8927.0	13339.0
		21982.0			
VARIG	Belem	5553.0	8936.0	8939.0	
	Brasilia	5553.0			
	Recife	5553.0			
	Rio de Janeiro	3010.0	5541.0	6547.0	8924.0
		8936.0	8939.0	10069.0	11305.0
		11325.0	11327.0	11346.0	11366.0
		11375.0	13309.0	13327.0	17913.0
		17919.0	17931.0	21955.0	21991.0
	Sao Paulo	8939.0			
VASP - Viacao Aerea Sao Paulo	Rio de Janeiro	4666.0	11375.0	17943.0	19943.0
	Sao Paulo	4666.0	11375.0	17943.0	19943.0
VIASA	Maiquetia	6643.0	8924.0	11305.0	11345.0
		17937.0			
West Indian	Piarco	3010.0	5535.0	8924.0	11345.0
		13336.0	17928.0	21955.0	
Westbury	Santo Domingo	5425.0			
Zambia Airways	Lusaka	3013.0	3413.0	6640.0	8843.0
		11342.0	13300.0	13348.0	13354.0
		17925.0	21964.0		

LDOC - Common Carrier

Carrier	Frequencies			
ARINC - New York	3413.0	3494.0	6526.0	6640.0
	8843.0	8933.0	11342.0	13300.0
	13354.0	17925.0	21964.0	
ARINC - San Francisco	3013.0	6640.0	10033.0	11342.0
	13330.0	13348.0	13354.0	17925.0
	21964.0			
ARINC- Honolulu	3013.0	6640.0	10033.0	11342.0
	13330.0	13348.0	13354.0	17925.0
	21964.0			
ARINC- HF Ramp Check	5574.0	5598.0	5603.0	13324.0
Houston Radio (Universal Aviation)	5529.0	6637.0	10075.0	13330.0
	17940.0	21964.0		
Rainbow Radio	3378.0	3446.0	3458.0	3845.0
	5604.0	8819.0	10264.0	12348.6
	13119.4	13285.0	13356.5	13373.5
	13420.0	14545.0	17282.5	17910.0
Berne ("Berna") Radio	3010.0	4654.0	4670.0	4702.0
	6526.0	6643.0	6705.0	6742.0
	8936.0	9211.0	10069.0	13205.0
	13266.0	13324.0	13593.0	15046.0
	15050.0	15835.0	17931.0	18023.0
	18480.0	19554.0	20035.0	20870.0
	21933.0	21988.0	23285.0	25500.0
Portishead Radio	3482.0	3747.0	4521.0	4807.0
	4810.0	5610.0	5670.0	5690.0
	6556.0	6634.0	6854.0	7870.0
	8170.0	8180.0	8185.0	8960.0
	10291.0	10884.0	10960.0	11306.0
	11363.0	12133.0	12168.0	13865.0
	14890.0	15964.0	16003.0	16370.0
	16443.0	17405.0	18210.0	19510.0
	20065.0	20665.0	21765.0	23142.0
	23210.0	23412.0	24655.0	25109.0
	27218.0			
Stockholm Radio	3341.0	3494.0	4041.0	4595.0
	4654.0	4690.0	5541.0	5589.0
	7433.0	7453.0	8930.0	8972.0
	10165.0	10575.0	10805.0	10884.0
	11222.0	11225.0	11345.0	13300.0
	13330.0	13342.0	13576.0	13942.5
	14645.0	15021.0	15046.0	15685.0
	16207.0	17916.0	17982.0	20770.0
	21977.0	21997.0	23040.0	23210.0
	25035.0	25385.0		
Sydney SkyComms	3007.0	4666.0	4687.0	6532.0
	8140.0	8903.0	8930.0	8936.0
	8972.0	9040.0	10072.0	11132.0
	11342.0	13330.0	17440.0	17934.0
	17940.0	20160.0	23070.0	

VOLMET Stations

Area/Station	Times	Frequencies			
AFI-VOL					
Brazzaville , Congo	(H+10,+25,+30,+55)	5499.0	10057.0	13261.0	
Algiers, Algeria		11279.0			
Kano, Nigeria					
CAR-VOL					
Tegucigalpa, Honduras	(H+50)	4710.0			
EA-VOL					
Beijing, China	(H+05,45)	3458.0	5673.0	8849.0	13285.0
Guangzhou ,China	(H+10,50)				
EU-VOL					
Shannon , Ireland	(H+00,+25,+30,+55)	3413.0	5505.0	5640.0	8957.0
13264.0					
MID-VOL					
Beirut, Lebanon	(H+15,45)	3001.0	5561.0	8819.0	
Damascus, Syria	(H+00,30)	2992.0	5667.0	8918.0	13312.0
Karachi, Pakistan	(H+15,45)	3432.0	6680.0	10017.0	
Kuwait, Kuwait		3404.0	5603.0	6624.0	8847.0
		10009.0	13336.0		
NAT-VOL					
Gander, Canada	(H+20, 50)	3485.0	6604.0	10051.0	13270.0
New York, USA	(H+00,30)				
NCA-VOL					
CIS English Language Network					
Khabarovsk, Russia	(H+05,35)	4663.0	5676.0	10090.0	13279.0
Tashkent, Uzbekistan	(H+10,40)				
Kiev, Ukraine	(H+15,45)				
Moscow, Russia	(H+25,55)				
Novosibirsk, Russia	(H+20,50)				
Russian Network A					
Riga, Latvia	(H+00,30)	2941.0	6617.0	8939.0	11297.0
St. Petersburg, Russia	(H+05,35)				
Moscow, Russia	(H+10,15,40,45)				
Kiev, Ukraine	(H+20,50)				
Rostov, Ukraine	(H+25,55)				

Area/Station	Times	Frequencies			
Russian Network B					
Tbilisi, Georgia	(H+00,30)	3407.0	6730.0	8819.0	11279.0
Aktyubinsk, Kazakhstan	(H+05,35)				
Krasnodar, Azerbaijan	(H+10,40)				
Alma Ata, Kazakhstan	(H+15,45)				
Tashkent, Uzbekistan	(H+20,50)				
Baku, Azerbaijan	H+25,55)				
Russian Network C					
Syktyvkar, Russia	(H+00,30)	2869.0	6693.0	8888.0	11318.0
Sverdlovsk, Russia	(H+05,35)				
Novosibirsk, Russia	(H+10,40)				
Kuybyshev, Russia	(H+15,45)				
Tyuman, Russia	(H+20,50)				
Russian Network D					
Kirensk, Russia	(H+00,30)	5691.0	8861.0	13267.0	
Yakutsk, Russia	(H+10,40)				
Khabarovsk, Russia	(H+15,45)				
Magadan, Russia	(H+20,50)				
Irkutsk, Russia	(H+25,55)				
Russian Network E					
Pevek, Russia	(H+10,40)	8852.0			
Katanga, Russia	(H+15,45)				
PAC-VOL					
Honolulu, Hawaii	(H+00,+30)	2863.0	6679.0	8828.0	
Tokyo, Japan	(H+10,+40)				
Hong Kong , Hong Kong	(H+15,+45)				
Auckland , New Zealand	(H+20,50)				
SAM-VOL					
Asuncion , Paraguay	(H+05)	5601.0			
Ezeiza, Argentina	(H+15)				
Asuncion , Paraguay	(H+15)	10067.0			
Belem, Brazil		6603.0	10057.0	13352.0	
Brasilia, Brazil		6603.0	10057.0	13352.0	
Galeao, Brazil		6603.0		13352.0	
Guarulhos, Brazil			10057.0	13352.0	
Manaus, Brazil		6603.0		13352.0	
Porto Alegre, Brazil				13352.0	
Recife, Brazil		6603.0	10057.0	13352.0	
Rio de Janeiro, Brazil			10057.0	13352.0	
Buenos Aires, Argentina (Ezeiza)	(H+15)	2881.0	11369.0		
Buenos Aires, Argentina	(H+55)	13279.0			
Comodoro Rivadavia, Argentina	(H+30,40)	4675.0	8938/0		
Resistencia, Argentina	(H+20,50)	4675.0			

Area/Station	Times	Frequencies		
Cordoba, Argentina	(H+25)	5475.0	8952.0	
Salta, Argentina	(H+15)	5475.0		
Montevideo, Uruguay	(H+15)	5803.0		
Puerto Montt, Chile	(H+20)	3787.5	6745.5	
SEA-VOL				
Sydney, Australia	(H+00,+30)	2965.0	6676.0	11387.0
Calcutta, India	(H+05,35)			
Bangkok, Thailand	(H+10,+40)			
Karachi, Pakistan	(H+15,+45)			
Singapore, Singapore	(H+20,+50)			
Bombay, India	(H+25,55)			

Avro Lancaster
Royal Air Force

MWARA Country/City Listing

Aden							
Aden	AFI-3	3467.0	5658.0	10018.0	11300.0	13288.0	17961.0
	MID-1	2992.0	4669.0	5667.0	6631.0	8951.0	11375.0
		17961.0					
Afghanistan							
Kabul	MID-2	3467.0	5658.0	10018.0	11300.0	13288.0	17961.0
Algeria							
Algiers	AFI-2	3419.0	5652.0	8894.0	13273.0	17961.0	
Tamanrasset	AFI-2	3419.0	5652.0	8894.0	13273.0	17961.0	
Timimoun	AFI-2	3419.0	5652.0	8894.0	13273.0	17961.0	
Angola							
Luanda	AFI-4	2878.0	5493.0	8903.0	13294.0	17961.0	
Salazar	AFI-4	2878.0	5493.0	8903.0	13294.0	17961.0	
Argentina							
Bariloche	SAM-SW	2944.0	4669.0	6549.0	10024.0	11360.0	17907.0
Buenos Aires	SAM-SW	2944.0	4669.0	6549.0	10024.0	11360.0	17907.0
	SAM-SE	3479.0	5526.0	8855.0	10096.0	13297.0	17907.0
Comodoro Rivadavia	SAM-SW	2944.0	4669.0	6549.0	10024.0	11360.0	17907.0
Cordoba	SAM-SW	2944.0	4669.0	6549.0	10024.0	11360.0	17907.0
Mendoza	SAM-SW	2944.0	4669.0	6549.0	10024.0	11360.0	17907.0
Resistencia	SAM-SE	3479.0	5526.0	8855.0	10096.0	13297.0	17907.0
	SAM-SW	2944.0	4669.0	6549.0	10024.0	11360.0	17907.0
Ushuaia	SAM-SW	2944.0	4669.0	6549.0	10024.0	11360.0	17907.0
Armenia							
Yerevan	MID-1	2992.0	4669.0	5667.0	6631.0	8951.0	11375.0
		17961.0					
	MID-2	3467.0	5658.0	10018.0	11300.0	13288.0	17961.0
	MID-3	2994.0	4669.0	6631.0	8951.0	11375.0	17961.0
Australia							
Darwin	SEA-3	3470.0	5733.0	6556.0	10066.0	11396.0	13318.0
		17907.0					
Perth	INO-1	3476.0	5634.0	8879.0	13306.0	17961.0	
	SEA-3	3470.0	5733.0	6556.0	10066.0	11396.0	13318.0
		17907.0					
Sydney	SP-6/7	3467.0	5643.0	8867.0	13273.0	17904.0	
Azores							
Santa Maria	NAT-A	3016.0	5598.0	13306.0	17946.0		
	NAT-B	2899.0	5616.0	8864.0	13291.0	17946.0	
	NAT-E	2962.0	6628.0	8825.0	11309.0	13354.0	
Bahrain							
Manama	AFI-3	3467.0	5658.0	10018.0	11300.0	13288.0	17961.0
	MID-1	2992.0	4669.0	5667.0	6631.0	8951.0	11375.0
		17961.0					
Bangladesh							
Dhaka	SEA-1	3470.0	6556.0	10066.0	13318.0	17907.0	

Benin							
Contonou	AFI-4	2878.0	5493.0	8903.0	13294.0	17961.0	
Bolivia							
La Paz	SAM-SE	3479.0	5526.0	8855.0	10096.0	13297.0	17907.0
	SAM-SW	2944.0	4669.0	6549.0	10024.0	11360.0	17907.0
Santa Cruz	SAM-SW	2944.0	4669.0	6549.0	10024.0	11360.0	17907.0
	SAM-SE	3479.0	5526.0	8855.0	10096.0	13297.0	17907.0
Botswana							
Francistown	AFI-4	2878.0	5493.0	8903.0	13294.0	17961.0	
Brazil							
Belem	SAM-C	3479.0	5526.0	8855.0	10096.0	13297.0	17907.0
	SAM-NE	3479.0	5526.0	8855.0	10096.0	13297.0	17907.0
	SAM-SE	3479.0	5526.0	8855.0	10096.0	13297.0	17907.0
Brasilia	SAM-C	3479.0	5526.0	8855.0	10096.0	13297.0	17907.0
	SAM-SE	3479.0	5526.0	8855.0	10096.0	13297.0	17907.0
	SAT-1	3452.0	6535.0	8861.0	13357.0	17955.0	
Campo Grande	SAM-SE	3479.0	5526.0	8855.0	10096.0	13297.0	17907.0
Curtiba	SAM-SE	3479.0	5526.0	8855.0	10096.0	13297.0	17907.0
Manaus	SAM-C	3479.0	5526.0	8855.0	10096.0	13297.0	17907.0
	SAT-1	3452.0	6535.0	8861.0	13357.0	17955.0	
	SAT-2	2854.0	5565.0	11291.0	13315.0	17955.0	
Porto Alegre	SAM-SE	3479.0	5526.0	8855.0	10096.0	13297.0	17907.0
Porto Velho	SAM-C	3479.0	5526.0	8855.0	10096.0	13297.0	17907.0
	SAM-SE	3479.0	5526.0	8855.0	10096.0	13297.0	17907.0
Recife	SAM-NE	3479.0	5526.0	8855.0	10096.0	13297.0	17907.0
	SAM-SE	3479.0	5526.0	8855.0	10096.0	13297.0	17907.0
	SAT-1	3452.0	6535.0	8861.0	13357.0	17955.0	
	SAT-2	2854.0	5565.0	11291.0	13315.0	17955.0	
Rio de Janeiro	SAM-C	3479.0	5526.0	8855.0	10096.0	13297.0	17907.0
	SAT-1	3452.0	6535.0	8861.0	13357.0	17955.0	
	SAT-2	2854.0	5565.0	11291.0	13315.0	17955.0	
Salvador	SAT-1	3452.0	6535.0	8861.0	13357.0	17955.0	
	SAM-SE	3479.0	5526.0	8855.0	10096.0	13297.0	17907.0
	SAT-2	2854.0	5565.0	11291.0	13315.0	17955.0	
Bulgaria							
Sofia	EUR-A	3479.0	5661.0	6598.0	10084.0	13288.0	17961.0
Burkina Faso							
Bobo Dioulasso	AFI-1	3452.0	6535.0	8861.0	13357.0	17955.0	
Ouagadougou	AFI-1	3452.0	6535.0	8861.0	13357.0	17955.0	
Burundi							
Bujumbura	AFI-3	3467.0	5658.0	10018.0	11300.0	13288.0	17961.0
Byelarus							
Minsk	EUR-A	3479.0	5661.0	6598.0	10084.0	13288.0	17961.0
Vitebsk	EUR-A	3479.0	5661.0	6598.0	10084.0	13288.0	17961.0

Cameroon							
Douala	AFI-4	2878.0	5493.0	8903.0	13294.0	17961.0	
Garoua	AFI-4	2878.0	5493.0	8903.0	13294.0	17961.0	
Maroua	AFI-4	2878.0	5493.0	8903.0	13294.0	17961.0	
Yaounde	AFI-4	2878.0	5493.0	8903.0	13294.0	17961.0	
Canada							
Cambridge Bay	NAT-D	2971.0	4675.0	8891.0	11279.0	13291.0	17946.0
Churchill	NAT-D	2971.0	4675.0	8891.0	11279.0	13291.0	17946.0
Gander	NAT-A	3016.0	5598.0	13306.0	17946.0		
	NAT-B	2899.0	5616.0	8864.0	13291.0	17946.0	
	NAT-C	2862.0	5649.0	8879.0	13306.0	17946.0	
	NAT-D	2971.0	4675.0	8891.0	11279.0	13291.0	17946.0
	NAT-F	3476.0	6622.0	8831.0	11336.0	13291.0	
Iqualuit (Frobisher Bay)	NAT-D	2971.0	4675.0	8891.0	11279.0	13291.0	17946.0
Canary Islands							
Canarias	AFI-1	3452.0	6535.0	8861.0	13357.0	17955.0	
	NAT-A	3016.0	5598.0	13306.0	17946.0		
	SAT-1	3452.0	6535.0	8861.0	13357.0	17955.0	
	SAT-2	2854.0	5565.0	11291.0	13315.0	17955.0	
Cental African Republic							
Bangui	AFI-1	3452.0	6535.0	8861.0	13357.0	17955.0	
	AFI-4	2878.0	5493.0	8903.0	13294.0	17961.0	
Chad							
N'djamena	AFI-2	3419.0	5652.0	8894.0	13273.0	17961.0	
	AFI-3	3467.0	5658.0	10018.0	11300.0	13288.0	17961.0
	AFI-4	2878.0	5493.0	8903.0	13294.0	17961.0	
Chile							
Antofagasta	SAM-SW	2944.0	4669.0	6549.0	10024.0	11360.0	17907.0
Puerto Montt	SAM-SW	2944.0	4669.0	6549.0	10024.0	11360.0	17907.0
Punta Arenas	SAM-SW	2944.0	4669.0	6549.0	10024.0	11360.0	17907.0
Santiago	SAM-SW	2944.0	4669.0	6549.0	10024.0	11360.0	17907.0
China							
Beijing	EA-1	3016.0	6571.0	8897.0	10042.0	17958.0	
Canton	EA-1	3016.0	6571.0	8897.0	10042.0	17958.0	
	EA-2	3485.0	5649.0	5655.0	8942.0	11396.0	13309.0
		17907.0					
Guangzhou	SEA-1	3470.0	6556.0	10066.0	13318.0	17907.0	
	SEA-2	3485.0	5649.0	5655.0	8942.0	11396.0	13309.0
		17907.0					
Jinan	EA-1	3016.0	6571.0	8897.0	10042.0	17958.0	
Kunming	EA-1	3016.0	6571.0	8897.0	10042.0	17958.0	
	SEA-1	3470.0	6556.0	10066.0	13318.0	17907.0	
Lanzhou	EA-1	3016.0	6571.0	8897.0	10042.0	17958.0	
Shanghai	EA-1	3016.0	6571.0	8897.0	10042.0	17958.0	
Shenyang	EA-1	3016.0	6571.0	8897.0	10042.0	17958.0	
Urumqi	EA-1	3016.0	6571.0	8897.0	10042.0	17958.0	
	MID-2	3467.0	5658.0	10018.0	11300.0	13288.0	17961.0
Wuhan	EA-1	3016.0	6571.0	8897.0	10042.0	17958.0	
Zhengzhou	EA-1	3016.0	6571.0	8897.0	10042.0	17958.0	

Cocos Islands							
Cocos Islands	INO-1	3476.0	5634.0	8879.0	13306.0	17961.0	
	SEA-3	3470.0	5733.0	6556.0	10066.0	11396.0	13318.0
		17907.0					
Colombia							
Barranquilla	CAR-A	2887.0	5550.0	6577.0	8918.0	11396.0	13297.0
		17907.0					
	CAR-B	3455.0	5520.0	6586.0	8846.0	11330.0	17907.0
	SAM-NW	2944.0	4669.0	6549.0	10024.0	11360.0	17907.0
Bogota	SAM-C	3479.0	5526.0	8855.0	10096.0	13297.0	17907.0
	SAM-NW	2944.0	4669.0	6549.0	10024.0	11360.0	17907.0
Leticia	SAM-C	3479.0	5526.0	8855.0	10096.0	13297.0	17907.0
San Andrés Is.	CAR-A	2887.0	5550.0	6577.0	8918.0	11396.0	13297.0
		17907.0					
	CAR-B	3455.0	5520.0	6586.0	8846.0	11330.0	17907.0
Comoros Islands							
Moroni	AFI-3	3467.0	5658.0	10018.0	11300.0	13288.0	17961.0
	INO-1	3476.0	5634.0	8879.0	13306.0	17961.0	
Congo							
Brazzaville	AFI-2	3419.0	5652.0	8894.0	13273.0	17961.0	
	AFI-4	2878.0	5493.0	8903.0	13294.0	17961.0	
Cook Islands							
Rarotonga	SP-6/7	3467.0	5643.0	8867.0	13273.0	17904.0	
Costa Rica							
San José	CAR-A	2887.0	5550.0	6577.0	8918.0	11396.0	13297.0
		17907.0					
Cuba							
Boyeros	CAR-A	2887.0	5550.0	6577.0	8918.0	11396.0	13297.0
		17907.0					
	CAR-B	3455.0	5520.0	6586.0	8846.0	11330.0	17907.0
Djibouti							
Djibouti	AFI-3	3467.0	5658.0	10018.0	11300.0	13288.0	17961.0
Easter Island							
Pascua	SAM-SE	3479.0	5526.0	8855.0	10096.0	13297.0	17907.0
	SAM-SW	2944.0	4669.0	6549.0	10024.0	11360.0	17907.0
	SP-6/7	3467.0	5643.0	8867.0	13273.0	17904.0	
Ecuador							
Quito	SAM-NW	2944.0	4669.0	6549.0	10024.0	11360.0	17907.0
Egypt							
Cairo	AFI-3	3467.0	5658.0	10018.0	11300.0	13288.0	17961.0
	MID-1	2992.0	4669.0	5667.0	6631.0	8951.0	11375.0
		17961.0					

Ethiopia							
Addis Ababa	AFI-3	3467.0	5658.0	10018.0	11300.0	13288.0	17961.0
Asmara	AFI-3	3467.0	5658.0	10018.0	11300.0	13288.0	17961.0
Fiji Islands							
Nandi	SP-6/7	3467.0	5643.0	8867.0	13273.0	17904.0	
French Guiana							
Cayenne	CAR-B	3455.0	5520.0	6586.0	8846.0	11330.0	17907.0
	SAM-NE	3479.0	5526.0	8855.0	10096.0	13297.0	17907.0
	SAT-1	3452.0	6535.0	8861.0	13357.0	17955.0	
	SAT-2	2854.0	5565.0	11291.0	13315.0	17955.0	
Gabon							
Franceville	AFI-4	2878.0	5493.0	8903.0	13294.0	17961.0	
Libreville	AFI-4	2878.0	5493.0	8903.0	13294.0	17961.0	
Port Gentil	AFI-4	2878.0	5493.0	8903.0	13294.0	17961.0	
Georgia							
Tbilisi	MID-1	2992.0	4669.0	5667.0	6631.0	8951.0	11375.0
		17961.0					
	MID-2	3467.0	5658.0	10018.0	11300.0	13288.0	17961.0
Germany							
Berlin	EUR-A	3479.0	5661.0	6598.0	10084.0	13288.0	17961.0
Ghana							
Accra	AFI-4	2878.0	5493.0	8903.0	13294.0	17961.0	
Greenland							
Sondrestrom	NAT-D	2971.0	4675.0	8891.0	11279.0	13291.0	17946.0
Guam							
Guam	CWP-1/2	2998.0	4666.0	6532.0	6562.0	8903.0	11384.0
		13300.0	17904.0	21985.0			
Guatemala							
Guatemala City	CAR-A	2887.0	5550.0	6577.0	8918.0	11396.0	13297.0
		17907.0					
Guinea							
Conakry	AFI-1	3452.0	6535.0	8861.0	13357.0	17955.0	
Guinea-Bissau							
Bissau	AFI-1	3452.0	6535.0	8861.0	13357.0	17955.0	
Guyana							
Georgetown	CAR-B	3455.0	5520.0	6586.0	8846.0	11330.0	17907.0
	SAM-NE	3479.0	5526.0	8855.0	10096.0	13297.0	17907.0

Hawaii							
Honolulu	CEP-1/2	2869.0	3413.0	5547.0	8843.0	11282.0	13261.0
		17904.0					
	CWP-1/2	2998.0	4666.0	6532.0	6562.0	8903.0	11384.0
		13300.0	17904.0	21985.0			
	NP-3/4	2932.0	5628.0	5677.0	6665.0	8915.0	10048.0
		13294.0	13339.0	17904.0	17946.0	21925.0	
	SP-6/7	3467.0	5643.0	8867.0	13273.0	17904.0	
Honduras							
Tegucigalpa	CAR-A	2887.0	5550.0	6577.0	8918.0	11396.0	13297.0
		17907.0					
Hong Kong							
Hong Kong	CWP-1/2	2998.0	4666.0	6532.0	6562.0	8903.0	11384.0
		13300.0	17904.0	21985.0			
	SEA-2	3485.0	5649.0	5655.0	8942.0	11396.0	13309.0
		17907.0					
Iceland							
Reykjavik	NAT-B	2899.0	5616.0	8864.0	13291.0	17946.0	
	NAT-C	2862.0	5649.0	8879.0	13306.0	17946.0	
	NAT-D	2971.0	4675.0	8891.0	11279.0	13291.0	17946.0
India							
Bombay	AFI-3	3467.0	5658.0	10018.0	11300.0	13288.0	17961.0
	NO-1	3476.0	5634.0	8879.0	13306.0	17961.0	
	MID-2	3467.0	5658.0	10018.0	11300.0	13288.0	17961.0
Calcutta	SEA-1	3470.0	6556.0	10066.0	13318.0	17907.0	
Delhi	MID-2	3467.0	5658.0	10018.0	11300.0	13288.0	17961.0
Madras	INO-1	3476.0	5634.0	8879.0	13306.0	17961.0	
	SEA-1	3470.0	6556.0	10066.0	13318.0	17907.0	
Mahajanga	INO-1	3476.0	5634.0	8879.0	13306.0	17961.0	
Indonesia							
Bali	SEA-1	3470.0	6556.0	10066.0	13318.0	17907.0	
	SEA-2	3485.0	5649.0	5655.0	8942.0	11396.0	13309.0
		17907.0					
	SEA-3	3470.0	5733.0	6556.0	10066.0	11396.0	13318.0
		17907.0					
Denpasar	SEA-2	3485.0	5649.0	5655.0	8942.0	11396.0	13309.0
		17907.0					
Jakarta	SEA-1	3470.0	6556.0	10066.0	13318.0	17907.0	
	SEA-2	3485.0	5649.0	5655.0	8942.0	11396.0	13309.0
		17907.0					
	SEA-3	3470.0	5733.0	6556.0	10066.0	11396.0	13318.0
		17907.0					
Ujung Pandang	SEA-3	3470.0	5733.0	6556.0	10066.0	11396.0	13318.0
		17907.0					
Iran							
Abadan	MID-2	3467.0	5658.0	10018.0	11300.0	13288.0	17961.0
Tehran	MID-1	2992.0	4669.0	5667.0	6631.0	8951.0	11375.0
		17961.0					
	MID-2	3467.0	5658.0	10018.0	11300.0	13288.0	17961.0

Iraq							
Baghdad	MID-1	2992.0	4669.0	5667.0	6631.0	8951.0	11375.0
		17961.0					
Basrah	MID-1	2992.0	4669.0	5667.0	6631.0	8951.0	11375.0
		17961.0					
Ivory Coast							
Abidjan	AFI-1	3452.0	6535.0	8861.0	13357.0	17955.0	
Bouake	AFI-1	3452.0	6535.0	8861.0	13357.0	17955.0	
Japan							
Naha	CWP-1/2	2998.0	4666.0	6532.0	6562.0	8903.0	11384.0
		13300.0	17904.0	21985.0			
Tokyo	CWP-1/2	2998.0	4666.0	6532.0	6562.0	8903.0	11384.0
		13300.0	17904.0	21985.0			
	NP-3/4	2932.0	5628.0	5677.0	6665.0	8915.0	10048.0
		13294.0	13339.0	17904.0	17946.0	21925.0	
	SEA-2	3485.0	5649.0	5655.0	8942.0	11396.0	13309.0
		17907.0					
Jordan							
Amman	MID-1	2992.0	4669.0	5667.0	6631.0	8951.0	11375.0
		17961.0					
Kazakhstan							
Aktyubinsk	MID-3	2994.0	4669.0	6631.0	8951.0	11375.0	17961.0
Alma Ata	MID-2	3467.0	5658.0	10018.0	11300.0	13288.0	17961.0
	MID-3	2994.0	4669.0	6631.0	8951.0	11375.0	17961.0
Uralsk	MID-3	2994.0	4669.0	6631.0	8951.0	11375.0	17961.0
Kzyl-Orda	MID-3	2994.0	4669.0	6631.0	8951.0	11375.0	17961.0
Kenya							
Nairobi	AFI-3	3467.0	5658.0	10018.0	11300.0	13288.0	17961.0
	AFI-4	2878.0	5493.0	8903.0	13294.0	17961.0	
	INO-1	3476.0	5634.0	8879.0	13306.0	17961.0	
Khartoum							
Khartoum	AFI-3	3467.0	5658.0	10018.0	11300.0	13288.0	17961.0
Kuwait							
Kuwait	MID-1	2992.0	4669.0	5667.0	6631.0	8951.0	11375.0
		17961.0					
	MID-2	3467.0	5658.0	10018.0	11300.0	13288.0	17961.0
Kyrgyzstan							
Frunze	MID-2	3467.0	5658.0	10018.0	11300.0	13288.0	17961.0
	MID-3	2994.0	4669.0	6631.0	8951.0	11375.0	17961.0
Laos							
Vientiane	SEA-2	3485.0	5649.0	5655.0	8942.0	11396.0	13309.0
		17907.0					
Latvia							
Riga	EUR-A	3479.0	5661.0	6598.0	10084.0	13288.0	
		17961.0					

Lebanon							
Beirut	EUR-A	3479.0	5661.0	6598.0	10084.0	13288.0	17961.0
	MID-1	2992.0	4669.0	5667.0	6631.0	8951.0	11375.0
		17961.0					
Lesotho							
Maseru	AFI-4	2878.0	5493.0	8903.0	13294.0	17961.0	
Liberia							
Monrovia (Roberts)	AFI-1	3452.0	6535.0	8861.0	13357.0	17955.0	
	AFI-4	2878.0	5493.0	8903.0	13294.0	17961.0	
Libya							
Benghazi	AFI-3	3467.0	5658.0	10018.0	11300.0	13288.0	17961.0
Tripoli	AFI-2	3419.0	5652.0	8894.0	13273.0	17961.0	
	AFI-3	3467.0	5658.0	10018.0	11300.0	13288.0	17961.0
Lithuania							
Vilnius	EUR-A	3479.0	5661.0	6598.0	10084.0	13288.0	17961.0
Madagascar							
Antananarivo	INO-1	3476.0	5634.0	8879.0	13306.0	17961.0	
Toamasina	INO-1	3476.0	5634.0	8879.0	13306.0	17961.0	
Malawi							
Blantyre	INO-1	3476.0	5634.0	8879.0	13306.0	17961.0	
Lilongwe	INO-1	3476.0	5634.0	8879.0	13306.0	17961.0	
Malaysia							
Kota Kinabalu	SEA-2	3485.0	5649.0	5655.0	8942.0	11396.0	13309.0
		17907.0					
Kuala Lumpur	SEA-1	3470.0	6556.0	10066.0	13318.0	17907.0	
	SEA-2	3485.0	5649.0	5655.0	8942.0	11396.0	13309.0
		17907.0					
Maldive Islands							
Male	INO-1	3476.0	5634.0	8879.0	13306.0	17961.0	
	MID-2	3467.0	5658.0	10018.0	11300.0	13288.0	17961.0
	SEA-1	3470.0	6556.0	10066.0	13318.0	17907.0	
Mali							
Bamako	AFI-1	3452.0	6535.0	8861.0	13357.0	17955.0	
Gao	AFI-2	3419.0	5652.0	8894.0	13273.0	17961.0	
Malta							
Valetta	EUR-A	3479.0	5661.0	6598.0	10084.0	13288.0	17961.0
Mauritania							
Nouadhibou	AFI-1	3452.0	6535.0	8861.0	13357.0	17955.0	
Nouakchott	AFI-1	3452.0	6535.0	8861.0	13357.0	17955.0	
Mauritius							
Mauritius	INO-1	3476.0	5634.0	8879.0	13306.0	17961.0	

Mexico							
Merida	CAR-A	2887.0	5550.0	6577.0	8918.0	11396.0	13297.0
		17907.0					
Mongolia							
Hailar	EA-1	3016.0	6571.0	8897.0	10042.0	17958.0	
Ulaanbaatar	EA-1	3016.0	6571.0	8897.0	10042.0	17958.0	
	EA-2	3485.0	5649.0	5655.0	8942.0	11396.0	13309.0
		17907.0					
	NCA-3	3004.0	5664.0	10039.0	13303.0	17958.0	
Morocco							
Casablanca	AFI-1	3452.0	6535.0	8861.0	13357.0	17955.0	
Mozambique							
Beira	INO-1	3476.0	5634.0	8879.0	13306.0	17961.0	
Myanmar							
Yangon	SEA-1	3470.0	6556.0	10066.0	13318.0	17907.0	
Namibia							
Windhoek	AFI-4	2878.0	5493.0	8903.0	13294.0	17961.0	
Nepal							
Kathmandu	MID-2	3467.0	5658.0	10018.0	11300.0	13288.0	17961.0
	SEA-1	3470.0	6556.0	10066.0	13318.0	17907.0	
New Zealand							
Auckland	SP-6/7	3467.0	5643.0	8867.0	13273.0	17904.0	
Niger							
Niamey	AFI-1	3452.0	6535.0	8861.0	13357.0	17955.0	
	AFI-2	3419.0	5652.0	8894.0	13273.0	17961.0	
	AFI-4	2878.0	5493.0	8903.0	13294.0	17961.0	
Nigeria							
Kano	AFI-1	3452.0	6535.0	8861.0	13357.0	17955.0	
	AFI-2	3419.0	5652.0	8894.0	13273.0	17961.0	
	AFI-4	2878.0	5493.0	8903.0	13294.0	17961.0	
Lagos	AFI-4	2878.0	5493.0	8903.0	13294.0	17961.0	
North Korea							
Pyongyang	EA-1	3016.0	6571.0	8897.0	10042.0	17958.0	
	EA-2	3485.0	5649.0	5655.0	8942.0	11396.0	13309.0
		17907.0					
	NCA-3	3004.0	5664.0	10039.0	13303.0	17958.0	
Norway							
Bodo	NAT-D	2971.0	4675.0	8891.0	11279.0	13291.0	17946.0
Oman							
Muscat	MID-2	3467.0	5658.0	10018.0	11300.0	13288.0	17961.0

Pakistan								
Karachi	MID-2	3467.0	5658.0	10018.0	11300.0	13288.0	17961.0	
Lahore	MID-2	3467.0	5658.0	10018.0	11300.0	13288.0	17961.0	
Panama								
Panama	CAR-A	2887.0	5550.0	6577.0	8918.0	11396.0	13297.0	
		17907.0						
	CAR-B	3455.0	5520.0	6586.0	8846.0	11330.0	17907.0	
Papua New Guinea								
Port Moresby	CWP-1/2	2998.0	4666.0	6532.0	6562.0	8903.0	11384.0	
		13300.0	17904.0	21985.0				
Paraguay								
Asuncion	SAM-SE	3479.0	5526.0	8855.0	10096.0	13297.0	17907.0	
	SAM-SW	2944.0	4669.0	6549.0	10024.0	11360.0	17907.0	
Peru								
Iquitos	SAM-C	3479.0	5526.0	8855.0	10096.0	13297.0	17907.0	
Lima	SAM-NW	2944.0	4669.0	6549.0	10024.0	11360.0	17907.0	
	SAM-SE	3479.0	5526.0	8855.0	10096.0	13297.0	17907.0	
	SAM-SW	2944.0	4669.0	6549.0	10024.0	11360.0	17907.0	
Talara	SAM-SW	2944.0	4669.0	6549.0	10024.0	11360.0	17907.0	
Philippines								
Manila	CWP-1/2	2998.0	4666.0	6532.0	6562.0	8903.0	11384.0	
		13300.0	17904.0	21985.0				
	SEA-2	3485.0	5649.0	5655.0	8942.0	11396.0	13309.0	
		17907.0						
Polynesia								
Wallis Island	SP-6/7	3467.0	5643.0	8867.0	13273.0	17904.0		
Russia								
Arkhangelsk	EUR-A	3479.0	5661.0	6598.0	10084.0	13288.0	17961.0	
Barnaul	NCA-2	2851.0	4678.0	6592.0	10096.0	17958.0		
Chita	NCA-3	3004.0	5664.0	10039.0	13303.0	17958.0		
Chulman	NCA-3	3004.0	5664.0	10039.0	13303.0	17958.0		
Ekimchan	NCA-3	3004.0	5664.0	10039.0	13303.0	17958.0		
Irkutsk	EA-1	3016.0	6571.0	8897.0	10042.0	17958.0		
	EA-2	3485.0	5649.0	5655.0	8942.0	11396.0	13309.0	
		17907.0						
	NCA-2	2851.0	4678.0	6592.0	10096.0	17958.0		
	NCA-3	3004.0	5664.0	10039.0	13303.0	17958.0		
Ivdel	NCA-1	3019.0	5646.0	13315.0	17958.0			
Khabarovsk	NCA-3	3004.0	5664.0	10039.0	13303.0	17958.0		
Khanty Mansiysk	NCA-1	3019.0	5646.0	13315.0	17958.0			
	NCA-2	2851.0	4678.0	6592.0	10096.0	17958.0		
Kirensk	NCA-2	2851.0	4678.0	6592.0	10096.0	17958.0		
	NCA-3	3004.0	5664.0	10039.0	13303.0	17958.0		
Kolpashevo	NCA-2	2851.0	4678.0	6592.0	10096.0	17958.0		
Krasnoyarsk	NCA-2	2851.0	4678.0	6592.0	10096.0	17958.0		
Kuybyshev	MID-3	2994.0	4669.0	6631.0	8951.0	11375.0	17961.0	

	Moscow	EUR-A	3479.0	5661.0	6598.0	10084.0	13288.0	17961.0
		MID-3	2994.0	4669.0	6631.0	8951.0	11375.0	17961.0
		NCA-1	3019.0	5646.0	13315.0	17958.0		
	Murmansk	EUR-A	3479.0	5661.0	6598.0	10084.0	13288.0	17961.0
	Novosibirsk	NCA-2	2851.0	4678.0	6592.0	10096.0	17958.0	
	Podkamennaya	NCA-2	2851.0	4678.0	6592.0	10096.0	17958.0	
	St. Petersburg	EUR-A	3479.0	5661.0	6598.0	10084.0	13288.0	17961.0
	Surgut	NCA-2	2851.0	4678.0	6592.0	10096.0	17958.0	
	Sverdlovsk	NCA-1	3019.0	5646.0	13315.0	17958.0		
	Syktyvkar	EUR-A	3479.0	5661.0	6598.0	10084.0	13288.0	17961.0
		NCA-1	3019.0	5646.0	13315.0	17958.0		
	Ulan Ude	NCA-3	3004.0	5664.0	10039.0	13303.0	17958.0	
	Velikiye	EUR-A	3479.0	5661.0	6598.0	10084.0	13288.0	17961.0
	Volodga	NCA-1	3019.0	5646.0	13315.0	17958.0		
		EUR-A	3479.0	5661.0	6598.0	10084.0	13288.0	17961.0
	Yeniseysk	NCA-2	2851.0	4678.0	6592.0	10096.0	17958.0	
Rwanda								
	Kigali	AFI-3	3467.0	5658.0	10018.0	11300.0	13288.0	17961.0
		INO-1	3476.0	5634.0	8879.0	13306.0	17961.0	
Sal Island								
	Sal	SAT-1	3452.0	6535.0	8861.0	13357.0	17955.0	
		SAT-2	2854.0	5565.0	11291.0	13315.0	17955.0	
Saudi Arabia								
	Jeddah	AFI-3	3467.0	5658.0	10018.0	11300.0	13288.0	17961.0
		NO-1	3476.0	5634.0	8879.0	13306.0	17961.0	
		MID-1	2992.0	4669.0	5667.0	6631.0	8951.0	11375.0
			17961.0					
Senegal								
	Dakar	AFI-1	3452.0	6535.0	8861.0	13357.0	17955.0	
		SAT-1	3452.0	6535.0	8861.0	13357.0	17955.0	
		SAT-2	2854.0	5565.0	11291.0	13315.0	17955.0	
Seychelles								
	Seychelles	AFI-3	3467.0	5658.0	10018.0	11300.0	13288.0	17961.0
		AFI-4	2878.0	5493.0	8903.0	13294.0	17961.0	
		INO-1	3476.0	5634.0	8879.0	13306.0	17961.0	
Sierra Leone								
	Freetown	AFI-1	3452.0	6535.0	8861.0	13357.0	17955.0	
Singapore								
	Singapore	SEA-1	3470.0	6556.0	10066.0	13318.0	17907.0	
		SEA-2	3485.0	5649.0	5655.0	8942.0	11396.0	13309.0
			17907.0					
		SEA-3	3470.0	5733.0	6556.0	10066.0	11396.0	13318.0
			17907.0					
Somalia								
	Hargesia	AFI-3	3467.0	5658.0	10018.0	11300.0	13288.0	17961.0
	Kisimayu	AFI-3	3467.0	5658.0	10018.0	11300.0	13288.0	17961.0
	Mogadishu	AFI-3	3467.0	5658.0	10018.0	11300.0	13288.0	17961.0

South Africa							
Johannesburg	AFI-4	2878.0	5493.0	8903.0	13294.0	17961.0	
	INO-1	3476.0	5634.0	8879.0	13306.0	17961.0	
South Korea							
Seoul	CWP-1/2	2998.0	4666.0	6532.0	6562.0	8903.0	11384.0
		13300.0	17904.0	21985.0			
	SEA-2	3485.0	5649.0	5655.0	8942.0	11396.0	13309.0
		17907.0					
Taegu	EA-1	3016.0	6571.0	8897.0	10042.0	17958.0	
Sri Lanka							
Colombo	INO-1	3476.0	5634.0	8879.0	13306.0	17961.0	
	SEA-1	3470.0	6556.0	10066.0	13318.0	17907.0	
St. Denis & Reunion Islands							
St. Denis	INO-1	3476.0	5634.0	8879.0	13306.0	17961.0	
Surinam							
Paramaribo	CAR-B	3455.0	5520.0	6586.0	8846.0	11330.0	17907.0
	NAT-A	3016.0	5598.0	13306.0	17946.0		
	SAM-NE	3479.0	5526.0	8855.0	10096.0	13297.0	17907.0
	SAT-1	3452.0	6535.0	8861.0	13357.0	17955.0	
	SAT-2	2854.0	5565.0	11291.0	13315.0	17955.0	
Syria							
Damascus	MID-1	2992.0	4669.0	5667.0	6631.0	8951.0	11375.0
		17961.0					
Tahiti							
Tahiti	SP-6/7	3467.0	5643.0	8867.0	13273.0	17904.0	
Taiwan							
Taipei	CWP-1/2	2998.0	4666.0	6532.0	6562.0	8903.0	11384.0
		13300.0	17904.0	21985.0			
Tajikistan							
Dushanbe	MID-2	3467.0	5658.0	10018.0	11300.0	13288.0	17961.0
	MID-3	2994.0	4669.0	6631.0	8951.0	11375.0	17961.0
Tanzania							
Dar es Salaam	AFI-3	3467.0	5658.0	10018.0	11300.0	13288.0	17961.0
	INO-1	3476.0	5634.0	8879.0	13306.0	17961.0	
Thailand							
Bangkok	SEA-1	3470.0	6556.0	10066.0	13318.0	17907.0	
	SEA-2	3485.0	5649.0	5655.0	8942.0	11396.0	13309.0
		17907.0					
Togo							
Lomé	AFI-4	2878.0	5493.0	8903.0	13294.0	17961.0	
Niamtougou	AFI-4	2878.0	5493.0	8903.0	13294.0	17961.0	

Trinidad							
Piarco (Port of Spain)	CAR-A	2887.0	5550.0	6577.0	8918.0	11396.0	13297.0
		17907.0					
	CAR-B	3455.0	5520.0	6586.0	8846.0	11330.0	17907.0
	NAT-A	3016.0	5598.0	13306.0	17946.0		
	SAM-NE	3479.0	5526.0	8855.0	10096.0	13297.0	17907.0
Tunisia							
Tunis	AFI-2	3419.0	5652.0	8894.0	13273.0	17961.0	
	EUR-A	3479.0	5661.0	6598.0	10084.0	13288.0	17961.0
Turkey							
Ankara	MID-1	2992.0	4669.0	5667.0	6631.0	8951.0	11375.0
		17961.0					
Uganda							
Entebbe	AFI-3	3467.0	5658.0	10018.0	11300.0	13288.0	17961.0
	AFI-4	2878.0	5493.0	8903.0	13294.0	17961.0	
Ukraine							
Kiev	EUR-A	3479.0	5661.0	6598.0	10084.0	13288.0	17961.0
L'vov	EUR-A	3479.0	5661.0	6598.0	10084.0	13288.0	17961.0
Odessa	EUR-A	3479.0	5661.0	6598.0	10084.0	13288.0	17961.0
	MID-1	2992.0	4669.0	5667.0	6631.0	8951.0	11375.0
		17961.0					
	MID-2	3467.0	5658.0	10018.0	11300.0	13288.0	17961.0
Simferopol	EUR-A	3479.0	5661.0	6598.0	10084.0	13288.0	17961.0
	MID-1	2992.0	4669.0	5667.0	6631.0	8951.0	11375.0
		17961.0					
United Kingdom							
Shanwick	NAT-A	3016.0	5598.0	13306.0	17946.0		
	NAT-B	2899.0	5616.0	8864.0	13291.0	17946.0	
	NAT-C	2862.0	5649.0	8879.0	13306.0	17946.0	
	NAT-F	3476.0	6622.0	8831.0	11336.0	13291.0	
Uruguay							
Montevideo	SAM-SE	3479.0	5526.0	8855.0	10096.0	13297.0	17907.0
USA							
New York	CAR-A	2887.0	5550.0	6577.0	8918.0	11396.0	13297.0
		17907.0					
	CAR-B	3455.0	5520.0	6586.0	8846.0	11330.0	17907.0
	NAT-A	3016.0	5598.0	13306.0	17946.0		
	NAT-B	2899.0	5616.0	8864.0	13291.0	17946.0	
	NAT-E	2962.0	6628.0	8825.0	11309.0	13354.0	
San Francisco	CEP-1/2	2869.0	3413.0	5547.0	8843.0	11282.0	13261.0
		17904.0					
	NP-3/4	2932.0	5628.0	5677.0	6665.0	8915.0	10048.0
		13294.0	13339.0	17904.0	17946.0	21925.0	
Uzbekistan							
Samarkand	MID-2	3467.0	5658.0	10018.0	11300.0	13288.0	17961.0
	MID-3	2994.0	4669.0	6631.0	8951.0	11375.0	17961.0
Tashkent	MID-2	3467.0	5658.0	10018.0	11300.0	13288.0	17961.0
	MID-3	2994.0	4669.0	6631.0	8951.0	11375.0	17961.0

Vanuatu							
Port Vila	SP-6/7	3467.0	5643.0	8867.0	13273.0	17904.0	
Venezuela							
Maiquetia (Caracas)	CAR-B	3455.0	5520.0	6586.0	8846.0	11330.0	17907.0
	SAM-C	3479.0	5526.0	8855.0	10096.0	13297.0	17907.0
	SAM-NE	3479.0	5526.0	8855.0	10096.0	13297.0	17907.0
	SAM-NW	2944.0	4669.0	6549.0	10024.0	11360.0	17907.0
Vietnam							
Hanoi	SEA-2	3485.0	5649.0	5655.0	8942.0	11396.0	13309.0
		17907.0					
Ho Chi Minh	SEA-2	3485.0	5649.0	5655.0	8942.0	11396.0	13309.0
		17907.0					
Yemen							
Sana'a	AFI-3	3467.0	5658.0	10018.0	11300.0	13288.0	17961.0
	MID-1	2992.0	4669.0	5667.0	6631.0	8951.0	11375.0
		17961.0					
Zaire							
Goma	AFI-4	2878.0	5493.0	8903.0	13294.0	17961.0	
Kinshasa	AFI-4	2878.0	5493.0	8903.0	13294.0	17961.0	
Kisangani	AFI-4	2878.0	5493.0	8903.0	13294.0	17961.0	
Lumbumbashi	AFI-4	2878.0	5493.0	8903.0	13294.0	17961.0	
N'djili	AFI-4	2878.0	5493.0	8903.0	13294.0	17961.0	
Zambia							
Lusaka	AFI-4	2878.0	5493.0	8903.0	13294.0	17961.0	
	INO-1	3476.0	5634.0	8879.0	13306.0	17961.0	
Zimbabwe							
Bulawayo	AFI-4	2878.0	5493.0	8903.0	13294.0	17961.0	
Harare	INO-1	3476.0	5634.0	8879.0	13306.0	17961.0	
Salisbury	AFI-4	2878.0	5493.0	8903.0	13294.0	17961.0	

Other Services

Aeronautical Fixed Telecommunications Network (AFTN)

4611.0	4905.0	6813.5	6821.3	6821.4	7490.0
7740.0	9116.0	9336.0	9424.5	10028.0	10846.0
13700.0	13812.0	14500.0	14900.0	19500.0	

ASECNA

17995.0

Australian Royal Flying Doctor Service

2020.0	2260.0	2280.0	2656.0	2760.0	2805.0
2972.0	4010.0	4030.0	4045.0	4055.0	4350.0
4606.0	4880.0	4926.0	4935.0	4940.0	4980.0
5110.0	5145.0	5300.0	5355.0	5410.0	6785.0
6825.0	6840.0	6845.0	6866.0	6880.0	6890.0
6920.0	6925.0	6945.0	6950.0	6960.0	6965.0
6975.0	7307.0	7392.0	7410.0	7465.0	7475.0
7517.0	7550.0	7975.0	8144.0	8147.0	8165.0

Canadian Coast Guard (Air Vessel)

6513.0

NASA

2405.0	2505.0	2622.0	2664.0	2678.0	2716.0
2744.0	2764.0	2800.0	2836.0	3024.0	3120.0
3187.0	3365.0	4376.0	4500.0	4510.0	4704.0
4714.0	4755.0	4825.0	4856.0	4860.0	4900.0
4992.0	5060.0	5180.0	5187.0	5190.0	5235.0
5246.0	5350.0	5436.0	5680.0	5718.0	5775.0
5810.0	5822.0	6720.0	6750.0	6753.0	6810.0
6837.0	6880.0	6896.0	6897.0	6919.0	7313.0
7412.0	7461.0	7525.0	7605.0	7676.0	7697.0
7742.0	7765.0	7804.0	7807.0	7833.0	7860.0
7910.0	7919.0	7985.0	8077.0	8993.0	9018.0
9022.0	9043.0	9115.0	9132.0	9138.0	9170.0
9910.0	10159.0	10215.0	10230.0	10270.0	10301.0
10305.0	10310.0	10327.0	10475.0	10780.0	10850.0
10880.0	10905.0	10949.0	11104.0	11252.0	11407.0
11414.0	11548.0	11615.0	11621.0	11634.0	11984.0
11988.0	12107.0	12160.0	12277.0	12287.0	12876.0
13210.0	13227.0	13237.0	13244.0	13380.0	13468.0
13495.0	13600.0	13676.0	13735.0	13742.0	13878.0
13942.0	14497.0	14585.0	14615.0	14650.0	14896.0
14937.0	14967.0	15698.0	16216.0	16246.0	17470.0
17554.0	17668.0	17940.0	18009.0	18022.0	18051.0
18196.0	18310.0	18331.0	18354.0	18434.0	18700.0
18769.0	18801.0	18990.0	19126.0	19143.0	19149.5
19303.0	19371.0	19390.0	19640.0	19928.0	19963.0
19966.0	20185.0	20186.0	20192.0	20198.0	20266.0
20272.0	20390.0	20475.0	20690.0	21810.0	22683.0
22755.0	22990.0	23035.0	23281.0	23325.0	23413.0

23479.0	23485.0	23661.0	23840.0	23940.0	24240.0
24512.0	24530.0	24780.0	24914.0	25130.0	25161.0
25198.0	25245.0	25597.0	26356.0	26389.0	26515.0
26684.0	27065.0	27720.0			

Goddard Space Center

3860.0	7185.0	14295.0	21395.0	28650.0

Jet Propulsion Labs

14280.0	21280.0

Johnson Space Center

3840.0	14280.0

Offshore Drilling Rigs - Helicopter Support

2860.0	2878.0	3019.0	3434.0	3449.0	3452.0
3453.0	3488.0	4645.0	4672.0	5463.0	5472.0
5480.0	5508.0	5568.0	5645.0		

United Kingdom - Air/Sea Rescue

5690.0	5695.0	13205.0

United States Coast Guard - Air Operations

2141.0	2182.0	2261.0	2678.0	3023.0	3120.0
3123.0	3132.0	4125.0	4376.0	5272.0	5320.0
5680.0	5692.0	5696.0	6230.0	6513.0	8980.0
8984.0	11195.0	11201.0	15081.0	15084.0	15087.0

United States - Counter-Drug Operations

a) U.S. Customs

3123.0	7527.0	8100.0	8912.0	10242.0	11494.0
13312.0	13907.0	15081.0	15084.0	15867.0	18594.0
20890.0	20943.0	23214.0	25350.0		

c) U.S. Department of Defense

2808.5	3369.0	3428.0	4500.0	4991.0	5058.5
5571.0	5732.0	5912.0	7475.0	7527.0	7778.5
8912.0	9238.5	9802.0	10242.0	11071.0	11073.5
11191.0	11195.0	11198.0	11288.0	11494.0	12138.5
12215.0	12222.0	13312.0	13457.0	13658.5	13907.0
15084.0	15867.0	15953.5	15964.0	17601.0	17952.0
18594.0	19131.0	20631.0	20890.0	23214.0	25350.0
27870.0					

b) U.S. Drug Enforcement Agency

5277.0	5841.0	7300.0	7657.0	9497.0	11076.0
14350.0	14686.0	14690.0	18171.0	18666.0	19131.0
23402.5	23675.0				

d) U.S. Joint Task Force - 4

3130.0	4735.0	5399.5	6788.0	8972.0	11191.0

United -States - Federal Aviation Administration

3331.0	3428.0	4055.0	4675.0	5571.0	5860.0
6870.0	7475.0	7611.0	8125.0	8912.0	9914.0
11288.0	11401.0	11637.0	13312.0	13457.0	13630.0
15851.0	16348.0	17952.0	19410.0	27575.0	27585.0
27625.0	27665.0				

United States - Flight Tests

a) Aero Corporation

5571.0	6550.0	8822.0

b) Aerospatiale Helicopter

5451.0	13312.0

c) Boeing Company

2851.0	2994.0	3004.0	3281.0	3343.0	3443.0
5451.0	5469.0	5571.0	6550.0	8822.0	8918.0
9017.0	10045.0	11288.0	11306.0	11375.0	13312.0
17964.0	21931.0				

d) Curtis Wilbur

3109.0

e) Falcon Jet Corporation

2851.0	8822.0	17964.0

f) Grumman Aerospace

3279.5	3281.0	6694.5	9010.5	11210.5	13225.0
13225.5	15027.5	23331.0	23332.5		

g) Lockheed Corporation

3443.0	3821.0	5469.0	6550.0	6730.0	8822.0
10045.0	11306.0	13312.0	17964.0	21931.0	

h) McDonnell Douglas

2851.0	3004.0	3443.0	5451.0	5469.0	5571.0
6550.0	8822.0	8918.0	10045.0	11288.0	11306.0
13312.0	17964.0	21931.0			

i) Northern Technical

3449.0	5472.0

j) Rockwell International

2851.0	2869.0	2994.0	3004.0	3443.0	3474.0
4675.0	4682.0	5451.0	5469.0	5571.0	5596.0
6550.0	6659.0	8822.0	8918.0	10099.0	11288.0
11306.0	13312.0	17964.0	21931.0		

k) United Technologies

3039.0	3281.0	9011.5	9013.0	17983.0

United States - National Oceanographic and Atmospheric Administration (NOAA)

3407.0	4701.0	5562.0	5696.0	6673.0	8876.0
9020.0	10015.0	11398.0	13267.0	13354.0	17901.0
21937.0					

Fairchild Republic A-10a Thunderbolt II
United States Air Force

World Military/Air Forces

Belgian Air Force

8989.0	11268.0	11275.0	18002.0

Brazilian Air Force

6708.0	7782.0	8834.0	9001.0	9009.0	9093.0
11172.0	11247.0	11273.0	13221.0	13225.0	13250.0
17957.0	17983.0	21994.0			

Canadian Forces

3046.0	3092.0	3095.0	3151.0	4560.0	4700.0
4704.0	4730.0	4739.0	4746.0	4752.0	5595.0
5684.0	5690.0	5703.0	5718.0	5850.0	6693.0
6705.0	6708.0	6712.0	6716.0	6746.0	6753.0
6764.0	8873.0	8989.0	9006.0	9010.0	9023.0
9027.0	11186.0	11209.0	11214.0	11217.0	11233.0
11236.0	11240.5	11249.0	11265.0	11271.0	11272.0
13207.0	13231.0	13254.0	13257.0	13315.0	15031.0
15035.0	15038.0	17995.0	17999.0	18012.0	18027.0
23250.0					

Chilean Air Force

5710.5	7357.5

CIS (former Soviet) Air Force

11216.0

Cuban Air Force

9018.0

Danish Air Force

6732.0	11245.0

Danish Navy (Naval Air)

4663.0

Panavia Pa-200 Tornado Ids
German Air Force

French Air Force

3069.0	3896.0	5696.0	5708.0	5725.0	6712.0
6738.0	6747.0	6752.0	8964.0	8981.0	8987.0
9015.0	11223.0	13239.0	23249.0	23254.0	

German Air Force

3144.0	5691.0	5691.5	5713.0	6693.0	6718.0
6743.0	6747.0	6762.0	6832.0	8967.0	8985.0
9000.0	9011.0	9025.0	11179.0	11187.0	11217.0
11266.0	11272.0	11287.0	13200.0	13245.0	13248.0
17992.0	18006.0	23342.0			

German Navy (Naval Air)

13248.0

Indian Air Force

10049.0

Italian Air Force

5685.0	5690.0	5721.0	6715.0	6740.0	6743.0
6760.0	8991.0	9013.0	11214.0	11357.0	13220.0
15026.0	23134.0				

Mexican Air Force

6693.0

Netherlands (Dutch) Air Force

4768.0	5690.0	5705.0	6689.0	6726.0	6729.0
8970.0	11182.0				

NORAD

3071.0	3295.0	3306.0	4435.0	4443.0	4495.0
4735.0	4872.0	5068.0	5297.0	5812.0	5960.0
6708.0	6735.0	6750.0	6757.0	7811.0	9023.0
9027.0	9232.0	9235.0	9315.0	9500.0	9510.0
9586.0	9650.0	9723.0	9793.0	9993.0	10194.0
10452.0	11007.0	11141.0	11214.0	11226.0	11240.0
11284.0	11441.0	11607.0	13207.0	13291.0	13547.0
14364.0	14894.0	16363.0	17999.0	18027.0	20042.0
20420.0	20433.0	20855.0	23265.0	23419.0	25340.0

Norwegian Navy (Naval Air)

11182.0

Pakistani Air Force

2931.0

Philippine Air Force

6525.0

Portuguese Air Force

8992.0

Bae Harrier Gr.5a
Royal Air Force

Royal Australian Air Force

3032.0	5688.0	5695.0	5713.0	5718.0	6738.0
8976.0	8990.0	9006.0	9023.0	9027.0	11195.0
11209.0	11235.0	11236.0	11267.0	13205.0	13207.0
18023.0					

Royal Australian Navy (Naval Air)

6224.0

Royal Air Force

2641.0	3007.0	3026.0	3039.0	3050.0	3051.0
3085.0	3102.0	3110.0	3112.0	3116.0	3120.0
3126.0	3130.0	3218.0	3345.0	3380.0	3481.0
3512.0	3864.0	3867.0	3880.0	3893.0	3916.0
3939.0	3947.0	4043.0	4397.0	4484.0	4540.0
4707.0	4710.0	4716.0	4719.0	4722.0	4730.0
4739.0	4742.0	4746.0	4790.0	4822.0	4830.0
4845.0	5095.0	5178.0	5211.0	5270.0	5361.0
5403.0	5420.0	5429.0	5430.0	5436.0	5441.0
5446.0	5447.0	5462.0	5471.0	5610.0	5685.0
5712.0	5713.0	5717.0	5721.0	5729.0	5747.0
6526.0	6690.0	6693.0	6697.0	6715.0	6730.0
6734.0	6738.0	6742.0	6748.0	6751.0	6757.0
6760.0	6765.0	8156.0	8190.0	8790.0	8921.0
8965.0	8967.0	8971.0	8975.5	8980.0	8984.0
8987.0	8990.0	8992.0	8993.0	8996.0	9011.0
9014.0	9022.0	9024.0	9032.0	9036.0	10093.0
10194.0	10937.0	11176.0	11180.0	11200.0	11204.0
11212.0	11214.0	11217.0	11234.0	11243.0	11270.0
13237.0	13245.0	13250.0	13257.0	13294.0	13342.0
13924.0	15031.0	15040.0	17982.0	18018.0	23220.0

Royal Navy (Naval Air)

3885.0	4775.0	5450.0	8977.0	8993.0	9014.0

Royal New Zealand Air Force

3481.0	4448.0	4703.0	5356.0	5688.0	5707.0
5718.0	6723.0	6738.0	6761.0	8055.0	8907.0
8967.0	8976.0	8984.0	8992.0	8997.0	9016.0
9018.0	9027.0	11180.0	11224.0	11236.0	11246.0
13205.0	13207.0	13295.0	13251.0	15044.0	15053.0
17982.0	18012.0	23150.0	23210.0		

South African Air Force

3116.0	3932.0	4703.0	5680.0	5695.0	6687.0
8975.0	8984.0	8992.0	11237.0	15056.0	17993.0
21860.0	23287.0				

Saudi Arabian Air Force

3095.0	5526.0	7300.0	8967.0	8990.0	9130.0
11100.0	12112.0	18019.0			

United States Air National Guard

4760.0	5703.0	5745.0	5805.0	5827.0	6100.0
6713.5	6714.0	6769.0	6800.0	6890.0	6895.0
6940.0	7450.0	7460.0	7853.0	8731.0	14650.0
17975.0					

United States Civil Air Patrol

2371.0	2374.0	4273.0	4464.5	4466.0	4467.5
4469.0	4506.0	4507.5	4509.0	4582.0	4585.0
4601.0	4602.5	4604.0	4627.0	4630.0	7635.0
7920.0	11975.0	14902.0	18025.0	20873.0	26617.0
26620.0					

United States Air Force - Air Combat Command

3032.0	3060.0	3231.0	3299.0	3364.0	3383.0
3394.0	4449.0	4474.0	4500.0	4630.0	4721.0
4732.0	4742.0	4746.0	4760.0	4772.0	4865.0
4872.0	4874.0	4896.0	4986.0	5068.0	5171.0
5700.0	5703.0	5766.0	5800.0	6121.0	6136.0
6141.0	6708.0	6727.0	6730.0	6735.0	6753.0
6757.0	6904.0	6940.0	6942.0	6947.0	7397.0
7460.0	7632.0	7675.0	7811.0	8711.0	8964.0
9014.0	9017.0	9234.0	9474.0	9568.0	10267.0
10665.0	10895.0	10987.0	11007.0	11016.0	11130.0
11214.0	11240.0	11510.0	11610.0	11623.0	11740.0
12203.0	13204.0	13207.0	13426.0	13457.0	13670.0
14650.0	14905.0	15091.0	16362.0	18002.0	18019.0
18027.0	20019.0	20406.0	21866.0	23206.0	23264.0
23419.0	25340.0				

United States Air Force - Air Mobility Command

3100.5	3878.0	4702.5	5185.5	5197.0	5895.0
5992.0	6691.5	6701.0	7713.0	7844.0	8192.0
8993.0	9175.0	9987.0	10930.0	11214.0	11226.0
12290.0	13204.0	14655.0	16191.0	18027.0	18240.0
18399.0					

United States Air Force - Air Rescue Service

6712.0	6714.0	6715.0	7813.0	11440.0	13207.0
15011.0					

United States Air Force - Commando Escort Net

3032.0	3137.0	6712.0	6750.0	6944.0	7415.0
9129.0	10452.0	10510.0	11697.0	17414.0	17464.0
18005.0	20737.0	20740.0	21754.0	23441.0	23689.0
26515.0					

United States Air Force - Crash Investigation

4277.0

United States Air Force - Global High Frequency System

4725.0	6738.0	8910.0	8964.0	8967.0	8993.0
11150.0	11176.0	11226.0	11413.0	13201.0	15015.0
17975.0					

United States Air Force - "Hurricane Hunters"

4701.0

United States Air Force - Pacific Missile Range

10305.0	11110.0	15793.0

United States Air Force - Special Air Mission

3116.0	4444.0	4445.0	4455.0	4487.0	4505.0
4721.0	4760.0	4865.0	4925.0	4938.0	4982.0
5026.0	5078.0	5152.0	5270.0	5305.0	5340.0
5395.0	5398.0	5412.0	5432.0	5434.0	5437.0
5700.0	5760.0	5775.0	5800.0	5820.0	5822.0
5910.0	5937.0	6683.0	6693.0	6716.0	6728.0
6730.0	6731.0	6750.0	6756.0	6757.0	6760.0
6780.0	6790.0	6793.0	6812.0	6813.0	6814.0
6817.0	6927.0	6989.0	6993.0	7305.0	7316.0
7466.0	7469.0	7497.0	7605.0	7660.0	7690.0
7693.0	7735.0	7765.0	7813.0	7827.0	7873.0
7907.0	7910.0	7922.0	7930.0	7975.0	7982.0
7997.0	8029.0	8039.0	8045.0	8047.0	8050.0
8055.0	8060.0	8080.0	8086.0	8162.0	8170.0
8176.0	8939.0	8992.0	8993.0	9006.0	9007.0
9017.0	9018.0	9023.0	9043.0	9057.0	9180.0
9188.0	9215.0	9270.0	9320.0	9414.0	9425.0
9475.0	9866.0	9885.0	9921.0	9958.0	9991.0
10112.0	10153.0	10202.0	10247.0	10357.0	10427.0
10530.0	10550.0	10583.0	10586.0	10590.0	10603.0
10720.0	10765.0	10780.0	10880.0	10881.0	11035.0
11052.0	11053.0	11055.0	11056.0	11058.0	11118.0
11153.0	11156.0	11180.0	11209.0	11210.0	11220.0
11226.0	11228.0	11229.0	11249.0	11407.0	11413.0
11441.0	11448.0	11466.0	11484.0	11488.0	11494.0
11498.0	11545.0	11615.0	11627.0	11634.0	11667.0
11988.0	11995.0	12029.0	12058.0	12060.0	12090.0
12105.0	12106.0	12107.0	12155.0	12170.0	12240.0

12242.0	12250.0	12254.0	12258.0	12270.0	12277.0
12317.0	12324.0	13204.0	13205.0	13210.0	13211.0
13217.0	13247.0	13283.0	13285.0	13412.0	13440.0
13445.0	3457.0	13484.0	13485.0	13565.0	13582.0
13585.0	13604.0	13710.0	13752.0	13760.0	13765.0
13825.0	13878.0	14364.0	14412.0	14417.0	14448.0
14497.0	14572.0	14576.0	14670.0	14715.0	14766.0
14829.0	14863.0	14867.0	14876.0	14887.0	14896.0
14897.0	14902.0	14913.0	14957.0	15018.0	15036.0
15041.0	15048.0	15058.0	15550.0	15555.0	15595.0
15664.0	15672.0	15687.0	15710.0	15724.0	15733.0
15742.0	15760.0	15776.0	15821.0	15860.0	15908.0
16011.0	16041.0	16070.0	16077.0	16080.0	16100.0
16117.0	16120.0	16121.0	16160.0	16186.0	16230.0
16246.0	16320.0	16385.0	16407.0	17386.0	17427.0
17433.0	17457.0	17460.0	17480.0	17496.0	17547.0
17554.0	17562.0	17565.0	17625.0	17679.0	17840.0
17972.0	17985.0	18023.0	18060.0	18095.0	18100.0
18146.0	18175.0	18218.0	18230.0	18270.0	18320.0
18331.0	8400.0	18478.0	18490.0	18532.0	18590.0
18629.0	18675.0	18790.0	18795.0	18980.0	19005.0
19008.0	19047.0	19050.0	19060.0	19092.0	19160.0
19180.0	19237.0	19270.0	19340.0	19373.0	19447.0
19513.0	19653.0	19758.0	19800.0	19895.0	20016.0
20053.0	20124.0	20150.0	20154.0	20165.0	20195.0
20313.0	20321.0	20340.0	20395.0	20400.0	20415.0
20425.0	20452.0	20475.0	20535.0	20640.0	20650.0
20665.0	20758.0	20953.0	20972.0	21770.0	21843.0
22723.0	22913.0	22940.0	23035.0	23132.0	23243.0
23397.0	23643.0	23687.0	24127.0	24274.0	24483.0
24933.0	25130.0	25227.0	25433.0		

United States Air Force - U.S. Strategic Command

3032.0	3048.0	3113.0	3295.0	4495.0	4725.0
4742.0	5700.0	5800.0	5826.0	6683.0	6730.0
6757.0	6761.0	7330.0	7475.0	7831.0	9023.0
9027.0	9057.0	9806.0	9809.0	11220.0	11226.0
11243.0	11408.0	11494.0	12070.0	13211.0	13213.0
13217.0	13241.0	13247.0	15038.0	15044.0	15962.0
17972.0	17975.0	17992.0	18937.0	20124.0	20167.0
20407.0	23265.0				

United States Air Force - Additional Frequencies

2950.0	4845.0	5670.0	5710.0	6705.0	6732.0
6805.0	6969.0	7527.0	8888.0	8945.0	9018.0
9020.0	18023.0	18046.0	18397.0		

United States Marine Corps

11270.0	13250.0

United States Navy (Naval Air)

2326.0	2426.0	2476.0	2576.0	2789.0	3023.0
3036.0	3039.0	3050.0	3052.0	3087.0	3088.0
3109.0	3127.0	3130.0	3151.0	3261.0	4014.0
4015.0	4043.0	4372.0	4373.0	4416.0	4700.0
4702.0	4703.0	4704.0	4706.0	4707.0	4709.0
4710.5	4711.0	4714.0	4716.0	4718.0	4730.0
4732.0	4737.0	4738.0	5076.0	5680.0	5686.5
5694.0	5696.0	5718.0	5720.0	5724.0	5726.0
5728.0	6636.0	6681.0	6683.0	6686.0	6690.0
6697.0	6699.0	6701.0	6705.0	6708.0	6720.0
6721.0	6723.0	6750.0	6788.0	7535.0	7595.0
7883.0	7893.0	8778.0	8873.0	8884.0	8900.0
8918.0	8943.0	8967.0	8972.0	8976.0	8981.5
8988.0	8997.0	9001.0	9002.0	9006.0	9008.0
9010.0	9012.0	9023.0	9032.0	9035.0	9036.0
9037.0	9191.0	9892.0	10246.0	10258.0	10805.0
11186.0	11191.0	11195.0	11198.0	11199.0	11201.0
11205.0	11209.0	11214.0	11221.0	11255.0	11256.0
11263.0	11265.0	11266.0	11267.0	11270.0	11377.0
11430.0	12234.0	12237.0	13181.0	13207.0	13213.0
13222.0	13223.5	13224.0	13227.5	13231.0	13251.0
13254.0	13257.0	13261.0	13380.0	13520.0	13530.0
13542.0	13545.0	13558.0	14400.0	15021.0	15024.0
15026.0	15027.0	15028.0	15036.0	15051.0	15054.0
15057.0	15058.0	15061.0	15064.0	15066.0	15067.0
15071.0	15074.0	15076.0	15078.0	15081.0	15084.0
15086.0	15087.0	15500.0	15522.0	15535.0	17904.0
17979.0	17982.0	17985.0	18009.0	18012.0	18014.0
18015.0	18036.0	18080.0	18100.0	18125.0	18128.0
18624.5	18800.0	23177.0	23221.0	23224.0	23227.0
23242.0	23281.0	23284.0	23287.0	23290.0	23293.0
23303.0	23306.0	23312.0	23315.0	23442.0	23500.0
24430.0	26610.0	26615.0	26722.0	26725.0	26965.0

Zairian Air Force

8913.0

Antonov An-225 Mriya Cossack
Soviet Air Force

United States Civil Air Patrol Call Signs and Identifiers

STATE	CALL	C/SIGN	BASE ID	MOBILE ID	AIRBORNE ID
AL	A62U	KIG442	Golden Rod	Hot Rod	Ram Rod
AK	BE90	KWA667	Sour Dough	Mukluk	Aurora
AR	B620	KKI719	Dogwood	Razorback	Diamond
AZ	BZ8S	KOF424	Thunderbird	Geronimo	Tomahawk
CA	B650	KME284	Whitebear	Blackbear	Brownbear
CO	DI13	KAF357	Pikes Peak	Red River	Blue River
CT	DJ46	KCC590	Nutmeg	Rambler	Rocket
DE	D793	KGC462	Gabby	Vagabond	Barfly
GA	EJ1G	KIG443	Red Star	White Star	Blue Star
FL	IL9U	KIG444	Sparrow	Crane	Eagle
HI	F23I	KUA341	Firebrand	Mobile	Hiboy
ID	GQ7E	KOP334	Magpie	Rabbit	Hornet
IL	JT96	KSC952	Red Fox	Yellow Fox	Blue Fox
IN	JY79	KSC953	Red Fire	Blue Fire	Green Fire
IA	KF1L	KAF358	Corn State	Bull Dog	Cyclone
KS	KI5T	KAF359	Jayhawk (Post)	Jayhawk Bug	Jayhawk Bat
KY	K53A	KIG445	Middleground	Whirlaway	Jet Pilot
LA	L11R	KKI720	Magnolia	Muskrat	Pelican
ME	L43P	KCC591	Pinetree	Pinecar	Pineair
MD	N290	KGC464	Plant	Tug	Jet
MA	N74U	KCC592	Freedom	Pilgrim	Clipper
MI	OJ3U	KQD405	Red Robin	White Robin	Blue Robin
MN	O24N	KAF360	Star Fish	Dog Fish	Cat Fish
MO	PZ37	KAF361	Blue Bird	Red Bird	Black Bird
MS	PN92	KKI721	Mocking Bird	Jay Bird	Snow Bird
MT	P83W	KOF426	Father	Mother	Angel
NB	RO87	KAF362	Wigwam	Buffalo	Meadowlark
NC	UF6M	KIG446	Red Dog	Blue Dog	Mad Dog
ND	UI6Y	KAF363	Blackfoot	Sioux	Mohawk
NH	SN5S	KCC593	Profile	Bob Cat	Saucer
NJ	S54P	KEC994	Zig Zag	Domino	Aircap
NM	T865	KKI772	Pueblo	Zuni	Navajo
NV	RQ29	KOP335	Northwind	Yellow Jacket	Red Spider
NY	UE5K	KEC995	Empire	Tomcat	Wild Cat
OH	VX2G	KQD406	Blackhawk	Grayhawk	Whitehawk
OK	V92U	KKI723	Sooner	Oil Well	Gas Well
OR	XE7F	KOF428	Beaver Fox	Beaver Muskrat	Beaver Bird
PA	YB9I	KCC465	Keystone	Rolling Stone	Flight Stone
RI	Y188	KCC594	Rhody	Little Rhody	Air Rhody
SC	ZK6T	KIG447	Kiddie Car	Side Car	Box Car
SD	OJCZ	KAF364	Dacotah	Mandan	Cheyenne
TN	OV19	KIG448	Blue Chip	Red Chip	Gold Chip
TX	83CR	KKI724	Eagle Nest	Gold Eagle	Blue Eagle
UT	89VX	KOF429	Uncle Willie	Uncle Mike	Uncle Able
VA	9F6J	KIG449	Blue Flight	Green Flight	Red Flight
VT	9DXH	KCC595	Pico	Marble	Mansfield
WA	9KYJ	KOF430	Fir	Maple	Ash
WI	9OZ1	KSC954	Badger	Scooter	Buzzard
WV	9N7T	KQD407	Low Land	Over Land	High Land
WY	91OY	KOF431	King	Queen	Jack
PR	93UI	WWA353	Pineapple	Sugar	Pava
HQ	QZ3W	KGC463	Aero	Aerodyne	Aeronaut

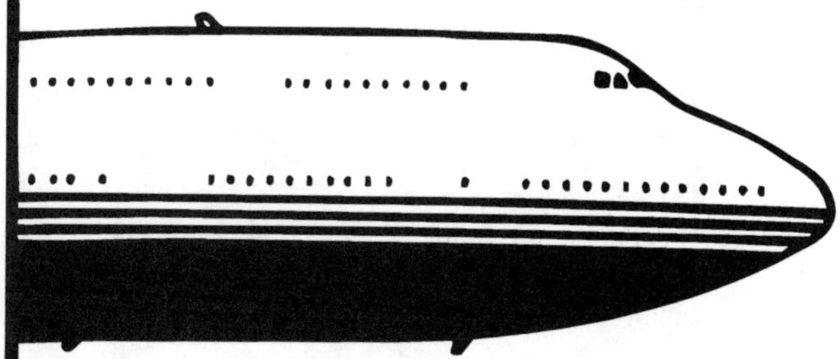

Section 2

HF (Shortwave) Digital Communications

Aeronautical Fixed Telecommunications Network

The **Aeronautical Fixed Service (AFS)** is a telecommunications link between specific fixed points provided primarily for the safety of air navigation and for the regular, efficient and economical operation of air services. It comprises various types of voice and data circuits. The major part of the digital (as distinct from voice) messages is organized as the **Aeronautical Fixed Telecommunications Network (AFTN).**

These circuits employ the entire spectrum of available communication mEthiopiaods, including HF radio, landline, microwave, submarine cable and satellite. Transmission modes encompass CW, RTTY, and other data communications protocols.

These messages are in coded format and are usually decoded by a computer at the receiving station. However, an excellent publication, the *Air and Meteo Code Manual* by Klingenfuss, provides the user with the means to manually decode this type of traffic.

AFTN Message Format

The following is an actual message transmitted in RTTY (50 Baud 850 Shift) by CSY, Santa Maria Air, Azores on 9994.0 kHz.

```
ZCZC MCA028 060050
FF GMMMZQ GCCCZQ GVSCZQ GOOOZQ
SBREZQ SBBLZQ SBBSZQ SBRFTP
060055 LPPTTPZI
(DEP-TP385-LPPT0043-SBRF)
NNNN
```

Decoded, the message states that Air Portugal flight 285 left Lisbon at 0043 UTC bound for Guararapes Airport at Recife in Brazil. The message was sent by Air Portugal Operations at Lisbon and advises the enroute Flight Information Centres (FIRs) at Casablanca, Canarias, Sal Island, Dakar, Recife, Belem and Brasilia as well as Air Portugal Operations at Guararapes Airport. This was the 28th message transmitted on this circuit for the day by Santa Maria and the forwarding/receiving station is Sal Island.

A listing of AFTN RTTY stations monitored to date follows on the next few pages. The Circuit Identifier (CID), time and RTTY data are shown. The polarity has been deliberately omitted, as it will depend on which receiver you are using. (For example, an RTTY signal that decodes as *normal* on a Japan Radio NRD-535D will decode as *reverse* when using an ICOM R71A or a Kenwood 5000).

Some stations also use both the ARQ-M2 and ARQ-E3 digital transmission modes.

Each RTTY circuit is intended for one way communications between two stations. The circuit identifier identifies both the sending and receiving station as well as the number of circuits available between them. Many circuits are arranged in pairs.

Consider the following examples:

14458.0	Karachi Air	KEA	Karachi to Cairo
14631.0	Cairo Air	EKA	Cairo to Karachi
18165.5	Khartoum Air	SMA	Khartoum to Luqa
19958.5	Luqa Air	MSA	Luqa to Khartoum

For eastern North America, a good time to monitor is late afternoon to early evening. In the past, extremely strong signals have been received from Santa Maria, Nairobi, Jeddah and several west coast African stations. Unfortunately, North American west coast monitors report little success in decoding the African broadcasts. Transmissions tend to be continuous at times closest to the hour and half hour.

Most stations have more than one frequency allocated and you should follow the general rule that the higher frequencies will be used during their local day with movement to the lower ones as night approaches.

North Atlantic Track information is usually also broadcast each day from Santa Maria, Azores.

You will note that the majority of AFTN RTTY stations are located in Africa. North American and European facilities do not rely on HF shortwave radio for transmissions. Many of the African stations listed will have moved to satellite by the end of 1994.

The United States Air Force also maintains a RTTY and FAX Automated Weather Service (AWS) on the shortwave bands. A listing of current frequencies is included.

Lockheed C-5b Galaxy
United States Air Force

FREQ.	C/S	STATION	COUNTRY	MODE	SETTNG	CID
2682.0	9HA	Luqa Air	Malta	RTTY	50/425	
2822.0	5AF	Tripoli Air	Libya	RTTY	50/400	
3177.5	AWC	Calcutta Air	India	RTTY	50/425	
3595.0	9HA	Luqa Air	Malta	RTTY	50/425	
3602.0	STK	Khartoum Air	Sudan	RTTY	50/425	
3650.0	6VU	ASECNA Dakar	Senegal	RTTY	50/425	
3710.8	3XA	Conakry Air	Guinea	RTTY	50/425	
3886.0	HDS	Bangkok Air	Thailand	RTTY	50/425	
3898.0	TNL	ASECNA Brazzaville	Congo	ARQ-M2	96/400	
3999.0	HZJ	Jeddah Air	Saudi Arabia	RTTY	50/425	JVA
4014.0	HDS	Bangkok Air	Thailand	RTTY	50/425	
4014.7	5ST	ASECNA Antananarivo	Madagascar	ARQ-E3	48/425	
4015.0	XZW	Yangon Air	Myanmar	RTTY	50/425	
4023.5	3BZ	Plaisance Air	Mauritius	ARQ-E3	48/850	
4056.0	TJK	ASECNA Douala	Cameroon	ARQ-E3	48/850	
4195.5	TUH	ASECNA Abidjan	Ivory Coast	RTTY	50/425	
4464.5	TRK	ASECNA Libreville	Gabon	ARQ-E3	48/400	
4788.0	6VU	ASECNA Dakar	Senegal	RTTY	50/400	
4788.0	TJK	ASECNA Douala	Cameroon	RTTY	50/425	
4846.0	5UA	ASECNA Niamey	Niger	RTTY	50/425	
4870.0	TNL	ASECNA Brazzaville	Congo	RTTY	50/425	
4960.0	SUC	Cairo Air	Egypt	RTTY	50/850	ESA
5107.0	EPD	Tehran Air	Iran	RTTY	50/425	
5117.0	STK	Khartoum Air	Sudan	RTTY	50/425	
5117.7	TYE	ASECNA Contonou	Benin	ARQ-M2	96/400	
5117.7	TYE	ASECNA Contonou	Benin	RTTY	50/425	
5187.0	ETD3	Addis Ababa Air	Ethiopiaiopia	RTTY	50/425	
5266.0	YAV	Kabul Air	Afghanistan	RTTY	50/425	
5287.0	FBSK	Gaborone Air	Botswana	RTTY	50/425	
5334.0	DJR	Jibouti Air	Djibouti	RTTY	50/650	DJR
5364.0	9HA	Luqa Air	Malta	RTTY	50/425	
5393.5	ELRB	Monrovia Air	Liberia	RTTY	50/425	LOA
5474.0	CSY	Santa Maria Air	Azores	RTTY	50/850	
5503.0	TZH	ASECNA Bamako	Mali	RTTY	50/425	
5610.5	5UA	ASECNA Niamey	Niger	RTTY	50/425	
5733.0	HZJ	Jeddah Air	Saudi Arabia	RTTY	50/425	JSA
5804.0	9GC	Accra Air	Ghana	RTTY	50/425	
5818.5	9HA	Luqa Air	Malta	RTTY	50/425	MLA
5848.0	TUH	ASECNA Abidjan	Ivory Coast	RTTY	50/425	IGA
5879.0	70C	Khormaksar Air	Yemen	RTTY	50/300	
5904.0	9GC	Accra Air	Ghana	RTTY	50/425	
6736.0	ETD3	Addis Ababa Air	Ethiopia	RTTY	50/850	VSA
6765.8	70C	Khormaksar Air	Yemen	RTTY	50/300	
6775.0	XTU	ASECNA Ouagadougou	Burkina Faso	ARQ-M2	96/400	
6784.0	STK	Khartoum Air	Sudan	RTTY	50/425	
6882.0	S2D	Dhaka Air	Bangladesh	RTTY	50/425	
6902.5	TLO	ASECNA Bangui	Cenrtal Afr. Rep.	RTTY	50/850	
6912.0	ETD3	Addis Ababa Air	Ethiopia	RTTY	50/425	
6925.0	8BN	Medan Air	Indonesia	RTTY	50/425	
6941.5	TRK	ASECNA Libreville	Gabon	ARQ-M2	96/425	GFA
6943.0	5TX	ASECNA Nouadhibou	Mauritania	ARQ-E3	48/400	
6975.0	6VU	ASECNA Dakar	Senegal	RTTY	50/425	
6989.0	8Q9	Male Air	Maldive Is.	RTTY	50/200	
6999.0	CSY	Santa Maria Air	Azores	RTTY	50/850	MCA
7340.0	70C	Khormaksar Air	Yemen	RTTY	50/300	

FREQ.	C/S	STATION	COUNTRY	MODE	SETTNG	CID
7342.0	5NK	Kano Air	Nigeria	RTTY	50/600	
7419.0	XZW	Yangon Air	Myanmar	RTTY	50/425	
7423.0	5YD	Nairobi Air	Kenya	RTTY	50/425	KVA
7426.0	5NL	Lagos Air	Nigeria	RTTY	50/425	
7474.0	TNL	ASECNA Douala	Cameroon	RTTY	50/425	
7483.0	6VU	ASECNA Dakar	Senegal	RTTY	50/425	DBA
7524.0	TYE	ASECNA Contonou	Benin	ARQ-M2	96/400	
7596.0	5UA	ASECNA Niamey	Niger	RTTY	50/425	
7609.0	3XA	Conakry Air	Guinea	RTTY	50/425	
7614.0	5UA	ASECNA Niamey	Niger	RTTY	50/425	
7618.0	6VU	ASECNA Dakar	Senegal	RTTY	50/850	
7626.0	TZH	ASECNA Bamako	Mali	RTTY	50/425	
7630.0	TTL	ASECNA N'Djamena	Chad	RTTY	50/170	
7690.0	TUH	ASECNA Abidjan	Ivory Coast	RTTY	50/405	IBA
7714.0	TJK	ASECNA Douala	Cameroon	ARQ-M2	96/400	
7763.5	3BZ	Plaisance Air	Mauritius	ARQ-E3	48/850	
7795.5	9HA	Luqa Air	Malta	RTTY	50/425	
7803.5	STK	Khartoum Air	Sudan	RTTY	50/425	JSA
7817.5	5NK	Kano Air	Nigeria	RTTY	50/425	
7832.0	9GC	Accra Air	Ghana	RTTY	50/425	
7913.0	9JZ	Lusaka Air	Zambia	RTTY	50/500	
7990.0	5HD	Dar es Salaam Air	Tanzania	RTTY	50/850	
8031.0	5UA	ASECNA Niamey	Niger	RTTY	50/425	
8071.5	AWD2	Delhi Air	India	RTTY	50/650	IKA
8101.0	STK	Khartoum Air	Sudan	RTTY	50/425	SEA
8113.0	TNL	ASECNA Brazzaville	Congo	RTTY	50/850	
8118.0	9JZ	Lusaka Air	Zambia	RTTY	50/500	
8123.0	TNL	ASECNA Brazzaville	Congo	ARQ-M2	96/400	
8137.0		Larnaca Air	Cyprus	RTTY	500/400	
8145.0	EIP	Shannon Air	Ireland	RTTY	50/850	SMA
8146.0	TNL	ASECNA Brazzaville	Congo	RTTY	50/425	
8165.0	5YD	Nairobi Air	Kenya	RTTY	50/170	KSA
8819.0	CAI7E	Hanga Roa Air	Easter Island	RTTY	50/425	
9058.0	9PL	Kinshasa Air	Zaire	RTTY	50/850	ZDA
9070.0	6VU	ASECNA Dakar	Senegal	RTTY	50/425	OLA
9072.5	TLO	ASECNA Bangui	Cenrtal Afr. Rep.	RTTY	50/850	
9105.0	5NL	Lagos Air	Nigeria	RTTY	50/850	
9136.0	TJK	ASECNA Douala	Cameroon	RTTY	50/425	KLA
9144.0	TUH	ASECNA Abidjan	Ivory Coast	RTTY	50/425	INA
9154.0	D4B	Amilcar Cabral Air	Cape Verde	RTTY	50/850	SLA
9160.0	5UA	ASECNA Niamey	Niger	RTTY	50/425	NIA
9183.7	TLO	ASECNA Bangui	Cenrtal Afr. Rep.	RTTY	50/850	LDA
9194.0	5ST	ASECNA Antananarivo	Madagascar	ARQ-E3	48/425	
9195.0	3BZ	Plaisance Air	Mauritius	ARQ-E3	48/850	
9217.5	TTL	ASECNA N'Djamena	Chad	ARQ-M2	96/450	
9223.5	TJK	ASECNA Douala	Cameroon	RTTY	50/425	
9226.0	TJK	ASECNA Douala	Cameroon	RTTY	50/850	
9228.0	9HA	Luqa Air	Malta	RTTY	50/425	
9252.0	ELRB	Monrovia Air	Liberia	RTTY	50/425	LOA
9285.0	TNL	ASECNA Brazzaville	Congo	ARQ-M2	96/400	
9285.0	TNL	ASECNA Brazzaville	Congo	RTTY	50/425	FGA
9378.5	3BZ	Plaisance Air	Mauritius	ARQ-E3	48/850	
9423.0	TUH	ASECNA Abidjan	Ivory Coast	RTTY	50/425	
9437.7	STK	Khartoum Air	Sudan	RTTY	50/425	
9846.0	TUH	ASECNA Abidjan	Ivory Coast	RTTY	50/850	ILA

FREQ.	C/S	STATION	COUNTRY	MODE	SETTNG	CID
9848.0	5UA	ASECNA Niamey	Niger	RTTY	50/425	DBF
9874.0	ETD3	Addis Ababa Air	Ethiopia	RTTY	50/425	
9994.0	CSY	Santa Maria Air	Azores	RTTY	50/850	MCA
10047.0	6VU	ASECNA Dakar	Senegal	RTTY	50/425	OLA
10104.0	3XA	Conakry Air	Guinea	RTTY	50/425	
10123.0	TNL	ASECNA Brazzaville	Congo	RTTY	50/425	
10134.0	TZH	ASECNA Bamako	Mali	RTTY	50/425	
10391.0	5NL	Lagos Air	Nigeria	RTTY	50/425	
10539.0	CSY	Santa Maria Air	Azores	RTTY	50/850	
10613.0	S2D	Dhaka Air	Bangladesh	RTTY	50/425	
10635.0	SUC	Cairo Air	Egypt	RTTY	50/850	ESB
10654.5	HDS	Bangkok Air	Thailand	RTTY	50/425	
10779.0	ETD3	Addis Ababa Air	Ethiopia	RTTY	50/425	
11027.5	9PL	Kinshasa Air	Zaire	RTTY	50/425	ZLA
11056.0	70C	Khormaksar Air	Yemen	RTTY	50/300	
11065.0	YAV	Kabul Air	Afghanistan	RTTY	50/425	KTA
11100.0	CAK	Santiago Air (AF)	Chile	RTTY	50/850	SIA
11112.8	ETD3	Addis Ababa Air	Ethiopia	RTTY	50/850	VSA
11175.8	5HD	Dar es Salaam Air	Tanzania	RTTY	50/850	
11439.4	EIP	Shannon Air	Ireland	RTTY	50/850	
11440.0	5NK	Kano Air	Nigeria	RTTY	50/600	
11443.0	9JZ	Lusaka Air	Zambia	RTTY	50/500	
11486.0	TUH	ASECNA Abidjan	Ivory Coast	RTTY	50/300	IBA
11495.0	5AF	Tripoli Air	Libya	RTTY	50/425	
11507.5	STK	Khartoum Air	Sudan	RTTY	50/425	
11515.2	TZH	ASECNA Bamako	Mali	RTTY	50/425	
11541.0	70C	Khormaksar Air	Yemen	RTTY	50/300	
11546.0	5YD	Nairobi Air	Kenya	RTTY	50/425	
11575.0	5UA	ASECNA Niamey	Niger	RTTY	50/425	NBA
11634.5	STK	Khartoum Air	Sudan	RTTY	50/425	
11640.0	70C	Khormaksar Air	Yemen	RTTY	50/850	
11676.5	TJK	ASECNA Douala	Cameroon	RTTY	50/425	
12065.0	EPD	Tehran Air	Iran	RTTY	50/425	
12174.2	ETD3	Addis Ababa Air	Ethiopia	RTTY	50/850	VJA
12256.0	5YD	Nairobi Air	Kenya	RTTY	50/270	
12263.0	TTL	ASECNA N'Djamena	Chad	RTTY	50/170	TNA
12323.0	CSY	Santa Maria Air	Azores	RTTY	50/850	
13200.0	CAI7E	Hanga Roa Air	Easter Island	RTTY	50/850	ISA
13366.0	5YD	Nairobi Air	Kenya	RTTY	50/170	KVA
13372.8	5YD	Nairobi Air	Kenya	RTTY	50/200	KSA
13737.0	5YD	Nairobi Air	Kenya	RTTY	50/850	KSA
13742.5	HDS	Bangkok Air	Thailand	RTTY	50/425	
13752.0	HZJ	Jeddah Air	Saudi Arabia	RTTY	50/425	JHA
13991.5	STK	Khartoum Air	Sudan	RTTY	50/425	
13996.5	STK	Khartoum Air	Sudan	RTTY	50/425	SKA
14370.5	HZJ	Jeddah Air	Saudi Arabia	RTTY	50/425	JSA
14395.0	70C	Khormaksar Air	Yemen	RTTY	50/300	
14458.0	ARA	Karachi Air	Pakistan	RTTY	50/850	KEA
14463.0	TNL	ASECNA Brazzaville	Congo	RTTY	50/425	
14490.0	TNL	ASECNA Brazzaville	Congo	ARQ-M2	96/400	
14497.5	CSY	Santa Maria Air	Azores	RTTY	50/850	MCA
14498.0	SUC	Cairo Air	Egypt	RTTY	50/850	
14508.0	D4B	Amilcar Cabral Air	Cape Verde	RTTY	50/850	CMA
14631.0	SUC	Cairo Air	Egypt	RTTY	50/850	EKA
14633.0	9UA	ASECNA Bujumbura	Burundi	RTTY	50/425	

AFTN

FREQ.	C/S	STATION	COUNTRY	MODE	SETTNG	CID
14722.5	TNL	ASECNA Brazzaville	Congo	RTTY	50/425	FNA
14776.0	SUC	Cairo Air	Egypt	RTTY	50/850	EWA
14786.5	9PL	Kinshasa Air	Zaire	RTTY	50/425	ZNA
14937.5	5UA	ASECNA Niamey	Niger	RTTY	50/850	NBA
14989.0	TNL	ASECNA Brazzaville	Congo	ARQ-M2	96/400	
14989.0	TNL	ASECNA Brazzaville	Congo	RTTY	50/850	BNA
15655.0	S2D	Dhaka Air	Bangladesh	RTTY	50/425	
16202.0	STK	Khartoum Air	Sudan	RTTY	50/425	
18047.0	TTL	ASECNA N'Djamena	Chad	RTTY	50/170	
18064.5	STK	Khartoum Air	Sudan	RTTY	50/425	
18165.0	STK	Khartoum Air	Sudan	RTTY	50/425	SMA
18173.5	STK	Khartoum Air	Sudan	RTTY	50/425	
18288.6	5AF	Tripoli Air	Libya	RTTY	50/400	
18363.5	9PL	Kinshasa Air	Zaire	RTTY	50/425	ZSA
18544.0	STK	Khartoum Air	Sudan	RTTY	50/425	
18924.8	ETD3	Addis Ababa Air	Ethiopia	RTTY	50/425	
19822.5	5AF	Tripoli Air	Libya	RTTY	50/400	
19958.0	9HA	Luqa Air	Malta	RTTY	50/850	MSA

USAF Automated Weather Service

FREQ:	MODE	UTC	CALL	STATION	CTY	SETTINGS
3233.00	FAX	0110	KWGC	USAF AWS Offutt AFB	USA	120/576
6821.00	FAX	0215	AFA	USAF AWS Ramstein	GRM	120/576
6902.00	RTTY	0000	KAWN	USAF AWS Omaha	USA	75/850
6906.00	FAX	2300	KWGC	USAF AWS Offutt AFB	USA	120/576
10875.00	FAX	2000	AJE	USAF Croughton	UKE	120/576
11118.70	RTTY	0000	KAWN	USAF Carswell AFB	USA	75/850
11122.00	FAX	0000	KWGC	USAF AWS Offutt AFB	USA	120/576
15783.00	FAX	2330	KWGC	USAF AWS Offutt AFB	USA	120/576
15799.00	RTTY	0000	KAWN	USAF Carswell AFB	USA	75/850
19361.00	RTTY	2330	KAWN	USAF Carswell AFB	USA	75/850
19365.00	FAX	2330	KWGC	USAF AWS Offutt AFB	USA	120/576

Note: Several of the frequencies are arranged in RTTY/FAX broadcast pairs.
For example, tune your receiver to 11120.0 kHz.
Set your receiver to USB mode - you'll hear the FAX transmission.
Set your receiver to LSB mode - you'll hear the RTTY transmission.

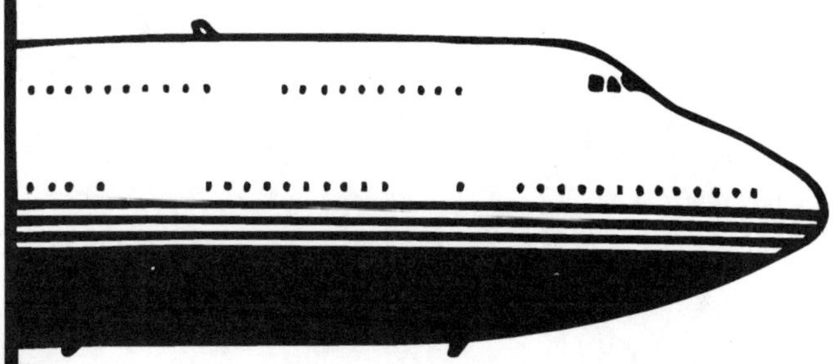

Section 3

VHF/UHF Voice Communications

Introduction

The VHF (Very High Frequency) Aero Band extends from 108.000 to 135.975 MHz, while the UFH (Ultra High Frequency) Bands falls between 225.0 and 400 .0 MHz.

Communication distances of normally 200 to 250 miles are possible between air/ground stations. Due to altitude, air/ground communications with the Concordes average about 300 miles. The Concorde to Concorde in flight range has reached 600 miles at times. Unusual propagation conditions, such as "E-Skip" during the summer months may account for aircraft transmissions being audible from distances of 500 to 800 miles.

AM (Amplitude Modulation) is used for both VHF/UHF traffic for two reasons. FM signals coming and going to an aircraft would be subject to the Doppler Effect, which can shift them off the established communications channels. The greater the aircraft speed, the greater would be the shift. Secondly, AM mode permits all stations working the facility at the same time to all be heard simultaneously. (In FM Mode, only the station with the strongest signal would be heard. All others would be "drowned out".)

Navigation Aids

The lower portion of the VHF aero band (108.00 to 118.00) is reserved for various navigational aids. These include DME and ILS beacons, VOR and some ATIS broadcasts. Generally these special transmissions can only be heard in close proximity to their associated airport.

Voice Communications

The upper portion of the VHF aero band is where all the voice communication activity takes place. This portion begins at 118.00 and extends to 135.975 MHz. Frequencies are spaced in increments of 25 kHz. Consequently you will find transmissions at 118.000, 118.025, 118.050, and so on. The VHF aero band is primarily used by private aviation and commercial air carriers.

While some commercial traffic can be found in the UHF band, this frequency range is primarily devoted to military and paramilitary operations. It is not unusual for facilities at major airports to transmit simultaneously on one frequency in the VHF band and one in the UHF band. In turn, they will monitor both frequencies, and work aircraft on whichever band they use to reply.

To monitor commercial VHF traffic (118.0 to 136.0 MHz) and military UHF traffic (225.0 to 400.0 MHz), you will need a scanner capable of tuning these bands in AM mode in 25 kHz increments. Most of today's entry level scanners do not support the UHF aero band.

If you live within a 20 mile radius of an airport, you probably will be able to hear both ground and aircraft communications. Natural and man-made obstructions may interfere with your reception of the ground-based facilities.

The 118.0 to 136.0 MHz range is roughly divided by usage according to the table on the next page.

FREQUENCY	COMMUNICATIONS USAGE
118.000 - 121.400	**Air Traffic Control** ATC Towers and ATC Centers
121.500	**International VHF Emergency** Utilized for voice and ELT purposes. Monitored by pilots for aircraft in distress.
121.600 - 121.950	**Ground Control** Runways, taxiways, traffic to and from hangars.
121.975 - 122.675	**Flight Service Stations (FSS)** Provide general aviation (private pilots) with information on airport conditions, radio, navigational and flight aids.
122.700 - 122.825	**UNICOM Frequencies** Aero advisory facilities located near small airports that do not have individual airport frequencies.
122.975 - 123.075	**Helicopter UNICOM Frequencies** Used by helicopters
123.100 - 123.125	**Search and Rescue** Used by Coast Guard, Civil Air Patrol and the like
123.125 - 123.425	**Flight Test** Used by manufacturers engaged in the design and testing of aircraft. May also be used by MULTICOMS.
123.450	**Air-To-Air** Unofficial pilots' chit-chat channel. Very interesting conversations at times.
123.500	**Flight Schools** Also used by glider pilots and towing craft.
123.525 - 123.575	**Flight Test** Same use as above.
123.600 - 123.650	**Arrivals and Departures** Used by large airports.
123.675 - 128.800	**Air Traffic Control** Used by a variety of ATC stations.
128.225 - 132.000	**Aeronautical Enroute** ARINC, Flight Support , Company Operations, ACARS
132.025 - 135.975	**Air Traffic Control**

Commercial VHF Aero Frequency Assignments

Aeronautical Telephone Channels

Channel	Ground	Aircraft
Airtel F1	454.950	459.950
Airtel F2	454.900	459.900
Airtel F3	454.850	459.850
Airtel F4	454.800	459.800
Airtel F5	454.750	459.750
Airtel F6	454.700	459.700
Airtel F7	454.725	459.725
Airtel F8	454.825	459.825
Airtel F9	454.925	459.925
Airtel F10	454.875	459.875
Airtel F11	454.925	459.925
Airtel F12	454.975	459.975
Hailing Freq	454.675	459.675

Original Air Telephone Frequency Assignments

Mode FM or FMN

Channel	Ground	Aircraft
F# Aircraft Phones	849.4100	894.4100
F1 Aircraft Phones	849.4160	894.4160
F2 Aircraft Phones	849.4220	894.4220
F3 Aircraft Phones	849.4280	894.4280
F4 Aircraft Phones	849.4340	894.4340
F5 Aircraft Phones	849.4400	894.4400
F6 Aircraft Phones	849.4460	894.4460
F7 Aircraft Phones	849.4520	894.4520
F8 Aircraft Phones	849.4580	894.4580
F9 Aircraft Phones	849.4640	894.4640
F10 Aircraft Phones	849.4700	894.4700
F11 Aircraft Phones	849.4760	894.4760
F12 Aircraft Phones	849.4820	894.4820
F13 Aircraft Phones	849.4880	894.4880
F14 Aircraft Phones	849.4940	894.4940
F15 Aircraft Phones	849.5000	894.5000
F16 Aircraft Phones	849.5060	894.5060
F17 Aircraft Phones	849.5120	894.5120
F18 Aircraft Phones	849.5180	894.5180
F19 Aircraft Phones	849.5240	894.5240
F20 Aircraft Phones	849.5300	894.5300
F21 Aircraft Phones	849.5360	894.5360
F22 Aircraft Phones	849.5420	894.5420
F23 Aircraft Phones	849.5480	894.5480
F24 Aircraft Phones	849.5540	894.5540
F25 Aircraft Phones	849.5600	894.5600
F26 Aircraft Phones	849.5660	894.5660
F27 Aircraft Phones	849.5720	894.5720
F28 Aircraft Phones	849.5780	894.5780
F29 Aircraft Phones	849.5840	894.5840
F30 Aircraft Phones	849.5900	894.5900
F31 Aircraft Phones	849.5960	894.5960

AIRFONE
Mobile Telephone Channels

Channel Spacing .006 MHz

Mode SSB

Additional Air/Ground Service
under development
944.000 to 946.000 MHz Ground
899.000 to 901.000 MHz Aircraft
Channel Spacing .006 MHz
Mode SSB

Common North American VHF/UHF Frequencies

Freq.	Service
121.500	Air Emergency/Calling - Civilian
122.000	Enroute Flight Advisory Service (Weather)
122.200	Enroute Flight Advisory Service (Weather)
122.750	U. S. Government Air-to-Air
122.800	UNICOM at airports without Control Towers
122.900	U.S. Government Aircraft, Training Search & Rescue
122.950	UNICOM at airports with Control Towers
123.025	Helicopter Air-to-Air
123.050	Heliports
123.100	Air Search and Rescue
123.450	Pilot's chit chat/air-to-air
126.200	U. S. Military Air Towers
129.200	ARINC
129.400	ARINC
148.150	U.S. Civil Air Patrol Direct Operations
149.925	U.S. Civil Air Patrol Repeaters
156.300	Aircraft to Ship, Ch #6, Safety Purposes Only
156.375	Aircraft to Ship, Ch #67
156.400	Aircraft to Ship, Ch #8, Commercial
156.425	Aircraft to Ship, Ch #68, Non-Commercial
156.450	Aircraft to Ship, Ch #9, Commercial
156.625	Aircraft to Ship, Ch #72, Non-Commercial
156.800	Aircraft to Ship, Ch #16, Commercial
156.900	Aircraft to Ship, Ch #18, Commercial
157.425	Aircraft to Ship, Ch #88, Commercial Fishing
228.700	NORAD Channel 1
233.600	NORAD Channel 2
234.800	Canadian Military Aircraft
236.600	USAF Towers
238.200	USAF Air-to-Air
239.200	NORAD unlisted
243.000	Military Aircraft Calling/Distress/ELT
251.800	NORAD Call Sign "Huntress"
255.400	U.S. Military Flight Weather, Enroute Flight Advisory Service
257.800	U.S. Military Tower Hailing Frequency/Civilian Tower Common

Freq.	Service
258.000	NORAD Call Sign "Huntress"
259.400	USAF Air-to-Air
259.700	Space Shuttle
264.900	NORAD F2
266.500	USAF former SAC Refuelling
267.800	U.S. National Guard Air-to-Air
272.700	U.S. Military Air Weather
278.400	NORAD Channel 5
282.800	U.S. Military Search and Rescue
283.300	USAF Air-to-Air
288.000	NORAD unlisted
291.800	USAF former SAC Special Purpose
292.800	NORAD Channel 6
296.800	Space Shuttle NASA Operations F3
297.700	NORAD unlisted
301.600	USAF Air-to-Air
303.900	NORAD unlisted
311.000	USAF former SAC primary F1
314.200	USAF Air-to-Air
318.400	NORAD Channel 7
321.000	USAF former SAC secondary F2
333.300	Canadian Military Air-to-Air
340.200	U. S. Navy Air Towers
342.200	USAF former SAC frequency
342.500	U.S. Military Air Weather
344.600	U.S. Military Flight Weather
348.900	USAF Air-to-Air
349.400	USAF former MAC primary
364.200	NORAD F1
364.200	NORAD F1 Channel 9
372.100	USAF Flight Dispatch
381.300	USAF former Tactical Air Command
381.800	USCG Air Operations/CANFORCE Search & Rescue
406.025	Search and Rescue/ Emergency Location Transmitter
415.700	USAF Mystic Star (Air Force 1)

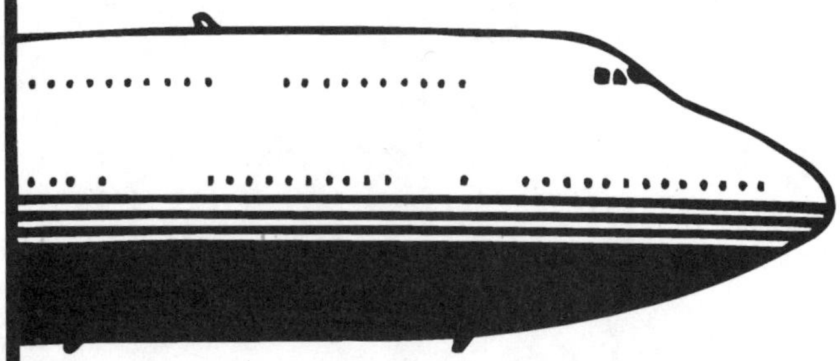

Section 4

VHF Digital Communications

Introducing ACARS

Background

During peak air traffic periods, over 1,000 commercial flights may be found just in the skies over North America alone.

Air Traffic Control Centers operated by the FAA in the United States and the MTC in Canada are entrusted with the gargantuan task of air traffic command and control management. No less onerous an undertaking is the myriad of voice contacts between flight deck crews and ground controllers/flight operations managers that keep the airborne fleet flying safely and efficiently.

Much of the voice contact traffic in the past was devoted to describing routine aircraft manoeuvres such as push back from the gate, take off, landing and gate arrival at the destination. Added to this were messages on aircraft performance, fuel consumption, position reports, etc.

Voice contacts generally require that the message receiver repeat the message content in its entirety so that the sender can confirm successful transmission.

As Flight Engineers were eliminated from the flight decks of many aircraft, the reporting part of their job now fell to the Pilots and Copilots. Indeed, the need existed to find a method to handle these routine air/ground communications and reduce the manpower involved.

The ACARS solution was developed and implemented for the aviation industry by ARINC (Aeronautical Radio Inc.) in the mid 1970's. The system was designed to cut down on flight crew work load by utilizing computers on board aircraft and at ground facilities to exchange routine reports and messages. However, it took nearly two decades for computer technology and equipment cost effectiveness to catch up with the reality.

While not every Airline Carrier is ACARS-equipped, nor is every aircraft in a Carrier's fleet outfitted with the system for those Carriers who do have it, the number of aircraft utilizing the system is growing significantly. ACARS is now a standard package on all new Airbus and Boeing deliveries.

What is ACARS?

ACARS is the acronym for **Aircraft Communications Addressing and Reporting System**. This system is an air/ground network which enables aircraft to function as mobile computer terminals linked to a ground-based command and control management system. Information collected from sensors onboard ACARS-equipped aircraft is automatically transferred by VHF radio link to ACARS ground facilities. It is then relayed via the ground stations to a central computer processor where the data is converted into inter-airline operational messages through the ARINC ESS Electronic Switching System.

Over 8 million ACARS messages are currently processed in any given month.

• Components

Three major elements comprise the ACARS Network.

1. The Airborne Subsystem (onboard the aircraft), which consists of the Management and Control units.

2. The ARINC Ground System, consisting of the ACARS VHF Remote Networks, the ACARS Front-end Processor System (AFEPS) and the ARINC Electronic Switching System (ESS).

3. The Air Carrier C_2 (Command and Control) and Management Subsystems which include ground-based flight operations, maintenance centers, dispatch offices, etc., of the various airline carriers who are ACARS-equipped.

Airborne Sub-system Configuration

Management Unit (MU)

The Airborne Sub-system Management Unit (MU) receives ground-to air messages from the radio transceiver to which it is connected and controls the transmission of air-to-ground digital messages through the same device. It is capable of operation in two modes. During Demand Mode, it transmits messages when the need arises and when it determines that the ACARS RF channel is free of traffic; in Polled Mode, it transmits only in response to a message (poll) from the ground station that is addressed to the specific aircraft (the procedure is similar to that of Selective Call Paging).

The MU gathers data for transmissions to the ground station from the Airborne Sub-system Control Unit (CU) and the Event Sensors on the aircraft (used for automatic Out, Off, On and In time reporting - known as OOOI). An additional message source may also be provided through an Optional Auxiliary Terminal (OAT).

Event Recording

OFF and ON events are typically recorded through sensors in the aircraft's landing gear. IN and OUT Events are usually triggered by the closing or opening of passenger doors, or the release or application of aircraft brakes. Separate Event Sensors are used which automatically record the event condition and the GMT time. Event times can then be called up on demand by the pilot as well as being automatically transmitted to the ground station without the need of aircrew intervention. To ensure that the sensors have not recorded a false event, ARINC has specified that these event sensors must record the event condition for a period of ten seconds, before the event condition can be declared to be "true".

An OUT event normally refers to the time the aircraft is "Off the Gate", or when the aircraft is pushed back by the tug. The term "time off the block" has also been used to describe this procedure - as this is generally the time when the wheel blocks are removed. Technically, for many airlines, it is recorded when two conditions are met: (1) all the passenger doors are closed and (2) the aircraft's brakes are released.

The OFF or "Wheels-Off" event is linked to performance of the landing gear. ARINC standards specify that an OFF event is to be initiated when the landing gear switch first annunciates extension of the strut. It is declared as true after the strut has been extended continuously for the required timeframe. Variations of this procedure may be utilized. For example, Boeing 767's operated by Air Canada capture the Start of Take-off (STO) when the RH landing light is switched on. The OFF time is captured at the nose oleo extension. Both events are recorded automatically.

An ON or "Wheels-On" event is started when the landing gear first annunciates compression of the strut following the OFF event. It is declared as true after 10 seconds of continuous strut compression. For the Boeing 767 used in the above example, the datalink system captures the ON time automatically as the nose oleo compresses on landing.

An IN or "At-the-Gate" event is generally declared when the aircraft has stopped at the gate and the passenger door(s) are opened. After gate arrival, a complete flight profile showing operating times, times leaving flight levels, fuel burns, etc., is generally printed automatically.

ARINC standards provide for the transmission delay of OOOI events until the appropriate VHF ground station is capable of receiving the signal. The writer often monitors the OUT and OFF event messages of transatlantic flights from Europe to eastern North America from his Toronto location. Since VHF cannot propagate over this distance, the obvious conclusion is that these messages are transmitted only when the aircraft is within VHF range of North America (New York, for example).

Control Unit (CU)

The Control Unit (CU) provides the pilot interface with ACARS. It supplies the facilities necessary to enter the text elements of the departure/arrival and ETA reports as well as the addresses (phone numbers) of parties on the ground with whom the aircrew desires voice communications.

The CU contains a display which is used as a "scratchpad" in the above data entry process and for the call-up presentation of OOOI event times, flight number and GMT (UTC). System status and ground-to-air voice signalling functions are also annunciated on the CU.

Optional Additional Components

The basic ACARS Airborne Sub-system consists of the MU and CU as previously described. The MU, however, can provide interfaces for additional sub-system elements with which the aircraft may be equipped, at the airline's option. Two such elements include the following:

1. An Uplink Message Hard-copy Printer located in the cockpit.
2. An Optional Auxiliary Terminal (OAT). This unit may take the form of a CRT/Keyboard device (Video Display Terminal) that may be located in the passenger cabin or mounted on the electronics rack which provides interfaces for other sources and sinks of data on the aircraft. One of these source/sink devices may itself be a display/keyboard terminal and either type of OAT may also be capable of supplying data to the Hard-copy Printer.

Operating Modes

The Airborne part of ACARS operates in conjunction with a ground-based digital data processor in either Polled or Demand Mode.

In Polled Mode, the ground processor controls the transmission of all messages from the Airborne Sub-system to the ground. This mode is used in environments in which unacceptable contention levels cannot be otherwise avoided.

In Demand Mode, the Airborne Sub-system itself, initiates transmissions. This mode is used in environments in which the volume of communications is sufficiently low for contention so as to pose no problems.

Airborne Sub-system Operation

A) Demand Mode Operation

Communication transactions may be initiated by either the ground processor or the Airborne Sub-system.

In the absence of ground-initiated messages requiring a response, the airborne sub-system remains quiet until (1) the occurrence of a pre-defined event or (2) a pilot-entered command to send a message to the ground.

In either case, the airborne sub-system is armed for transmission. It then monitors the RF channel for traffic, and if there is none, transmits the message. If the channel is found to be busy (with other traffic), the airborne sub-system waits for the channel to clear and then transmits the message.

Should two or more airborne sub-systems attempt to transmit at the same time, the message will be garbled at the ground station. Since no message acknowledgement will be sent from the ground station if this occurs, the airborne sub-system will attempt a retry. A random interval timer for each airborne sub-system normally ensures that transmission retries do not occur at the same instant. (Remember that these digital messages, transmitted at 2400 baud, normally occupy less than a second of actual on-air time.)

In the jargon of computer communications protocol, either unit initiating the message traffic (the airborne sub-system or the ground-based processor), will transmit a preamble technical acknowledgement field (positive acknowledgement - ACK or negative acknowledgement - NAK) as the first element of the message.

Demand Mode Operations - Air-to-Ground

The following series of events takes place during Air-to-Ground transmissions.

1. The airborne sub-system transmits the message. The preamble technical acknowledgement field of the downlink contains a "NAK" so as not to destroy any uplink messages awaiting transmission from the ground processor to the airborne sub-system.

2. Upon receipt of the message, the ground processor performs a BCS error check on the data received.

3. If the message is found to be error-free, it is routed to its proper destination.

4. The ground processor generates a positive acknowledgement (ACK) which it transmits to the airborne sub-system when the RF channel is clear using a Demand Mode general response uplink.

5. On receipt of the acknowledgement, the airborne sub-system clears the original message from its memory storage and returns to a quiescent state, awaiting further activity.

6. If the original transmitted message was garbled or contains errors (BCS check fails), the ground processor generated no response. The airborne sub-system will continue to hold the message in its memory storage. After a pre-determined time, the airborne sub-system will re-transmit the message. Several retries are permitted (normally up to six) before the unit alerts the aircrew that it is unable to obtain a response.

Demand Mode Operations - Ground-to-Air

The procedure for the initiation of messages by the ground processor in Demand Mode is similar to the foregoing. Messages likely to be initiated in this manner include ground-to-air calls for voice communications, messages for the optional printer and optional auxiliary terminal, as well as data transceiver autotune frequency selection commands.

Once again, the preamble technical acknowledgement field of each uplink that is not the response to a downlink will contain a "NAK". This will preclude the possibility of destroying a message stored in the airborne sub-system which is awaiting RF channel availability for transmission to the ground processor. On receipt of this message in the aircraft, the airborne sub-systems likewise performs a BCS error check and, if the message is determined to be error-free, generates a positive acknowledgement which will be downlinked immediately (subject to RF channel availability), either in the preamble of the next air-to-ground message, if the airborne sub-system is armed to transmit, or in the preamble of a demand mode general response.

When a downlink message is the vehicle for the "positive acknowledgement", the ground processor, after performing an error check on the message and finding it error-free, returns to the aircraft with another "positive acknowledgement" contained in either a demand mode general response, or a message, if it has one for the aircraft. If the demand mode general response is used, the airborne sub-system returns to the quiescent state upon receiving it.

Use of an uplink message for positive acknowledgement will result in another acknowledgement cycle being initiated. When the original positive acknowledgement is downlinked in a demand mode general response, however, the airborne sub-system returns to the quiescent state as soon as the transmission is complete.

If the uplink message is found to contain errors, the airborne sub-system generates a negative technical acknowledgement "NAK", for the downlink message or general response. Upon receiving the NAK, the ground processor re-transmits the uplink message. A number of retries are permitted before the aircrew is alerted.

B) Polled Mode Operations

The airborne sub-system will interpret a general poll uplink from the ground processor as an instruction to transfer from the demand mode of system operation to that of polled mode. In this mode, the airborne sub-system transmits only in response to received uplink messages or polls. It does not initiate any communications traffic itself.

Having commanded the airborne sub-system to switch to operation in polled mode, the ground processor maintains continuous communications with it by transmitting general polls (or messages) to it at time intervals not exceeding in length the time interval specified as the "no communications" alert criteria for polled mode. When the RF channel is clear, the aircraft responds to these polls or messages with its own messages, or if it has no message on hand, with the polled mode general response. BCS error checks are performed on all polls and messages received, both on the ground and in the air, and a positive or negative acknowledgement, (ACK or NAK) is generated for inclusion in the next transmission.

The ground processor will command an airborne sub-system operating in polled mode to transfer to demand mode by transmitting a demand mode general response message which must be acknowledged by the aircraft. An "ON" event will also trigger the airborne sub-system operating in polled mode to return to demand mode.

Radio Frequency Usage and Environment

ACARS was initially intended to be used in a line-of-sight VHF band radio environment. Since its inception, both HF (Shortwave) and Satellite transmission have been used experimentally.

Depending on VHF propagation conditions, line-of-sight for high altitude aircraft can be as much as 200 to 300 miles in distance.

ACARS transmissions can be found on the following channels in the AM VHF Aircraft Band.

131.550 MHz - The initial implementation and primary channel for ACARS in the United States and Canada

130.025 MHz - Secondary ACARS channel for busy areas of the United States

129.125 MHz - Tertiary ACARS channel for busy areas of the United States

131.475 MHz - The proprietary company channel for Air Canada

131.725 MHz - The primary channel for ACARS in Europe.

What Can You Monitor?

For most ACARS monitors (except those living within close proximity to a major airport), transmissions from the aircraft's Airborne Subsystem are audible only when the aircraft is actually airborne. On good VHF propagation days, with aircraft flying at Flight Levels FL350 and above, you can expect to receive transmissions from up to 300/400 miles away.

Generally these transmissions fall into one of three broad categories:

1. ACARS traffic occurring immediately after departure.

2. ACARS traffic from high altitude flights crossing the Center's Flight Information Region.

3. ACARS traffic from aircraft on approach to land.

By monitoring the Approach and Departure VHF voice frequencies for your local airport and comparing them to the ACARS traffic you are receiving, you will soon learn two things.

1. Which Airline Carriers and type of aircraft are ACARS-equipped.

2. What message formats/content are used for Approach and Departure.

You must have two VHF scanners (receivers) to accomplish this. You may also wish to scan to your local Air Traffic Control Center's voice frequencies for aircraft flying through their zone.

You may also optionally scan the frequencies of distant ATC VHF facilities.

For example, from the writer's location in Toronto, ACARS transmissions have been monitored from flights departing from and arriving at New York, Chicago, Cleveland, Detroit, Buffalo, Rochester, etc. Scanning the New York ATC voice frequencies often turns up an aircraft that appeared on the ACARS net.

The general rule of thumb regarding distant ACARS transmissions is that if VHF voice transmissions can be heard from your location, you will also be able to receive ACARS traffic from the same location. With the writer living in close proximity to the busiest international airport in Canada, he has observed that roughly about 50% of the traffic monitored has been from distant aircraft. This bodes well for ACARS monitors who do not live anywhere near a major airport.

ACARS transmissions from aircraft on the ground will not generally be audible unless you live within sight of a major airport.

What Equipment Do You Need?

To monitor ACARS transmissions you require a VHF scanner/receiver capable of tuning the AM Aircraft band (118.00 MHz to 136.00 MHz). A suitable VHF antenna is also required. While table-top scanner/receivers are preferred, they certainly are not necessary.

ACARS decoding and the concept of "scanning" are mutually exclusive. Because ACARS transmissions are split-second in nature, the squelch control on your radio must be turned completely off. Otherwise the transmission will be half over before the squelch circuit opens.

The Universal M-400, M-1200 and M-8000v5 Decoders are currently the only commercially available decoders for ACARS.

The M-400 is a self-contained unit that has a 40 character, 2 line LCD display. A generous 4000 character buffer permits scrolling to previously received messages. The parallel printer interface permits a standard Centronics-type parallel printer to be connected to the unit. To reap the full benefit of the decoder, you really do need a printer. Other digital modes can also be decoded by this unit.

The Universal M-1200 is a decoder card that fits inside a *PC-type* computer. It then displays the decoded material to the computer's monitor (and printer, if connected). The M-1200 card decodes ACARS plus a wide variety of other VFH and HF communications protocols.

The Universal M-8000v5 is the one of the most sophisticated digital decoding units available to the hobbyist. Connected to a VGA color monitor and a dot matrix or laser printer, the unit can also be controlled through a standard RS-232 computer interface. ACARS represents only one of the many modes this unit can handle.

ACARS Message Structure

The characters of ACARS messages are coded according to the Standard Seven-Unit Code specified by the ICAO. An eighth bit is added to each character that renders character parity as odd. An error detection scheme, known as Block Check Sequence (BCS), composed of 16 bits, does not comply to this coding convention and is distinguished from other communications control characters by its relative position within ACARS messages. BCS is the vehicle that ensures transmission integrity of all ACARS messages.

ACARS Message Formats

There are two general Message Formats in use:

1) Category A
2) Category B

Both formats are utilized in air-to-ground and ground-to-air messages. Note that ACARS does not support air-to-air communications.

Differences between the "Category A" format and that of "Category B" exist only in the Technical Acknowledgement and Block Identifier fields of the message.

As the **Technical Acknowledgement field** controls the ACK (Acknowledgement) and NAK (Negative Acknowledgement) communications protocol of the ACARS hardware, and cannot be viewed by the ACARS monitor, nothing more will be mentioned concerning this item.

The **Uplink Block Identifier** is used in both "Category A" and "Category B" formats. It is comprised of a single character that is provided in all uplinks (ground-to-air) from the ground station. The ground-based processor changes the bit patterns each time a general response or a new message block is uplinked to the specific aircraft.

The **Downlink Block Identifier** is used for "Category B" format only. It also is a single character located in the Message Sequence field at the beginning of the text portion of the word and is provided in all downlinks. Its function is to enable the ground-based processor to detect duplicate messages or message blocks. The Airborne Sub-system changes the bit pattern transmitted in this character position each time a general response or new message or new message block is downlinked to the ground.

The Downlink Block Identifier consists of a single character in the range of "0" to "9". Since ACARS allows for up to five retries at downlinking an unsuccessful transmitted message, you will often copy the same message.

The clue that it has been retransmitted lies in the fact that the Message Sequence Identifier (more on that later) and the Downlink Block Identifier continue to have the same values as the first time the message was originally downlinked.

When monitoring subsequent "Category B" downlink messages from the same aircraft, you will typically notice that for each new message or message block, the Downlink Block Identifier increases in value by one. For example, the first message sent may be identified by a DBI value of "0", the second message by a DBI value of "1", the third message by a "2" and so on. When a DBI value of "9" is reached, the next new message starts the sequence over again at "0".

When present, the Downlink Block Identifier character is easily spotted in an ACARS message. See the discussion on ACARS message components below.

During uplink transmissions, the ground-based processor sends a special control character to the Airborne Sub-system to indicate its preference for either "Category A" or "Category B" communications format. The aircraft's Airborne Sub-system then configures itself automatically for the preferred format.

ACARS Message Text

Not all ACARS transmissions contain visible text. Some only contain special control characters that are meant to trigger special actions in the receiving ACARS transceiver. Such transmissions are beyond the scope of Universal decoders.

For those messages, however, that do contain text, the maximum text length may not exceed 220 characters. The M-400 allows display of two lines of 20 characters each, and scrolls text to store a maximum of 4000 characters in its buffer. Serious monitoring really requires a printer to be on-line at all times, unless you've managed to interface your computer to the M-400's parallel printer port.

The various message types are defined by a unique two-character label. Generally the various message types contain a mandatory fixed-format text field, as defined by ARINC, followed by an optional "free talk" portion that may be utilized by each airline carrier as they see fit.

ACARS Message Components

Generally speaking, ACARS messages are comprised of the following elements in the following order. Some elements are mandatory, others may be optional. For the purposes of illustration, we will concentrate on downlink messages only.

POSITION	ELEMENT NAME	LENGTH	REQUIREMENT
1.	Address Field	7	Mandatory
2.	Message Label	2	Mandatory
3.	Downlink Block Identifier	1	Optional (Category B)
4.	Message Sequence Number	4	Mandatory
5.	Carrier/Flight Number	6	Mandatory

Consider the following "**Q0**" label ACARS message. This is probably the most frequent message you will encounter. It serves as a Link Test to ensure that the ground-based processor recognizes the Airborne Sub-system on the aircraft. No text is exchanged. A typical Link Test displayed on the M-400 would appear as follows:

```
.N123UA Q01
2032UA0045
```

Line 1	**.N123UA**	Address Field
	Q0	Message Label
	1	Downlink Block Identifier
Line 2	**2032**	Message Sequence Number
	UA0045	Carrier/Flight Number

Address Field

The Address field identifies the aircraft with which the ground station is communicating. For uplink (ground-to-air) messages it will be either the aircraft's official registration mark or the flight number of the service operating the aircraft. For downlinked (air-to-ground) messages it always must be the aircraft's official registration mark.

By international agreement, the official registration marks are coded according to a country of origin one or two letter ICAO prefix. The single letter "N" is the prefix for all aircraft registered in the United States. Some other prefixes include "C" for Canada, "G" for Great Britain, "F" for France and "HB" for Switzerland.

American registered aircraft may also contain a unique carrier suffix that forms an integral part of the official registration. For example N176UA is Boeing 747-400 owned and operated by United Airlines while N176DN is a Boeing 767 owned an operated by Delta Airlines.

For ACARS purposes, the Address field must be seven characters in length and is always right-justified. If the aircraft's registration mark is less than seven characters, it must be left-filled with periods. Hence the following valid addresses:

```
N1825TU
.N123UA         .C-FDCA
..N1901         .F-GHGF
...N409         .HB-IGC
```

An aircraft's official registration mark is generally painted somewhere on the aircraft. Do not confuse it with the "Tail Number" which normally is a carrier-assigned fleet number.

Message Label

ARINC has defined a series of two character message labels that identify message type. In addition, many airlines have defined their own sets of labels for company operations purposes. The Message Label is always the second element in any ACARS message. It is separated from the Aircraft Registration Mark by a space.

Downlink Block Identifier

As previous mentioned, the DBI is present only for "Category B" format messages and is used primarily as a means of indicating the retransmission of a previously downlinked message, If the DBI suffix is present, it will always be directly appended to the Message Label. There will not be a space between the label and the DBI. Examples are shown below:

EXAMPLE	MESSAGE LABEL	DBI
Q00	Q0 Link Test	0
Q71	Q7 Delay Message	1
QH2	QH Out Report	2
5U3	5U Weather Request	3
5D4	5D ATIS Request	4
7A5	7A Engine Data	5
H19	H1 OAT Message	9

Message Sequence Number

For most downlink messages, the Message Sequence Number is a four digit value that represents the time in minutes and seconds past the hour that the message was transmitted. (Note that the hour is not given). There are a few exceptions to this general rule.

ARINC defines the start of the Message Sequence Number as the first character in the message "text" field. Thus, starting with the Message Sequence Number, up to 220 characters may be present. Note that the Aircraft Registration Mark, Message Label and Downlink Block Identifier (if present) are excluded from consideration as part of the text field.

The Message Sequence Number will always be found at the beginning of the second line of an ACARS message. Consider the following example:

```
.N955DL QB0
4248DL1919YYZ1842
```

.N955DL	Aircraft Registration Mark: Delta Airlines MD-88, Fleet #955
QB	Message Label: QB - Downlinked Off Report
0	Downlink Block Identifier
4248	**Message Sequence Number: 42 minutes, 48 seconds past the hour (1800)**
DL1919	Carrier and Flight Number: Delta Airlines #1919
YYZ	Station of Activity: Pearson International, Toronto, Ont.
1842	Off Time: 1842 UTC

The Message Sequence Number in this message was delivered from the GMT clock in the MU at the instant of first transmission of this message. To enable the ground processor to maintain proper message accountability in Demand Mode operations, this number must be maintained with this message until a positive technical acknowledgement is received from the ground and the whole message cleared from store. The sequence number assigned to a message by the MU must remain unchanged through the second and any subsequent attempts to obtain positive acknowledgement following the presentation of a "No Communications Alert" in Demand Mode.

For example, suppose this message took four tries before the ground station acknowledged receipt of the transmission. Due to the short duration of ACARS messages, you would likely find transmissions from other aircraft interspersed among the retries.

❶	**.N955DL QB0** **4248DL1919YYZ1842**	Delta Airlines Flight 1919 First Downlink Attempt: 42 minutes, 48 seconds
	.N66US Q03 **4250NW0018**	Northwest Airlines Flight 18 Successful Downlink at 42 minutes, 50 seconds
❷	**.N955DL QB1** **4248DL1919YYZ1842**	Delta Airlines Flight 1919 First Downlink Retry: original message time = 42:48
	.N617UA 5Z3 **4301UA0026/W1 SFOJFK JFK**	United Airlines Flight 26 Successful Downlink at 43 minutes, 1 second
	.N330AA 5Z8 **4310AA0160OS JFK /ACK3935**	American Airlines Flight 160 Successful Downlink at 43 minutes, 10 seconds
❸	**.N955DL QB2** **4248DL1919YYZ1842**	Delta Airlines Flight 1919 Second Downlink Retry:original message time = 42:48
❹	**.N955DL QB3** **4248DL1919YYZ1842**	Delta Airlines Flight 1919 Third Downlink Retry:original message time = 42:48 (Receipt of message finally acknowledged)

ACARS Time Representation

Most times found in ACARS messages are GMT or UTC format. However, be aware that strictly regional carriers often use local times as well in the "free talk" portion of their messages.

Aircraft Flight Number

The six-character Flight Number field is comprised of a two-character airline identity code followed by a four-character alpha/numeric flight number. The two-character airline code conforms to the IATA two-character Airline Designator.

If the Flight Number is less than four characters in length, it generally will be right-justified and left-filled with leading zeroes. See the examples below.

AC1030	BA0294	UA0038	AA0006

Flight Numbers for Northwest Airlines appear to be an exception to the ARINC standard. They will often leave a leading space (blank) before a three-digit flight number - for example: **NW 201**.

Scheduled carriers may also conduct charter flights. The letter "**F**" is normally appended to the two-letter airline code to indicate that the flight is a charter. The author has only noted a few examples of this procedure. The example below was an Air Canada charter from Toronto to Cancun, Mexico. The flight number was 95.

ACF095

As well as commercial carriers, you will encounter a number of business jets using the ACARS network. Since these are not scheduled commercial flights, they do not have assigned flight numbers. The general carrier and flight number designation for business jets is always **GS0001**. see the example below.

..N10AT Q01
2320GS0001

..N10AT	Aircraft Registration Mark: Falcon 50 - Quaker Oats Co., Wheeling IL
Q0	Message Label: Q0 - Link Test
1	Downlink Block Identifier
2320	Message Sequence Number: 23 minutes, 20 seconds past the hour
GS0001	Generic Flight Number for non-commercial/private flight

Getting More Information on ACARS

For detailed information regarding the decoding of ACARS message traffic, refer to the publication "*Understanding ACARS*" authored by Ed Flynn and published by Universal Radio Research.

A few examples of ACARS messages types appear on the following pages.

Off Report

This transmission from the aircraft indicates the "Wheels Up" time from the departure airport. The first 17 characters of the text field are fixed format. Characters 18 through 220 are available for "free talk".

.N1844U QB
1108UA0731YYZ0310

.N1844U	Address: Aircraft Registration Mark
QB	Message Label: QB - Off Report
1108	Message Sequence Number: 11 minutes and 8 seconds past the hour
UA0731	Carrier and Flight Number: United Airlines #731
YYZ	Station of Activity: Pearson International, Toronto, Ont.
0310	Off (Wheels Up) Time 0310 UTC

On Report

This transmission from the aircraft indicates the time when the wheels "touched down" at the destination runway.

.N6807 QC8
1851AA0319ORD0018

.N6807	Address: Aircraft Registration Mark
QC	Message Label: QC - On Report
8	Downlink Block Identifier
1851	Message Sequence Number: 18 minutes 51 seconds past the hour
AA0319	Carrier and flight number: American Airlines flight #319
ORD	Departure Station: Chicago, O'hare
0018	On Time: 0018 UTC

Note that the station of activity field contains the departure station code. This message is transmitted automatically following the declaration of an ON event.

Out/Return In Report

This transmission from the aircraft results from the aircraft returning to the gate after an OUT event has been declared. The text portion of the message contains a 21-character fixed format followed by optional "free talk"

.N93105 QG
4916TW0721LGW09110922

.N93105	Address: Aircraft Registration Mark
QG	Message Label: QG - Out/Return In
4916	Message Sequence Number: 49 minutes and 16 seconds past the hour
TW0721	Carrier and Flight Number: Trans World #721
LGW	Departure Station: London, Gatwick, UKE
0911	OUT Time (time off gate): 0911 UTC
0922	Return In Time: 0922 UTC

Aircraft Routing Messages

These transmissions from the aircraft occur after the aircraft has become airborne after take-off. A considerable period of time may elapse between the first and second transmissions (up to one hour has been observed). It is important to catch the first destination message as it contains both the aircraft registration and carrier and flight number. Subsequent transmissions only contain the registration number, with the flight number always appearing as "**0000**".

To date, only American Airlines has been noted using this type of Routing message.

Message 1 - Flight Destination (22:05:04 UTC)

This transmission from the aircraft occurs shortly after take-off. Its chief purpose appears to be to indicate the destination of the flight. It is the only transmission in the series that contains both the aircraft's registration number as well as the flight number. Likewise, it seems to be the only message that contains the flight's destination.

```
.N321AA 5Z6
5910AA038OS ZRH
```

.N321AA	Address: Aircraft Registration Mark - American Airlines Boeing 767
5Z	Downlink Message Label: 5Z - Airline Designated Downlink
6	Downlink Block Identifier
5910	Message Sequence Number: 59 minutes, 10 seconds past the hour (21:59:10)
AA038	American Airlines flight # 38
OS	???
ZRH	Destination: Zurich, Switzerland

Message 2 - Flight Routing (22:49:30 UTC)

This transmission from the aircraft occurs after the aircraft has been airborne for some time. It has been observed as much as one hour after the original destination message. The majority of the message identifies the VORTAC navigational beacons and Waypoint names that the aircraft will follow on its flight to the destination airport.

Monitoring the same flight on different days yields interesting comparisons of differing flight routes to the same destination.

Waypoint and beacon names are often observed joined together. Beacon names are usually three characters in length, while Waypoints are generally five characters long. Aircraft positions over the Atlantic Ocean are normally given in degrees Latitude. Note the use of non-standard Message Sequence Numbers generated by the Optional Auxiliary Terminal.

If the same longitudinal radial is being followed from the last land position, the Longitude co-ordinates are not usually given.

```
.N321AA H10
F004AA0000#M1APWDA370YYZ VQC YUP YMX CEFOUYNA JUGARYAY 5350N5440N5430N54
20N5315NBURAKCRK TIVLILND NAKIDLIZADJSY SENEQCAN RBT BRY TRO RLP
```

N321AA	Address: Aircraft Registration Mark: American Airlines Boeing 767
H1	Downlink Message Label: H1 - Optional Auxiliary Terminal Message
0	Downlink Block Identifier
F004	Message Sequence Number
AA0000	AA Flight Number always appears as 0000. You must catch previous message with registration and Flight Number to identify this transmission
#M1A	???
PWDA	???
370	(possible flight cruising level FL 370)
YYZ	Position: Toronto, Ont
VQC	Position: Sterling, Ont VOR
YUP	Position: Uplands, Ont VOR
YMX	Position: Montreal, Que VOR
CEFOU	Position: Waypoint "CEFOU" (somewhere in Quebec)
YNA	Position: Natashquan, Que VOR
JUGAR	Position: Waypoint "JUGAR", Nfld
YAY	Position: St. Anthony, Nfld VOR
5350N	Position: 53:50 North
5440N	Position: 54:40 North
5430N	Position: 54:30 North
5420N	Position: 54:20 North
5315N	Position: 53:15 North
BURAK	Position: Waypoint "BURAK" off coast of United Kingdom
CRK	Position: Beacon at Cork, Ireland
TIVLI	Position: Waypoint "TIVLI" - southern coast of England
LND	Position: Beacon at Land's End, England
NAKID	Position: Waypoint "NAKID"
LIZAD	Position: Waypoint "LIZAD"
JSY	Position: Beacon at Jersey
SENEQ	Position: Waypoint "SENEQ"
CAN	Position: Beacon at Caen, France
RBT	Position: Beacon at Rambouillet, France
BRY	Position: Beacon at Bray, France
TRO	Position: Beacon at Troyes France
RLP	Position: Beacon at Rolampont, France

Message 3 - Position Report (22:50:37 UTC)

This position report was transmitted approximately 45 minutes after the first destination report message. Current position, flight level, wind and outside air temperature are usually given. Time and flight level at the next position also appear.

```
.N321AA H11
F005AA0000#M1AAEPN433524W08021362250370M5729759YAY/0105/370
```

.N321AA	Address: Aircraft Registration Mark: American Airlines Boeing 767
H1	Downlink Message Label: H1 - Optional Auxiliary Terminal Downlink Message
1	Downlink Block Identifier
F005	Message Sequence Number
AA0000	AA Flight Number always appears as 0000. You must catch previous message with registration and Flight Number to identify this transmission
#M1A	???
AEP	Fixed ICAO Format Position Report with Weather
N433524	Current North Position: 43:35.24 degrees
W0802136	Current West position: 80:21:36 degrees
2250	Time over current position 22 hours 50 minutes
370	Flight Level FL370
M57	Outside Air Temperature - Minus 57 Celsius
297	Wind Direction; Blowing from 297 degrees
59	Wind Speed in Knots: 59
YAY	Next Position : St. Anthony Nfld VOR
/0105	Time at next position (St. Anthony) 0105
/370	Flight level at next position (St. Anthony) FL370

Message 4 - Engine Data Report (22:51:51 UTC)

This message, transmitted by the aircraft, contains information on aircraft engine performance. Content will vary depending on the type of aircraft. For now, the actual engine data is not decipherable.

```
.N321AA H11
D635AA0000#DFBEDA/E184,411,322,E3B,,61E621,5FE5FD,5FE5FD,58C585,2AE2AD,03C03F,2B02E0
,2192E8,2571BF,12401240,3E8,0E30E2,00C,001,0,6AD449,225146
```

.N321AA	Address: Aircraft Registration Mark: American Airlines Boeing 767
H1	Downlink Message Label: H1 - Optional Auxiliary Terminal Downlink Message
1	Downlink Block Identifier
D635	Message Sequence Number
AA0000	AA Flight Number always appears as 0000. You must catch previous message with registration and Flight Number to identify this transmission
#DFB	???
EDA	Engine Performance Data follows: (Hexadecimal format)

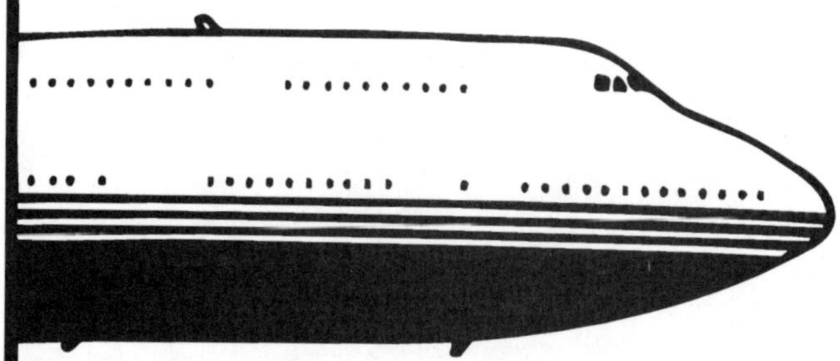

Glossary

Appendices

Glossary

AB	Air Base
ACC	Air (Traffic) Control Center
Aeradio	Aeronautical Radio
AF	Air Force
AFB	Air Force Base
AFI-1	African MWARA 1
AFI-2	African MWARA 2
AFI-3	African MWARA 3
AFI-3(R)	African RDARA 3
AFI-4	African MWARA 4
AFI-4(R)	African RDARA 4
AFI-ATC	African Air Traffic Control
AFI-LDOC	African Long Distance Operational Control
AFI-VOL	African VOLMET
AFTN	Aeronautical Fixed Telecommunications Network
AGAR + nbrs	USAF EC-135 Advanced Range Instrumentation Aircraft (ARIA)
AIR FORCE 1	SAM aircraft with U.S. President on board
AIR FORCE 2	SAM aircraft with U.S. Vice-president on board
Airway	Designated air traffic route
ALMIGHTY	U.S. Customs, Guantanamo Bay NAS, Cuba
ALPHA + 1 nbr	Maintenance Status of USAF aircraft
ALPHA MONITOR	Broadcast period for USAF EAM Foxtrot message
AMBUSH	USAF/ANG Radar Unit, Dominican Republic
ANDY	Andrews AFB (USAF SAM)
APU	Auxiliary Power Unit
ARCHITECT	RAF Strike Command and Control
ARINC	Aeronautical Radio Incorporated
ARRS	Air Rescue and Recovery Service (USAF)
ASCOT + nbrs	RAF transport/cargo flights
ASECNA	Agence Pour La Securite de la Navigation
ASW	Anti-Submarine Warfare (U.S. Navy)
ATC	Air Traffic Control
ATCC	Air Traffic Control Center
ATG	Air Transport Group (Canadian Forces)
ATLAS	Rockwell/Collins net control (anti-drug agencies)
AUS-RFDS	Australian Flying Doctor Service
AUSSIE + nbrs	RAAF flights
AWACS	Advanced Weapons and Combat Systems (USAF)
BANDIT	Target Aircraft (Military)
BC	Broadcast
BEL-AF	Belgian Air Force
BLIND	"Transmitting in the blind" (not sure if anyone is listening)
BOGEY	Target aircraft (Military and Customs/DEA)
BRZ-AF	Brazilian Air Force
CAM	Central America
CAMSATLANT	Communications Area Master Station - Atlantic (USCG)
CAMSPAC	Communications Area Master Station - Pacific (USCG)
CAN-CG	Canadian Coast Guard
CAN-FSS	Canadian Flight Service Station
CANFORCE	Canadian Forces
CANFORCE + nbrs	Canadian Forces Aircraft
CAR-A	Caribbean A MWARA
CAR-B	Caribbean B MWARA
CAR-LDOC	Caribbean Long Distance Operational Control
CAR-RDARA	Caribbean Regional and Domestic Air Route Area

Glossary

CAR-VOL	Caribbean Volmet
CAVOK	Ceiling and Visibility OK (VOLMET Wx)
CC	Common Carrier
CEP-1/2	Central East Pacific MWARA 1/2
CEP-2	Central East Pacific MWARA 2
CEP-5	Central East Pacific MWARA 5
CEP-CC-LDOC	Central East Pacific Common Carrier Long Distance Operational Control
CIS	Commonwealth of Independent States (former Soviet Union)
CLIPPER + nbrs	Pan American Airways flight
COM3RDFLT	Commander - Third Fleet (U.S. Navy)
COM7THFLT	Commander - Seventh Fleet (U.S. Navy)
COMMSTA	Communications Master Station (USCG)
COTHERN	U.S. Customs Over-the-Horizon Radar Network
CROWN	White House Communications Agency
CWP-1/2	Central West Pacific MWARA 1/2
DIAGONAL	Slash Character (/)
DISCARD	MAC 22nd AF Operations, Travis AFB
DIW	Dead In Water (Delta India Whiskey)
DV + number	VIP passenger code (used on USAF SAM flights)
EA-1	East Asia MWARA 1
EA-2	East Asia MWARA 2
EA-LDOC	East Asia Long Distance Operational Control
EA-RDARA	East Asia Regional and Domestic Air Route Area
EA-VOL	East Asia Volmet
EAM FOXTROT	Emergency Action Message
ELECTRIC	National Emergency Airborne Command Post
Endurance	Time in hours that an aircraft can remain aloft with sufficient fuel
ESA	European Space Agency
ETA	Estimated Time of Arrival
ETD	Estimated Time of Departure
EU-CC-LDOC	European Common Carrier Long Distance Operation Control
EU-FSS	European Flight Service Station
EU-LDOC	European Long Distance Operational Control
EU-VOL	European VOLMET
EXECUTIVE 1	Commercial Airliner with U.S. President on board
EXECUTIVE 1 FOXTROT	Commercial airliner with member of U.S. Presidential family on board
EXECUTIVE 2	Commercial Airliner with U.S. Vice-president on board
EXECUTIVE 2 FOXTROT	Commercial Airliner with member of U.S. Vice- Presidential family on board
FACSFAC	USN Fleet Area Control & Surveillance Facility
FAF	French Air Force
FIR	Flight Information Region
FIS	Flight Information Service
FL	Flight Level
FORMAT	HQ 21st Air Force, McGuire AFB NJ
FOXTROT	Frequency Designator (as in "Foxtrot 391")
FRIED CHICKEN	U.S. Customs AOB, New Orleans LA
FSS	Flight Service Station
G-NAVY	German Navy
GAF	German Air Force
GREEN	Scrambled Voice Communications ("in the green", "go green")
GUARD	"Assume your guard" - Controlling ground station to an aircraft
GULL + nbrs	USAF Weather Recon flight-Keesler AFB
H + 2 nbrs	Broadcast time past the hour in minutes
HAMMER	U.S. Customs
	Command, Control, Communications & Intelligence Center West, Riverside CA

HAVEN	Ascension AB call sign (RAF)
HI-FI + nbrs	U.S. Air National Guard KC-135 Refuelling aircraft
HICOM	High Frequency Communications (U.S. Navy)
HOMEPLATE	U.S. Customs AOB, Homestead FL
HOTEL FOXTROT	High Frequency (Shortwave)
HQ	Headquarters
IAF	Indian Air Force
ICAO	International Civil Aviation Organization
IFSS	International Flight Service Stations
INDIA-OSCAR	Radioteletype circuit maintained during USAF SAM VIP flights
INO-1	Indian Ocean MWARA 1
INO-LDOC	Indian Ocean Long Distance Operational Control
INO-RDARA	Indian Ocean Regional and Domestic Air Route Area
INS	Inertial Navigation System on board an aircraft
ITALY-AF	Italian Air Force
KIWI + nbrs	Royal New Zealand Air Force aircraft
LDOC	Long Distance Operational Control-Company Ops
LIMA CHARLIE	Loud and Clear
LSB	Lower Side Band
MAC	Military Airlift Command (USAF)
Mach	Air speed expressed as Mach number (Mach 1 = speed of sound)
MAG	Military Air Group (Canadian Forces)
MAINSAIL	General call sign for any GHFS ground station
MARLIN 395	DEA Intelligence Center, El Paso TX
MARS	Military Affiliate Radio System (U.S. Forces)
MAVERICK	Target aircraft (Military)
MEDEVAC	Medical Evacuation Flight
METRO	Weather service at military air base (pronounced meetro)
MEX-AF	Mexican Air Force
MID-1	Middle East MWARA 1
MID-2	Middle East MWARA 2
MID-3	Middle East MWARA 3
MID-LDOC	Middle East Long Distance Operational Control
MID-VOL	Middle East VOLMET
MIKE SIERRA	Maintenance Status
MSA	Maintenance Status Alpha (all aircraft systems OK)
MSB	Maintenance Status Bravo (equipment problems)
MWARA	Major World Air Route Area
MYSTIC STAR	USAF Special Air Mission Network name
NA-CC-LDOC	North American Common Carrier Long Distance Operational Control
NA-LDOC	North American Long Distance Operational Control
NA-RDARA	North American Regional and Domestic Air Route Area
NAS	Naval Air Station
NASA	National Aeronautics and Space Administration
NAT	North Atlantic
NAT-A	North Atlantic MWARA Family A
NAT-B	North Atlantic MWARA Family B
NAT-C	North Atlantic MWARA Family C
NAT-D	North Atlantic MWARA Family D
NAT-E	North Atlantic MWARA Family E
NAT-F	North Atlantic MWARA Family F
NAT-RDARA	North Atlantic Regional and Domestic Air Route Area
NAT-VOL	North Atlantic Volmet
NAVCOMSTA	Naval Communications Station (U.S. Navy)
nbrs	numbers

NCA-1 MWARA	North Central Asia Major World Air Route Area 1
NCA-2 MWARA	North Central Asia Major World Air Route Area 2
NCA-3 MWARA	North Central Asia Major World Air Route Area 3
NCA-LDOC	North Central Asia Long Distance Operational
NCA-RDARA	North Central Asia Regional and Domestic Air Route Area
NCA-VOL	North Central Asia VOLMET
NDB	Non-directional Beacon
NEGATIVE	No - Do Not
NETH-AF	Netherlands (Dutch) Air Force
NIGHT HAWK	USMC helicopter with U.S. President on board
NO JOY	No response to transmitting station
NO SIG	No Significant Weather
NOAA 23/24	NOAA "Hurricane Hunters" aircraft
NORAD	North American Aerospace Defense Command
NOTAM	Notice To Airmen
NP-3/4	North Pacific MWARA 3/4
NP-RDARA	North Pacific Regional and Domestic Air Route Area
NW-SAM	North West South America MWARA
NWG-NAVY	Norwegian Navy
OCEANSIDE 300	U.S. Customs/USCG "Blue Lighting Ops", Miami
OCTAS	Cloud cover measured in eighths
OD-RDARA	Offshore Drilling Regional and Domestic Air Route Area
OMAHA + nbrs	U.S. Customs anti-drug smuggling aircraft
OP name	Operation "name of operation"
OPS	Operations (as in Company Ops)
OTH	Over-The-Horizon Radar
PAC-LDOC	Pacific Long Distance Operational Control
PAC-VOL	Pacific Volmet
PAK-AF	Pakistani Air Force
PANTHER	U.S. DEA Regional HQ, Nassau, Bahamas
PAX	Passengers
PHANTOM	European Command (USAF SAC)
PHIL-AF	Philippine Air Force
PIREP	Pilot's Report (position, wind direction/speed, outside air temp. etc.)
PRT	Portuguese Air Force
QNH	Barometric Pressure
RAAF	Royal Australian Air Force
RAF	Royal Air Force (United Kingdom)
RAN	Royal Australian Navy
RANCH HOUSE	U.S. military radar, Providenciales, Caicos Islands
RAYMOND 24	52 nd AWACS , Tinker AFB (USAF)
RCC	Rescue Co-ordination Centre
RDARA	Regional and Domestic Air Route Area
REACH	USAF AMC "Hilda" Tanker/Refuel Facility, Scott AFB
REACH + nbrs	USAF AMC Tanker/Refueler aircraft based at Hilda (Scott AFB)
RECON	Reconnaissance
RED	Non-scrambled voice communications ("go red, in the red")
RESCUE	Aircraft/Helicopter on Search and Rescue mission
RNAS	Royal Naval Air Station (Royal Navy - United Kingdom)
RNAVY	Royal Navy (United Kingdom)
RNZAF	Royal New Zealand Air Force
ROGER	Communications Acknowledgement
ROMEO	Local Time
RON	Remain Overnight (Romeo Oscar November)
RTB	Return to Base (Romeo Tango Bravo)

RTTY	Radioteletype
RVR	Runway Visible Range (Wx reports)
SABENA	Belgian World Airlines
SAC	former USAF Strategic Air Command (now part of other USAF Commands)
SAF-AF	South African Air Force
SAGE	Semi-automatic Ground Environment (NORAD)
SAM	Special Air Mission (USAF VIP flights)
SAM + nbrs	Special Air Mission flight (SAM - Mystic Star) SAM 28,000 and SAM 29,000 used for Air Force 1 & 2
SAM COMMAND	HQ - Special Air Mission (Andrews AFB)
SAM-ACC	South American Air (Traffic) Control Center
SAM-AFTN	South American Aeronautical Fixed Telecommunications Network
SAM-AGS	South American Air/Ground System
SAM-ATC	South American Air Traffic Control
SAM-C MWARA	South America - Central MWARA
SAM-FSS	South American Flight Service Station
SAM-LDOC	South American Long Distance Operational Control
SAM-NE MWARA	South American North East MWARA
SAM-NW MWARA	South American North West MWARA
SAM-RDARA	South American Regional and Domestic Air Route Area
SAM-SE MWARA	South American South East MWARA
SAM-SW MWARA	South American South West MWARA
SAM-VOL	South American VOLMET
SAR	Search and Rescue
SAT-1	South Atlantic MWARA 1
SAT-2	South Atlantic MWARA 2
SAT-AFTN	South Atlantic Aeronautical Fixed Telecommunications Network
SAT-RDARA	South Atlantic Regional and Domestic Air Route Area
SAUDI-AF	Saudi Arabian Air Force
SEA-1	South East Asia MWARA 1
SEA-2	South East Asia MWARA 2
SEA-3	South East Asia MWARA 3
SEA-CC-LDOC	South East Asia Common Carrier Long Distance Operational Control
SEA-LDOC	South East Asia Long Distance Operational Control
SEA-RDARA	South East Asia Regional and Domestic Air Route Area
SEA-VOL	South East Asia VOLMET
SELCAL	Selective Call Paging System
SELSCAN	Selective Scanning Frequency System (U.S. Customs & FAA)
SENTRY + nbrs	AWACS aircraft, Tinker AFB
SHARES	Shared Emergency System Network (U.S.A.)
SIERRA + nbrs	U.S. Customs Administrative flight
SIGMET	Significant Meteorological Weather
SKYBIRD	General call sign to any USSTRATCOM ground station
SKYKING	General call sign to any USSTRATCOM forces aircraft
SLINGSHOT	U.S. Customs Command, Control, Communications & Intelligence Center East , Miami FL
SP-6	South Pacific MWARA 6
SP-7	South Pacific MWARA 7
SP-9(R)	South Pacific RDARA 9
SP-AFTN	South Pacific Aeronautical Fixed Telecommunications Network
SP-LDOC	South Pacific Long Distance Operational Control
SP-RDARA	South Pacific Regional and Domestic Air Route Area
SPAF	Spanish Air Force
SPAR + nbrs	USAF SAM flight with military or diplomatic attachés onboard
SPEEDBIRD + nbrs	British Airways flight

SPRINGBOK + nbrs	South African Airways flight
Squawk	Set transponder to (code)
STCICS	Strike Command Integrated Communications
SWD-AF	Swedish Air Force
SWORDFISH	USCG aircraft on Customs/DEA mission
TANGO + nbrs	U.S. Customs aircraft on training mission
TEAL	815th Weather Recon Squadron, Keesler AFB (USAF)
U.S. Flight Test	American-based aircraft manufacturer flight test facilities
UFIR	Upper Flight Information Region
UK-RCC	United Kingdom Air Search and Rescue Coordination Centres
UK-RESEARCH	United Kingdom Antarctic Research Operations and Bases
UKADGE	United Kingdom Air Defense Ground Environment
ULYSSES	U.S. Coast Guard, Miami FL
unid-LDOC	unidentified Long Distance Operational Control frequencies
UNIFORM	UHF frequency band
UNIFORM SIERRA	Unusable (as in "This frequency is UNIFORM SIERRA")
US-ANG	United States Air National Guard
US-CAP	United States Civil Air Patrol
US-Customs	United States Customs Agency
US-DEA	United States Drug Enforcement Agency
US-DOD	United States Department of Defence
US-FAA	United States Federal Aviation Authority
US-JCS	United States Joint Chiefs of Staff
US-JTF-4	United States Joint Task Force 4 on Drug Enforcement
US-NOAA	United States National Oceanographic and Atmospheric Agency
USAF	United States Air Force
USAF-ACC	United States Air Force Air Combat Command
USAF-AMC	United States Air Force Air Mobility Command
USAF-AMC-OP	USAF AMC Operation Restore Hope (Somalia)
USAF-ARRS	United States Air Force Air Rescue and Recovery Service
USAF-CEN	United States Air Force Commando Escort Net
USAF-CI	United States Air Force Crash Investigation
USAF-GHFS	United States Air Force Global High Frequency System
USAF-HH	United States Air Force "Hurricane Hunters"
USAF-SAM	United States Air Force Special Air Mission
USAF-USSTRATCOM	United States Air Force - United States Strategic Command
USB	Upper Side Band
USCG	United States Coast Guard
USCG-AIR	United States Coast Guard Air Operations
USMC	United States Marine Corps
USN	United States Navy
UTC	Universal Co-ordinated Time
VHF	Very High Frequency band
VICTOR	VHF frequency Band
VIPER	Mount Pleasant Base, Falklands (RAF)
VOLMET	Aviation Weather Broadcasts (French contraction "Flying Weather")
Waypoint	Mandatory reporting position on an airway
WESTPAC	Western Pacific (U.S. Navy)
WILCO	Contraction of "Will Comply"
Wx	Weather
ZAIRE-AF	Zairian Air Force
ZULU	Universal Co-ordinated Time

International Phonetic Alphabet

A	ALPHA	N	NOVEMBER	1	WON
B	BRAVO	O	OSCAR	2	TOO
C	CHARLIE	P	PAPA	3	TREE
D	DELTA	Q	QUEBEC	4	FOWER
E	ECHO	R	ROMEO	5	FIFE
F	FOXTROT	S	SIERRA	6	SIX
G	GOLF	T	TANGO	7	SEVEN
H	HOTEL	U	UNIFORM	8	AIT
I	INDIA	V	VICTOR	9	NINER
J	JULIET	W	WHISKEY	0	ZERO
K	KILO	X	X-RAY		
L	LIMA	Y	YANKEE		
M	MIKE	Z	ZULU		

Appendix A

Location Indicators by Code

Code	Location	Code	Location
AA	Australia	FMM	Madagascar
AB	Australia	FMN	Madagascar
AG	Solomon Islands	FMQ	Madagascar
AM	Australia	FMS	Madagascar
AN	Nauru	FN	Angola
AP	Australia	FO	Gabon
AS	Australia	FP	Sao Tomé and Principe
AY	Papua New Guinea	FQ	Mozambique
BA	China	FS	Seychelles
BC	China	FT	Chad
BG	Greenland	FV	Zimbabwe
CI	Iceland	FW	Malawi
CU	Canada	FX	Lesotho
CW	Canada	FY	Antarctic
CY	Canada	FZ	Zaire
CZ	Canada	GA	Mali
DA	Algeria	GB	Gambia
DB	Benin	GC	Canary Islands
DE	India	GE	Spain
DF	Burkina Faso	GF	Sierra Leone
DG	Ghana	GG	Guinea-Bissau
DI	Ivory Coast	GL	Liberia
DK	North Korea	GM	Morocco
DN	Nigeria	GO	Senegal
DR	Niger	GQ	Mauritania
DT	Tunisia	GS	Western Sahara
DX	Togo	Gu	Guinea
EB	Belgium	GV	Cape Verde
ED	Germany	HA	Ethiopia
EE	European Space Agency	HB	Burundi
EF	Finland	HC	Somalia
EG	United Kingdom	HE	Egypt
EH	Netherlands	HF	Djibouti
EI	Ireland	HK	Kenya
EK	Denmark	HL	Libya
EL	Luxembourg	HR	Rwanda
EN	Norway	HS	Sudan
EP	Poland	HT	Tanzania
ES	Sweden	HU	Uganda
ET	Germany	K	United States
FA	Namibia	LA	Albania
FA	South Africa	LB	Bulgaria
FB	Botswana	LC	Cyprus
FC	Congo	LD	Croatia
FD	Swaziland	LE	Spain
FE	Central African Republic	LF	France
FG	Equatorial Guinea	LG	Greece
FH	Ascension	LH	Hungary
FI	Mauritius	LI	Italy
FJ	Diego Garcia	LJ	Slovenia
FK	Cameroon	LK	Czech Republic
FL	Zambia	LK	Slovakia
FMC	Comoros	LL	Israel
FME	Reunion	LM	Malta

Appendix A

Location Indicators by Code

Code	Location	Code	Location
LN	Monaco	PG	Guam & Mariana Islands
LO	Austria	PH	Hawaii
LP	Azores	PJ	Johnston Island
LP	Madeira	PK	Marshall Islands
LP	Portugal	PL	Kiribati
LR	Romania	PM	Midway Island
LS	Switzerland	PO	Alaska
LT	Turkey	PP	Alaska
LX	Gibraltar	PT	Micronesia & Palau
LY	Bosnia & Hercegovina	PW	Wake Island
LY	Serbia & Montenegro	RC	Taiwan
LZ	Bulgaria	RJ	Japan
MB	Turks & Caicos Islands	RK	South Korea
MD	Dominican Republic	RO	Japan (Ryukyu Islands)
MG	Guatemala	RP	Philippines
MH	Honduras	RU	Commonwealth of Independent States
MI	Cuba	SA	Argentina
MK	Jamaica	SB	Brazil
MM	Mexico	SC	Chile
MN	Nicaragua	SE	Ecuador
MP	Panama	SF	Falkland Islands
MR	Costa Rica	SG	Paraguay
MS	El Salvador	SK	Colombia
MT	Haiti	SL	Bolivia
MW	Cayman Islands	SM	Surinam
MY	Bahamas	SO	French Guiana
MZ	Belize	SP	Peru
NC	Cook Islands	ST	Falkland Islands
NF	Fiji & Tonga	SU	Uruguay
NG	Kiribati & Tuvalu	SV	Venezuela
NI	Niue Island	SY	Guyana
NL	Wallis & Futuna Islands	TA	Antigua & Barbuda
NT	Polynesia (French)	TB	Barbados
NV	Vanuatu	TD	Dominica
NW	New Caledonia & Dependencies	TF	French Antilles
NZ	New Zealand	TG	Grenada
OA	Afghanistan	TI	Virgin Islands (USA)
OB	Bahrain	TJ	Puerto Rico
OE	Saudi Arabia	TK	St. Kitts & Nevis
OI	Iran	TL	Saint Lucia
OJ	Jordan	TN	Aruba & Netherlands Antilles
OK	Kuwait	TQ	Anguilla
OL	Lebanon	TR	Montserrat
OM	United Arab Emirates	TT	Trinidad & Tobago
OO	Oman	TU	Virgin Islands (British)
OP	Pakistan	TV	Saint Vincent & the Grenadines
OR	Iraq	TX	Bermuda
OS	Syria	UA	Kazakstan & Kirghizia
OT	Qatar	UB	Azerbaijan
OY	Yemen	UE	Russian Federation
PA	Alaska	UG	Armenia
PB	Baker Island	UG	Georgia
PC	Phoenix Islands	UH	Russian Federation
PF	Alaska	UI	Russian Federation

Location Indicators by Code

Code	Location	Code	Location
UK	Moldovia	VN	Nepal
UK	Ukraine	VO	India
UL	Estonia	VQ	Bhutan
UL	Russian Federation	VR	Maldives
UM	Byelerus	VT	Thailand
UN	Russian Federation	VV	Vietnam
UO	Russian Federation	VY	Myanmar
UR	Russian Federation	WA	Indonesia
US	Russian Federation	WB	Brunei, Sabah & Sarawak
UTA	Turkmenistan	WI	Indonesia
UTD	Tajikistan	WM	Malaysia (Peninsular)
UTE	Uzbekistan	WP	Indonesia
UTK	Uzbekistan	WR	Indonesia
UTN	Uzbekistan	WS	Singapore
UTS	Uzbekistan	YR	Romania
UTT	Uzbekistan	ZA	Albania
UU	Russian Federation	ZB	China
UW	Russian Federation	ZG	China
VA	India	ZH	China
VC	Sri Lanka	ZK	North Korea
VD	Cambodia	ZL	China
VE	India	ZM	Mongolia
VG	Bangladesh	ZP	China
VH	Hong Kong	ZS	China
VI	India	ZU	China
VL	Laos	ZW	China
VM	Macau	ZY	China

Location Indicators by Location

Location	Code	Location	Code
Afghanistan	OA	Chad	FT
Alaska	PA	Chile	SC
Alaska	PF	China	BA
Alaska	PO	China	BC
Alaska	PP	China	ZB
Albania	LA	China	ZG
Albania	ZA	China	ZH
Algeria	DA	China	ZL
Angola	FN	China	ZP
Anguilla	TQ	China	ZS
Antarctic	FY	China	ZU
Antigua & Barbuda	TA	China	ZW
Argentina	SA	China	ZY
Armenia	UG	Colombia	SK
Aruba & Netherlands Antilles	TN	Commonwealth of Independent States	RU
Ascension	FH	Comoros	FMC
Australia	AA	Congo	FC
Australia	AB	Cook Islands	NC
Australia	AM	Costa Rica	MR
Australia	AP	Croatia	LD
Australia	AS	Cuba	MI
Austria	LO	Cyprus	LC
Azerbaijan	UB	Czech Republic	LK
Azores	LP	Denmark	EK
Bahamas	MY	Diego Garcia	FJ
Bahrain	OB	Djibouti	HF
Baker Island	PB	Dominica	TD
Bangladesh	VG	Dominican Republic	MD
Barbados	TB	Ecuador	SE
Belgium	EB	Egypt	HE
Belize	MZ	El Salvador	MS
Benin	DB	Equatorial Guinea	FG
Bermuda	TX	Estonia	UL
Bhutan	VQ	Ethiopia	HA
Bolivia	SL	European Space Agency	EE
Bosnia & Hercegovina	LY	Falkland Islands	SF
Botswana	FB	Falkland Islands	ST
Brazil	SB	Fiji & Tonga	NF
Brunei, Sabah & Sarawak	WB	Finland	EF
Bulgaria	LB	France	LF
Bulgaria	LZ	French Antilles	TF
Burkina Faso	DF	Gabon	FO
Burundi	HB	Gambia	GB
Byelerus	UM	Georgia	UG
Cambodia	VD	Germany	ED
Cameroon	FK	Germany	ET
Canada	CU	Ghana	DG
Canada	CW	Gibraltar	LX
Canada	CY	Greece	LG
Canada	CZ	Greenland	BG
Canary Islands	GC	Grenada	TG
Cape Verde	GV	French Guiana	SO
Cayman Islands	MW	Guam & Mariana Islands	PG
Central African Republic	FE	Guatemala	MG

Location Indicators by Location

Location	Code	Location	Code
Guinea	GU	Mexico	MM
Guinea-Bissau	GG	Micronesia & Palau	PT
Guyana	SY	Midway Island	PM
Haiti	MT	Moldovia	UK
Hawaii	PH	Monaco	LN
Honduras	MH	Mongolia	ZM
Hong Kong	VH	Montserrat	TR
Hungary	LH	Morocco	GM
Iceland	CI	Mozambique	FQ
India	DE	Myanmar	VY
India	VA	Namibia	FA
India	VE	Nauru	AN
India	VI	Nepal	VN
India	VO	Netherlands	EH
Indonesia	WA	New Caledonia & Dependencies	NW
Indonesia	WP	New Zealand	NZ
Indonesia	WR	Nicaragua	MN
Indonesia	WI	Niger	DR
Iran	OI	Nigeria	DN
Iraq	OR	Niue Island	NI
Ireland	EI	North Korea	DK
Israel	LL	North Korea	ZK
Italy	LI	Norway	EN
Ivory Coast	DI	Oman	OO
Jamaica	MK	Pakistan	OP
Japan	RJ	Panama	MP
Japan (Ryukyu Islands)	RO	Papua New Guinea	AY
Johnston Island	PJ	Paraguay	SG
Jordan	OJ	Peru	SP
Kazakstan & Kirghizia	UA	Philippines	RP
Kenya	HK	Phoenix Islands	PC
Kiribati	PL	Poland	EP
Kiribati & Tuvalu	NG	Polynesia (French)	NT
Kuwait	OK	Portugal	LP
Laos	VL	Puerto Rico	TJ
Lebanon	OL	Qatar	OT
Lesotho	FX	Reunion	FME
Liberia	GL	Romania	LR
Libya	HL	Romania	YR
Luxembourg	EL	Russian Federation	UE
Macau	VM	Russian Federation	UH
Madagascar	FMM	Russian Federation	UI
Madagascar	FMN	Russian Federation	UL
Madagascar	FMQ	Russian Federation	UN
Madagascar	FMS	Russian Federation	UO
Madeira	LP	Russian Federation	UR
Malawi	FW	Russian Federation	US
Malaysia (Peninsular)	WM	Russian Federation	UU
Maldives	VR	Russian Federation	UW
Mali	GA	Rwanda	HR
Malta	LM	Saint Lucia	TL
Marshall Islands	PK	Saint Vincent & the Grenadines	TV
Mauritania	GQ	Sao Tomé and Principe	FP
Mauritius	FI	Saudi Arabia	OE

Location Indicators by Location

Location	Code	Location	Code
Senegal	GO	Tunisia	DT
Serbia & Montenegro	LY	Turkey	LT
Sweden	ES	Turkmenistan	UTA
Seychelles	FS	Turks & Caicos Islands	MB
Sierra Leone	GF	Uganda	HU
Singapore	WS	Ukraine	UK
Slovakia	LK	United Arab Emirates	OM
Slovenia	LJ	United Kingdom	EG
Solomon Islands	AG	United States	K
Somalia	HC	Uruguay	SU
South Korea	RK	Uzbekistan	UTE
South Africa	FA	Uzbekistan	UTK
Spain	GE	Uzbekistan	UTN
Spain	LE	Uzbekistan	UTS
Sri Lanka	VC	Uzbekistan	UTT
St. Kitts & Nevis	TK	Vanuatu	NV
Sudan	HS	Venezuela	SV
Surinam	SM	Vietnam	VV
Swaziland	FD	Virgin Islands (British)	TU
Switzerland	LS	Virgin Islands (USA)	TI
Syria	OS	Wake Island	PW
Taiwan	RC	Wallis & Futuna Islands	NL
Tajikistan	UTD	Western Sahara	GS
Tanzania	HT	Yemen	OY
Thailand	VT	Zaire	FZ
Togo	DX	Zambia	FL
Trinidad & Tobago	TT	Zimbabwe	FV

City/Airport	Country	IATA	ICAO
Aberdeen	Scotland	ABZ	EGPD
Abidjan/Port Bouet	Ivory Coast		DIAP
Abu Dhabi/Int'l	United Arab Emirates	AUH	OMAA
Acapulco	Mexico	ACA	MMAA
Accra/Kotoka Int'l	Ghana	ACC	DGAA
Addis Ababa/Bole Int'l	Ethiopia	ADD	HAAB
Adelaide	Australia		APAA
Aden/Int'l	Yemen		OYAA
Aguadilla/Borinquen	Puerto Rico	BQN	TJBQ
Akrotiri (RAF)	Cyprus		LCRA
Aktyubinsk	Kazakhstan		UATT
Al Jouf	Saudi Arabia	AJO	OESK
Alesund/Vigra	Norway	VIG	ENAL
Alexandria	Egypt		HEAX
Algiers	Algeria	ALG	DAAA
Alma Ata	Kazakhstan		UAAA
Alofi/Niue Int'l	Niue Island		NIUE
Amman/Queen Alia	Jordan	AMM	OJAI
Amsterdam/Schiphol	Netherlands	AMS	EHAM
Anchorage (Elmendorf AFB)	Alaska		PAED
Anchorage/Int'l	Alaska	ANC	PAMR
Anguilla	Anguilla	AXA	TQPF
Antananarivo/Ivato	Madagascar	TNR	FMMI
Antigua/V.C. Bird Int'l	Antigua	ANU	TAPA
Antofagasta/Int'l Cerro Moreno	Chile		SCFA
Antwerp/Deurne	Belgium	ANR	EBAW
Arkhangelsk	Russian Federation		ARHN
Aruba/Reina Beatrix	Aruba & Netherlands Antilles	AUA	TNCA
Asmara/Yohannes IV	Ethiopia		HAAS
Asturias	Spain	OVD	LEAS
Asuncion/Silvio Pettirossi	Paraguay	ASU	SGAS
Athens	Greece	ATH	LGAT
Atlanta/Hartsfield Int'l	USA	ATL	KATL
Auckland/Int'l	New Zealand	AKL	NZAA
Avarua/Rarotonga Int'l	Cook Islands		NCRG
Baghdad/Saddam Int'l	Iraq	BGW	ORBS
Bahrain/Int'l	Bahrain	BAH	OBBI
Baku/Bina	Azerbaijan		UBBB
Bali/Int'l Ngurah Rai	Indonesia		WRRR
Bamako	Mali	BKO	GAAB
Bangkok	Thailand	BKK	VTBD
Bangui/M'Poko	Central African Republic	BCF	FEFF
Banjul	Gambia		GBYD
Barbados/Grantley Adams Int'l	Barbados	BGI	TBPB
Barber's Point NAS	Hawaii	NAX	PHNA
Barcelona	Spain	BCN	LEBL
Barranquilla/Ernesto Cortissoz	Colombia	BAQ	SKBQ
Basle/Basle Mulhouse	France	BSL	LFSB
Bata	Equatorial Guinea		FGBT
Beijing	China	PEK	BABJ
Beira	Mozambique	BEW	FQBR
Beirut/Int'l	Lebanon	BEY	OLBA
Belem	Brazil	BEL	SBBL
Belfast/Aldergrove	England	BFS	EGAA

City/Airport	Country	IATA	ICAO
Belgrade (Beograd)	Serbia	BRG	LYBE
Belize City/Philip S. W. Goldson Int'l	Belize	BZE	MZBZ
Benbecula	England	BEB	EGPL
Benghazi/Benina	Libya	BEN	HLLB
Benin	Nigeria		DNBE
Bergen/Flesland	Norway	BGO	ENBR
Berlin	Germany	BER	EDBB
Berlin/Schönefeld	Germany		ETBS
Bermuda NAS	Bermuda	BDA	TXKF
Berne/Belp	Switzerland	BRN	LSZB
Birmingham	England	BHX	EGBB
Bissau/Oswaldo Vieira Int'l	Giunea-Bissau		GGOV
Blantyre/Chileka	Malawi		FWCL
Bobo-Dioulasso	Burkina Faso		DFOO
Bodo (Oceanic Clearance)	Norway	BOO	ENOB
Bogota/Eldorado	Colombia	BOG	SKBO
Bombay	India	BOM	VABB
Bonaire	Aruba & Netherlands Antilles	BON	TNCB
Bora Bora/Motu-Mute	French Polynesia		NTTB
Bordeaux/Merignac	France	BOD	LFBD
Boston, MA	USA	BOS	KBOS
Bouake	Ivory Coast		DIBN
Brasilia/Int'l	Brazil	BSB	SBBR
Bratislava	Czech Republic	BTS	LKIB
Brazzaville/Maya-Maya	Congo		FCBB
Brest/Guipavas	France	BES	LFRB
Brisbane	Australia		ABBB
Brunei/Int'l	Brunei		WBSB
Brussels/National	Belgium	BRU	EBBR
Bucharest/Otopeni	Romania	BUH	LROP
Budapest	Hungary	BUD	HABP
Buenos Aires/Ezeiza	Argentina	BUE	SAEZ
Bujumbura	Burundi		HBBA
Bulawayo/Induna	Zimbabwe		FVIN
Burgas	Bulgaria		LBBG
Butaritari	Kiribati & Tuvalu		NGTU
Cairo	Egypt	CAI	HECA
Calcutta	India	CCU	VECC
Calgary, ALTA	Canada	YYC	CYYC
Cali/Alfonso Bonilla Aragon	Colombia	CLO	SKCL
Campo Grande/Int'l	Brazil		SBCG
Canberra	Australia		ASCB
Cancun Int'l	Mexico	CUN	MMUN
Cape Town	South Africa	CPT	FACT
Caracas/Maiquetia	Venezuela	CCS	SVMI
Cartagena/Rafael Nuñez	Colombia	CTG	SKCG
Casablanca/Mohammed V	Morocco	CAS	GMMN
Cayenne/Rochambeau	French Guiana	CAY	SOCA
Cebu	Philippines	CEB	RPMC
Charlottetown, PEI	Canada	YVG	CYVG
Cherbourg/Maupertus	France	CER	LFRC
Chiang Mai	Thailand	CNX	VTCC
Chicago/O'hare, MI	USA	ORD	KORD
Chita	Russian Federation		UIAA

City/Airport	Country	IATA	ICAO
Christchurch/Int'l	New Zealand	CHC	NZCH
Chulman (Neriugri)	Russian Federation		UELL
Cognac/Chateaubernard	France	CGC	LFBG
Cologne/Bonn	Germany	CGN	EDDK
Colombo	Sri Lanka	CMB	VCBI
Comodoro Rivadavia ACC	Argentina		SAVU
Conakry/Gbessia	Guinea		GUNZ
Copenhagen/Kastrup	Denmark	CPH	EKCH
Cordoba ACC	Argentina		SACU
Cotonou	Benin		DBBB
Covington/Cincinatti OH/KY	USA	CVG	KCVG
Cozumel/Int'l	Mexico	CZM	MMCZ
Curacao	Aruba & Netherlands Antilles	CUR	TNCC
Curtiba	Brazil		SBCW
Dakar/Yoff	Senegal	DKR	GOOY
Dallas/Fort Worth Int'l	USA	DFW	KDFW
Damascus/Int'l	Syria	DAM	OSDI
Dar es Salaam	Tanzania	DAR	HTDA
Darwin	Australia		APDD
Delhi	India	DEL	VIDP
Denver, CO	USA	DEN	KDEN
Dhahran	Saudi Arabia	DHA	OEDR
Dhaka/Zia Int'l	Bangladesh		VGZR
Dijon/Longvic AB	France	DIJ	LFSD
Dominica/Melville Hall	Dominica	DOM	TDPD
Douala	Cameroon	DLA	FKKD
Dubai/Int'l	United Arab Emirates	DXB	OMDB
Dublin	Ireland	DUB	EIDW
Dubrovnik	Croatia		LDDU
Durban	South Africa	DUR	FADN
Dushanbe	Tajikistan		UTDD
Dusseldorf	Germany	DUS	EDDL
Edmonton, ALTA	Canada	YEG	CYEG
Ekimchan	Russian Federation		UHBP
Entebbe Int'l	Uganda		HUEN
Faro	Portugal	FAO	LPFR
Fez/Sefrou	Morocco	FEZ	GMFU
Fort-de-France/Le Lamentin	Martinique	FDF	TFFF
Franceville/Mvengue	Gabon		FOON
Francistown	Botswana		FBFT
Frankfurt	Germany	FRA	EDDF
Freeport	Bahamas	FPO	MYGF
Freetown/Lungi	Sierra Leone		GFLL
Funafuti/Int'l	Kiribati & Tuvalu		NGFU
Futuna/Pointe Vele	Wallis & Futuna Islands		NLWF
Gaborone/Sir Seretse Khama	Botswana		FBSK
Gander, NFLD	Canada	YQX	CYQX
Gao	Mali		GAGO
Geneva/Cointrin	Switzerland	GVA	LSGG
Genoa/Sestri	Italy	GOA	LIMJ
Georgetown/Owen Roberts Int'l	Gayman Islands		MWCR
Georgetown/Timehri Int'l	Guyana	GEO	SYTM
Gibraltar	Gibraltar	GIB	LXGB
Glascow	Scotland	GLA	EGPF

City/Airport	Country	IATA	ICAO
Godthab	Greenland		BGGH
Goose Bay, NFLD	Canada	YYR	CYYR
Gran Canarias	Canary Islands	LPA	GCLP
Grand Cayman/Cayman Is.	Grand Cayman	GCM	MWCR
Grand Turk/Turks & Caicos	Turks & Caicos	GDT	MBGT
Grenada/St. Georges	Grenada	GND	TGPG
Guam/Taguac	Guam & Mariana Islands	GUM	PGAC
Guangzhou	China		BCGZ
Guatemala City/La Aurora	Guatemala	GUA	MGGT
Halifax, NS	Canada	YHZ	CYHZ
Hamburg	Germany	HAM	EDDH
Hanoi/Noibai	Vietnam	HAN	VVNB
Hanover	Germany	HAJ	EDVV
Harare/Prince Charles	Zimbabwe	HRE	FVCP
Hargeisa	Somalia		HCMH
Havana/José Marti	Cuba	HAV	MUHA
Helsinki	Finland	HEL	EFHF
Hilo/General Lyman	Hawaii	ITO	PHTO
Ho Chi Mihn Ville	Vietnam		VVVS
Hong Kong/Int'l	Hong Kong	HKG	VHHH
Honiara	Solomon Islands		AGGF
Honolulu	Hawaii	HML	PHNL
Honolulu (Hickham AFB)	Hawaii		PHIK
Houston, TX	USA	IAH	KIAH
Innsbruck	Austria	INN	LOWI
Iraklion/Nikos Kazantzakis	Greece	HER	LGIR
Irkutsk	Russian Federation		UIII
Isla de Pascua/Int'l Mataveri (Easter Island)	Chile		SCIP
Istanbul/Ataturk	Turkey	IST	LTBA
Jakarta/Soekarno Hatta Int'l	Indonesia		WIII
Jeddah/King Abdul Aziz Int'l	Saudi Arabia	JED	OEJN
Jibouti/Ambouli	Djibouti	JIB	HFFF
Jonkoping	Malaysia	JKG	ESGJ
Kabul ACC	Afghanistan		OAKX
Kamina-Base	Zaire		FZSA
Kano/Mallam Aminu Int'l	Nigeria		DNMA
Karachi/Quaid-e-Azam Int'l	Pakistan	HKI	OPKC
Kathmandu/Int'l	Nepal		VNKT
Keflavik	Iceland	KEF	BIKF
Khabarovsk	Russian Federation		RUHB
Khanty-Mansiysk	Russian Federation		USHH
Khartoum	Sudan	KRT	HSSS
Kiev/Borispol	Ukraine	IEV	UKBB
Kigali/Gregoire Kayibanda	Rwanda	KGL	HRYR
Kingston/Norman Manley Int'l	Jamaica	KIN	MKJP
Kinshasa/N'djili	Zaire	FIH	FZAA
Kisangani/Bangoka	Zaire		FZIC
Kisimayu	Somalia		HCMK
Kitona-Base	Zaire		FZAI
Kolpashevo	Russian Federation		UNLL
Kota Kinabalu/Int'l	Sarawak		WBKK
Kuala Lumpur	Malaysia	KUL	WMKK
Kuwait/Int'l	Kuwait	KWI	OKBK
Kzyl-Orda	Kazakhstan		UAOO

City/Airport	Country	IATA	ICAO
L'vov	Ukraine		UKLL
La Paz/Kennedy Int'l	Bolivia	LPB	SLLP
Lagos/Murtala Muhammed	Nigeria	LOS	DNMM
Lamezia/Terme	Italy	SUF	LICA
Lanzhou	China		BCLZ
Larnaca	Cyprus	LCA	LCLK
Libreville/Leon M'Ba	Gabon	LBV	FOOL
Lilongwe/Kamuzu Int'l	Malawi		FWKI
Lima-Callao/Int'l Jorge Chavez	Peru	LIM	SPIM
Lisbon	Portugal	LIS	LPPT
Liverpool	England	LPL	EGGP
Ljubljana	Serbia	LJU	LYLJ
Lomé	Togo	LFW	DXXX
London/Gatwick	England	LGW	EGKK
London/Heathrow	England	LHR	EGLL
Los Angeles, CA	USA	LAX	KLAX
Luanda/4 de Fevereiro	Angola		FNLU
Lubumbashi/Luano	Zaire		FZQC
Lusaka	Zambia		FLHQ
Luxembourg	Luxembourg	LUX	ELLX
Luxor	Egypt		HELX
Macau	Macau		VMMC
Madrid	Spain	MAD	LEAR
Malaga	Spain		LEMG
Male/Int'l	Maldive Islands	MLE	VRMM
Malta/Luqa	Malta	MLA	LMML
Managua/Augusto Cesar Sandino	Nicaragua	MGA	MNMG
Manaus/Eduardo Gomez	Brazil	MAO	SBEG
Manchester	England	MAN	EGCC
Manila/Int'l	Philippines	MNL	RPMM
Manzini/Matsapa	Swaziland		FDMS
Maputo	Mozambique		FQMA
Marrakech/Menara	Morocco	RAK	GMMX
Maseru/Moshoeshoe Int'l	Lesotho		FXMM
Mauritius/Sir Seewoosagur Ramgoolam Int'l	Mauritius	MRU	FIMP
Mazatlan/General Rafael Bueina Int'l	Mexico	MZT	MMMZ
Melbourne	Australia	MEL	AMMM
Mexico City/Benito Juarez Int'l	Mexico	MEX	MMMX
Miami, FL	USA	MIA	KMIA
Milan/Malpensa	Italy	MIL	LIMC
Mineralynye Vody	Russian Federation		URMM
Mogadishu	Somalia	MGQ	HCMM
Molodezhnaja	Russian Federation		RUML
Mombasa/Moi Int'l	Kenya	MBA	HKMO
Monrovia/Roberts Int'l	Liberia	ROB	GLRB
Monte Carlo	Monaco	MCM	LNMC
Monte Caseros	Argentina		SARM
Montego Bay/Sangster Int'l	Jamaica	MBJ	MKJS
Montevideo/Carrasco Int'l	Uruguay	MVD	SUMU
Montreal/Dorval, QUE	Canada	YUL	CYUL
Montreal/Mirabel, QUE	Canada	YMX	CYMX
Montserrat	Montserrat	MNI	TRPM
Moroni/Iconi	Comoros		FMCN
Moscow	Russian Federation	MOW	MSKW

City/Airport	Country	IATA	ICAO
Munich	Germany	MUC	EDDM
Mururoa	French Polynesia		NTTX
Muscat/Seeb Int'l	Oman		OOMS
N'Djamena	Chad	NDJ	FTTJ
Nagoya	Japan	NGO	RJNN
Nairobi/Jomo Kenyatta Int'l	Kenya	NBO	HKNA
Nandi (Nadi)	Fiji	NAN	NFFN
Nassau	Bahamas	NAS	MYNN
Nassau/Paradise Is	Bahamas	QZY	MYGM
Nauru Island	Nauru		ANAU
Nevis/Newcastle	Saint. Kitts & Nevis	NEV	TKPN
New Delhi	India		DEMS
New York/Kennedy, NY	USA	JFK	KJFK
New York/La Guardia, NY	USA	LGA	KLGA
Niamey	Niger	NIM	DRRN
Nouadhibou	Mauritania		GQPP
Nouakchott	Mauritania	NKC	GQNN
Noumea/La Tontouta	New Caledonia		NWWW
Novosibirsk/Tolmachevo	Russian Federation		RUNW
Odessa/Tsentrainy	Ukraine		UKOO
Offutt AFB, Omaha NE	USA		KGWC
Osaka	Japan	OSA	RJOY
Oslo	Norway	OSL	ENOS
Ottawa, ONT	Canada	YOW	CYOW
Ouagadougou	Burkina Faso	OUA	DFFD
Padang/Tabing	Indonesia		WIMG
Pago Pago/Int'l	Samoa		NSTU
Palma/Mallorca Is.	Canary Islands	PMI	GCCC
Panama City/Tocumen	Panama	PTY	MPTO
Paramaribo/Zog en Hoop	Surinam	PBM	SMZO
Paris/Charles de Gaulle	France	CDG	LFPG
Penang	Malaysia	PEN	WMKP
Perth	Australia		APPH
Pori	Finland	POR	EFPO
Port au Prince	Haiti	PAP	MTPP
Port Gentil	Gabon		FOOG
Port Vila/Bauerfield	Vanuatu		NVVV
Port-of-Spain/Piarco	Trinidad	POS	TTPP
Porto Alegre/Canoas	Brazil		SBCO
Prague/Letnany	Czech Republic	PRG	LKLT
Principe	Sao Tomé & Principe		FPPR
Puerto Vallarta/Gustavo Dias Ordaz Int'l	Mexico	PVR	MMPR
Punta Arenas/Int'l Carlos Ibanez del Campo	Chile		SCCI
Pyongyang	North Korea	FNJ	DKPY
Quito/Mariscal Sucre	Ecuador	UIO	SEQU
Rangiroa	French Polynesia		NTTG
Recife/Guararapes	Brazil		SBRF
Resistencia ACC	Argentina		SARR
Reykjavik	Iceland		BIRD
Riga/Skulte	Latvia		UMRW
Rio de Janeiro/Int'l Galeao	Brazil	RIO	SBGL
Rio Gallegos	Argentina		SAWG
Riyan	Yemen		OYAR
Rome/Da Vinci	Italy	FCO	

City/Airport	Country	IATA	ICAO
Rome/Fiumicino	Italy	ROM	LIRF
Rota/Int'l	Guam & Mariana Islands		PGRO
Rotterdam	Netherlands	RTM	EHRD
Saint-Denis/Gillot	Reunion		FMEE
Sal Oceanic	Cape Verde		GVSC
Sal/Amilcar Cabral Int'l	Cape Verde	SID	GVAC
Salt Lake City, UT	USA	SLC	KSLC
Salvador/Dois de Julho	Brazil		SBSV
San Andros	Bahamas	SAQ	MYAN
San Diego, CA	USA	SAN	KSAN
San Francisco, CA	USA	SFO	KSFO
San José/Tobias Bolanos Int'l	Costa Rica	SJO	MRPV
San Juan/Luis Muñoz Marin Int'l	Puerto Rico		TJSJ
San Salvador/El Salvador Int'l	El Salvador	SAL	MSLP
Sana'a/Int'l	Yemen		OYSN
Santa Maria	Azores	SMA	LPAZ
Santiago/Int'l Arturo Merino/Benitez	Chile	SCL	SCEM
Santo Domingo/De las Americas Int'l	Dominican Republic	SDQ	MDSD
Sao Paulo/Congonhas	Brazil	SAO	SBSP
Sao Tomé	Sao Tomé & Principe		FPST
Saskatoon, SASK	Canada	YXE	CYXE
Seoul/Kimo Int'l	South Korea	SEL	RKSS
Seychelles Int'l	Seychelles		FSIA
Shanghai	China	SHA	ZSSL
Shannon	Ireland	SNN	EIAA
Simferopol	Ukraine		UKFF
Singapore	Singapore	SIN	WSJC
Sofia	Bulgaria	SOF	LZSO
Sondre Stromfjord	Greenland		BGSF
St. Croix/Alexander Hamilton	Virgin Islands	STX	TISX
St. John's, NFLD	Canada	YYT	CYYT
St. Petersburg	Russian Federation	LED	LGTD
St. Kitts/Golden Rock	Saint. Kitts & Nevis	SKB	TKPK
St.Maarten	Aruba & Netherlands Antilles	SXM	TBCM
St. Vincent	Saint Vincent	SVD	TVSV
Stockholm/Tullinge	Sweden	STO	ESCN
Sydney	Australia	SYD	ASSS
Tahiti	French Polynesia		NTAA
Taipei/Int'l	Taiwan	TPE	RCTP
Tampa, FL	USA	TPA	KTPA
Tangier/Boukhalf	Morocco	TNG	GMTT
Tashkent	Uzbekistan		UTTT
Tbilisi/Novoalexeyevka	Georgia		UGGG
Tegucigalpa/Toncontin Int'l	Honduras		MHTG
Tehran/Mehrabad Int'l	Iran		OIII
Tel Aviv/D. Ben Gurion	Israel	TLV	LLBG
Tenerife	Canary Islands	TCI	GCXO
Timimoun	Algeria		DAUT
Tirana/Rinas	Albania		LATI
Tokyo-Narita	Japan	NRT	RJAA
Tokyo/Int'l	Japan	TYO	RJTT
Tongatapu/Fua'amoutu Int'l	Tonga		NFTF
Toronto, ONT	Canada	YYZ	CYYZ
Tripoli	Libya		HLLL

City/Airport	Country	IATA	ICAO
Tunis/Carthage	Tunisia	TUN	DTTA
Ujung Pandang/Hasanuddin	Indonesia		WAAA
Ulan Ude/Mukhino	Russian Federation		UIUU
Ulaanbaatar	Mongolia		ZMUB
Uralsk	Kazakhstan		UARR
Urumqi	China		BCUQ
Vancouver, BC	Canada	YVR	CYVR
Vienna	Austria	VIE	LOVV
Vientiane	Laos	VTE	VLAO
Vieux-Fort/Hewanorra Int'l	Saint Lucia	SLU	TLPL
Vilnius	Lithuania		UMWW
Vitebsk	Belarus		UMII
Vologda	Russian Federation		ULWW
Wallis/Hihifo	Wallis & Futuna Islands		NLWW
Warsaw/Okecie	Poland		EPWA
Washington-Dulles Int'l	USA	IAD	KIAD
Wellington	New Zealand	WLG	NZKL
West End	Bahamas	WTD	MYGW
Yakutsk	Russian Federation		UEEE
Yangon/Int'l	Myanmar	YGN	VYYY
Yerevan/Zvartnos	Armenia		UGEE
Zagreb	Croatia		LDZA
Zandery/Johan Adolfo Pengel Int'l	Surinam		SMJP
Zanzibar	Tanzania	ZNZ	HTZA
Zarzaitine/In Armenas	Algeria		DAUZ
Zurich	Switzerland	ZRH	LSZH

Appendix C - Airline Carriers by Carrier

AIRLINE CARRIER	COUNTRY	IATA	ICAO
A.L.M. - Antillean Airlines	Netherlands Antilles	LM	ALM
Adria Airways	Slovenia	JP	ADR
Aer Lingus ,"Shamrock"	Ireland	EI	EIN
Aero Caribbean	Cuba	CR	CRN
Aero Caribe	Mexico	QA	
Aero Lloyd Luftverkehrs	Germany	YP	AEF
Aero Peru - Empresa de Transporte Aereo del Peru	Peru	PL	PLI
Aero Transporti Italiani	Italy	BM	ATI
Aeroejecutivos SA de CV	Mexico		
Aeroflot	Russia	SU	AFL
Aerolineas Argentinas	Argentina	AR	ARG
Aeromexico (Aeovias de Mexico)	Mexico	AM	AMX
Aeronica - Aerolineas Nicaraguenses	Nicaragua	NI	ANI
Aeropostal - Linea Aeropostal Venezolana	Venezuela	LV	LAV
Aerosucre Colombia	Colombia		KRE
African Airlines International	Kenya		
African Safari Airways	Kenya	QS	QSC
Air 2000, "Jetset"	United Kingdom	DP	AMM
Air Afrique	Ivory Coast	RK	RKA
Air Algerie	Algeria	AH	DAH
Air Alliance	Canada	3J	AAQ
Air Aruba	Aruba	FQ	ARU
Air Atlantic	Canada	9A	ATL
Air B.C. ,"Aircoach"	Canada	ZX	ABL
Air Belgium International	Belgium	VY	ABB
Air Benin	Benin	TS	TSB
Air Berlin	Germany	AB	BER
Air Botswana	Botswana	BP	BOT
Air Burkina	Burkina Faso	VH	VBW
Air Burundi	Burundi	PB	PBU
Air Caledonie International, "Aircal"	New Caledonia	SB	RKL
Air Canada	Canada	AC	ACA
Air Chad	Tchad	HT	HTT
Air Charter	France	SF	ACF
Air China	China	CA	CCA
Air Comoros	Comoros Islands	OR	AOR
Air Creebec, "Cree"	Canada	YN	CRQ
Air Europa	Spain	UX	AEA
Air Europe Italy	Italy	AX	AEL
Air France	France	AF	AFR
Air Gabon	Gabon	GN	AGN
Air Gambia, "Atas"	Gambia	1V	AGS
Air Guinee	Guinea	GI	GIB
Air Holland Charter	Netherlands	GG	AHR
Air Hong Kong	Hong Kong		AHK
Air India	India	AI	AIC
Air Inter (Lignes Aerienes Interieures)	France	IT	ITF
Air Inuit	Canada	3H	AIE
Air Jamaica	Jamaica	JM	AJM
Air Kenya	Kenya	QP	CSS
Air Koyro	North Korea		
Air Lanka	Sri Lanka	UL	ALK
Air Madagascar, "Madair"	Madagascar	MD	MDG
Air Malawi	Malawi	QM	AML
Air Maldives	Maldives	PN	AMI

AIRLINE CARRIER	COUNTRY	IATA	ICAO
Air Malta	Malta	KM	AMC
Air Manitoba, "Manitoba"	Canada	7N	NAM
Air Mauritania	Mauritania	MR	MRT
Air Mauritius	Mauritius	MK	MAU
Air Namibia	Namibia	SW	NMB
Air Nauru	Nauru	ON	RON
Air New Zealand	New Zealand	NZ	ANZ
Air Niagara Express, "Databird"	Canada	DB	DBD
Air Nippon Kasushika Gaisha	Japan	WK	ANK
Air Niungini	Papua New Guinea	PX	ANG
Air Nova	Canada	QK	ARN
Air Ontario, "Ontario"	Canada	GX	ONT
Air Pacific, "Pacific"	Fiji	FJ	FJI
Air Portugal, "TAP"	Portugal	TP	TAP
Air Rarotonga	Cook Islands	GZ	
Air Rwanda	Rwanda	UW	RWD
Air Senegal	Senegal	DS	DSR
Air Sinai	Egypt	DP	ASD
Air Swazi Cargo	Swaziland	CW	CWS
Air Tahiti	Tahiti	VT	TAH
Air Tanzania	Tanzania	TC	ATC
Air Transafrik	Sao Tomé	PQ	TRF
Air Transat	Canada	TS	TSC
Air Tungaru	Kiribati	RT	TUN
Air Ukraine International	Ukraine	PS	UKR
Air Vanuatu, "Air Van"	Vanuatu	NF	AVN
Air Zaire	Zaire	QC	AZR
Air Zimbabwe	Zimbabwe	WX	AZW
Airborne Express, "Abex"	United States of America	QB	ABX
Alaska Airlines	Alaska	AS	ASA
Alhoa Airlines	Hawaii	AQ	AHA
Alitalia	Italy	AZ	AZA
All Nippon Airways	Japan	NH	ANA
America West Airlines, "Cactus"	United States of America	HP	AWE
American Airlines	United States of America	AA	AAL
American Eagle/Flagship Airlines	United States of America	8N	NAE
American International Airways	United States of America	CB	CKS
American Trans Air, "Amtran"	United States of America	TZ	AMT
Amerijet Int'l Inc.	United States of America	JH	AJT
Ansett - New Zealand, "Anza"	New Zealand	AN	NMA
Ansett Australia	Australia	AA	AAA
Ariana Afghan Airlines	Afghanistan	FG	AFG
Asiana Airlines	South Korea	OZ	AAR
Atlantic Southeast Airlines	United States of America	EV	ASE
Austral Lineas Aereas	Argentina	AU	AUT
Australian Airlines Ltd	Australia	TN	AUS
Austrian Airlines	Austria	OS	AUA
Avensa - Aerovias Venezolanas	Venezuela	VE	AVE
AVIACO Aviacion y Comercio	Spain	AO	AYC
Avianca - Aerovias Nacionales de Colombia	Colombia	AV	AVA
Aviateca Aerolineas de Guatemala	Guatemala	GU	GUG
AZAL - Azerbaijan Airlines	Azerbaijan		
Bahamasair	Bahamas	BH	BHS
Balkan - Bulgarian Airlines	Bulgaria	LZ	LAZ
Baltic International Airlines	Latvia	TI	BIA

AIRLINE CARRIER	COUNTRY	IATA	ICAO
Basil Central Lineas Aereos Regional, "Central"	Brazil	JJ	BLC
Bearskin Airlines	Canada	JV	BLS
Biman Bangladesh Airlines	Bangladesh	BG	BBC
Birgenair	Turkey	KT	BHY
Bouraq Indonesia Airlines	Indonesia	BO	BOU
Braathens S.A.F.E.	Norway	BU	BRA
Bradley Air Services/First Air	Canada	7F	FAN
Britannia Airways	United Kingdom	BY	BAL
British Airways, "Speedbird"	United Kingdom	BA	BAW
British Midland Airways, "Midland"	United Kingdom	BD	BMA
Burlington Air Express (Burlington Northern Air Freight)	United States of America	8W	
Business Airlines	Netherlands	WZ	ATQ
Business Express, "Bizex"	United States of America	HQ	GAA
Caledonian Airways	United Kingdom	KT	BKT
Cambodian International Airlines	Cambodia		
Cameroon Airlines	Cameroon	UY	UYC
Canada 300 Airlines, "Elite"	Canada	MM	CMM
Canadian Airlines International	Canada	CP	CDN
Cargolux Airlines International	Luxembourg	CV	CLX
Caribbean Air Transport	St. Lucia	SX	
Caribjet Inc.	Antigua		
Carnival Airlines	United States of America	KW	CAA
Cathay Pacific Airways	Hong Kong	CX	CPA
Cayman Airways	Cayman Islands	KX	CAY
Ceskoslovenske Aerolinie	Czech Republic	OK	CSA
China Airlines, "Dynasty"	Taiwan	CI	CAL
China Eastern Airlines	China	MU	CEA
China Northern Airlines	China	CJ	CBF
China Northwest Airlines	China	WH	CNW
China Southern Airlines	China	CZ	CSN
China Southwest Airlines	China	SZ	CXN
China United Airlines	China		CUA
Comair	United States of America	OH	COM
Conair of Scandinavia	Denmark	OY	OYC
Condor Flugdienst	Germany	DE	CFG
Continental Air Lines	United States of America	CO	COA
COPA Compania Panamena de Aviacion	Panama	CM	CMP
Corsair International	France	SS	CRL
Croatia Airlines	Croatia		CTN
Crossair AG	Switzerland	LX	CRX
Cubana (Empresa Consolidada Cubana de Aviacion)	Cuba	CU	CUB
Cyprus Airways	Cyprus	CY	CYP
D.H.L. Worldwide Courier Express	United States of America	ER	DHL
Dairo Air Services, "Dairair"	Uganda	SE	DSR
Delta Air Lines	United States of America	DL	DAL
Deutsche BA	Germany	DI	BAG
Dominicana (Compania Dominicana de Aviacion)	Dominican Republic	DO	DOA
Dragonair (Hong Kong Dragon Airlines)	Hong Kong	KA	HDA
Druk Air (Royal Bhutan Airlines)	Bhutan	KB	DRK
Eagle Airways	New Zealand	EX	NZE
Eastern Australia Airlines	Australia	TN	ECO
Eastwest Airlines	Australia	EW	EWA
Ecuato-Guineana de Aviacion	Equatorial Guinea	ZH	EGA
Ecuatoriana - Compania Ecuatoriana de Aviacion	Ecuador	EU	EEA
Egyptair	Egypt	MS	MSR

AIRLINE CARRIER	COUNTRY	IATA	ICAO
El Al - Israel Airlines	Israel	LY	ELY
Emery Air Freight Corp	United States of America	EB	EAF
Emirates Airlines	United Arab Emirates	EK	UAE
Equatorial International Airlines	Sao Tomé	GL	EQL
Ethiopian Airlines, "Holloway"	Ethiopia	ET	ETH
Euralair	France	RN	EUI
Euro Berlin	Germany	EE	EEB
EuroBelgian Airlines, "Belstar"	Belgium		EBA
Europe Aero Service	France	EY	EYT
European Airlines	Belgium		FRO
Evergreen International Airlines	United States of America	EV	EIA
Excalibur Airways, "Camelot"	United Kingdom	EQ	EXC
Express One International, "Spartus"	United States of America		YPX
Falcon Air Cargo/Falcon Executive	Sweden	IH	FCN
Far Eastern Air Transport Corp.	Taiwan	EF	FEA
Faucett Peru - Compania de Aviacion Faucett	Peru	CF	CFP
Federal Express Corporation	United States of America	MB	FDX
FIGAS - Falkland Islands Government Air Service	Falkland Islands		
Finnair	Finland	AY	FIN
Flitestar	South Africa	KP	ACP
G.B. Airways Ltd., "Gibair"	Gibraltar	GT	GBL
German Cargo Services	Germany	GE	GEC
Germania Fluggesellschaft Koln, "Joker"	Germany	JO	GFG
Ghana Airways	Ghana	GH	GHA
Green Air	Turkey	WK	GRN
Gulf Air	Oman	GF	GFA
Guyana Airways. "Guyair"	Guyana	GY	GYA
Haiti Trans Air	Haiti	TV	HTC
Hapag Lloyd Fluggesellschaft	Germany	HF	HLF
Hawiian Airlines	Hawaii	HA	HAL
Hazelton Air Services Pty	Australia	ZL	HZL
Heli Air Monaco	Monaco	YO	MCM
Horizon Air	United States of America	QX	QXE
Iberia - Lineas Aereas de España	Spain	IB	IBE
Icelandair Flugledir, "Iceair"	Iceland	FI	ICE
Indian Airlines Corp, "Indair"	India	IC	IAC
Inter European Airways, "Aspro"	United Kingdom	IP	IEA
Iran Air (Iran National Airlines)	Iran	IR	IRA
Iraqi Airways	Iraq	IA	IAW
Istanbul Airlines/Hava Yollari	Turkey	IL	IST
JAL - Japan Air Lines	Japan	JL	JAL
Japan Air System Company	Japan	JD	JAS
Japan Asia Airways, "Asia"	Japan	EG	JAA
K.L.M - Royal Dutch Airlines	Netherlands	KL	KLM
Kabo Air Travels	Nigeria	QN	QNK
KAL - Korean Air Lines	South Korea	KE	KAL
Kampuchea Airlines	Cambodia	DK	
Kazakstan Airlines	Kazakstan		SAX
Kendell Airlines	Australia	KD	KDA
Kenya Airways	Kenya	KQ	KQA
Key Airlines	United States of America	9D	KEY
Kinair Cargo	Zaire		
Kuwait Airways Corp	Kuwait	KU	KAC
L.A.P. - Lineas Aereas Paraguayas	Paraguay	PZ	LAP
L.A.R. Liniile Aeriene Romane	Romania	RL	RLA

AIRLINE CARRIER	COUNTRY	IATA	ICAO
LAB Lloyd Aero Boliviano	Bolivia	LB	LLB
LACSA - Lineas Aereas Costarricenses	Costa Rica	LR	LRC
LADECO Linea Aerea del Cobre	Chile	UC	LCO
LAM Lineas Aereas Mozambique	Mozambique	TM	LAM
LAN Chile Linea Aerea Nacional de Chile	Chile	LA	LAN
Lao International	Laos	QV	LAO
LAPA - Lineas Aereas Privadas Argentinas	Argentina	MJ	LPR
Latvian Airlines	Latvia		LTL
Lauda Air Luftfahrt	Austria	LW	LDA
Lesotho Airways	Lesotho	QL	LAI
LIAT - Leeward Islands Air Transport	Antigua	LI	LIA
Liberia World Airways	Liberia	HY	LWA
Libyan Arab Airlines, "Libair"	Libya	LN	LAA
Lina Congo - Lignes Nationales Aeriennes Congolaises	Congo	GC	GCB
Lithuanian Airlines	Lithuania	TE	LIL
Loganair Ltd.	United Kingdom	LC	LOG
LOT - Polskie Linie Lotnicze, "Pollot"	Poland	LO	LOT
LTE International Airways, "Bluejet"	Spain	XO	LTE
LTU Lufttransport Unternehmen	Germany	LT	LTU
LTU Sud	Germany	BV	LTS
Lufthansa (Deutsche Lufthansa)	Germany	LH	DLH
Luxair	Luxembourg	LG	LGL
Macedonian Air Services	Macedonia		MDO
Maersk Air	Denmark	DM	DMA
Makair Inc., "Interalas"	Alaska	BF	MRK
Malaysia Airlines	Malaysia	MH	MAS
Malev Hungarian Airlines	Hungary	MA	MAH
Mandarin Airlines	Taiwan	AE	MDA
Manx Airlines	United Kingdom	JE	MNX
Martinair Holland	Netherlands	MP	MPH
Maya Airways	Belize	MW	MAY
Meridiana SpA.	Italy	IG	ISS
Merpati Nusantara Airlines	Indonesia	MZ	MNA
META Aviotransport Macedonia	Macedonia		MAM
Mexicana - Compania Mexicana de Aviacion	Mexico	MX	MXA
MGM Grand Air	United States of America	MG	MGM
Miami Air International, "Biscayne"	United States of America		
MIAT Mongolian Airlines	Mongolia	OM	
Middle East Airlines, "Cedar Jet"	Lebanon	ME	MEA
Monarch Airlines	United Kingdom	ZB	MON
Myanma Airlines	Myanmar	UB	UBA
Newair Airservice, "Newden"	Denmark	OZ	NAW
Nigeria Airways	Nigeria	WT	NGA
Nippon Cargo Airlines	Japan	KZ	NCA
Nomads Inc. (Travel Club)	United States of America		
Nordeste Linhas Regionias	Brazil	RE	NES
NorOntair	Canada	NR	NOA
North American Airlines	United States of America	XG	
Northwest Airlines	United States of America	NW	NWA
Northwest Airlink/Mesaba Airlines	United States of America	XJ	MES
NWT Air, "Territorial"	Canada	NV	NWT
Okada Air Service	Nigeria	OX	OKJ
Olympic Airways	Greece	OA	OAL
Ontario Express Ltd	Canada	9X	OEL
Onur Air	Turkey	TK	OHY

Appendix C - Airline Carriers by Carrier

AIRLINE CARRIER	COUNTRY	IATA	ICAO
P.T. Gatari Hutuma Air Services	Indonesia		GHS
PALAIR Macedonian	Macedonia		PMK
Patriot Airlines	United States of America		
Pegasus Airlines	Turkey		PGT
Pelita Air Service	Indonesia	EP	PAS
Philippine Air Lines	Philippines	PR	PAL
PIA - Pakistan Int'l Airlines	Pakistan	PK	PIA
PLUNA Primerias Lineas Uruguayas de Navegacion Aerea	Uruguay	PU	PUA
PN. Garuda Indonesia Airways, "Garuda"	Indonesia	GA	GIA
Polynesian Airlines	Western Samoa	PH	PAO
Pride African International	Zaire		PAI
PT Sempati Air Transport	Indonesia	VD	SMP
Qantas Australian Airlines	Australia	QF	QFA
Reeve Aleutian Airways	Alaska	RV	RVV
Rio Sul Serviços Aereos Regionais	Brazil	SL	RSL
Royal Air Maroc, "Marocair"	Morocco	AT	RAN
Royal Brunei Airlines	Brunei	BI	RBA
Royal Nepal Airlines	Nepal	RA	RNA
Royal Swazi National Airways	Swaziland	WA	RSN
Royal Tongan Airways	Tonga	JK	HRH
Saarland Airlines	Germany		SSL
SABENA	Belgium	SN	SAB
SAETA - Soc. Anonima Ecuatoriana de Transportes Aereos	Ecuador	EH	SET
Safair, "Cargo"	South Africa	CG	SFR
SAHSA Servicio Aero de Honduras	Honduras	SH	SHA
SAM Colombia - Soc. Aeronautica de Medellin Consolidada	Colombia	MM	SAM
SARO - Servicios Aereos Rutas Oriente	Mexico		SRO
SAS - Scandinavian Airlines System	Sweden	SK	SAS
Saudi - Saudi Arabian Airlines	Saudi Arabia	SV	SVA
Scibe Airlift Cargo Zaire (SBZ Cargo)	Zaire	ZM	
Seagreen Air Transport	Antigua	ES	ESA
Shanghai Airlines	China	SF	CSH
Sierra Pacific Airlines	United States of America		SPA
Silkair	Singapore	MI	SLK
Singapore Airlines	Singapore	SQ	SIA
Sky West Airlines	United States of America	OO	SKW
Skywest Airlines	Australia	YT	SLL
Sobelair - Societe Belge de Transportes Aeriens	Belgium	OO	SLR
Solomon Airlines	Solomon Islands	IE	SOL
Somali Airlines	Somalia	HH	MSO
South African Airways, "Springbok"	South Africa	SA	SAA
Southwest Air Lines, "Nansei"	Japan	NU	SWL
Southwest Airlines Company	United States of America	WN	SWA
Spanair	Spain	JK	SPP
Ste de Transportes Aerien du Mali	Mali	SB	SBA
Sterling Airways	Denmark	NB	SAW
Sudan Airways	Sudan	SD	SUD
Sultan Air	Turkey		STN
Sun Country Airlines, "Sunshine"	United States of America	SY	SCX
Sun Express (Gunes Ekspreii Havacink)	Turkey	XQ	SXS
Sun-Air of Scandinavia	Denmark	EZ	
Swedair AB	Sweden	JG	SWE
Swissair AG	Switzerland	SR	SWR
Syrianair (Syrian Arab Airlines)	Syria	RB	SYR
TAAG Angola Airlines	Angola	DT	DTA

AIRLINE CARRIER	COUNTRY	IATA	ICAO
TABA - Transportes Aereos de Bacia Amazonica	Brazil	TT	TAB
TACA International Airlines	El Salvador	TA	TAI
TAESA - Transportes Aereos Ejecutivos	Mexico		TEJ
TAM - Lineas Aereos Regional	Brazil	TF	TAM
TAME - Transportes Aereos Militares Nac. Ecuatorianos	Ecuador	EQ	TAE
Tampa Colombia Aerolineas	Colombia	QT	TPA
Tarom - Transporturile Aeriene Romane	Romania	RO	ROT
TAT European Airlines	France	IJ	TAT
TEA Basle (Trans European Airways), "Transway"	Switzerland		TSW
Thai Airways International, "Thainter"	Thailand	TG	THA
The Royal Jordanian Airline Corp.	Jordan	RJ	RJA
THT - Turk Hava Tasimaciligi	Turkey		THT
THY - Turkish Airlines, "Turkair"	Turkey	TK	THY
Tower Air Inc., "Tee Air"	United States of America	FF	TOW
Tradewinds International Air Line	United States of America	WI	WRN
Trans Arabian Air Transport	Sudan	MI	TRT
Trans Mediterranean Airways	Lebanon	TL	TMA
Trans World Airlines	United States of America	TW	TWA
Transasia	Taiwan	GE	FHA
Transavia Airlines	Netherlands	HV	TRH
Transbrasil SA. Lineas Aereas/Aerobrasil	Brazil	TR	TMA
Transmed	Egypt	MT	TMD
Transportes Aereos de Cabo Verde, "Transverde"	Cape Verde	VR	TCV
Transports Aeriens de la Guinea-Bissau	Guinea-Bissau	GB	GBU
Tunis Air, "Tunair"	Tunisia	TU	TAR
Turks & Caicos National Airline	Turks & Caicos	QW	TCI
Tyrolean Airways	Austria	TQ	TYR
U. S. Air	United States of America	US	USA
U.P.S. United Parcel Service, "Upsco"	United States of America	SX	UPS
Uganda Airlines	Uganda	QU	UGA
United Airlines	United States of America	UA	UAL
United Express	United States of America	UA	UAL
Uzbekistan Airlines	Uzbekistan	HY	UZB
VARIG - Viacao Aerea Rio-Grandense	Brazil	RG	VRG
VASP - Viacao Aerea Sao Paulo	Brazil	VP	VSP
VB Air (Varda Bosna Air)	Bosnia		BAA
VIASA - Venezolana Internacional de Aviacion	Venezuela	VA	VIA
Vietnam Airlines	Vietnam	VN	HVN
Virgin Atlantic Airways	United Kingdom	VS	VIR
VIVA Air - Vuelos Internacionales de Vacaciones	Spain	FV	VIV
West Indian (BWIA)	Trinidad & Tobago	BW	BWA
World Airways	United States of America	WO	WOA
Xiamen Airlines	China	MF	CXA
Xinjiang Airlines	China	XO	CXJ
Yemenia Airways	Yemen	IY	IYE
Zambia Airways	Zambia	QZ	ZAC
Zantop International Airlines	United States of America	VK	ZAN
ZAS Airlines of Egypt	Egypt	WW	ZAS
Airbus Industrie	Manufacturers' Fleets	VK	AIB
Beech Aircraft Corp	Manufacturers' Fleets		BEC
Boeing Commercial Airplane Group	Manufacturers' Fleets		BOE
Bombardier Aerospace Group	Manufacturers' Fleets		
British Aerospace PLC	Manufacturers' Fleets	HO	BAE
Deutsche Aerospace/Dornier	Manufacturers' Fleets		DOR
McDonnel-Douglas, "Daco"	Manufacturers' Fleets		DAC

Appendix C - Airline Carriers by Country

COUNTRY/AIRLINE CARRIER	IATA	ICAO
Afghanistan		
Ariana Afghan Airlines	FG	AFG
Alaska		
Alaska Airlines	AS	ASA
Makair Inc., "Interalas"	BF	MRK
Reeve Aleutian Airways	RV	RVV
Algeria		
Air Algerie	AH	DAH
Angola		
TAAG Angola Airlines	DT	DTA
Antigua		
Caribjet Inc.		
LIAT - Leeward Islands Air Transport	LI	LIA
Seagreen Air Transport	ES	ESA
Argentina		
Aerolineas Argentinas	AR	ARG
Austral Lineas Aereas	AU	AUT
LAPA - Lineas Aereas Privadas Argentinas	MJ	LPR
Aruba		
Air Aruba	FQ	ARU
Australia		
Ansett Australia	AA	AAA
Australian Airlines Ltd	TN	AUS
Eastern Australia Airlines	TN	ECO
Eastwest Airlines	EW	EWA
Hazelton Air Services Pty	ZL	HZL
Kendell Airlines	KD	KDA
Qantas Australian Airlines	QF	QFA
Skywest Airlines	YT	SLL
Austria		
Austrian Airlines	OS	AUA
Lauda Air Luftfahrt	LW	LDA
Tyrolean Airways	TQ	TYR
Azerbaijan		
AZAL - Azerbaijan Airlines		
Bahamas		
Bahamasair	BH	BHS
Bangladesh		
Biman Bangladesh Airlines	BG	BBC

COUNTRY/AIRLINE CARRIER	IATA	ICAO
Belgium		
Air Belgium International	VY	ABB
EuroBelgian Airlines, "Belstar"		EBA
European Airlines		FRO
SABENA	SN	SAB
Sobelair - Societe Belge de Transportes Aeriens	OO	SLR
Belize		
Maya Airways	MW	MAY
Benin		
Air Benin	TS	TSB
Bhutan		
Druk Air (Royal Bhutan Airlines)	KB	DRK
Bolivia		
LAB Lloyd Aero Boliviano	LB	LLB
Bosnia		
VB Air (Varda Bosna Air)		BAA
Botswana		
Air Botswana	BP	BOT
Brazil		
Brasil Central Lineas Aereos Regional, "Central"	JJ	BLC
Nordeste Linhas Regionias	RE	NES
Rio Sul Serviços Aereos Regionais	SL	RSL
TABA - Transportes Aereos de Bacia Amazonica	TT	TAB
Transbrasil SA. Lineas Aereas/Aerobrasil	TR	TMA
VARIG - Viacao Aerea Rio-Grandense	RG	VRG
VASP - Viacao Aerea Sao Paulo	VP	VSP
Brunei		
Royal Brunei Airlines	BI	RBA
Bulgaria		
Balkan - Bulgarian Airlines	LZ	LAZ
Burkina Faso		
Air Burkina	VH	VBW
Burundi		
Air Burundi	PB	PBU
Cambodia		
Cambodian International Airlines		
Kampuchea Airlines	DK	
Cameroon		
Cameroon Airlines	UY	UYC

COUNTRY/AIRLINE CARRIER	IATA	ICAO
Canada		
Air Alliance	3J	AAQ
Air Atlantic	9A	ATL
Air B.C. ,"Aircoach"	ZX	ABL
Air Canada	AC	ACA
Air Creebec, "Cree"	YN	CRQ
Air Inuit	3H	AIE
Air Manitoba, "Manitoba"	7N	NAM
Air Niagara Express, "Databird"	DB	DBD
Air Nova	QK	ARN
Air Ontario, "Ontario"	GX	ONT
Air Transat	TS	TSC
Bearskin Airlines	JV	BLS
Bradley Air Services/First Air	7F	FAN
Canada 300 Airlines, "Elite"	MM	CMM
Canadian Airlines International	CP	CDN
NorOntair	NR	NOA
NWT Air, "Territorial"	NV	NWT
Ontario Express Ltd	9X	OEL
Cape Verde		
Transportes Aereos de Cabo Verde, "Transverde"	VR	TCV
Cayman Islands		
Cayman Airways	KX	CAY
Chile		
LADECO Linea Aerea del Cobre	UC	LCO
LAN Chile Linea Aerea Nacional de Chile	LA	LAN
China		
Air China	CA	CCA
China Eastern Airlines	MU	CEA
China Northern Airlines	CJ	CBF
China Northwest Airlines	WH	CNW
China Southern Airlines	CZ	CSN
China Southwest Airlines	SZ	CXN
China United Airlines		CUA
Shanghai Airlines	SF	CSH
Xiamen Airlines	MF	CXA
Xinjiang Airlines	XO	CXJ
Colombia		
Aerosucre Colombia		KRE
Avianca - Aerovias Nacionales de Colombia	AV	AVA
SAM Colombia - Sociedad Aeronautica de Medellin Consolidada	MM	SAM
Tampa Colombia Aerolineas	QT	TPA
Comoros Islands		
Air Comoros	OR	AOR
Congo		
Lina Congo - Lignes Nationales Aeriennes Congolaises	GC	GCB

COUNTRY/AIRLINE CARRIER	IATA	ICAO
Cook Islands		
Air Rarotonga	GZ	
Costa Rica		
LACSA - Lineas Aereas Costarricenses	LR	LRC
Croatia		
Croatia Airlines		CTN
Cuba		
Aero Caribbean	CR	CRN
Cubana (Empresa Consolidada Cubana de Aviacion)	CU	CUB
Cyprus		
Cyprus Airways	CY	CYP
Czech Republic		
Czeskoslovenske Aerolinie	OK	CSA
Denmark		
Conair of Scandinavia	OY	OYC
Maersk Air	DM	DMA
Newair Airservice, "Newden"	OZ	NAW
Sterling Airways	NB	SAW
Sun-Air of Scandinavia	EZ	
Dominican Republic		
Dominicana (Compania Dominicana de Aviacion)	DO	DOA
Ecuador		
Ecuatoriana - Compania Ecuatoriana de Aviacion	EU	EEA
SAETA - Sociedad Anonima Ecuatoriana de Transportes Aereos	EH	SET
TAME - Transportes Aereos Militares Nacionales Ecuatorianos	EQ	TAE
Egypt		
Air Sinai	DP	ASD
Egyptair	MS	MSR
Transmed	MT	TMD
ZAS Airlines of Egypt	WW	ZAS
El Salvador		
ACA International Airlines	TA	TAI
Equatorial Guinea		
Ecuato-Guineana de Aviacion	ZH	EGA
Ethiopia		
Ethiopian Airlines, "Holloway"	ET	ETH
Falkland Islands		
FIGAS - Falkland Islands Government Air Service		
Fiji		
Air Pacific, "Pacific"	FJ	FJI

COUNTRY/AIRLINE CARRIER	IATA	ICAO
Finland		
Finnair	AY	FIN
France		
Air Charter	SF	ACF
Air France	AF	AFR
Air Inter (Lignes Aerienes Interieures)	IT	ITF
Corsair International	SS	CRL
Euralair	RN	EUI
Europe Aero Service	EY	EYT
TAT European Airlines	IJ	TAT
Gabon		
Air Gabon	GN	AGN
Gambia		
Air Gambia, "Atas"	1V	AGS
Germany		
Aero Lloyd Luftverkehrs	YP	AEF
Air Berlin	AB	BER
Condor Flugdienst	DE	CFG
Deutsche BA	DI	BAG
Euro Berlin	EE	EEB
German Cargo Services	GE	GEC
Germania Fluggesellschaft Koln, "Joker"	JO	GFG
Hapag Lloyd Fluggesellschaft	HF	HLF
LTU Lufttransport Unternehmen	LT	LTU
LTU Sud	BV	LTS
Lufthansa (Deutsche Lufthansa)	LH	DLH
Saarland Airlines		SSL
Ghana		
Ghana Airways	GH	GHA
Gibraltar		
G.B Airways Ltd., "Gibair"	GT	GBL
Greece		
Olympic Airways	OA	OAL
Guatemala		
Aviateca Aerolineas de Guatemala	GU	GUG
Guinea		
Air Guinee	GI	GIB
Guinea-Bissau		
Transports Aeriens de la Guinea-Bissau	GB	GBU
Guyana		
Guyana Airways. "Guyair"	GY	GYA
Haiti		
Haiti Trans Air	TV	HTC

COUNTRY/AIRLINE CARRIER	IATA	ICAO
Hawaii		
Alhoa Airlines	AQ	AHA
Hawiian Airlines	HA	HAL
Honduras		
SAHSA Servicio Aero de Honduras	SH	SHA
Hong Kong		
Air Hong Kong		AHK
Cathay Pacific Airways	CX	CPA
Dragonair (Hong Kong Dragon Airlines)	KA	HDA
Hungary		
Malev Hungarian Airlines	MA	MAH
Iceland		
Icelandair Flugledir, "Iceair"	FI	ICE
India		
Air India	AI	AIC
Indian Airlines Corp, "Indair"	IC	IAC
Indonesia		
Bouraq Indonesia Airlines	BO	BOU
Merpati Nusantara Airlines	MZ	MNA
P.T. Gatari Hutuma Air Services		GHS
Pelita Air Service	EP	PAS
PN. Garuda Indonesia Airways, "Garuda"	GA	GIA
PT Sempati Air Transport	VD	SMP
Iran		
Iran Air (Iran National Airlines)	IR	IRA
Iraq		
Iraqi Airways	IA	IAW
Ireland		
Aer Lingus ,"Shamrock"	EI	EIN
Israel		
El Al - Israel Airlines	LY	ELY
Italy		
Aero Transporti Italiani	BM	ATI
Air Europe Italy	AX	AEL
Alitalia	AZ	AZA
Meridiana SpA.	IG	ISS
Ivory Coast		
Air Afrique	RK	RKA
Jamaica		
Air Jamaica	JM	AJM

COUNTRY/AIRLINE CARRIER	IATA	ICAO
Japan		
Air Nippon Kasushika Gaisha	WK	ANK
All Nippon Airways	NH	ANA
JAL - Japan Air Lines	JL	JAL
Japan Air System Company	JD	JAS
Japan Asia Airways, "Asia"	EG	JAA
Nippon Cargo Airlines	KZ	NCA
Southwest Air Lines, "Nansei"	NU	SWL
Jordan		
The Royal Jordanian Airline Corp.	RJ	RJA
Kazakstan		
Kazakstan Airlines		SAX
Kenya		
African Airlines International		
African Safari Airways	QS	QSC
Air Kenya	QP	CSS
Kenya Airways	KQ	KQA
Kiribati		
Air Tungaru	RT	TUN
Kuwait		
Kuwait Airways Corp	KU	KAC
Laos		
Lao International	QV	LAO
Latvia		
Baltic International Airlines	TI	BIA
Latvian Airlines		LTL
Lebanon		
Middle East Airlines, "Cedar Jet"	ME	MEA
Trans Mediterranean Airways	TL	TMA
Lesotho Airways	QL	LAI
Liberia World Airways	HY	LWA
Libya		
Libyan Arab Airlines, "Libair"	LN	LAA
Lithuania		
Lithuanian Airlines	TE	LIL
Luxembourg		
Cargolux Airlines International	CV	CLX
Luxair	LG	LGL
Macedonia		
Macedonian Air Services		MDO
META Aviotransport Macedonia		MAM
PALAIR Macedonian		PMK

COUNTRY/AIRLINE CARRIER	IATA	ICAO
Madagascar		
Air Madagascar, "Madair"	MD	MDG
Malawi		
Air Malawi	QM	AML
Malaysia		
Malaysia Airlines	MH	MAS
Maldives		
Air Maldives	PN	AMI
Mali		
Ste de Transportes Aerien du Mali	SB	SBA
Malta		
Air Malta	KM	AMC
Mauritania		
Air Mauritania	MR	MRT
Mauritius		
Air Mauritius	MK	MAU
Mexico		
Aero Caribe	QA	
Aeroejecutivos SA de CV		
Aeromexico (Aeovias de Mexico)	AM	AMX
Mexicana - Compania Mexicana de Aviacion	MX	MXA
SARO - Servicios Aereos Rutas Oriente		SRO
AESA - Transportes Aereos Ejecutivos		TEJ
Monaco		
Heli Air Monaco	YO	MCM
Mongolia		
MIAT Mongolian Airlines	OM	
Morocco		
Royal Air Maroc, "Marocair"	AT	RAN
Mozambique		
LAM Lineas Aereas Mozambique	TM	LAM
Myanmar		
Myanma Airlines	UB	UBA
Namibia		
Air Namibia	SW	NMB
Nauru		
Air Nauru	ON	RON
Nepal		
Royal Nepal Airlines	RA	RNA

COUNTRY/AIRLINE CARRIER	IATA	ICAO
Netherlands		
Air Holland Charter	GG	AHR
Business Airlines	WZ	ATQ
K.L.M - Royal Dutch Airlines (Koninklijke Luchtvaart Maatschappij)	KL	KLM
Martinair Holland	MP	MPH
Transavia Airlines	HV	TRH
Netherlands Antilles		
A.L.M. - Antillean Airlines	LM	ALM
New Caledonia		
Air Caledonie International, "Aircal"	SB	RKL
New Zealand		
Air New Zealand	NZ	ANZ
Ansett - New Zealand, "Anza"	AN	NMA
Eagle Airways	EX	NZE
Nicaragua		
Aeronica - Aerolineas Nicaraguenses	NI	ANI
Nigeria		
Kabo Air Travels	QN	QNK
Nigeria Airways	WT	NGA
Okada Air Service	OX	OKJ
North Korea		
Air Koyro		
Norway		
Braathens S.A.F.E.	BU	BRA
Oman		
Gulf Air	GF	GFA
Pakistan		
PIA - Pakistan Int'l Airlines	PK	PIA
Panama		
COPA Compania Panamena de Aviacion	CM	CMP
Papua New Guinea		
Air Niungini	PX	ANG
Paraguay		
L.A.P. - Lineas Aereas Paraguayas	PZ	LAP
Peru		
Aero Peru - Empresa de Transporte Aereo del Peru	PL	PLI
Faucett Peru - Compania de Aviacion Faucett	CF	CFP
Philippines		
Philippine Air Lines	PR	PAL

COUNTRY/AIRLINE CARRIER	IATA	ICAO
Poland		
LOT - Polskie Linie Lotnicze, "Pollot"	LO	LOT
Portugal		
Air Portugal, "TAP"	TP	TAP
Romania		
L.A.R. Liniile Aeriene Romane	RL	RLA
Tarom - Transporturile Aeriene Romane	RO	ROT
Russia		
Aeroflot	SU	AFL
Rwanda		
Air Rwanda	UW	RWD
Sao Tomé		
Air Transafrik	PQ	TRF
Equatorial International Airlines	GL	EQL
Saudi Arabia		
Saudi - Saudi Arabian Airlines	SV	SVA
Senegal		
Air Senegal	DS	DSR
Singapore		
Silkair	MI	SLK
Singapore Airlines	SQ	SIA
Slovenia		
Adria Airways	JP	ADR
Solomon Islands		
Solomon Airlines	IE	SOL
Somalia		
Somali Airlines	HH	MSO
South Africa		
Flitestar	KP	ACP
Safair, "Cargo"	CG	SFR
South African Airways, "Springbok"	SA	SAA
South Korea		
Asiana Airlines	OZ	AAR
KAL - Korean Air Lines	KE	KAL
Spain		
Air Europa	UX	AEA
AVIACO Aviacion y Comercio	AO	AYC
Iberia - Lineas Aereas de España	IB	IBE
LTE International Airways, "Bluejet"	XO	LTE
Spanair	JK	SPP
VIVA Air - Vuelos Internacionales de Vacaciones	FV	VIV

COUNTRY/AIRLINE CARRIER	IATA	ICAO
Sri Lanka		
Air Lanka	UL	ALK
St. Lucia		
Caribbean Air Transport	SX	
Sudan		
Sudan Airways	SD	SUD
Trans Arabian Air Transport	MI	TRT
Swaziland		
Air Swazi Cargo	CW	CWS
Royal Swazi National Airways	WA	RSN
Sweden		
Falcon Air Cargo/Falcon Executive	IH	FCN
SAS - Scandinavian Airlines System	SK	SAS
Swedair AB	JG	SWE
Switzerland		
Crossair AG	LX	CRX
Swissair AG	SR	SWR
TEA Basle (Trans European Airways), "Transway"		TSW
Syria		
Syrianair (Syrian Arab Airlines)	RB	SYR
Tahiti		
Air Tahiti	VT	TAH
Taiwan		
China Airlines, "Dynasty"	CI	CAL
Far Eastern Air Transport Corp.	EF	FEA
Mandarin Airlines	AE	MDA
Transasia	GE	FHA
Tanzania		
Air Tanzania	TC	ATC
Tchad		
Air Chad	HT	HTT
Thailand		
Thai Airways International, "Thainter"	TG	THA
Tonga		
Royal Tongan Airways	JK	HRH
Trinidad & Tobago		
West Indian (BWIA)	BW	BWA
Tunisia		
Tunis Air, "Tunair"	TU	TAR

COUNTRY/AIRLINE CARRIER	IATA	ICAO
Turkey		
Birgenair	KT	BHY
Green Air	WK	GRN
Istanbul Airlines/Hava Yollari	IL	IST
Onur Air	TK	OHY
Pegasus Airlines		PGT
Sultan Air		STN
Sun Express (Gunes Ekspreii Havacink)	XQ	SXS
THT - Turk Hava Tasimaciligi		THT
THY - Turkish Airlines, "Turkair"	TK	THY
Turks & Caicos		
Turks & Caicos National Airline	QW	TCI
Uganda		
Dairo Air Services, "Dairair"	SE	DSR
Uganda Airlines	QU	UGA
Ukraine		
Air Ukraine International	PS	UKR
United Arab Emirates		
Emirates Airlines	EK	UAE
United Kingdom		
Air 2000, "Jetset"	DP	AMM
Britannia Airways	BY	BAL
British Airways, "Speedbird"	BA	BAW
British Midland Airways, "Midland"	BD	BMA
Caledonian Airways	KT	BKT
Excalibur Airways, "Camelot"	EQ	EXC
Inter European Airways, "Aspro"	IP	IEA
Loganair Ltd.	LC	LOG
Manx Airlines	JE	MNX
Monarch Airlines	ZB	MON
Virgin Atlantic Airways	VS	VIR
United States of America		
Airborne Express, "Abex"	QB	ABX
America West Airlines, "Cactus"	HP	AWE
American Airlines	AA	AAL
American Eagle/Flagship Airlines	8N	NAE
American International Airways	CB	CKS
American Trans Air, "Amtran"	TZ	AMT
Amerijet Int'l Inc.	JH	AJT
Atlantic Southeast Airlines	EV	ASE
Burlington Air Express (Burlington Northern Air Freight)	8W	
Business Express, "Bizex"	HQ	GAA
Carnival Airlines	KW	CAA
Comair	OH	COM
Continental Air Lines	CO	COA
D.H.L. Worldwide Courier Express	ER	DHL
Delta Air Lines	DL	DAL
Emery Air Freight Corp	EB	EAF
Evergreen International Airlines	EV	EIA

COUNTRY/AIRLINE CARRIER	IATA	ICAO
Express One International, "Spartus"		YPX
Federal Express Corporation	MB	FDX
Horizon Air	QX	QXE
Key Airlines	9D	KEY
MGM Grand Air	MG	MGM
Miami Air International, "Biscayne"		
Nomads Inc. (Travel Club)		
North American Airlines	XG	
Northwest Airlines	NW	NWA
Northwest Airlink/Mesaba Airlines	XJ	MES
Patriot Airlines		
Sierra Pacific Airlines		SPA
Sky West Airlines	OO	SKW
Southwest Airlines Company	WN	SWA
Sun Country Airlines, "Sunshine"	SY	SCX
Tower Air Inc., "Tee Air"	FF	TOW
Tradewinds International Air Line	WI	WRN
Trans World Airlines	TW	TWA
U. S. Air	US	USA
U.P.S. United Parcel Service, "Upsco"	SX	UPS
United Airlines	UA	UAL
United Express	UA	UAL
World Airways	WO	WOA
Zantop International Airlines	VK	ZAN
Uruguay		
PLUNA Primerias Lineas Uruguayas de Navegacion Aerea	PU	PUA
Uzbekistan		
Uzbekistan Airlines	HY	UZB
Vanuatu		
Air Vanuatu, "Air Van"	NF	AVN
Venezuela		
Aeropostal - Linea Aeropostal Venezolana	LV	LAV
Avensa - Aerovias Venezolanas	VE	AVE
VIASA - Venezolana Internacional de Aviacion	VA	VIA
Vietnam		
Vietnam Airlines	VN	HVN
Western Samoa		
Polynesian Airlines	PH	PAO
Yemen		
Yemenia Airways	IY	IYE
Zaire		
Air Zaire	QC	AZR
Kinair Cargo		
Pride African International		PAI
Scibe Airlift Cargo Zaire (SBZ Cargo)	ZM	

COUNTRY/AIRLINE CARRIER	IATA	ICAO
Zambia		
Zambia Airways	QZ	ZAC
Zimbabwe		
Air Zimbabwe	WX	AZW
Aircraft Manufacturers' Fleets		
Airbus Industrie	VK	AIB
Beech Aircraft Corp		BEC
Boeing Commercial Airplane Group		BOE
Bombardier Aerospace Group		
British Aerospace PLC	HO	BAE
Deutsche Aerospace/Dornier		DOR
Embraer		EMB
Fohker		FOP
McDonnel-Douglas, "Daco"		DAC
Short Brothers	IM	SBL

Appendix D - Aircraft Registration

COUNTRY	PREFIX	COUNTRY	PREFIX
Afghanistan	YA	Ecuador	HC
Albania	ZA	Egypt	SU
Algeria	7T	El Salvador	YS
American Samoa	N	Equatorial Guinea	3C
Andorra	C3	Eritrea	-
Angola	D2	Estonia	ES
Anguilla	VP-LA	Ethiopia	ET
Antigua	V2	Falkland Islands	VP-F
Argentina	LV	Fiji	DQ
Armenia	-	Finland	OH
Aruba	P4	France	F
Australia	VH	French Guiana	F
Austria	OE	Gabon	TR
Azerbaijan	4K	Gambia	C5
Bahamas	C6	Georgia	-
Bahrain	A9C	Germany	D
Bangladesh	S2	Ghana	9G
Barbados	8P	Gibraltar	VR-G
Barbuda	V2	Great Britain	G
Belarus	EW	Greece	SX
Belgium	OO	Grenada	J3
Belize	V3	Guadeloupe	F
Benin	TY	Guam	N
Bermuda	VR-B	Guatemala	TG
Bhutan	A5	Guinea	3X
Bolivia	CP	Guinea Bissau	J5
Bophuthatswana	ZS	Guyana	8R
Botswana	A2	Haiti	HH
Brazil	PP/PT	Honduras	HR
British Virgin Islands	VP-LV	Hong Kong	VR-H
Brunei	V8	Hungary	HA
Bulgaria	LZ	Iceland	TF
Burkina Faso	XT	India	VT
Burundi	9U	Indonesia	PK
Cameroon	TJ	Iran	EP
Canada	C/CF	Iraq	YI
Cape Verde Islands	D4	Ireland	EI
Caroline Islands	N	Israel	4X
Cayman Islands	VR-C	Italy	I
Central African Republic	TL	Ivory Coast	TU
Chad	TT	Jamaica	6Y
Chile	CC	Japan	JA
China	B	Jordan	JY
Colombia	HK	Kampuchea	XU
Comoros Islands	D6	Kazakhstan	-
Congo	TN	Kenya	5Y
Costa Rica	TI	Kiribati	T3
Croatia	9A	Krygyzstan	-
Cuba	CU	Kuwait	9K
Cyprus	5B	Laos	RDPL
Czech Republic	OK	Latvia	YL
Denmark	OY	Lebanon	OD
Djibouti	J2	Lesotho	7P
Dominica	J7	Liberia	EL
Dominican Republic	HI	Libya	5A

Appendix D - Aircraft Registration

COUNTRY	PREFIX	COUNTRY	PREFIX
Liechtenstein	HB	Sao Tomé	S9
Lithuania	LY	Saudi Arabia	HZ
Luxembourg	LX	Senegal	6V
Macedonia	-	Serbia	-
Madagascar	5R	Seychelles	S7
Malawi	7Q	Sierra Leone	9L
Malaysia	9M	Singapore	9V
Maldives	8Q	Slovenia	S5
Mali	TZ	Solomon Islands	H4
Malta	9H	Somalia	6O
Mariana Islands	N	South Africa	ZS
Marshall Islands	V7	South Korea	HL
Martinique	F	Spain	EC
Mauritania	ST	Sri Lanka	4R
Mauritius	3B	St. Kitts-Nevis	V4
Mexico	XA/XB/XC	St. Lucia	J6
Moldova	ER	St. Vincent & Grenadines	J8
Monaco	3A	Sudan	ST
Mongolia	MT	Surinam	PZ
Montserrat	VP-LM	Swaziland	3D
Morocco	CN	Sweden	SE
Mozambique	C9	Switzerland	HB
Myanmar	XY	Syria	YK
Namibia	V5	Taiwan	B
Nauru	C2	Tajikistan	EY
Nepal	9N	Tanzania	5H
Netherlands	PH	Thailand	HS
Netherlands Antilles	PJ	Togo	5V
New Caledonia	F	Tonga	A3
New Zealand	ZK	Transkei	ZS
Nicaragua	YN	Trinidad & Tobago	9Y
Niger	5U	Tunisia	TS
Nigeria	5N	Turkey	TC
North Korea	P	Turkmenistan	EZ
Norway	LN	Turks & Caicos	VQ-T
Oman	A40	Tuvalu	T2
Pakistan	AP	U.S. Virgin Islands	N
Palau	-	Uganda	5X
Panama	HP	Ukraine	UR
Papua New Guinea	P2	United Arab Emirates	A6
Paraguay	ZP	United Nations	4U
Peru	OB	Uruguay	CX
Philippines	RP	USA	N
Poland	SP	Uzbekistan	UK
Polynesia	F	Vanuatu	YJ
Portugal	CS	Vatican	HV
Puerto Rico	N	Venda	ZS
Qatar	A7	Venezuela	YV
Réunion Islands	F	Vietnam	VN
Romania	YR	Western Samoa	5W
Russia	RA	Yemen	7O
Rwanda	9XR	Yugoslavia	YU
Saint-Barthelemy	F	Zaire	9Q/9T
Saint-Pierre & Miquelon	F	Zambia	9J
San Marino	T7	Zimbabwe	Z

PREFIX	COUNTRY
3A	Monaco
3B	Mauritius
3C	Equatorial Guinea
3D	Swaziland
3X	Guinea
4K	Azerbaijan
4R	Sri Lanka
4U	United Nations
4X	Israel
5A	Libya
5B	Cyprus
5H	Tanzania
5N	Nigeria
5R	Madagascar
5U	Niger
5V	Togo
5W	Western Samoa
5X	Uganda
5Y	Kenya
6O	Somalia
6V	Senegal
6Y	Jamaica
7O	Yemen
7P	Lesotho
7Q	Malawi
7T	Algeria
8P	Barbados
8Q	Maldives
8R	Guyana
9A	Croatia
9G	Ghana
9H	Malta
9J	Zambia
9K	Kuwait
9L	Sierra Leone
9M	Malaysia
9N	Nepal
9Q/9T	Zaire
9U	Burundi
9V	Singapore
9XR	Rwanda
9Y	Trinidad & Tobago
A2	Botswana
A3	Tonga
A40	Oman
A5	Bhutan
A6	United Arab Emirates
A7	Qatar
A9C	Bahrain
AP	Pakistan
B	China
B	Taiwan
C/CF	Canada
C2	Nauru
C3	Andorra

PREFIX	COUNTRY
C5	Gambia
C6	Bahamas
C9	Mozambique
CC	Chile
CN	Morocco
CP	Bolivia
CS	Portugal
CU	Cuba
CX	Uruguay
D	Germany
D2	Angola
D4	Cape Verde Islands
D6	Comoros Islands
DQ	Fiji
EC	Spain
EI	Ireland
EL	Liberia
EP	Iran
ER	Moldova
ES	Estonia
ET	Ethiopia
EW	Belarus
EY	Tajikistan
EZ	Turkmenistan
F	France
F	French Guiana
F	Guadeloupe
F	Martinique
F	New Caledonia
F	Polynesia
F	Réunion Islands
F	Saint-Barthelemy
F	Saint-Pierre & Miquelon
G	Great Britain
H4	Solomon Islands
HA	Hungary
HB	Liechtenstein
HB	Switzerland
HC	Ecuador
HH	Haiti
HI	Dominican Republic
HK	Colombia
HL	South Korea
HP	Panama
HR	Honduras
HS	Thailand
HV	Vatican
HZ	Saudi Arabia
I	Italy
J2	Djibouti
J3	Grenada
J5	Guinea Bissau
J6	St. Lucia
J7	Dominica
J8	St. Vincent & Grenadines

Appendix D - Aircraft Registration

PREFIX	COUNTRY	PREFIX	COUNTRY
JA	Japan	TT	Chad
JY	Jordan	TU	Ivory Coast
LN	Norway	TY	Benin
LV	Argentina	TZ	Mali
LX	Luxembourg	UK	Uzbekistan
LY	Lithuania	UR	Ukraine
LZ	Bulgaria	V2	Antigua
MT	Mongolia	V2	Barbuda
N	American Samoa	V3	Belize
N	Caroline Islands	V4	St. Kitts-Nevis
N	Guam	V5	Namibia
N	Mariana Islands	V7	Marshall Islands
N	Puerto Rico	V8	Brunei
N	U.S. Virgin Islands	VH	Australia
N	USA	VN	Vietnam
OB	Peru	VP-F	Falkland Islands
OD	Lebanon	VP-LA	Anguilla
OE	Austria	VP-LM	Montserrat
OH	Finland	VP-LV	British Virgin Islands
OK	Czech Republic	VQ-T	Turks & Caicos
OO	Belgium	VR-B	Bermuda
OY	Denmark	VR-C	Cayman Islands
P	North Korea	VR-G	Gibraltar
P2	Papua New Guinea	VR-H	Hong Kong
P4	Aruba	VT	India
PH	Netherlands	XA/XB/XC	Mexico
PJ	Netherlands Antilles	XT	Burkina Faso
PK	Indonesia	XU	Kampuchea
PP/PT	Brazil	XY	Myanmar
PZ	Surinam	YA	Afghanistan
RA	Russia	YI	Iraq
RDPL	Laos	YJ	Vanuatu
RP	Philippines	YK	Syria
S2	Bangladesh	YL	Latvia
S5	Slovenia	YN	Nicaragua
S7	Seychelles	YR	Romania
S9	Sao Tomé	YS	El Salvador
SE	Sweden	YU	Yugoslavia
SP	Poland	YV	Venezuela
ST	Mauritania	Z	Zimbabwe
ST	Sudan	ZA	Albania
SU	Egypt	ZK	New Zealand
SX	Greece	ZP	Paraguay
T2	Tuvalu	ZS	Bophuthatswana
T3	Kiribati	ZS	South Africa
T7	San Marino	ZS	Transkei
TC	Turkey	ZS	Venda
TF	Iceland	-	Armenia
TG	Guatemala	-	Eritrea
TI	Costa Rica	-	Georgia
TJ	Cameroon	-	Kazakhstan
TL	Central African Republic	-	Krygyzstan
TN	Congo	-	Macedonia
TR	Gabon	-	Palau
TS	Tunisia	-	Serbia

Appendix E - Waypoints

WAYPOINT	LATITUDE	LONGITUDE	LOCATION	MWARA
ABACO	27:00.0 N	77:34.2 W	S.E. coast of USA	NAT
ACKIL	54:00.0 N	10:00.0 W	N.W. coast of Ireland	EUR
ADOOR	29:24.0 N	78:33.4 W	S.E. coast of USA	NAT
AGUJA	10:59.0 N	77:25.0 W	North Atlantic/Caribbean	NAT
AKLAN	26:31.0 N	18:44.0 W	North Atlantic/Canary Is.	AFI
ALANO	39:26.0 N	25:52.0 W	Azores	NAT
ALDAN	62:57.9 N	18:45.5 W	Iceland	EUR
ALINE	38:27.5 N	71:13.2 W	N.E. coast of USA	NAT
ALORA	19:27.0 N	79:00.0 W	North Atlantic/Caribbean	NAT
ALVAG	16:00.0 N	68:49.0 W	North Atlantic/Caribbean	NAT
AMBIN	15:41.0 N	74:00.0 W	North Atlantic/Caribbean	NAT
ANADA	15:03.3 N	64:10.3 W	North Atlantic/Caribbean	NAT
ANTEX	18:29.0 N	68:00.0 W	North Atlantic/Caribbean	NAT
ARMUR	15:33.0 N	66:38.0 W	North Atlantic/Caribbean	NAT
ATUVI	20:00.0 N	81:25.0 W	North Atlantic/Caribbean	NAT
BACUS	34:26.0 N	73:51.0 W	N.E. coast of USA	NAT
BAKIS	31:00.3 N	14:39.5 W	North Atlantic/Canary Is.	AFI
BANCS	45:39.0 N	52:06.2 W	E. coast of Canada	NAT
BANLO			S. E. coast of England	NAT
BAREE			Eastern Canada	NAT
BDA**	32:21.8 N	64:41.4 W	Bermuda	NAT
BEMOL	19:18.0 N	77:01.0 W	North Atlantic/Caribbean	NAT
BENET	18:15.0 N	74:40.0 W	North Atlantic/Caribbean	NAT
BERGH	39:08.0 N	72:03.2 W	N.E. coast of USA	NAT
BEXER	14:12.0 N	68:11.0 W	North Atlantic/Caribbean	NAT
BLUFI	26:52.6 N	79:49.1 W	S.E. coast of USA	NAT
BOSOM	17:51.0 N	78:02.0 W	North Atlantic/Caribbean	NAT
Bravo	38:52.0 N	25:15.0 W	Azores	NAT
BREKI	62:32.3 N	19:32.5 W	Iceland	EUR
BRIMS	28:15.0 N	91:13.5 W	Gulf of Mexico	NAT
BRUNZ	39:00.0 N	65:00.0 W	N.E. coast of USA	NAT
BURGO	24:25.0 N	74:33.9 W	North Atlantic/Caribbean	NAT
CANOA	24:00.0 N	83:04.0 W	North Atlantic/Caribbean	NAT
CARPE	53:05.0 N	54:05.0 W	N.E. coast of Canada	NAT
CARPS	30:24.5 N	77:45.0 W	S.E. coast of USA	NAT
CATCH	31:59.0 N	70:03.0 W	S.E. coast of USA	NAT
CAVEL	19:35.0 N	67:15.0 W	North Atlantic/Caribbean	NAT
CHAMP	37:31.0 N	71:41.0 W	N.E. coast of USA	NAT
Charlie	38:22:0 N	24:42.0 W	Azores	NAT
COLBY	15:00.0 N	78:32.0 W	North Atlantic/Caribbean	NAT
COLOR	46:40.4 N	52:30.9 W	E. coast of Canada	NAT
CORAN	32:01.0 N	73:36.0 W	E. coast of USA	NAT
CRABB	42:12.8 N	65:45.2 W	N.E. coast of USA	NAT
CROAK	36:56.3 N	73:00.0 W	N.E. coast of USA	NAT
CRUTA	15:17.0 N	82:57.0 W	North Atlantic/Caribbean	NAT
CUDAS	42:37.4 N	64:14.1 W	N.E. coast of USA	NAT
CVS**	16:44.0 N	22:58.0 W	North Atlantic/Cape Verde Is.	AFI
DAKES	17:03.0 N	67:00.0 W	North Atlantic/Caribbean	NAT
DANER	35:16.0 N	69:04.0 W	N.E. coast of USA	NAT
DAVES	42:56.7 N	67:30.5 W	N.E. coast of USA	NAT
DAYSE			Eastern Canada	NAT
DAYSY	31:25.2 N	16:18.8 W	North Atlantic/Canary Is.	AFI
DEENO	30:31.0 N	67:28.0 W	S.E. coast of USA	NAT
Delta	37:46.0 N	24:05.0 W	Azores	NAT
DESIL	41:00.0 N	15:00.0 W	N.W. coast of Spain	AFI

Appendix E - Waypoints

WAYPOINT	LATITUDE	LONGITUDE	LOCATION	MWARA
DIRMA	40:51.0 N	09:30.0 W	W. coast of Portugal	AFI
DIVAN	39:25.8 N	72:26.0 W	N.E. coast of USA	NAT
DOGGA			North Sea, 70 nm on 106 from OTR	EUR
DOLPH	28:15.0 N	90:01.4 W	Gulf of Mexico	NAT
DOTTY	50:38.0 N	55:35.0 W	N.E. coast of Canada	NAT
DUNNO	23:00.0 N	76:04.0 W	North Atlantic/Caribbean	NAT
DUXUN	15:00.0 N	79:15.0 W	North Atlantic/Caribbean	NAT
Echo	37:19.0 N	23:45.0 W	Azores	NAT
EDROD	15:00.0 N	74:44.0 W	North Atlantic/Caribbean	NAT
EDUMO	22:55.0 N	23:36.0 W	North Atlantic/Canary Is.	AFI
EKROL	37:17.0 N	23:45.0 W	Azores	NAT
ELBOW	26:25.5 N	76:43.2 W	S.E. coast of USA	NAT
ELKAS	27:28.0 N	73:19.0 W	S.E. coast of USA	NAT
ELOPO	17:38.0 N	62:31.0 W	North Atlantic/Caribbean	NAT
ELTIN	35:21.0 N	64:19.0 W	N.E. coast of USA	NAT
ELWOD	29:35.0 N	69:22.0 W	S.E. coast of USA	NAT
EMARY	33:31.0 N	71:41.0 W	E. coast of USA	NAT
EMBLA	63:28.2 N	26:58.5 W	Iceland	EUR
ENAMO	23:34.2 N	77:22.3 W	North Atlantic/Caribbean	NAT
ENDER	27:00.0 N	68:39.0 W	S.E. coast of USA	NAT
EPOKA	17:31.0 N	24:30.0 W	North Atlantic/Cape Verde Is.	AFI
EPOSO	30:51.7 N	14:22.3 W	North Atlantic/Canary Is.	AFI
ERIKO	14:08.0 N	74:08.0 W	North Atlantic/Caribbean	NAT
ESPOT	18:00.0 N	83:38.0 W	North Atlantic/Caribbean	NAT
ETALA	14:03.0 N	64:57.0 W	North Atlantic/Caribbean	NAT
ETBOD	18:31.0 N	71:53.0 W	North Atlantic/Caribbean	NAT
ETRAM	30:22.6 N	13:17.6 W	North Atlantic/Canary Is.	AFI
EXTER	25:46.4 N	76:12.9 W	S.E. coast of USA	NAT
FISSH	38:53.5 N	74:23.1 W	N.E. coast of USA	NAT
FLANN	38:20.0 N	69:57.0 W	N.E. coast of USA	NAT
FORRD	25:00.0 N	72:24.0 W	S.E. coast of USA	NAT
Foxtrot 2	36:27.0 N	23:45.0 W	Azores	NAT
FRATT	21:51.5 N	180:00.0 W	Pacific	PAC
GABAR	17:22.0 N	62:59.0 W	North Atlantic/Caribbean	NAT
GABES	34:00.0 N	67:41.0 W	E. coast of USA	NAT
GADUN	20:30.6 N	20:37.7 W	North Atlantic/Cape Verde Is.	AFI
GAGLY	32.01.0 N	72:01.0 W	S.E. coast of USA	NAT
GAMBA	18:57.2 N	26:03.6 W	North Atlantic/Cape Verde Is.	AFI
GAPOL	14:16.0 N	26:28.0 N	North Atlantic/Cape Verde Is.	AFI
GDV**	28:04.6 N	15:25.6 W	North Atlantic/Canary Is.	AFI
GEJAY	25:00.0 N	70:15.0 W	S.E. coast of USA	NAT
GEKRA	16:23.5 N	21:59.2 W	North Atlantic/Cape Verde Is.	AFI
GIMLI	64:38.4 N	26:58.3 W	Iceland	EUR
GINNY	27:00.0 N	66:45.0 W	S.E. coast of USA	NAT
GIPER			S. E. coast of England	NAT
GLIBS	30:56.0 N	74:15.0 W	S.E. coast of USA	NAT
Golf	35:50.0 N	24:53.0 W	Azores	NAT
GONIS	20:00.0 N	78:58.0 W	North Atlantic/Caribbean	NAT
GRADI	20:35.0 N	69:45.0 W	North Atlantic/Caribbean	NAT
GRANN	23:30.0 N	65:48.0 W	North Atlantic/Caribbean	NAT
GRATX	26:54.6 N	74:17.5 W	S.E. coast of USA	NAT
GRUPI	43:52.0 N	58:50.3 W	N.E. coast of USA	NAT
HADOK	54:26.5 N	59:55.3 W	N.E. coast of Canada	NAT
HENCH	33:30.0 N	61:24.0 W	E. coast of USA	NAT
HENLI	16:54.0 N	65:25.0 W	North Atlantic/Caribbean	NAT

WAYPOINT	LATITUDE	LONGITUDE	LOCATION	MWARA
HERIN	42:00.2 N	67:47.5 W	N.E. coast of USA	NAT
HOBEE	29:13.3 N	79:09.1 W	S.E. coast of USA	NAT
Hotel	36:00.0 N	25:58.0 W	Azores	NAT
HUDRA	44:25.0 N	13:00.0 W	N.W. coast of Spain	EUR
ILURI	16:18.0 N	63:00.0 W	North Atlantic/Caribbean	NAT
INDEE	23:08.4 N	74:07.2 W	North Atlantic/Caribbean	NAT
India	37:07.0 N	27:53.0 W	Azores	NAT
IRKID	33:55.5 N	18:04.4 W	North Atlantic/Madeira	AFI
ITSOS	16:07.4 N	22:07.9 W	North Atlantic/Cape Verde Is.	AFI
JESSE	29:30.0 N	75:04.0 W	S.E. coast of USA	NAT
JFK**	40:38.0 N	73:46.4 W	N.E. coast of USA	NAT
JOBOC	40:07.0 N	67:00.0 W	N.E. coast of USA	NAT
Juliett	38:07.0 N	29:42.0 W	Azores	NAT
KAKNI	30:00.0 N	147:38.0 E	Pacific	PAC
KARUM	16:00.0 N	69:24.0 W	North Atlantic/Caribbean	NAT
KASOR	15:00.0 N	77:47.0 W	North Atlantic/Caribbean	NAT
KBV**	32:21.8 N	64:41.7 W	E. coast of USA	NAT
KELVI			Eastern Canada	NAT
KENDA	39:21.2 N	70:30.0 W	N.E. coast of USA	NAT
KENOX	14:48.0 N	28:29.0 W	North Atlantic/Cape Verde Is.	AFI
KIKER	15:05.9 N	65:17.7 W	North Atlantic/Caribbean	NAT
KILER	15:00.0 N	76:52.0 W	North Atlantic/Caribbean	NAT
Kilo	38:28.0 N	39:22.0 W	Azores	NAT
KLAMM	52:34.6 N	58:22.6 W	N.E. coast of Canada	NAT
KOBOT	16:00.0 N	69:47.0 W	North Atlantic/Caribbean	NAT
KONCH	44:33.3 N	55:29.0 W	E. coast of Canada	NAT
KOTEN	08:15.0 N	58:35.0 W	North Atlantic/Caribbean	NAT
KRAFT	23:30.0 N	67:43.0 W	North Atlantic/Caribbean	NAT
LACKS	40:00.0 N	68:12.0 W	N.E. coast of USA	NAT
LADUE	30:24.0 N	67:43.0 W	S.E. coast of USA	NAT
LEARS	28:30.0 N	71:27.0 W	S.E. coast of USA	NAT
LENOM	17:00.0 N	72:40.0 W	North Atlantic/Caribbean	NAT
LEOES	39:58.5 N	72:38.9 W	N.E. coast of USA	NAT
LEPOD	08:29.0 N	58:59.0 W	North Atlantic/Caribbean	NAT
LEVER	33:52.0 N	72:29.0 W	E. coast of USA	NAT
LEVOR	15:00.0 N	81:35.0 W	North Atlantic/Caribbean	NAT
Lima	39:30.0 N	31:41.0 W	Azores	NAT
LIMMI	31:40.0 N	69:58.0 W	S.E. coast of USA	NAT
LINDA	62:37.3 N	10:00.0 W	Iceland	NAT
LINND	39:24.6 N	71:42.8 W	N.E. coast of USA	NAT
LIZARD			North Sea	UER
LOACH	55:31.0 N	57:01.0 W	N.E. coast of Canada	NAT
LOPPS	29:35.0 N	63:21.0 W	S.E. coast of USA	NAT
LOTUS	29:46.5 N	79:01.2 W	S.E. coast of USA	NAT
LOUIZ	28:28.4 N	77:00.0 W	S.E. coast of USA	NAT
LUMPO	15:40.9 N	20:00.0 W	North Atlantic/Cape Verde Is.	AFI
LYNUS	38:00.9 N	72:39.3 W	N.E. coast of USA	NAT
MAMEL	25:31.8 N	76:38.1 W	S.E. coast of USA	NAT
MANNA	31:25.0 N	71:35.0 W	S.E. coast of USA	NAT
MANOT	06:44.0 S	162:12.0 E	Pacific	PAC
MAPYL	27:50.0 N	75:59.0 W	S.E. coast of USA	NAT
MAROT	18:30.0 N	72:55.0 W	North Atlantic/Caribbean	NAT
MAZZA	11:41.5 N	180:00.0 W	Pacific	PAC
MELLA	18:12.0 N	68:00.0 W	North Atlantic/Caribbean	NAT
MERCI	35:00.0 N	71:45.0 W	N.E. coast of USA	NAT

WAYPOINT	LATITUDE	LONGITUDE	LOCATION	MWARA
METTA	32:26.1 N	78:22.8 W	E. coast of USA	NAT
MIILS	42:56.4 N	67:02.9 W	Eastern Canada	NAT
Mike	39:36.0 N	31:38.0 W	Azores	NAT
MILKS	32:01.0 N	71:37.0 W	E. coast of USA	NAT
MILOE	32:17.3 N	77:58.5 W	E. coast of USA	NAT
MILOK	15:18.0 N	65:53.0 W	North Atlantic/Caribbean	NAT
MINNU	62:07.9 N	70:00.0 W	N.E. coast of Canada	NAT
MODUX	16:58.0 N	63:00.0 W	North Atlantic/Caribbean	NAT
MOFFY	29:23.0 N	65:05.0 W	S.E. coast of USA	NAT
MOGSA	14:41.4 N	20:12.6 W	North Atlantic/Cape Verde Is.	AFI
MORNA	03:00.0 S	165:10.0 E	Pacific	PAC
NAPEE			Eastern Canada	NAT
NELSO	31:42.0 N	17:26.5 W	North Atlantic/Madeira	AFI
NERVA	11:14.0 N	73:41.0 W	North Atlantic/Caribbean	NAT
November	39:53.0 N	28:31.0 W	Azores	NAT
NUCAR	28:07.6 N	77:38.0 W	S.E. coast of USA	NAT
ODKAM	17:51.7 N	62:13.1 W	North Atlantic/Caribbean	NAT
OLDEY	32:15.6 N	77:50.9 W	E. coast of USA	NAT
OLGIS	10:00.0 N	160.56.1 E	Pacific	PAC
OMOKO	48:50.0 N	12:00.0 W	North East Atlantic	EUR
ONOBI	13:41.4 N	24:35.8 W	North Atlantic/Cape Verde Is.	AFI
OROSA	14:19.0 N	73:58.0 W	North Atlantic/Caribbean	NAT
OTAMO	15:00.0 N	75:59.0 W	North Atlantic/Caribbean	NAT
OWENZ	39:49.4 N	72:50.0 W	N.E. coast of USA	NAT
OWSKI	27:00.0 N	65:23.0 W	S.E. coast of USA	NAT
OYSTR	53:52.0 N	54:58.0 W	N.E. coast of Canada	NAT
OZENA	30:25.5 N	78:20.9 W	S.E. coast of USA	NAT
PALAS	16:33.0 N	71:40.0 W	North Atlantic/Caribbean	NAT
PELRA	14:15.0 N	82:27.0 W	North Atlantic/Caribbean	NAT
PENKO	15:05.0 N	70:19.0 W	North Atlantic/Caribbean	NAT
PENYT	39:13.9 N	68:30.0 W	N.E. coast of USA	NAT
PEXOR	15:00.0 N	157:57.0 E	Pacific	PAC
PISAX	23:30.0 N	62:33.0 W	North Atlantic/Caribbean	NAT
PLATY	25:14.6 N	17:24.6 W	North Atlantic/Canary Is.	AFI
PLING	19:54.0 N	66:47.0 W	North Atlantic/Caribbean	NAT
POGGO	41:08.0 N	67:00.0 W	N.E. coast of USA	NAT
PORGY	56:19.0 N	58:05.0 W	N.E. coast of Canada	NAT
PRAWN	57:12.2 N	59:10.8 W	N.E. coast of Canada	NAT
PRISS	31:56.0 N	68:11.0 W	S.E. coast of USA	NAT
PUTAR	23:59.0 N	77:59.0 W	North Atlantic/Caribbean	NAT
PUTUL	20:00.0 N	78:20.0 W	North Atlantic/Caribbean	NAT
RAYAS	15:42.7 N	65:29.9 W	North Atlantic/Caribbean	NAT
REDBY	52:03.8 N	57:07.9 W	N.E. coast of Canada	NAT
RINGS	37:55.2 N	70:49.4 W	N.E. coast of USA	NAT
RISBA	21:00.0 N	154:08.0 E	Pacific	PAC
ROSEL	29:13.0 N	70:05.0 W	S.E. coast of USA	NAT
ROSTA	28:12.0 N	20:00.0 W	North Atlantic/Canary Is.	AFI
RUBIE	32:53.0 N	71:40.0 W	E. coast of USA	NAT
SA374	43:55.8 N	60:01.4 W	E. coast of Canada	NAT
SAILE	41:11.1 N	67:53.8 W	N.E. coast of USA	NAT
SARJE	29:30.0 N	73:27.9 W	S.E. coast of USA	NAT
SASON	17:54.0 N	74:12.0 W	North Atlantic/Caribbean	NAT
SCAPA	15:50.0 N	67:30.0 W	North Atlantic/Caribbean	NAT
SCROD	54:37.0 N	55:52.0 W	N.E. coast of Canada	NAT
SEGRO	25:00.0 N	151:23.5 E	Pacific	PAC

WAYPOINT	LATITUDE	LONGITUDE	LOCATION	MWARA
SEKAR	20:25.1 N	70:47.7 W	North Atlantic/Caribbean	NAT
SELAN	13:51.0 N	73:18.0 W	North Atlantic/Caribbean	NAT
SERNA	16:51.0 N	66:33.0 W	North Atlantic/Caribbean	NAT
SIDER	61:00.0 N	05:08.2 W	Iceland	NAT
SILVA	14:27.0 N	66:42.0 W	North Atlantic/Caribbean	NAT
SLAPP	24:59.0 N	71:18.0 W	S.E. coast of USA	NAT
SLATN	39:07.0 N	67:00.0 W	N.E. coast of USA	NAT
SLATO	27:00.0 N	76:26.0 W	S.E. coast of USA	NAT
SLURP	20:05.0 N	66:13.0 W	North Atlantic/Caribbean	NAT
SMELT	31:58.0 N	77:00.0 W	S.E. coast of USA	NAT
SPING	30:36.0 N	75:55.0 W	S.E. coast of USA	NAT
STEAM	52:24.1 N	70:00.0 W	Eastern Canada	NAT
SWAPS	32:55.0 N	70:19.0 W	E. coast of USA	NAT
TADPO	24:00.0 N	81:13.0 W	North Atlantic/Caribbean	NAT
TALLO	29:30.0 N	71:30.0 W	S.E. coast of USA	NAT
TARBA	16:30.0 N	73:29.0 W	North Atlantic/Caribbean	NAT
TARGA	35:05.0 N	66:13.0 W	N.E. coast of USA	NAT
TEAMS	33:12.0 N	72:54.0 W	E. coast of USA	NAT
TFN**	28:31.7 N	16:15.6 W	North Atlantic/Canary Is.	AFI
TFS**	28:00.1 N	16:41.2 W	North Atlantic/Canary Is.	AFI
TIVLI	51:17.0 N	07:30.7 W	North Sea	EUR
TONIK	32:00.0 N	146:00.0 E	Pacific	PAC
TOOMS	23:00.0 N	69:45.0 W	North Atlantic/Caribbean	NAT
TORRY	30:25.3 N	78:51.9 W	S.E. coast of USA	NAT
TOTEM	18:00.0 N	61:52.9 W	North Atlantic/Caribbean	NAT
TOTON	19:41.0 N	77:48.0 W	North Atlantic/Caribbean	NAT
TRAPP	09:05.0 N	56:05.0 W	North Atlantic/Caribbean	NAT
TROUT	30:23.0 N	77:00.0 W	S.E. coast of USA	NAT
TUNNI	59:56.5 N	70:00.0 W	N.E. coast of Canada	NAT
ULISA	18:54.0 N	82:04.0 W	North Atlantic/Caribbean	NAT
ULTEM	21:29.7 N	29:48.0 W	North Atlantic/Cape Verde Is.	AFI
UMANN	33:53.0 N	70:37.0 W	E. coast of USA	NAT
URIBI	11:16.0 N	72:11.0 W	North Atlantic/Caribbean	NAT
URSUS	24:00.0 N	79:01.0 W	North Atlantic/Caribbean	NAT
VALDI	61:12.0 N	00:00.0 W	Iceland	NAT
VESKA	16:00.0 N	70:45.0 W	North Atlantic/Caribbean	NAT
VEXIN	37:00.0 N	15:00.0 W	W. coast of Portugal	AFI
VIPER	28:14.9 N	88:53.1 W	Gulf of Mexico	NAT
VODIN	14:34.0 N	67:18.0 W	North Atlantic/Caribbean	NAT
VORAS	21:38.0 N	21:59.0 W	North Atlantic/Cape Verde Is.	AFI
VOTOL	17:30.7 N	24:02.1 W	North Atlantic/Cape Verde Is.	AFI
VYSTA	48:30.8 N	52:44.7 W	E. coast of Canada	NAT
WHALE	42:11.9 N	67:00.0 W	N.E. coast of USA	NAT
XUNIX	18:38.9 N	25:37.6 W	North Atlantic/Cape Verde Is.	AFI
ZIBUT	36:56.3 N	72:40.0 W	N.E. coast of USA	NAT

Sources

General Utility Guides

Dexter, Larry	Shortwave Listening With The Experts	1987	$19.95
Halligey, Geoff	Confidential Frequency List, 8th Edition	1992	$19.95
Klingenfuss, J.	Guide To Utility Stations, 12th Edition	1993	$37.95
Poly-Verlag (Switzerland)	Internationales Kurzwellen-Frequenz-Handbuch	1992	70 Sf
SPEEDX	SPEEDX Reference Guide To The Utilities	1988	$25.00
Symington & Henault	Utility QSL Address Guides, Volumes 1 & 2	1987	$12.95
Van Horn, Larry	Grove Shortwave Directory, 8th Edition	1993	$29.95

HF Aeronautical

Battles, Bill	World Air Carrier Radio Callsign Directory	1992	$22.00
Evans, Robert E.	The Aeronautical Communications Handbook - HF Edition	1989	$19.95
Evans, Robert E.	Worldwide Aeronautical Communications Frequency Directory	1991	$6.95
Schaay, Michael	Aeronautical Radio Handbook	1991	$13.95
Van Horn, Larry	Grove Shortwave Directory, 8th Edition	1993	$29.95

VHF Aeronautical

Air Guide Publications	Flight Guide (Airport & Frequency Manual) V 1 to 3	1993	$39.95
Coburn, R.A. & Lindley, R.	Official Aeronautical Frequency Directory	1990	$24.95
DC Enterprises	VHF/UHF Aircraft Directory	1989	$14.95
FOX	FOX Scanner Radio Listings	1990	$19.95
Flynn, Ed	Understanding ACARS	1993	$4.95
Kneitel, Tom	Air Scan	1990	$14.95

Coast Guard/Military/NASA

Curtis, Anthony R.	Monitoring NASA Communications	1992	$14.95
Evans, Robert E.	The Aeronautical Communications Handbook - HF Edition	1989	$19.95
Evans, Robert E.	Worldwide Aeronautical Communications Frequency Directory	1991	$6.95
Ing, Robert S.	Canadian Military Radio Frequency Guide	1993	$13.95
Mitchell, S. & Eastwood, A.	Military Aircraft Serials of North America	1991	$23.95
Pogue, James T.	Coast Guard Radio	1990	$12.95
Schaay, Michael	U.S. Military Radio Communications, Volumes 1 , 2, 3	1987	$12.95
Sullivan, Jack	Directory Of N. Am. Military Aviation Communications V 1-4	1990	$24.95
Symington, D.	Monitoring The Military	1990	$16.95
Van Horn, Gayle	International Callsign Handbook	1992	$19.95
Van Horn, Larry	Grove Shortwave Directory, 8th Edition	1993	$29.95

Radioteletype (Aero-related)

Evans, Robert E.	The Aeronautical Communications Handbook - HF Edition	1989	$19.95
Klingenfuss, J.	Air and Meteo Code Manual, 13th Edition	1993	$29.95
Klingenfuss, J.	Guide To Utility Stations, 12th Edition	1993	$37.95
Van Horn, Larry	Grove Shortwave Directory, 8th Edition	1993	$29.95

SELCAL, Carrier and Fleet Information

Bucher Publications	JP Airline -Fleets International 93/94	1993	$65.00
Davies/Barker/McKenzie	High In the Sky	1993	$16.50
Gates, Brian	JP Biz-Jet	1993	$16.95
The Aviation Hobby Shop (UK)	Airlines	1993	$20.00

Sources

Flight Schedules

Official Airline Guide	OAG World Wide Edition (Obtain last month's copy from your Travel Agent)

General Interest

Daoud, Hessman	Aviation Dictionary	1972	$10.00
Green, W. & Swanborough, G.	The World's Airliners	1982	$15.50
Larson, Ken	To Fly The Concorde	1985	$9.95
Pealing, Norman	Big Jets	1987	$12.95
Simon & Shuster	The Air Traveller's Handbook	1978	$11.95
Stewart, Stanley	Flying The Big Jets	1984	$26.00
Wood, Derek	Jane's World Aircraft Recognition Handbook	1987	$13.95
Yeager, Jeana & Rutan, Dick	Voyager	1987	$19.95

Government Publications

Canada DOT	A.I.P. Canada	1993	$35.00
Canada DOT	Canada Flight Supplement	1993	$25.00
Canada DOE, M &R	Canadian Forces Flight Supplement**	1994	
U.S DOT	Location Identifiers (7350.6H)**	1994	
US DOD	IFR Supplement United States**	1994	
US DOD	Flight Information Handbook**	1994	
US DOD	Military Training Routes**	1994	

Magazine and Club Publication Columns

Airliners	Airliners Magazine (USA)
Baker, Jean	Plane Talk - Monitoring Times Magazine (USA)
Evans, John & Baxter, Ian	Utility Shack - DSWCI (Denmark)
Evans, Robert	Digital Digest - Monitoring Times Magazine (USA)
Manning, Godfrey	Airband - Shortwave Magazine (England)
Moon, Dick	Utility Safari - South African DX Club (South Africa)
Naylor, Spence	Utility Column - Association of DX Reporters (USA)
Ross, David	Monitoring Services - DX Ontario (ODXA) (Canada)
Schimmel, Don	Communications Confidential - Popular Communications Magazine (USA)
Smith, John	HF Utilities - DX Post (Australia)
Van Horn, Larry	Utility Column - Monitoring Times Magazine (USA)
Yarbrough, Chuck	Utility World Column - SPEEDX (USA)

Aeronautical Charts and Maps

Aerial Development of New England, P.O. Box 661, Bangor Maine 04402-0661
(** Excellent reasonably-priced source of government aeronautical publications, maps and charts)

NOAA Distribution Branch, National Oceanic Service, (N-CG-33) 6501 Lafyette Ave, Riverdale, MD 20737 USA

Jeppesen & Company, 55 Inverness Drive East, Englewood, Colorado 80112 USA

Energy, Mines and Resources, Canada Map Office, 615 Booth Street, Ottawa, Ontario L1A 0E9 Canada

International Civil Aviation Organization, Document Sales Unit, 1000 Sherbrooke W, Suite 400., Montreal PQ M3A 2R2 Canada

Aerad Customer Services, Building 254, P.O. Box 10, London Heathrow Airport, Hounslow, Middlesex, TW6 2JA United Kingdom

Royal Air Force - 1 AIDU, RAF Northolt, West End Road, Ruislip, Middlesex HA4 6NG United Kingdom

About the Author

Bob Evans has been monitoring the shortwave spectrum for the last three decades. Interest in utility DXing, particularly aeronautical, was kindled at an early stage in his SWL career. In 1989, he authored the *Aeronautical Communications Handbook-HF Edition*, followed by the *Worldwide Aeronautical Communications Frequency Directory* in 1991. He has given a number of illustrated presentations on Aeronautical Communications to various groups including Monitoring Times and ANARCON conventions. He reviewed the NRD-535D for Fine Tuning's *92/93 Proceedings*. Bob also serves as the *Digital Digest* column editor for Monitoring Times and as the associate editor for *The RTTY Listener*, the customer newsletter of Universal Radio.

His listening post includes Japan Radio NRD-535D and NRD-525 communications receivers. Peripheral equipment includes Datong FL-3 audio filters and Ameco PT3 preamps on each of the JRC receivers. A Sony 2010 and SW-55 are available for portable operations. A Universal M-7000 communications terminal connected to a Koyo monitor and HAL RTTY Scope are used to decode digital mode transmissions. HF antenna systems include a 54/108 foot balcony-mounted longwire loop, a double "Slinky" 85 foot longwire as well as two active antennas, a Dressler ara 30, and a Sony AN-1. A Wiltek/Trak solid-state HF antenna multicoupler is used to distribute signals to the receivers via a Grove TUN-4. VHF/UHF equipment includes an ICOM R-7100, R-7000, and Uniden 2500XLT scanner/receivers. Magnetic-mounted Austin "Spectra" antennas are used with the ICOM receivers. A Universal M-400 decoder is devoted exclusively to VHF ACARS.

All receivers and decoding equipment are interfaced to an Apple Macintosh Quadra 650 16/230 computer connected to a 600 dpi laser printer. Computer control software was written by Bob himself.

A graduate of St. Augustine's College, Ryerson Polytechnical Institute and the University of Toronto, he taught business and computer studies at the college level for 15 years. He spent the next decade as a computer management information systems consultant in the automotive field. He has authored a number of application manuals for major North American computer and automotive manufacturers. Currently, he is self-employed as a technical writer and corporate trainer.

An accomplished photographer, his other passions include Egyptology, Astronomy, Classical Music and Wine Tasting and Appreciation. He has travelled extensively and has conducted educational tours in Egypt and photographic and wildlife safaris in East Africa.

Bob is a member of the Ontario DX Association, the Armed Forces Communications and Electronics Association, the Society for Technical Communication and the Society for the Study of Egyptian Antiquities.

Bob makes his home in Don Mills, a suburb of Toronto, Canada.